A Special Issue of
Memory

Semantic Knowledge and Semantic Representations

Edited by

Rosaleen A. McCarthy

University of Cambridge, UK

Erlbaum (UK) Taylor & Francis

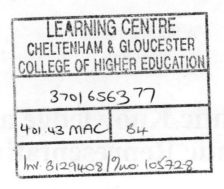
Erlbaum (UK) Taylor & Francis, Publishers
27 Church Road
Hove
East Sussex, BN3 2FA
UK

British Library Cataloguing in Publication Data

A catalogue record for this book is available from the British Library

    ISBN 0-86377-936-0
    ISSN 0965-8211

Subject Index compiled by Jackie McDermott
Cover design by SB Graphics, Hove
Typeset by DP Photosetting, Aylesbury
Printed and bound in the United Kingdom by BPC Wheatons Ltd., Exeter

Contents

*This book is also a double special issue of the journal *Memory* which forms Issues 3 and 4 of
Volume 3 (1995). The page numbers used here are taken from the journal and so begin with p.225.

iii

MEMORY, 1995, *3* (3/4), 225–246

Autobiographical Experience and Word Meaning

Julie S. Snowden, Helen L. Griffiths, and David Neary

Manchester Royal Infirmary, UK

The role of current personal experience in understanding of word meaning was investigated in a patient, WM, who suffers from semantic dementia. The study was prompted by the observation that WM, despite being severely impaired on formal tests of word comprehension and naming, retained a range of vocabulary pertaining to her daily life. If autobiographical experience has a general facilitatory effect, then this should affect which concepts are retained and which lost, but not influence the quality of that conceptual knowledge. Conversely, if personal autobiography has a direct role in investing concepts with meaning, then WM's understanding of nominal terms that she uses spontaneously in conversation ought not to be normal, but should be constrained by the autobiographical context in which she uses those terms. WM could define nouns and noun phrases drawn from her conversational vocabulary, but her definitions had a markedly autobiographical quality. Moreover, WM was extremely impaired in her ability to define new noun phrases, constructed by combining words from her conversational vocabulary (e.g. "dog licence", constructed from "driving licence" and "dog"; "oil field" constructed from "oil" and "field"). It was concluded that WM does not have normal conceptual understanding of nouns and noun phrases that she uses appropriately in conversation. Her understanding is narrow and autobiographically constrained. The findings, which suggest an interactive relationship between autobiographical and semantic memory, have implications for understanding of the progressive breakdown of semantic knowledge.

INTRODUCTION

The distinction between semantic and episodic memory was first put forward by Tulving (1972). Since then a body of neuropsychological evidence has accumulated to support the distinction. Patients with a classical amnesic syndrome, associated with damage to hippocampal and diencephalic structures have profound problems in memory for events even though their knowledge base remains intact (Cermak, 1984; Cermak & O'Connor, 1983; Kinsbourne & Wood, 1975; Schacter & Tulving, 1982). The converse, a selective disorder of semantics with intact episodic memory, was first described by Warrington

---

Requests for reprints should be sent to Julie S. Snowden, Cerebral Function Unit, Department of Neurology, Manchester Royal Infirmary, Manchester, M13 9WL, UK.

We are grateful to Elizabeth Anderson for providing background neuropsychological information.

(1975). Since Warrington's seminal report, semantic memory deficits have been reported in association with a number of conditions, including Alzheimer's disease (Chertkow & Bub, 1990; Hodges, Salmon, & Butters, 1992b), herpes simplex encephalitis (De Renzi, Liotti, & Nichelli, 1987; Pietrini et al., 1988; Sartori & Job, 1988; Sheridan & Humphreys, 1993; Warrington & Shallice, 1984) and temporal lobectomy (Ellis, Young, & Critchley, 1989; Wilkins & Moscovitch, 1978). However, with occasional exceptions (De Renzi et al., 1987; Ellis et al., 1989), episodic memory is typically also impaired.

A focal degenerative condition, involving circumscribed atrophy of the temporal lobes, appears unusual in that it gives rise to a profound disorder of semantics in the context of apparently well-preserved autobiographical "event" memory. The descriptive term "semantic dementia" has been adopted (Snowden, Goulding, & Neary, 1989) to highlight the salient clinical feature of this degenerative condition. Since then the designation has been adopted by others (Hodges, Patterson, Oxbury, & Funnell, 1992a; Patterson & Hodges, 1992; Saffran & Schwartz, 1993) and the central features of the condition outlined (Hodges et al., 1992a). Patients commonly present with problems in word comprehension and naming, reflecting a loss of word meaning. However, loss of meaning is not confined to verbal material. The semantic disorder encompasses non-linguistic sounds, faces, and objects, and affects all sensory modalities, including those of taste and smell. The patient progressively loses knowledge about the world, regardless of nature of the material and input modality. The disorder appears to reflect a degraded semantic system and not faulty semantic access (see Shallice, 1987, 1988): there is remarkable consistency in performance for individual items from one testing occasion to the next, and patients show no benefit from provision of prompts or from procedural manipulations such as the lengthening of inter-stimulus interval. In contrast to the patient's profound semantic disorder, cognitive skills that do not make semantic demands are well preserved. Patients speak fluently and effortlessly, without phonological or syntactic error. Patients perform well on perceptual matching and drawing tasks. Spatial skills are excellent. Although patients typically perform poorly on formal memory tests which employ stimulus material that has no meaning for them—words, faces, and pictures—memory on a day to day level is remarkably well preserved. Patients remain well oriented in time and place, can keep track of daily activities, recall accurately and without prompting appointments and autobiographical events, and have no difficulty finding their way around the locality. By virtue of these preserved abilities, patients retain a high degree of functional independence. They will continue, for example, to go shopping unaccompanied, either on foot or using public transport, at a time when their word comprehension is virtually nil. Semantic dementia appears to be part of the spectrum of lobar atrophies, pathologically distinct from Alzheimer's disease (Snowden et al., 1992). Certain well-documented patients in the literature, with degenerative disease of unspecified type (Schwartz, Marin, & Saffran 1979; Schwartz, Saffran, & Marin, 1980; Warrington, 1975) would appear to represent cases of semantic dementia.

One characteristic of a degraded semantic system is that loss of conceptual knowledge is not all or none: patients may have partial information about concepts. A frequent finding is that patients are able to classify concepts according to superordinate taxonomic category but fail to distinguish within-category members (Coughlan & Warrington, 1981; Hodges et al., 1992a; Warrington, 1975; Warrington & Shallice, 1984). The common interpretation is that patients retain broad categorical information, but lose the fine-grained featural information that permits specification of individual exemplars. Further distinctions between attributes of meaning have been made. Warrington and Shallice (1984), and Warrington and McCarthy (1987), have drawn a distinction between sensory properties (i.e. colour, shape, texture etc) and functional properties (i.e. object use), and suggest that differential performance for certain classes of information, such as superior knowledge of inanimate compared to biological concepts, may relate to the differential weight of sensory and functional properties in defining a concept. Other authors have made parallel distinctions: between perceptual and functional (Sartori & Job, 1988), visual and verbal (Silveri & Gainotti, 1988), and perceptual and associative knowledge (Chertkow, Bub, & Caplan, 1992). Studies of semantic degradation disorders have characteristically suggested breakdown of perceptual or sensory attributes, with relative sparing of functional or associative attributes (Sartori & Job, 1988; Silveri & Gainotti, 1988; Warrington & Shallice, 1984).

In semantic dementia, loss of word meaning is typically profound. From the time of initial evaluation patients' performance on traditional naming tasks, such as the Graded Naming Test (McKenna & Warrington, 1983) and Boston Naming Test (Kaplan, Goodlgass, Weintraub, & Segal, 1983) and on tests of word comprehension, such as the Peabody Picture Vocabulary Test (Dunn, 1959), typically approaches floor level, reflecting the severely degraded conceptual system. It has been noted previously, however, (Snowden, Griffiths, & Neary, 1994) that patients' conversational speech, although empty in quality, is not totally devoid of nominal terms. Patients may use a surprising range of both high- and low-frequency terms entirely appropriately and with precision. The question arose as to how a patient who is unable to name common objects on a standard naming task could produce in conversation such sentences as "I help the vicar by putting the chalice back in the vestry". The discrepancy cannot be attributed to test modality: patients exhibit a comparable difficulty in naming common objects from verbal description as in confrontation picture naming tasks. Nor does it appear to be the case that provision of a sentence context facilitates access to vocabulary that is otherwise unavailable. As noted previously, the semantic disorder in these patients represents a degradation in the semantic system, and there is a remarkable degree of consistency in performance for individual items, irrespective of how knowledge is probed. Vocabulary that is not known in one test setting is not known in another context. Indeed, the vocabulary that cannot be elicited on standard naming tasks is also not observed to occur in conversation.

One possible argument, in line with others, might be that disparities in what the patient knows and does not know reflect differences in the relative contribution of functional/associative and sensory/perceptual properties in defining the concept. However, this does not seem to provide a sufficient explanation. The functional properties of a chalice, to use the terminology of Warrington and McCarthy (1987), would seem to be of critical importance, just as are the functional properties of concepts such as "saw" and 'scissors" represented in standard naming tasks, concepts that the patient appears to have lost. Indeed, the patients' conversational vocabulary does not provide convincing evidence of selective preservation of certain classes or categories of information: a patient who uses the word "solicitor" has no understanding of the concept "plumber"; can understand "hospital" but not "cinema"; talks about "grammar school" but denies having heard of "public school" or "state school". An alternative interpretation is possible. An observed feature of patients with semantic dementia is that their conversation focuses exclusively on personally relevant topics, on events relating to their daily lives. Conversation has a stereotyped quality, revolving around an increasingly narrow range of personally relevant issues. Patients never embark on general, impersonal topics, and if such topics are introduced by an interviewer patients display a total lack of comprehension. This characteristic raises the possibility that autobiographical experience may contribute to the preservation of concept meaning.

An earlier study of five patients with semantic dementia (Snowden et al., 1994) provided support for an autobiographical role in meaning preservation. In an investigation of proper names, names of personal acquaintances were significantly better recognised than were names of celebrities, even though celebrity names were selected to be as high-profile as possible (e.g. Margaret Thatcher, Winston Churchill, Marilyn Monroe, Elvis Presley). The difference could not be attributed to inherent differences in task difficulty, as the discrepancy for personal *vs.* celebrity names was not observed in a control group of amnesic patients with Alzheimer's disease. The semantic dementia patients' superior performance for acquaintance names was most marked for names of current, as opposed to past, personal relevance. A similar effect of current autobiography was observed in a study that investigated knowledge of place names. Names of places of personal relevance to the patient were much better identified as places, than were places of no personal relevance, even though the latter were selected to be high-profile cities, such as Oxford, Cambridge, and Edinburgh. An effect of personal experience was also noted in a study of object recognition in one patient: the patient identified objects that belonged to her significantly better than different examples of the same object which belonged to the examiner. An interpretation of these data in terms of a frequency effect can be discounted: vocabulary that the patient uses in general conversation is often of much lower frequency than unknown vocabulary. Objects belonging to the patient and the examiner have the same name, and were all prototypical exemplars of the object category. It has been argued (Snowden et al., 1994) that the experiential effect, found in these studies was also not precisely equivalent to a familiarity effect, the importance of which has been demonstrated by others (Funnell & Sheridan, 1992). "Familiarity" as defined by Snodgrass and Vanderwart (1980) refers to accumulated life-time experience; however it appeared that present experience was the critical factor in the study by Snowden and colleagues, regardless of degree of past familiarity—the name of a new acquaintance might be recalled whereas the names of former life-long friends might not.

If current autobiographical experience has a role in the preservation of meaning, what precisely is the nature of that role? One possibility is that experiential memory has a general facilitatory, or activating effect: that by current use the concept is prevented from being eroded. The "experiential" effect would be construed as complementary to a frequency and familiarity effect, representing one of the independent variables that influence what information is maintained and what is lost in a degenerating semantic system. A second possibility is that autobiographical experience has a much more direct effect on the meaning system: that it serves to invest concepts with meaning, and conceptual information that the patient has is derived precisely from that experience. The implication of this second alternative is that the patient's understanding of concepts that are apparently available, such as "chalice" and "vestry" should not be normal, but should be restricted to those aspects of information directly related to their personal experience. The patient should not have a broad, generalised knowledge of verbal concepts, but a narrowed, personalised understanding. If, on the other hand, the experiential effect simply has a general facilitatory role then it should have no implications for the nature of the knowledge about a concept that is retained and lost.

The present study sought to investigate the role of present autobiographical experience in meaning. A standard word definition procedure was used to investigate the nature of the information available for nouns and nouns phrases within the patient's conversational vocabulary, by examining (a) the quality of her definitions and (b) generalisation of information to other concepts. The study focused on one patient whose range of vocabulary in general conversation provides scope for such an analysis. Aside from the extent of her spoken vocabulary, the patient is remarkably similar in terms of the characteristics of her semantic disorder and preservation of skills, to five other patients with semantic dementia currently under study.

CASE HISTORY

WM, a right-handed deputy headmistress, began at the age of 49 to have problems in word comprehension and naming, and she would make semantically related errors (e.g. saying/flaiz/for "birds"). Over the next six years her language problems increased insidiously and she also developed difficulty recognising acquaintances, resulting in her medical referral. General physical examination was entirely normal. She showed awareness of her language difficulties, although lacked an appropriate level of concern. Baseline psychometric evaluation revealed above average performances on Raven's Progressive Matrices (Raven, 1938), copying of the Rey-Osterrieth figure (Osterrieth, 1944), and on trail making (Reitan & Wolfson, 1985), and normal performance on the Digit Symbol Copying task and Digit Span of the WAIS-R (Wechsler, 1981) (Table 1).

TABLE 1
Background Neuropsychological Data

April 1992		Score	Percentile Range
Progressive Matrices	A	12/12	
	B	10/12	
	C	9/12	
	Predicted total	45/60	90–95%
WAIS-R	Digit span	11	
(Age-corrected scale scores)	Digit symbol	10	
NART	Errors	31	
	Predicted IQ	102	
Trail making	Part A	48 secs	25–50%
	Part B	90 secs	50–75%
Rey-Osterrieth	Copy	36/36	
	Immediate recall	28/36	80%
	Delayed recall	26/36	70%
AMIPB Info. processing	Form 2 Speed	37/90	25–50%
	Digit cancellation	67/105	75%
	Errors	2	50–75%
AMIPB List learning	Form 1	23/75	< 10% cut-off
AMIPB Story recall	Immediate recall	4/56	< 10% cut-off
	Delayed recall	0/56	< 10% cut-off
Recognition memory test	Words	37/50	< 5%
Hooper Visual Organisation Text		17.5/30	moderate impairment
Graded naming test		0/30	< 5%
Verbal fluency	S words/1 min.	14	$(X = 12.1, s.d. = 4.1)$
	J words/1 min.	5	$(X = 6, s.d. = 2.3)$
	Animals/1 min.	9	$(X = 17.3, s.d. = 5.0)$

However, she was unable to score on the Graded Naming Test (McKenna & Warrington, 1983), her verbal fluency performance was reduced and she had difficulty identifying the jigsaw figures of the Hooper Visual Organisation Test (Hooper, 1958). Her visual memory, as measured by immediate and delayed recall of the Rey Osterrieth figure was intact, but she performed poorly on the word list learning and story recall tests of the Adult Memory and Information Processing Battery (AMIPB) (Coughlan & Hollows, 1985), and on a test of word recognition (Warrington, 1984). Her premorbid ability could not be accurately assessed by the National Adult Reading test (Nelson & O'Connell, 1978) because she was noted to make regularisation errors, consistent with a mild surface dyslexia. A computed tomographic scan was reported as normal.

WM was referred for a specialist neurological opinion. Neurological examination was normal, aside from bilateral extensor plantar responses. Evaluation of her mental state revealed her to be garrulous and lacking in insight into the magnitude of her disorder: she was aware of difficulty with words but attributed this to lack of practice in speaking since living alone, and to surreptitious introduction of new words into the dictionary by men in order to confuse women. Her utterances were fluent and grammatically correct, without phonemic paraphasias. Content was, however, repetitive and stereotyped, centring on personally relevant topics. She showed good understanding of spatial prepositions and complex syntax, including items from the TROG (Bishop, 1989). In contrast, there was a notable impairment in her ability to comprehend nominal terms. She performed poorly on the PALPA spoken word–picture matching task (Kay, Lesser, & Coltheart, 1992), 10/15 errors being of semantic type (Table 2). In a four-choice written word–picture matching task, employing Snodgrass and Vanderwart line drawings and semantically related distractor items, she made errors for all the categories with the exception of transport (the matching task is easy and no errors would have been anticipated from her premorbidly). Performance on the Boston picture naming task (Kaplan et al., 1983) was severely impaired, errors comprising generic and coordinate category responses, functional descriptions, as well as perceptual associative errors. Verbal fluency test performance revealed a deterioration in her ability to generate animal names since her earlier assessment. Her reading of regular words from the Glushko word list (Glushko, 1979) was error-free, but she read correctly only 78% of exception words.

WM showed mild impairment of object recognition. On the Boston naming test, a complete absence of visual recognition occurred for 17 of the 60 pictures. Recognition of Snodgrass and Vanderwart line drawings of familiar household objects was rather better: recognition was judged by her ability to pantomime the object's use. Performance on the Pyramids and Palm Trees associative picture matching task (Howard & Patterson, 1992) was severely impaired. She had profound problems in identification of faces of celebrities, and could provide no functional descriptive or identifying information even for high-profile individuals. Her family confirmed that all faces were well-known to her

TABLE 2
Test Data Relating to Semantic Disorder

November 1992–March 1993			Repeat test March 1994
PALPA—Spoken word picture matching		25/40	
Written word–picture matching 4-choice (Snodgrass drawings)	Animals	4/10	3/10
	Fruit/vegetables	9/10	8/10
	Clothing	8/10	9/10
	Objects	7/10	5/10
	Body parts	9/11	
	Transport	12/12	
	Musical instruments	1/ 9	
Boston naming test		6/60	
Verbal fluency	F words/1 min.	9	
	Animals/1 min.	3	
Pyramids and Palm Trees Test	words	28/52	
	pictures	30/52	
Line drawing identification		22/24	
Famous face identification		0/10	
Famous building identification		0/20	
March 1994 BORB	Minimal feature match	22/25	
	Foreshortened match	22/25	
	Item match	32/32	
	Object decision (easy version B)	18/32	
	Association match	14/32	

prior to her illness. Similarly, she showed no recognition of famous buildings, being able to provide neither their names nor identifying information such as their location or function.

Drawing, constructional, spatial and praxic skills were excellent. WM had no difficulty telling the time, and scored 12/12 in a clockface reading task and 12/12 in setting the hands to denote a specified time. She indicated with remarkable accuracy towns on a map of Great Britain, and countries on a map of Europe, provided that the city and country names were meaningful to her. She carried out normally a picture sequencing task, requiring ordering of pictures to tell a logical story. Given the profound and selective disorder of word and face meaning, a diagnosis of semantic dementia was made. Electroencephalography was normal and SPECT scan revealed reduced uptake in the left fronto-temporal region, providing support for the diagnosis.

Over the ensuing 12 months there has been a mild deterioration in WM's condition, her conversation having become increasingly stereotyped and repetitive. Nevertheless, her performance on the word–picture matching task remains similar to that demonstrated previously. There is a suggestion of increased difficulty in object recognition. On the Birmingham Object Recognition Battery (Riddoch & Humphreys, 1993) performance is at chance level on the object decision and associative sub-tests, which make semantic demands. On object decision, errors are largely false positive: she accepts unreal items as real. Her semantic disorder remains circumscribed: she has no difficulty carrying out drawing and perceptual matching tasks and her spatial skills are excellent. She continues to live alone and is functionally independent. She maintains her house and garden in an immaculate state, she finds her way to local towns without becoming lost, and recalls the spatial location of items in the supermarket for which she does not know the names. Despite her poor scores on traditional verbal memory tests her day-to-day memory remains excellent. She is well oriented, invariably recalls the correct date, and estimates accurately the time of day. She has no difficulty recalling spontaneously arrangements that she has made some weeks earlier, and adheres rigorously to appointment times, without being prompted by others. She has learned the names of individuals with whom she has become acquainted in the preceding few months, and, within the confines of her expressive vocabulary, can provide an accurate account of autobiographical events, relating particularly to recent months, but also including details of her past life. She has spontaneously described her childhood period of wartime evacuation and recalled the name of the family with whom she resided (in contrast, she can provide no factual information about the war, and shows no recognition of the name Hitler). She spontaneously refers to former holiday destinations, and describes details of foreign trips. She names former work colleagues during her adult years, and describes events pertaining to those individuals. Although not quantified, her autobiographical memory would appear to encompass both personal semantic information and information about autobiographical events.

Despite the severity of WM's semantic disorder on a range of verbal and non-verbal tasks, she continues to produce spontaneously a range of vocabulary in conversation. The following are examples of her utterances extracted from recordings of her conversation during the last 12 months:

I help prepare the chalice for the Eucharist.
Anne is catering manager at the agricultural college.
This is a graded building in a Conservation area.
The only money I have is my pension to pay the mortgage, electricity and oil.
I need to talk to my solicitor about my driving licence. I wrote to the DVLC about it.

EXPERIMENTAL INVESTIGATIONS:
UNDERSTANDING OF NOUN PHRASES

WM's understanding of noun phrases that she uses in conversation was addressed, by examining (a) the quality of her definitions with respect to their autobiographical *vs.* generalised content, and (b) her ability to generalise information to other noun phrases.

Materials and Procedure

Transcripts of WM's conversation recorded during the preceding 12 months were examined and all nouns and noun phrases produced by WM were listed. From this pool, noun phrases were selected which, when combined with a single noun, also from WM's spoken vocabulary, would produce a new noun phrase, as shown in Fig. 1. Stimuli were selected such that meaning of the "new" noun phrase could be inferred from understanding of its constituent parts, i.e. normal understanding of "driving licence" and "dog" would allow accurate inference about the meaning of "dog licence" independent of whether the latter item had been directly experienced or not. Potential test items were avoided where the meaning of the new noun phrase could not be directly inferred from knowledge of its constituent parts. The assumption was that if the patient's understanding of nouns and noun phrases within her vocabulary were normal, then she ought to be

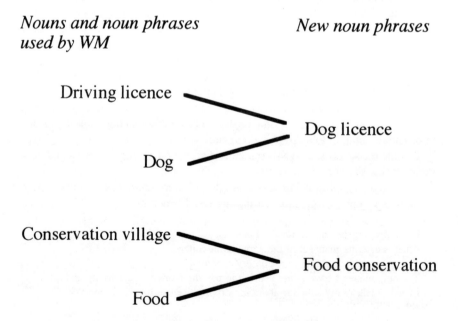

Nouns and noun phrases used by WM   *New noun phrases*

Driving licence

Dog licence

Dog

Conservation village

Food conservation

Food

FIG. 1.   Construction of test materials for first definition task.

able to define new noun phrases. Conversely, if her understanding of the vocabulary that she uses is limited to that aspect of information pertaining to her direct experience then she might not understand new noun phrases. "Old" and "new" nouns and noun phrases are shown in the Appendix (i).

"Old" and "new" noun phrases were presented, both orally and in written form, to WM in randomised order, using a standard word definition procedure. WM was encouraged to give as much information as possible about each phrase, and general open-ended prompts were employed, such as "What else do you know about it?", or "Can you guess, what do you think it could be?". Directed questioning regarding specific properties of a test item of the type "Does it have horns?" were avoided, as such questions could not be adequately controlled across test items, and interpretation of responses is potentially confounded by the patient's lack of understanding of the property concerned.

WM was also asked to define each of the component nouns making up the "new" noun phrases (e.g. "dog" and "licence" from the noun phrase "dog licence"). It was assumed that definition of single nouns, such as dog, drawn from WM's spoken vocabulary would be defined efficiently. Definition performance for the key component noun "licence" was less predictable, because this was being taken out of context of the noun phrase in which it was normally uttered by the patient. If WM's concept of the noun phrase "driving licence" were normal then the single word "licence" should be well understood and accurately defined. If, on the other hand, her concept of the noun phrase "driving licence" was understood as a conceptual unit with a specific autobiographical reference, then her understanding of the general term "licence" might be impaired.

Scoring of Responses

WM's spoken responses were recorded on audio-cassette tape, examined, and rated independently by two of the authors (JS and HG). There were two major dimensions of interest: (1) the quality of the definitions given for noun phrases drawn from her spoken vocabulary, and (2) her definition performance for "new" compared to "old" noun phrases. Definitions were scored as correct if they provided some indication of conceptual understanding, regardless of the depth or range of that understanding. Responses were scored as incorrect if no information could be provided, or if the information was patently false. For correct items, definitions were rated qualitatively according to whether the definition provided information related solely to the patient's own direct experience (autobiographical response), or provided information that extended beyond the patient's personal autobiography (general response). This distinction between autobiographical and general definitions was applied to noun phrases only. For single words the distinction is not readily made: for example, a definition of "dog" that includes information about different shapes and sizes could reflect intact general semantic knowledge, or personal experience of a range of examples of the dog species.

Results

WM made a clear distinction between test items that she did and did not know, either giving a rapid and confident definition or else denying emphatically all knowledge of the test item. There was no disagreement between the two examiners in rating responses as correct or incorrect.

Definition Performance for "Old" Nouns and Noun Phrases

Accuracy.   WM had no difficulty providing information about nouns and noun phrases, drawn from her spoken vocabulary. Performance for single nouns was 100% and for noun phrases 93%. The presence of occasional errors for noun phrases is unsurprising. Stimuli were drawn from transcripts of conversations recorded during the previous 12 months; there had been a slow, insidious deterioration in her condition during that time, with consequent increase in semantic loss.

Quality.   The pattern of her response for noun phrases is shown in Table 3, indicating that the majority of definitions provided information that was purely autobiographical in nature. Even with encouragement to expand her definition, she provided no information that was not directly personal in nature. Occasionally, the autobiographical *vs.* general nature of her response was ambiguous. In these cases, a lenient criterion was adopted for acceptance of a response as "general", in order to avoid exaggerated claims for the importance of autobiographical experience. For example, her definition of "Supply teaching" was: "I did supply teaching in different places, when other teachers have been poorly. They get somebody just to do supply teaching. Teaching very quickly." The "general" classification was applied because her definition included the notion of "Supply teaching" as an activity that people other than herself, i.e. "somebody", could engage in. As in this example, however, even "general" definitions had a personal slant.

TABLE 3
Definition of Noun Phrases

	Percentage of Response
Some general information provided	14%
Definition exclusively autobiographical	79%
Unable to define	7%

Definition of "New" vs. "Old" Noun Phrases

Definition performance for "new" noun phrases (e.g. "dog licence") was significantly inferior to performance for "old" noun phrases (e.g. "driving licence"), $\chi^2 = 9.58$, $P < 0.01$ (Fig. 2). In the majority of cases WM denied all knowledge of the new phrase and could make no attempt to infer or guess the meaning. On the occasions when new noun phrases were defined correctly, her definitions had an autobiographical quality. For example, given the phrase "money supply" she referred to her dwindling money supply since stopping work and the difficulty in paying her bills.

Definition of Key Nouns Extracted from Noun Phrases

Definition performance for single key nouns (e.g. licence), taken out of context of the noun phrase in which they were normally uttered, was significantly inferior to performance for the complete noun phrase (e.g. driving licence), Fisher's Exact test, $P < 0.05$ (Fig. 2).

Examples of WM's definitions are given below. The definitions highlight (a) the differential performance for nouns and noun phrases drawn from her spoken

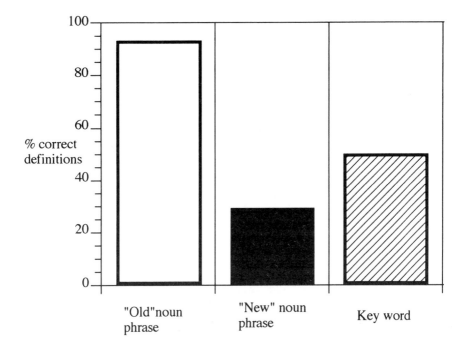

FIG. 2.   Correct definitions for "old" noun phrases (e.g. "driving licence"), "new" noun phrases (e.g. "dog licence"), and key constituent word (e.g. "licence").

vocabulary (first two items of each set) and for new noun phrase constructions (third item), and (b) the autobiographical quality to her responses:

Driving licence:	"I have the driving licence for driving cars, caravanettes and minibuses. I get it from the DVLC. It's labelled with my name."
Dog:	"They're out there [referring to dogs barking outside]. I take the vicar's dog for a walk at 2 o'clock."
Dog licence:	"I don't know the dog licence. I've never known the dog licence in all my life."
Church warden:	"I've been the church warden for 12 years. I do all different things, reading, picking up the money, and I have to wander round, and clean the church and sometimes put the flowers on."
Traffic:	"Driving—cars, buses, vans and tractors."
Traffic warden:	"Traffic warden. I don't know traffic warden. I only know the traffic, any car."
Conservation village:	"This is a conservation village. Any of these old houses."
Food:	"Loads of food. Whatever we're eating."
Food conservation:	"I don't know. I've lost the conservation. Was it preparing meals and things?"

EXPERIMENTAL INVESTIGATIONS: UNDERSTANDING OF NOUNS

Results from the previous task suggest that WM was treating known noun phrases such as driving licence, church warden, and conservation village as units of meaning: constituent key words, such as licence and warden were poorly understood. It would follow therefore that new noun phrases employing those key words would also be poorly understood. In the second task "new" compound words/noun phrases were constructed by combining single words from the corpus of her nominal vocabulary, as shown in Fig. 3. Understanding of this "old" and "new" vocabulary, shown in the Appendix (ii), was examined using the standard definition procedure, as described earlier.

Results

Definition performance for "old" words and "new" compounds is shown in Fig 4. WM had no difficulty defining words drawn from her conversation vocabulary and scored 100%. In contrast, she had significantly greater difficulty defining new compound words (Fisher's Exact test, $P < 0.05$). She would frequently cover each word in turn, saying "Well, I know this one, and I know this one, but I've never seen the two together. I've never known that in all my

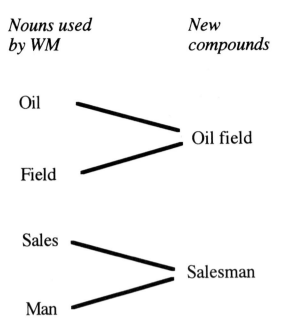

Nouns used
by WM

New
compounds

Oil

Oil field

Field

Sales

Salesman

Man

FIG. 3. Construction of test materials for second definition task.

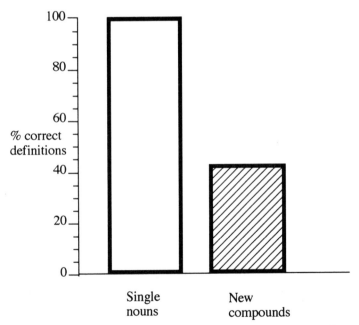

FIG. 4. Correct definitions for single nouns (e.g. "oil" and "field") and for "new" compounds (e.g. "oil field").

life'', and could make no attempt to guess or infer a meaning. Some examples of her responses are:

Oil:	"It's for this heating. It's in the outbuilding. Oil from Charringtons."
Field:	"I walk round the fields with the vicar's dog."
Oil field:	"I don't know what that is. I know the field, but we only use the oil for the radiator."
Sales:	"Up for sale. Anything up for sale, the house, car. Going for any amount of money."
Man:	"Different from us. We're all ladies [referring to three women in the room]."
Salesman:	"I've not seen the salesman before. I don't know that. I only know the man fitting something [refers to electrician coming to the house]."

DISCUSSION

The study addressed the nature of the role of autobiographical experience in maintenance of concepts. It was argued that if current personal experience has a general facilitatory effect then it would influence which concepts are retained and which lost, but would have no implications for the quality of that underlying conceptual knowledge. Conversely, if current experience has a direct effect in endowing concepts with meaning, then understanding of concepts, which are apparently available to the patient by virtue of their appropriate usage, should not be normal but should be limited to that aspect of meaning directly derived from personal experience. The study examined the understanding in one patient, WM, of nouns and noun phrases that she uses appropriately in general conversation.

WM, as anticipated, performed extremely well in defining nouns and noun phrases drawn from her conversational vocabulary, exemplifying the overall high degree of internal consistency in her performance. Nonetheless, her definitions had a markedly autobiographical quality. Despite encouragement to expand her definitions she rarely provided information that went beyond her own direct experience. Even those responses classified as "general" had an autobiographical emphasis. This quality of her definitions suggests that her understanding of terms, even though used appropriately in conversation, may not be normal, but may be autobiographically constrained. Such an interpretation cannot, however, rely on her definitions of "known" words alone. It is possible that WM has knowledge that she does not or cannot express.

The use of "new" noun phrases and compound nouns, constructed from "known' vocabulary permits greater examination of WM's understanding. If her understanding of the words and phrases that she uses is normal, then she ought to be able to infer meanings of other phrases constructed from that vocabulary. Her understanding of "new" phrases, such as "dog licence", "traffic warden" and "food conservation" was, however, extremely poor. Indeed, words such as "licence", "warden" and "conservation" taken out of the context of the noun phrase in which they are normally uttered were also poorly understood. Despite the fact that in conversation she uses the phrases "driving licence", "church warden" and "conservation village" consistently and entirely appropriately, she appears to have very poor grasp of the essential or core meaning of licence, warden and conservation. Her understanding of "driving licence" appears to be limited to the piece of paper on which is written her name, which she needs in order to drive her car; she appears not to have a general notion of "licence" as something that gives leave or permission. Similarly, her understanding of "conservation village" refers to the old houses in her village, but not the general idea of preservation or protection.

The construction of compound words from single nouns provides further evidence of restriction of conceptual understanding to what is directly experienced. WM provides good understanding of "oil" in so far as it pertains to her everyday life: that it is used in the radiators for heating, that it is stored in the outbuilding, that it comes from Charrington's. She appears to have no general knowledge of oil that extends beyond her personal experience, and is unable to conjecture what an oil field might be. Autobiographical experience appears to have a direct effect in determining what information is available and what is lost.

The findings have theoretical implications for the understanding of semantic memory function. Since the distinction with episodic memory was drawn (Tulving, 1972), semantic memory has characteristically been construed as a relatively stable knowledge base, acquired early in life and culturally shared, and models of semantic representation have tended to reflect this static view. Findings from the present study suggest a much more interactive relationship between semantic memory and autobiographical experience: a dynamic semantic memory system that is constantly updated with information from personal experience. In semantic dementia it appears that it is information of current autobiographical relevance that is selectively retained.

In WM, appropriate word usage does not imply normal conceptual understanding: she has impoverished or "partial" information about concepts. This finding is not new, and is entirely consistent with other reports which have suggested that semantic breakdown is not all or none (Hodges et al., 1992a; Warrington, 1975; Warrington & Shallice, 1984). Nevertheless, the nature of WM's partial information is somewhat at odds with that documented in previous reports. In WM, concepts appear to become progressively narrowed and constrained to the particular context in which they are experienced. Her conceptual information appears to be personal and specific, not broad and general. The contrasting notion has been advanced that broad categorical information is most resistant to disruption in a degenerating semantic system (Shallice, 1988). The latter view stems from the observation that patients may commonly be able to classify an object with respect to its superordinate category, but unable to distinguish it from co-ordinate category members (Hodges et al., 1992a; Warrington, 1975; Warrington & Shallice, 1984). A patient may know that a lion is an "animal", but be unable to provide lower-level featural information that permits accurate distinction from a tiger or a dog. With regard to a hierarchical model of semantic memory as outlined by Collins and Quillian (1969), it would be assumed that lower levels of the hierarchical tree are damaged first, the higher, superordinate level being most resistant to disruption. WM's apparently contradictory pattern cannot be attributed to inherent patient differences: she, like other patients with semantic dementia, may also identify a picture of a lion as "an animal", but not as a lion; a banana as "something to eat", but not as the specific fruit. Narrowed, personalised information, and broad categorical information seem, on the surface, to be present in the same patient.

It has been pointed out, however, (Rapp & Caramazza, 1989, 1993) that the fact that superordinate level questions are answered better than questions relating to subordinate level information, does not necessarily indicate that superordinate level information *per se* has been relatively spared. If attribute features for a given concept have been reduced, for example, to knowledge that a canary flies and has feathers, then this impoverished representation will better support superordinate type questions, such as "Is it a bird?" than questions such as "Is it yellow or brown?". We would argue in the same vein that the ability to name a lion as "an animal" but not as "a lion" does not imply that the patient has available a normal broad concept of the category of animals.

A confounding factor in determining patients' underlying semantic knowledge is that we are obliged to infer knowledge from their responses, whether verbal or non-verbal; but, as demonstrated by the present study, the assumptions on which such inferences are made may not be correct. In the case of verbal responses, appropriate word usage does not necessarily imply normal conceptual understanding. We would argue that WM's world view is progressively shrinking and concepts are becoming increasingly narrowed and personalised. With regard to the category of animals, we would suggest that she has lost knowledge of animals for which she does not have direct experience: that her concept of "animal" is reduced to knowledge, perhaps, of dogs and cats. If shown a picture of a lion, she is likely to search for the closest match within her experience, and associate the stimulus with a dog. She might name the picture as "a dog", or conversely might produce the superordinate category term "animal" (both types of responses are typical of this and other semantic dementia patients' naming performance). Her understanding of "animal" would be as impoverished as her understanding of particular examples of animal, but her superordinate level response would be classed as correct and her subordinate level response incorrect. It is perhaps noteworthy, in this regard, that patients with semantic dementia who provide superordinate level responses in naming tasks, such as "It's an animal", do not qualify this response with "but I don't know which one". We would suggest that the patient no longer has available the notion of the entire spectrum of animals; the patient's concept of the class of animals is severely diminished.

Semantic memory has been the focus of widespread theoretical interest in recent years, but relatively little attention has been paid to the possible influences of autobiographical experience. This undoubtedly stems from the frequently held assumption that semantic and episodic memory, which encompass autobiographical experience, are functionally independent systems, and that understanding of one can be achieved without regard to the other. There is, however, evidence of complex inter-relationships. It has been argued (Butters & Cermak, 1986) that "episodic" memories may, with time, become increasingly decontextualised and hence "semantic" in nature, thereby accounting for observed temporal gradients of retrograde amnesia. Studies of retrograde memory function in amnesic patients (Cermak & O'Connor, 1983; Warrington & McCarthy, 1988) have documented the generalised, factual nature of patients' autobiographical memories, suggesting that such memories have acquired the status of semantic knowledge. A more recent study by McCarthy and Warrington (1992), of the retrograde memory of a post-encephalitic amnesic patient, has demonstrated further that the distinction between "semantic" and "episodic" knowledge is not clear-cut. The patient's knowledge about people was differentially affected: the patient could retrieve factual knowledge about people, for whom he was unable to describe specific episodes.

A link between personal autobiographical information and semantic knowledge has also been suggested by studies of normal memory. Conway (1987) showed that positive response latencies to general autobiographical questions, such as "Do you often play football?" were speeded by provision of a semantically related prime, such as "sport" as much as for general semantic questions, such as "Is rugby a sport?". In a further study, Conway (1990) found that retrieval of autobiographical memories elicited by a cue word, such as "shirt", was facilitated by provision of a goal-derived category prime, such as "birthday present", suggesting that such conceptual "semantic" categories are closely associated in memory with the records of experienced events.

De Renzi et al. (1987) have provided evidence of an important semantic–autobiographic interaction, which is particularly pertinent to the present study. In an investigation of a female patient with a profound semantic disorder following herpes simplex encephalitis, De Renzi et al. noted that although their patient's knowledge of non-personal public events was severely impaired, such events could sometimes be recalled provided that they established a link with her personal experience or had a profound impact on her feelings. The study by De Renzi et al. highlighted, moreover, the important distinction between "autobiographical" memory, which was preserved in their patient, and non-personal episodic memory, which was impaired. In patients with a profound and putatively selective disorder of semantics, it would seem that non-personal episodes may be impaired while semantic information of personal, autobiographical relevance is retained. We would argue that autobiographical experience is a potent factor in influencing preserved knowledge in semantic dementia.

In characterising the nature of information lost and retained in semantic disorders, distinctions have been made between attributes of meaning: functional *vs.* sensory (Warrington & McCarthy, 1987; Warrington & Shallice, 1984);

functional and perceptual (Sartori & Job, 1988); verbal *vs.* visual (Silveri & Gainotti, 1988); associative *vs* perceptual (Chertkow et al., 1992). Deficits are commonly demonstrated at the sensory/perceptual level. One might consider the extent to which those functional or associative properties, which are reported to be preserved, are available by virtue of their link with personal, experiential memory: an object's function is determined by what the patient does with it, what is part of the patient's own daily routine. In any event, it would seem that personal autobiography is a factor of sufficient importance to warrant serious attention in studies of patients with disorders of semantic memory.

REFERENCES

Bishop, D. (1989). T.R.O.G. *Test of Reception of Grammar.* Abingdon, UK: Thomas Leach Ltd.
Butters, N., & Cermak, L.S. (1986). A case study of the forgetting of autobiographical knowledge: implications for the study of retrograde amnesia. In D.C. Rubin (Ed.), *Autobiographical memory.* Cambridge: Cambridge University Press.
Cermak, L.S. (1984). The episodic–semantic distinction in amnesia. In L.R. Squire & N. Butters (Eds.), *Neuropsychology of memory.* New York: The Guilford Press.
Cermak, L.S., & O'Connor, M. (1983). The anterograde and retrograde retrieval ability of a patient with amnesia due to encephalitis. *Neuropsychologia, 21,* 213–233.
Chertkow, H., & Bub, D. (1990). Semantic memory loss in dementia of Alzheimer's type. What do various measures measure? *Brain, 113,* 397–417.
Chertkow, H., Bub, D., & Caplan, D. (1992). Constraining theories of semantic memory processing: evidence from dementia. *Cognitive Neuropsychology, 9,* 327–365.
Collins, A.M., & Quillian, M.R. (1969). Retrieval time from semantic memory. *Journal of Verbal Learning and Verbal Behavior, 8,* 240–248.
Conway, M.A. (1987). Verifying autobiographical facts. *Cognition, 26,* 39–58.
Conway, M.A. (1990). Associations between autobiographical memories and concepts. *Journal of Experimental Psychology: Learning, Memory and Cognition, 16,* 799–812.
Coughlan, A.K., & Hollows, S.E. (1985). *The Adult Memory and Information Processing Battery (AMIPB).* Leeds, UK: A.K. Coughlan.
Coughlan, A.K., & Warrington, E.K. (1981). The impairment of verbal semantic memory: a single case study. *Journal of Neurology, Neurosurgery and Psychiatry, 44,* 1079–1083.
De Renzi, E., Liotti, M., & Nichelli, P. (1987). Semantic amnesia with preservation of autobiographic memory. A case report. *Cortex, 23,* 575–597.
Dunn, L.M. (1959). *Peabody Picture Vocabulary Test.* Minneapolis: American Guidance Service.
Ellis, A.W., Young, A.W., & Critchley, E.M.R. (1989). Loss of memory for people following temporal lobe damage. *Brain, 112,* 1469–1483.
Funnell, E., & Sheridan, J. (1992). Categories of knowledge? Unfamiliar aspects of living and non-living things. *Cognitive Neuropsychology, 9,* 135–153.
Glushko, R.J. (1979). The organization and activation of orthographic knowledge in reading aloud. *Journal of Experimental Psychology: Human Perception and Performance, 5,* 674–691.
Hodges, J.R., Patterson, K., Oxbury, S., & Funnell, E. (1992a). Semantic dementia. Progressive fluent aphasia with temporal lobe atrophy. *Brain, 115,* 1783–1806.
Hodges, J.R., Salmon, D.P., & Butters, N. (1992b). Semantic memory impairment in Alzheimer's disease: failure of access or degraded knowledge: *Neuropsychologia, 30,* 301–314.
Hooper, H.E. (1958). *The Hooper Visual Organization Test. Manual.* Los Angeles: Western Psychological Services.
Howard, D., & Patterson, K. (1992). *Pyramids and palm trees: A test of semantic access from pictures and words.* Bury St Edmunds, UK: Thames Valley Publishing Company.

Kaplan, E., Goodglass, H., Weintraub, S., & Segal, H. (1983). *Boston Naming Test*. Philadelphia: Lea & Febinger.

Kay, J., Lesser, R., & Coltheart, M. (1992). *Psycholinguistic Assessments of Language Processing in Aphasia (PALPA)*. Hove, UK: Lawrence Erlbaum Associates Ltd.

Kinsbourne, M., & Wood, F. (1975). Short-term memory processes and the amnesic syndrome. In D. Deutsch & J.A. Deutsch (Eds.), *Short-term memory* (pp. 258–291). New York: Academic Press.

McCarthy, R.A., & Warrington, E.K. (1992). Actors but not scripts: the dissociation of people and events in retrograde amnesia. *Neuropsychologia, 30*, 633–644.

McKenna, P., & Warrington, E.K. (1983). *Graded Naming Test*. Windsor, UK: NFER-Nelson.

Nelson, H.E., & O'Connell, A. (1978). Dementia: the estimation of premorbid intelligence levels using the new adult reading test. *Cortex, 14*, 234–244.

Osterrieth, P.A. (1944). Le test de copie d'une figure complexe: contribution a l'étude de la perception et de la memoire. *Archives de Psychologie, Geneve, 30*, 205–220.

Patterson, K., & Hodges, J.R. (1992). Deterioration of word meaning: implications for reading. *Neuropsychologia, 30*, 1025–1040.

Pietrini, V., Nertempi, P., Vaglia, A., Revello, M.G., Pinna, V., & Ferro-Milone, F. (1988). Recovery from herpes simplex encephalitis: selective impairment of specific semantic categories with neuroradiological correlation. *Journal of Neurology, Neurosurgery and Psychiatry, 51*, 1284–1293.

Rapp, B.A., & Caramazza, A. (1989). General to specific access to word meaning: a claim re-examined. *Cognitive Neuropsychology, 6*, 251–272.

Rapp, B.A., & Caramazza, A. (1993). On the distinction between deficits of access and deficits of storage: a question of theory. *Cognitive Neuropsychology, 10*, 113–141.

Raven, J.C. (1938). *Progressive matrices: A perceptual test of intelligence*. London: H.K. Lewis.

Reitan, R.M., & Wolfson, D. (1985). *The Halstead–Reitan Neuropsychological Test Battery*. Tucson: Neuropsychology Press.

Riddoch, J., & Humphreys, G.W. (1993). *Birmingham Object Recognition Battery*. Hove, UK: Lawrence Erlbaum Associates Ltd.

Saffran, E.M., & Schwartz, M.F. (1994). Of cabbages and things: semantic memory from a neuropsychological perspective—a tutorial review. In C. Umilta & M. Moscovitch (Eds.), *Attention & performance XV*. Cambridge, MA: MIT Press.

Sartori, G., & Job, R. (1988). The oyster with four legs: a neuropsychological study on the interaction between vision and semantic information. *Cognitive Neuropsychology, 5*, 105–132.

Schacter, D.L., & Tulving, E. (1982). Memory, amnesia and the episodic–semantic distinction. In R.L. Isaacson & N.E. Spear (Eds.), *Expression of knowledge*. New York: Plenum Press.

Schwartz, M.F., Marin, O.S.M., & Saffran, E.M. (1979). Dissociations of language function in dementia: a case study. *Brain & Language, 7*, 277–306.

Schwartz, M.F., Saffran, E.M., & Marin, O.S.M. (1980). Fractionating the reading process in dementia: evidence for word-specific print-to-sound associations. In M. Coltheart, K. Patterson, & J.C. Marshall (Eds.), *Deep dyslexia*. London: Routledge & Paul.

Shallice, T. (1987). Impairments of semantic processing: Multiple dissociations. In M. Coltheart, G. Sartori, & R. Job (Eds.), *The cognitive neuropsychology of language*. London: Lawrence Erlbaum Associates Ltd.

Shallice, T. (1988). *From neuropsychology to mental structure* (pp. 282–283). Cambridge: Cambridge University Press.

Sheridan, J., & Humphreys, G.W. (1993). A verbal-semantic category-specific recognition impairment. *Cognitive Neuropsychology, 10*, 143–184.

Silveri, M.C., & Gainotti, G. (1988). Interaction between vision and language in category-specific impairment. *Cognitive Neuropsychology, 5*, 677–709.

Snodgrass, J.G., & Vanderwart, M. (1980). A standardised set of 260 pictures: norms for name agreement, image agreement, familiarity and visual complexity. *Journal of Experimental Psychology: Human Learning and Memory, 6*, 174–215.

Snowden, J.S., Goulding, P.J., & Neary, D. (1989). Semantic dementia: a form of circumscribed cerebral atrophy. *Behavioural Neurology, 2,* 167–182.

Snowden, J.S., Griffiths, H., & Neary, D. (1994). Semantic dementia: autobiographical contribution to preservation of meaning. *Cognitive Neuropsychology, 11,* 265–288.

Snowden, J.S., Neary, D., Mann, D.M.A., Goulding, P.J., & Testa, H.J. (1992). Progressive language disorder due to lobar atrophy. *Annals of Neurology, 31,* 174–183.

Tulving. E. (1972). Episodic and semantic memory. In E. Tulving & W. Donaldson (Eds.), *Organization of memory* (pp. 382–404). New York: Academic Press.

Warrington, E.K. (1975). The selective impairment of semantic memory. *Quarterly Journal of Experimental Psychology, 27,* 635–637.

Warrington, E.K. (1984). *Recognition Memory Test.* Windsor, UK: NFER-Nelson.

Warrington, E.K., & McCarthy, R.A. (1987). Categories of knowledge: further fractionations and an attempted integration. *Brain, 110,* 1273–1296.

Warrington, E.K., & McCarthy, R.A. (1988). The fractionation of retrograde amnesia. *Brain & Cognition, 7,* 184–200.

Warrington, E.K., & Shallice, T. (1984). Category-specific semantic impairments. *Brain, 107,* 829–854.

Wechsler, D. (1981). *Wechsler Adult Intelligence Scale—Revised.* New York: Psychological Corporation.

Wilkins, A., & Moscovitch, M. (1978). Selective impairment of semantic memory after temporal lobectomy. *Neuropsychologia, 16,* 73–79.

APPENDIX

(i)

Vocabulary used in conversation by WM		*New noun phrases*
Driving licence	Dog	Dog licence
Brain scan	Body	Body scan
Victorian house	England	Victorian England
Teaching job	Holiday	Holiday job
Half term	Full	Full term
Conservation village	Food	Food conservation
Minibus	Water	Water bus
Supply teaching	Money	Money supply
Church warden	Traffic	Traffic warden
Deputy head	Government	Deputy government
Graded building	Fruit	Graded fruit
Brain damage	Weather	Weather damage
Catering manager	Hotel	Hotel manager
Healing group	Leg	Healing leg

(ii)

Words used in conversation by WM		*New compounds*
Pen	Friend	Penfriend
Car	Telephone	Car telephone
Oil	Field	Oil field
Sea	Bird	Seabird
Car	Body	Car body
Sales	Man	Salesman
Natural	World	Natural world

MEMORY, 1995, *3* (3/4), 247–264

Neuroanatomical Correlates of Category-specific Semantic Disorders: A Critical Survey

Guido Gainotti, Maria Caterina Silveri, Antonio Daniele
and Laura Giustolisi

Catholic University of Rome, Italy

Previous studies of category-specific semantic disturbances ·have focused their attention on the intrinsic cognitive structure of these disorders. The present survey aims to evaluate the relationships between disrupted semantic category and localisation of the underlying brain damage, in order to establish whether the injured brain areas house just those neurophysiological mechanisms that should have critically contributed to the acquisition of the disrupted semantic categories. We took into account in our review two double dissociations concerning respectively: (1) the impairment of a specific linguistic category—we contrast those disorders selectively affecting verbs (action names) with those selectively affecting nouns (object names); (2) the impairment of a specific conceptual/ semantic domain—we contrast disorders selectively affecting living beings with those preferentially affecting man-made artefacts.

The hypothesis that different categories of knowledge may be closely intertwined with different sources of sensory-motor information, was substantially confirmed. The lesion preferentially encroached on the left frontal lobe when the category "verbs" was selectively affected; it involved the left temporal lobe and the posterior association areas when the category "nouns" was preferentially disrupted; it involved bilateral temporo-limbic structures and inferior temporal lobes when the category "living beings" was selectively disrupted; it usually encroached on the left fronto-parietal areas when man-made artefacts and body parts were preferentially affected.

These data support the hypothesis that: (a) action schemata may critically contribute to the development of the semantic representation of verbs, (b) mechanisms of sensory integration may play an important role in establishing the semantic representation of nouns; (c) high-level visual processing and multi-modal sensory convergency may critically contribute to organising the semantic representation of living beings; (d) motor-kinaesthetic integration may play a leading role in developing the semantic representation of man-made artefacts.

Requests for reprints should be sent to Guido Gainotti, Institute of Neurology of the Catholic University of Rome, Policlinico Gemelli, Largo A. Gemelli, 8, 00168 Roma, Italy.

INTRODUCTION

The hypothesis that some kinds of representations may be located in the brain very near to the sensori-motor mechanisms on which they are grounded is certainly not a new one in the history of neurology. The classical theory of the "image centres" (Bastian, 1869, 1898; Wernicke, 1874/1908) was substantially based on this principle: the representations of the auditory sounds of words were deemed to be located in Wernicke's area, very close to the primary cortical auditory areas, whereas the representations of the motor sequences necessary for oral production of individual words were thought to be stored in Broca's area, very near to the portions of the motor cortex corresponding to the bucco-facial apparatus.

In spite of this background, the possibility that different realms of knowledge (namely different categories of words or concepts) may be stored in different parts of the brain was not considered. Such storage may be very close to the basic sensory-motor mechanisms that could have critically contributed to their acquisition.

In the last 10–15 years, however, the detailed clinical and experimental study of individual patients has convincingly shown not only that different categories of knowledge can be selectively disrupted by brain damage, but also that the preferential impairment of a given semantic category usually implicates damage to a well-defined part of the brain. However, it must be acknowledged that although description of the main categories of knowledge selectively disrupted by brain damage is well advanced, the study of their anatomical correlates is much less adequately developed. Thus, several authors using different categories of words as stimuli have shown that brain-damaged patients may demonstrate a selective impairment of some of these categories, such as *abstract or concrete words* (Shallice, 1988; Warrington, 1975, 1981); *proper names of people* (McKenna & Warrington, 1978; Semenza & Zettin, 1988, 1989; *action names/ verbs/or object names/nouns* (Baxter & Warrington, 1985; Caramazza & Hillis, 1991; Damasio & Tranel, 1993; Daniele, Silveri, Giustolisi, & Gainotti, 1993; McCarthy & Warrington, 1985; Miceli, Silveri, Nocentini, & Caramazza, 1989; Miceli, Silveri, Villa, & Caramazza, 1984; Zingeser & Berndt, 1988).

Other authors using as stimuli both verbal and non-verbal material have shown that a category-specific impairment can not only affect word classes, but may also involve specific semantic/conceptual domains. Examples include the broad categories of *living beings and food* (Basso, Capitani, & Laiacona, 1988; De Renzi & Lucchelli, 1994; Farah, Hammond, Metha, & Radcliff, 1989; Hart & Gordon, 1992; Sartori & Job, 1988; Silveri & Gainotti, 1988; Sirigu, Duhamel, & Poncet, 1991; Warrington & Shallice, 1984) and the categories of *non-living things/man-made artefacts* (Behrmann & Lieberthal, 1989; Hillis, Rapp, Romani, & Caramazza, 1990; Sacchett & Humphreys, 1992; Warrington & McCarthy, 1983, 1987). However, the great majority of these studies have ignored the anatomical correlates of these category-specific disorders, as they have been conducted within the framework of cognitive neuropsychology. As such they focus attention on the intrinsic cognitive structure of category-specific semantic disorders in order to check the existing cognitive models of the functional architecture of the semantic system or of lexical organisation. In the present survey we approach the problem from a different viewpoint, namely from that of cognitive neurosciences, and focus our attention on the relationships between disrupted semantic categories and the localisation of the underlying brain injury. Our working hypothesis was that the damaged brain areas subserve those sensorimotor mechanisms that could have contributed critically to the acquisition of the disrupted semantic categories.

This hypothesis is consistent with a line of thought recently developed by Warrington and McCarthy (1987) and by McCarthy and Warrington (1990, 1994). These authors have rightly pointed out that, even if different kinds of sensory-motor and functional information usually converge in the acquisition of our conceptual knowledge, the relative salience or weighting of various sources of information may be very different for different semantic categories. Different categories of meaning might, therefore, be "fed" by different sources of information; disruption of a particular source might lead to a selective disruption of a particular semantic category.

With this aim in mind, we have taken into account in the present survey only those category-specific disturbances that fulfilled the following criteria: (a) a consistency of results across investigations performed in different laboratories; (b) the presence of anatomo-clinical correlations allowing us to identify the locus of lesions causing this specific semantic impairment.

We have focused our attention on two double dissociations: the first apparently concerns two different grammatical/syntactic categories, namely verbs and nouns, whereas the second clearly concerns two domains of conceptual/semantic knowledge, namely living things (animals, flowers, vegetables, etc.) and man-made artefacts. We will argue, however, that in both cases the semantic level was probably basically involved, and that nouns and verbs were selectively impaired because they represent two different semantic categories (objects and actions respectively) and not because they belong to two different syntactic/grammatical classes.

DISORDERS IN PRODUCTION AND COMPREHENSION OF NOUNS AND VERBS IN APHASIC PATIENTS

The first study suggesting a differential impairment of nouns and verbs in patients with fluent and non-fluent aphasia was conducted by Goodglass, Klein, Carey, and Jones (1966), who noticed that fluent aphasics were more impaired in naming objects (producing nouns) than in naming actions (producing verbs), whereas non-fluent aphasics showed the opposite pattern of impairment. This double dissociation was afterwards further investigated, focusing attention on agrammatic patients (within the category of non-fluent aphasics) and on anomic patients (within the category of fluent aphasic). Thus, Myerson and Goodglass (1972), Marin, Saffran, and Schwartz (1976), and Miceli, Mazzuchi, Menn, and Goodglass (1983) noted that agrammatic patients tended to omit main (root) verbs, whereas Benson (1979) stressed the specific difficulty that anomic patients had in their selection of nouns. These early observations, gathered in the context of clinical investigations aiming to characterise the main features distinguishing agrammatism from anomia, were followed by studies specifically designed to investigate the differential impairment of nouns and verbs in aphasic patients.

In two well-conducted group studies, Miceli et al. (1984, 1988) have convincingly shown: (a) that agrammatic patients are more impaired in naming actions than objects, whereas anomic patients show the opposite pattern of impairment (Miceli et al., 1984); (b) that the same kind of dissociation can be observed in comprehension of nouns and verbs. Some agrammatic patients, however, show a deficit only in production (but not in comprehension) of verbs, whereas some anomic subjects show a deficit only in production of nouns (Miceli et al., 1988). In single case studies, McCarthy and Warrington (1985) have described an agrammatic patient who showed a selective impairment in the retrieval and comprehension of verbs, whereas Zingeser and Berndt (1988) have described an anomic patient who had a selective difficulty in producing nouns both in the oral and in the written modalities.

Broadening the field of investigation beyond the syndromes of agrammatism and anomia, Caramazza and Hillis (1991) reported an even more specific deficit in verb production. One of their patients (HW) was unable to produce verbs in the oral but not in the written modality, whereas another patient (SJD) showed a selective deficit in verb production only in the written but not in the oral modality. Finally, the problem of the localisation of lesions leading to a selective impairment for nouns and for verbs has been studied. Damasio and Tranel (1993) investigated patients with chronic stable symptoms following a focal brain injury, and Daniele et al. (1993) documented subjects with slowly progressive focal brain atrophy. In spite of the differences between these two studies with regard to the nature and temporal evolution of brain pathology, their results were surprisingly similar. A temporal lobe lesion has been consistently observed in patients with a selective breakdown of nouns, whereas frontal lobe involvement has been found in subjects with a selective impairment for verbs.

However, the interpretation of these data is still controversial, as according to some authors (e.g. Caramazza & Hillis, 1991; Miceli et al., 1984, 1988) the locus of cognitive impairment is at the lexical level, specifically concerning the phonological (or the graphemic) output lexicon, whereas according to other authors (e.g. McCarthy & Warrington, 1985, 1994) disorders of nouns and verb retrieval may be underpinned by a semantic level deficit. It is therefore necessary to give a brief consideration of the locus of cognitive impairments, before discussing the anatomical locus of lesions provoking a category-specific disorder for nouns or verbs.

Locus of Cognitive Impairment in Category-specific Disorders for Nouns and Verbs

The hypothesis that the selective impairment of nouns and verbs may be due to purely lexical defects is supported by two sets of data: (1) the observation of Miceli et al. (1988) that the category-specific impairment for verbs of some agrammatic patients (and for nouns of some anomic patients) can be circumscribed to the production stage, without affecting the comprehension level; (2) the evidence for selective modality-specific deficits in verb production reported by Caramazza and Hillis (1991) in patients HW and SJD.

As a matter of fact, if one accepts, as most authors do, that a central semantic disorder should express itself both at the expressive and at the receptive level in all the lexical tasks that require a consultation of the semantic system, (see, for example, Gainotti, 1976; Butterworth, Howard, & McLoughlin, 1984, and Hillis et al., 1990) then the observation that some category-specific defects are limited either to the expressive level or to a single lexical modality could suggest that the cognitive locus of lesion implicates the level of output lexical representations rather than the level of the semantic system. On the other hand, the observation of McCarthy and Warrington (1985) and of Miceli et al. (1988) that some anomic and some agrammatic patients show the same category-specific disorder (for nouns or for verbs) both in production and in comprehension, suggests that, at least in these patients, the defect should be located at the semantic level. Furthermore, longitudinal data obtained by Daniele et al. (1993), in patients with category-specific disorders arising in the context of degenerative diseases, suggest that even disturbances limited to the output level or to a single lexical modality do not necessarily originate from the disruption of independent lexical representations. Data reported by these authors and summarised in Table 1 shows, in fact, that in the early stages of the disease both patient GG and patient RA presented a category-specific defect for verbs limited either to production tasks or to a single output modality (in patient RA the selective impairment for verbs was present only in written but not in oral confrontation naming).

With the progression of the disease, however, the same category-specific defect also emerged in the other output modality (patient RA: second session) and/or at the receptive level (patient GG: second session; patient RA: third session). As it is very unlikely that during the progression of a disease the same pattern of deficit may develop independently with the same characteristics in different lexical modalities, these data suggest that a basic semantic disorder

TABLE 1
Patients GG and RA

Patient	Experimental Tasks	% of errors Noun	Verb		
GG					
July 1991	Oral Naming	6 (n = 48)	31 (n = 48)	$\chi^2 = 9.8$	$P < 0.002$
	Word–Picture Matching*	0 (n = 48)	8 (n = 48)	Fisher's test	ns
March 1992	Oral Naming	4 (n = 48)	23 (n = 48)	$\chi^2 = 7.2$	$P < 0.01$
	Word–Picture Matching*	0 (n = 48)	17 (n = 48)	$\chi^2 = 7.7$	$P < 0.005$
RA					
December 1988	Oral Naming	7 (n = 30)	19 (n = 36)	Fisher's test	ns
	Written Naming	0 (n = 24)	24 (n = 29)	Fisher's test	< 0.001
April 1989	Oral Naming	4 (n = 48)	35 (n = 48)	$\chi^2 = 14.8$	< 0.001
	Written Naming	8 (n = 24)	48 (n = 29)	$\chi^2 = 9.1$	< 0.002
	Word–Picture Matching*	0 (n = 48)	8 (n = 48)	Fisher's test	ns
March 1990	Oral Naming	69 (n = 48)	96 (n = 48)	$\chi^2 = 12.1$	< 0.001
	Word–Picture Matching*	4 (n = 24)	25 (n = 24)	Fisher's test	< 0.005

Performance across repeated tasks on nouns and verbs of patients GG and RA showing a slowly progressive category-specific disorder for verbs.
* Spoken Word–Picture Matching: chance level = 33%

may have different levels of clinical expression in the various lexical modalities. It can be hypothesised that a mild semantic impairment for actions or objects may be clinically apparent only on stringent production tasks, owing to their greater demands as compared to comprehension. A worsening of the central semantic impairment, however, might lead to a category-specific defect becoming apparent both at the expressive and at the receptive levels.

Anatomical Locus of Lesions in Patients with a Category-Specific Impairment for Verbs (Action Names) and Nouns (Object Names)

The study of the neuroanatomical correlates of category-specific semantic disorders for verbs and nouns is based in part on direct and in part on indirect evidence. The direct evidence consists of the small amount of neuroimaging data available from single case studies of patients with selective impairments of the categories nouns and verbs. The indirect evidence is based on inferences that can be drawn regarding the anatomical locus of lesions in patients whose category-specific disorder arises in the context of an aphasic syndrome with an established recognised localising significance. In the case of category-specific disorders for nouns, direct data (summarised in the lower part of Table 2) are very few but consistent. The lesion is often confined to the left temporal lobe involving in one case the posterior temporo-parieto-occipital association areas. These findings are also consistent with the usual lesion localisation in aphasic

TABLE 2
Neuroimaging Data From Patients With a Category-specific Impairment for
Verbs and Nouns

Authors	Case	Impaired Task	Lesion Site
Selective Impairment for Verbs			
Baxter and Warrington (1985)	GOS	Writing-to-dictation	Left F-T-P
McCarthy and Warrington (1985)	ROX	Naming Comprehension	Mainly anterior cortical atrophy
Miceli et al. (1988)	DP	Naming Comprehension	Left T-P
	CS	Naming Comprehension	Right F-T
	FS	Naming	Left F-T
	AM	Naming	Left F-T-P
Caramazza and Hillis (1991)	HW	Oral Naming only	Left P
	SJD	Written Naming only	Left F-T
Damasio and Tranel (1993)	KJ	Naming	Left F
Daniele et al. (1993)	GC	See Table 1	Left F
	RA		Left F
Selective Impairment for Nouns			
Miceli et al. (1988)	AA	Naming Comprehension	Left T / Right T
	SF	Naming	Left T
	AE	Naming	Left T / Right F
Zingeser and Berndt (1988)	HY	Oral and Written Naming	Left T-P-O
Damasio and Tranel (1993)	Boswell*	Naming	Left T / Right T
	AN	Naming	Left T
Daniele et al. (1993)	GP	Naming Comprehension	Left T

* In this patient the lesions were not confined to the temporal lobes, but also bilaterally involved the basal forebrain regions, the insular cortices, and the posterior orbital cortices.

anomia. We can, therefore, safely conclude that the temporal lobe and the posterior association areas are usually damaged in patients with a category-specific impairment for object names.

The anatomical correlates of category-specific defects for action names are less clear. Most of the direct data (summarised in the upper part of Table 2) consists of lesions involving both the frontal and the temporal lobes of the left hemisphere. However there are a few exceptions. The most obvious of these is patient HW, described by Caramazza and Hillis (1991) in whom neither the frontal nor the temporal lobe was involved. However it must be noted that this patient (who presented with a left parietal lesion) was rather atypical, because he showed a selective impairment for verbs that was confined to oral production, in the context of a verbal short-term memory disorder. Equally atypical (or subject to some caution with regard to the exact localisation of their anatomical lesions) were the patients GG and RA, described by Daniele et al. (1993), where lesions were restricted to the left frontal lobe, and patient DP, reported by Miceli et al. (1988), where the lesion did not involve this lobe. The former cases suffered from a degenerative disease which probably involved other lobes, albeit to a lesser extent, whereas the latter presented the atypical finding of an agrammatism provoked by a posterior (temporo-parietal) lesion! So, if we focus our attention on the other more typical cases, we can conclude that the lesions provoking a category-specific defect for action names usually encroach on the antero-superior portions of the temporal lobe and on the infero-posterior parts of the left frontal lobe. These conclusions are also consistent with the evidence for the prevalent localisation of lesions in agrammatism.

Taken together, anatomical data obtained in patients with a category-specific defect for nouns or verbs strongly suggest that a temporal lobe lesion is necessary to produce a word-finding defect. This difficulty interacts with the grammatical or semantic category to which the target items belongs.

When the lesion extends from the temporal towards the frontal lobe, the naming difficulty mainly concerns action names. When it expands, on the contrary, towards the posterior association areas, or it involves other parts of the temporal lobe, then object names are more difficult to produce or comprehend.

Tentative interpretations can be advanced to explain this differential impairment of action names in patients with lesions extending towards the frontal lobe, and of object names in patients with lesions extending towards the lateral and inferior parts of the temporal lobe or the posterior association areas. The hypothesis that we suggest consists in searching in the frontal lobe and in other parts of the temporal lobe (or in the posterior associative areas) for some general mechanisms that could play a critical role in the semantic representation of actions and of objects. It could be interesting to reconsider, from this point of view, a neurological model of naming proposed some years ago by Geschwind (1967) and which could be more appropriate to explain disorders in naming objects than to explain disorders in naming actions. According to Geschwind (1967), aphasic anomia results from damage to the angular gyrus because a large variety of sensory information converges in this region. This sensory convergence could supply the subject with the ''attributes'' necessary to arouse the verbal label corresponding to the semantic representation of the perceived object. Thus Geschwind's model, stressing the role of sensory attributes in establishing the semantic representations of objects, and assuming that such sensory information may converge in the posterior association areas, could explain why a lesion of these regions produces a selective inability to name objects. A similar model, stressing the importance of motor schemata in constructing the semantic representations of actions could explain why anterior (agrammatic) aphasic patients are more impaired in producing and comprehending verbs (action names) than in producing and comprehending nouns (object names).

This does not mean that we intend to accept Geschwind's model with the specification that it accounts only for nouns and that a similar neuroanatomical model could be proposed to account for disorders in verb production. The emphasis in Geschwind's model was primarily on activating "output" or "lexical" representations, whereas, in our opinion, category-specific disorders for nouns and verbs are primarily due to a degradation of the semantic representation for objects and actions. We cannot exclude the possibility, however, that in some cases a category-specific disorder for nouns or verbs may be due to disconnection between the semantic representation of these categories and their corresponding lexical representations. Furthermore, an interpretation based on the specific neuro-anatomical model proposed by Geschwind (rather than on his general idea that the convergence of different sensory attributes may feed the semantic representation of objects) might raise other important empirical objections.

Thus, for example, Geschwind's hypothesis that the angular gyrus may be the cortical region where sensory information converges to build the semantic representations of objects is only in part consistent with contemporary models of the processing and convergence of sensory information in the brain. (See, for example, Damasio & Tranel, 1993; Pandya & Yeterian, 1985; Ungerleider & Mishkin, 1982).

We will also see, in a further section of this review, that the hypothesis that the semantic representation of "objects" may be mainly based on a convergence of sensory attributes is almost certainly too broad, as it is more appropriate for some categories of "objects" than for others. It fits very well for some categories of "natural" objects (living things) whose semantic representation is mainly based on their sensory attributes, but less well for some categories of man-made artefacts, whose semantic representation is mostly based on functional attributes.

Nevertheless, and despite these reservations, we think that the general hypothesis that the same naming mechanism may interact with different sets of semantic representations based more on sensory information or on motor schemata remains appealing from the viewpoint of cognitive neurology, because it aims to trace some complex cognitive disorders back to some basic principles of brain organisation.

DISORDERS IN IDENTIFICATION OF LIVING THINGS (AND FOOD) AND OF MAN-MADE ARTEFACTS (AND BODY PARTS) IN BRAIN-DAMAGED PATIENTS

The second group of category-specific semantic disorders that we intend to discuss in this survey refers to the double dissociation between: (a) a more or less selective inability to identify *living things* (animals, flowers, fruits, vegetables, etc.) and food; and (b) a prevalent impairment in the identification of *man-made artefacts* (clothing, furniture, vehicles, tools, etc.) and of body parts.

A category-specific defect for living beings and food has been described by several authors in patients with herpes simplex encephalitis (e.g. Basso et al., 1988; DeRenzi & Lucchelli, 1994; Farah et al., 1989; Hart & Gordon, 1992; Sartori & Job, 1988; Silveri & Gainotti, 1988; Sirigu et al., 1991; Warrington & Shallice, 1984), whereas the prevalent impairment of man-made artefacts and body parts has been described by Warrington and McCarthy (1983, 1987), Behrman and Lieberthal (1989), Hillis et al. (1990), and Sacchett and Humphreys (1992) in patients with extensive lesions of the left frontal convexity. The first of these category-specific semantic disorders is the most striking for several reasons: (1) it is often observed in patients showing no defect of language or of visual-spatial functions; (2) the discrepancy between identification of living and non-living beings (and in particular between identification of animals and of man-made artefacts) is often very clear; (3) the same category-specific semantic impairment can often be observed with similar characteristics on the same items, using both verbal and non-verbal tasks in the visual and auditory modality. Thus, if a patient is unable to name the picture of a frog, he or she is also generally unable to give a verbal description of what the word "frog" means, to draw a picture of a frog from memory, or to colour a black and white picture of a frog green. The only information that these patients are usually able to give concerns the superordinate category to which the living items belongs ("a frog is an animal"), but they usually fail to retrieve the attributes that typically define this animal.

It must be acknowledged, however, that the expression "category-specific semantic impairment for living things" must be considered as a convenient shorthand, rather than as an explanation, as not all of the affected categories are "living" and not all living categories are affected. Warrington and Shallice (1984), Basso et al. (1988), Silveri and Gainotti (1988), Sirigu et al. (1991), Sheridan and Humphreys (1992), and De Renzi and Lucchelli (1994) have, in fact, shown that musical instruments and food are usually also impaired in these patients, whereas body parts are spared. This happens in spite of the fact that musical instruments and many sorts of food are man-made products, whereas body parts belong to the "living" categories. Warrington and Shallice (1984) have, therefore, proposed that the living/non-living dichotomy may conceal a more basic distinction, linked to the different weighting that visuo-perceptual and functional attributes have in the delineation of members of affected and unaffected categories.

In the case of living beings, identification of a category member may critically depend on visual features, such as the plain, striped, or spotted aspect of the skin which allows one to distinguish a lion from a tiger or from a leopard. In the case of man-made artefacts, on the contrary, identification of a category member crucially relies on functional attributes, i.e. the subtly different functions for which they were constructed. This hypothesis has been supported by experimental data obtained with different methodologies by Basso et al.

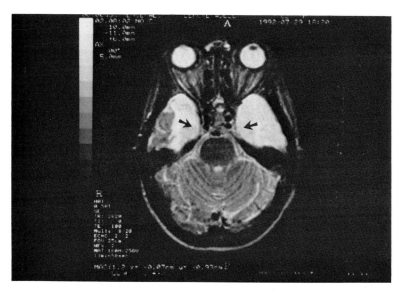

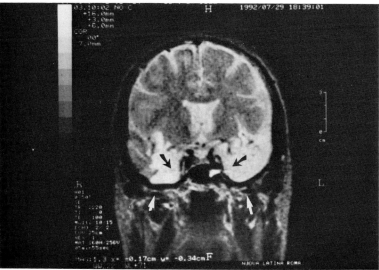

FIG. 1.   Axial (top) and coronal (bottom) T2-weighted MRI images of patient LA. The axial image cut across the lower parts of the temporal lobes, whereas the coronal slice was taken at the level of the anterior temporal regions. Both slices show that the parenchymal damage bilaterally involves the temporo-limbic structures (black arrows), but that they also encroach on the inferior temporal lobe (white arrows). The lesions prevail on the left side, where the anterior temporal lobe is completely destroyed, whereas the lateral portions of the right temporal lobe are partially spared.

(1988), Sartori and Job (1988), Silveri and Gainotti (1988), Farah et al. (1989), and DeRenzi and Lucchelli (1994). All of these investigations have shown that a fundamental deficit of patients with a selective disorder for living beings resides in their failure to retrieve the visual-perceptual features defining the different members of the living categories. A crucial question that can be raised from the viewpoint of the cognitive neurosciences is, therefore, the following: can the loss of stored visual information for living beings and the other features of semantic impairment shown by these patients be clarified by a careful study of the neuroanatomical correlates of their disorders?

The anatomical localisation of lesions associated with a category-specific semantic disturbance for living beings seems rather consistent, as almost all the prototypical instances of this disorder reported in the neuropsychological literature had made a partial recovery from herpes simplex encephalitis. This disease typically impairs the temporo-limbic structures of both hemispheres. Within the temporal lobe the lesions typically also extend to non-limbic structures, and in particular to the interior temporal lobe (Esiri, 1982). The hypothesis that lesion of these structures may play a critical role in the pathophysiology of semantic disorders specifically affecting living beings is confirmed by the small amount of neuroimaging data available from affected patients. All of the cases reported by Warrington and Shallice (1984), Sartori and Job (1988), Sirigu et al. (1991), and DeRenzi and Lucchelli (1994), showed bilateral damage to the antero-medial parts of both temporal lobes. Furthermore an extension of the lesion to the inferior temporal lobes was evident in all of those cases in whom this structure could be visualised. For example, Fig. 1 (p. 257) shows some typical MRI images taken from patient LA, described by Silveri and Gainotti (1988) and further investigated by Gainotti and Silveri (in press).

The principal connections and the main functions of the temporo-limbic structures and of the inferior temporal lobe, selectively damaged in patients with a semantic impairment for living beings, could help in clarifying the cognitive disorders of these patients. On the one hand, telencephalic temporo-limbic structures receive convergent, integrated input from all sensory systems, both directly, by way of projections from the unimodal association areas, and indirectly through multi-synaptic connections with polymodal and supramodal association cortices (Jones & Powell, 1970; Mesulam, Van Hoesen, Pandya, & Geschwind, 1977; Pandya & Yeterian, 1985; Van Hoesen, 1982). On the other hand, the inferior temporal lobe (IT) receives a major projection from area V_4 and is part of a visual processing system that plays a critical role in object recognition (Ungerleider & Mishkin, 1982). According to Mishkin, Malamut, and Bachevalier (1984) the anterior portion of IT (and in particular of area TE) could mediate the "central representations" of visual objects. It can, therefore, be speculated that the inferior temporal lobe and temporal limbic structures may play a critical role in processing, storing, and retrieving the semantic

TABLE 3
Lesion Location

Patient	Categories Impaired	Spared	Experimental Task	Lesion Site (Aphasic syndrome)
VER (1)	Man-made artefacts	Animals Flowers Food	Word–Picture Matching	Left F-p-T (Global Aphasia)
YOT (2)	Manipulable objects Body Parts	Animals Vegetables Food Flowers	Word–Picture Matching	Left F-p-T (Global Aphasia)
CH (3)	Furniture Body Parts	Animals	Category Sorting	Left F-p-T (Global Aphasia)
KE (4)	Furniture Clothing Body Parts	Animals Vegetables Food	Oral and Written Naming and Comprehension	Left F-P (Broca's Aphasia)
CW (5)	Man-made artefacts Body Parts	Animals Fruits Vegetables	Oral Naming and Comprehension	Left F-P (Broca's Aphasia)

Lesion location in patients presenting a differential impairment for man-made artefacts and a relative sparing of living beings.
(1) Warrington & McCarthy (1983)
(2) Warrington & McCarthy (1987)
(3) Behrmann & Lieberthal (1989)
(4) Hillis et al. (1990)
(5) Sacchett & Humphreys (1992)

representations of those semantic categories (such as animals or other kinds of living beings) knowledge of which is mainly based on sensory (and above all on visual) information.

Let us pass, now, to the main clinical features and to the lesion localisation in patients presenting with a selective impairment of man-made artefacts. As very few cases of this category-specific disorder have been reported in the neuropsychological literature, we have summarised in Table 3 the categories preferentially impaired or spared and the reported lesion location of patients who fulfil the criteria to be included in this group.

Some features emerge with clarity from the data reported in Table 3: The first is that the pattern of impaired and spared semantic categories closely mirrors that of patients with a selective semantic disorder for living beings. The impaired categories consist not only of man-made objects, but also of body parts, whereas the spared categories consist of living things and foods. Body parts were selectively spared in patients with category-specific semantic disorders for living things, whereas foods were in these patients as affected as the animals category. The second feature is that the anatomical correlates of these disorders are very consistent, as the lesions usually encroach on the fronto-parietal areas of the left hemisphere.

A possible link between the anatomical locus of lesions producing this selective disorder for man-made artefacts and the neurophysiological mechanisms that could have critically contributed to the acquisition of these categories of knowledge could consist in the fact that somato-sensory and motor functions are mainly represented in the fronto-parietal areas of the brain. It is, therefore, possible to speculate that the categories of man-made artefacts could be chiefly subserved by the fronto-parietal regions of the brain, because knowledge of these categories is at least in part based on handling, manual use or, in any case, physical contact and concrete utilisation of objects. This interpretation is further supported by two independent sets of data: (1) the consistent association (that we have just noted) between disruption of knowledge of man-made artefacts and impairment of body parts; (2) the observation of Warrington and McCarthy (1987) that knowledge of small manipulable objects was more impaired in their patient than identification of large (non-manipulable) "out-door objects".

CONCLUDING REMARKS

Both in aphasic patients showing a selective deficit for verbs (action names) or for nouns (object names) and in brain-damaged patients showing a selective disorder for living beings or for man-made artefacts, the lesions preferentially encroached on brain structures housing neurophysiological mechanisms that could have critically contributed to the acquisition of the disrupted semantic category. These mechanisms concern: motor functions in the case of action names; integration of sensory attributes in the case of object names; high-level visual processing and convergence of sensory information in the case of living beings; motor-kinaesthesic integration (handling of objects) in the case of man-made articles.

The hypothesis that different categories of knowledge may be closely intertwined with those brain mechanisms that have critically contributed to their acquisition can, therefore, be tentatively advanced.

Within this general hypothesis it is perhaps necessary to introduce some specifications to explain the large variance observed in patients with a category-specific semantic impairment, with respect both to symptomatology and to lesion location. As for symptomatology, an important distinction must probably be made between patients who present a category-specific impairment only on verbal tasks (usually on naming tasks) and patients who present a selective categorical impairment across different verbal and non-verbal tasks. As for neuroanatomy, the most important distinction concerns the localisation of lesions only on the left side or on both sides of the brain. Symptomatological and neuroanatomical issues are strongly interconnected, as patients who present a category-specific disorder on verbal tasks only, usually show left hemisphere lesions, whereas those who present this impairment both on verbal and non-verbal tasks, almost always show bilateral brain lesions. This state of affairs can, in our opinion, be explained if we make the following assumptions:

1. Category-specific disorders are in any case due to the degradation of a specific cluster of semantic representations, but this degradation can express itself through two different mechanisms: an insufficient activation of the lexical representations corresponding to the degraded semantic category; and a widespread inability to perform any kinds of tasks requiring the consultation of the degraded semantic representation.

2. Semantic categories are probably represented bilaterally in homologous structures of the right and left hemisphere, fed by the same kinds of information, whereas the mechanisms of lexical activation are represented only in critical areas of the left hemisphere.

3. When the brain damage disrupts a semantic category only at the level of the left hemisphere (as in the case of aphasic patients) this partial degradation provokes an inability to fully activate the corresponding lexical representation. A partly similar defect could be provoked by a mechanism of disconnection isolating the semantic representation of a given category from its lexical counterparts. This hypothetical mechanism could explain, for example, the very selective deficits in verb production reported by Caramazza and Hillis (1991).

4. When, on the contrary, the semantic representations corresponding to a given category are bilaterally disrupted (as in the case of herpes simplex encephalitis) then any kind of task involving these representations becomes impossible and the category-specific disorder becomes much more consistent and ubiquitous.

The general hypothesis that we have discussed in this paper, although admittedly preliminary and speculative, is well in line with some basic assumptions of contemporary connectionist models (e.g. Ballard, 1986; Churchland & Sejnowski, 1988; Farah & McClelland, 1991). These models maintain that information processing and storage are not separated but closely intertwined in a network, as information is stored as a pattern of activity in the connections between the units of the net processing the same information. The hypothesis that the representations of different semantic categories may be closely intertwined with the neurophysiological mechanisms that have critically contributed to their acquisition is, therefore, consistent with these basic connectionist assumptions.

REFERENCES

Ballard, D.H. (1986). Cortical connections and parallel processing: structure and function. *Behavioral and Brain Sciences, 9*, 67–120.

Basso, A., Capitani, E., & Laiacona, M. (1988). Progressive language impairment without dementia: a case with isolated category specific semantic defect. *Journal of Neurology, Neurosurgery and Psychiatry, 51*, 1201–1207.

Bastian, H.C. (1869). On the various forms of speech in cerebral disease. *British and Foreign Med. Chir. Rev.* (cited by Wernicke, 1874/1908).

Bastian, H.C. (1898). *A treatise on aphasia and other speech defects.* London: Lewis.

Baxter, D.M., & Warrington, E.K. (1985). Category specific phonological dysgraphia. *Neuropsychologia, 23,* 653–666.

Behrman, M., & Lieberthal, T. (1989). Category specific treatment of a lexical-semantic deficit: a single case study of global aphasia. *The British Journal of Disorders of Communication, 24,* 281–299.

Benson, F. (1979). Neurologic correlates of anomia. In H. Whitaker & H.A. Whitaker (Eds.), *Studies in neurolinguistics.* New York: Academic Press.

Butterworth, B., Howard, D., & McLoughlin, P. (1984). The semantic deficit in aphasia: the relationship between semantic errors in auditory comprehension and picture naming. *Neuropsychologia, 22,* 409–426.

Caramazza, A., & Hillis, A.E. (1991). Lexical organization of nouns and verbs in the brain. *Nature, 349,* 788–790.

Churchland, P.S., & Sejnowski, T.J. (1988). Neural representation and neural computation. In L. Nadel (Ed.), *Biological computation.* Cambridge, MA: MIT Press.

Damasio, A.R., & Tranel, D. (1993). Nouns and verbs are retrieved with differently distributed neural system. *Proceedings of the National Academy of Sciences USA, 90,* 4957–4960.

Daniele, A., Silveri, M.C., Giustolisi, L., & Gainotti, G. (1993). Category-specific deficits for grammatical classes of words: evidence for possible anatomical correlates. *The Italian Journal of Neurological Sciences, 14,* 87–94.

DeRenzi, E., & Lucchelli, F. (1994). Are semantic systems separately represented in the brain? The case of living category impairment. *Cortex, 30,* 3–25.

Esiri, M.M. (1982). Herpes Simplex Encephalitis: An immunohistological study of the distribution of viral antigen within the brain. *Journal of Neurological Science, 54,* 209–226.

Farah, M.J., Hammond, K.M., Mehta, Z., & Radcliff, G. (1989). Category-specificity and modality-specificity in semantic memory. *Neuropsychologia, 27,* 193–200.

Farah, M.J., & McClelland, J.L. (1991). A computational model of semantic memory impairment: modality specificity and emergent category specificity. *Journal of Experimental Psychology: General, 120,* 339–357.

Gainotti, G. (1976). The relationships between semantic impairment in comprehension and naming in aphasic patients. *The British Journal of Disorders of Communication, 11,* 77–81.

Gainotti, G., & Silveri, M.C. (in press). Anatomical and cognitive locus of lesion in patients with a category specific semantic impairment for living beings. *Cognitive Neuropsychology.*

Geschwind, N. (1967). The varieties of naming errors. *Cortex, 3,* 97–112.

Goodglass, H., Klein, B., Carey, P., & Jones, K. (1966). Specific semantic word categories in aphasia. *Cortex, 2,* 74–89.

Hart, J. Jr., & Gordon, B. (1992). Neural subsystem for object knowledge. *Nature, 359,* 60–64.

Hillis, A.E., Rapp, B., Romani, C., & Caramazza, A. (1990). Selective impairment of semantics in lexical processing. *Cognitive Neuropsychology, 7,* 191–243.

Jones, E.G., & Powell, T.P.S. (1970). An experimental study of converging sensory pathways within the cerebral cortex of the monkey. *Brain, 93,* 793–820.

Marin, O.S.M., Saffran, E.M., & Schwartz, M.F. (1976). Dissociations of language in aphasia: Implications for normal functions. *Annals of New York Academy of Sciences, 280,* 868–884.

McCarthy, R.A., & Warrington, E.K. (1985). Category specificity in an agrammatic patient: the relative impairment of verb retrieval and comprehension. *Neuropsychologia, 23,* 709–727.

McCarthy, R.A., & Warrington, E.K. (1990). *Cognitive neuropsychology.* New York: Academic Press.

McCarthy, R.A., & Warrington, E.K. (1994). Disorders of semantic memory. *Philosophical Transactions of the Royal Society of London, B346,* 89–96.

McKenna, P., & Warrington, E.K. (1978). Category specific preservation: a single case study. *Journal of Neurology, Neurosurgery and Psychiatry, 43,* 571–574.

Mesulam, M.M.G., Van Hoesen, G.W., Pandya, D.N., & Geschwind, N.   977). Limbic and sensory connections of the IPL in the rhesus Monkey. *Brain Research, 136*, 393–414.

Miceli, G., Mazzucchi, A., Menn, L., & Goodglass, H. (1983). Contrasting cases of Italian agrammatic aphasia without comprehension disorder. *Brain and Language, 19*, 65–97.

Miceli, G., Silveri, M.C., Nocentini, U., & Caramazza, A. (1988). Patterns of dissociation in comprehension and production of nouns and verbs. *Aphasiology, 2*, 351–358.

Miceli, G., Silveri, M.C., Villa, G., & Caramazza, A. (1984). On the basis for the agrammatic's difficulty in producing main verbs. *Cortex, 20*, 207–220.

Mishkin, M., Malamut, B., & Bachevalier, J. (1984). Memories and habits: Two neural systems. In G. Lynch, J.L. McGaugh & N.M. Weinberger (Eds.), *Neurobiology of learning and memory*. New York: The Guildford Press.

Myerson, R., & Goodglass, H. (1972). Transformational grammars of three agrammatic patients. *Language and Speech, 15*, 40–50.

Pandya, D.N., & Yeterian, E.H. (1985). Architecture and connections of cortical association areas. In A. Peters & E.G. Jones (Eds.), *Cerebral cortex*, Vol. 4. New York: Plenum Press.

Sacchett, C., & Humphreys, G.W. (1992). Calling a squirrel a squirrel but a canoe a wigwam: A category-specific deficit for artefactual objects and body parts. *Cognitive Neuropsychology, 9*, 73–86.

Sartori, G., & Job, R. (1988). The oyster with 4 legs: A neuropsychological study on the interaction of visual and semantic information. *Cognitive Neuropsychology, 5*, 105–132.

Semenza, C. & Zettin, M. (1988). Generating proper names: a case of selective inability. *Cognitive Neuropsychology, 5*, 711–721.

Semenza, C., & Zettin, M. (1989). Evidence from aphasia for the role of proper names as pure referring expressions. *Nature, 342*, 678–679.

Shallice, T. (1988). *From neuropsychology to mental structure*. Cambridge: Cambridge University Press.

Sheridan, J., & Humphreys, G.W. (1993). A verbal-semantic category-specific recognition impairment. *Cognitive Neuropsychology, 10*, 185–200.

Silveri, M.C., & Gainotti, G. (1988). Interaction between vision and language in category-specific semantic impairment. *Cognitive Neuropsychology, 5*, 677–709.

Sirigu, A., Duhamel, J.R., & Poncet, M. (1991). The role of sensorimotor experience in object recognition. A case of multimodal agnosia. *Brain, 114*, 2555–2573.

Ungerleider, L.G., & Mishkin, M. (1982). Two cortical visual system. In D.J. Ingle, M.A. Goodale, & R.J.W. Mansfield (Eds.), *Analysis of visual behavior*. Cambridge, MA: MIT Press.

Van Hoesen, G.W. (1982). The primate parahippocampal gyrus: new insights regarding its cortical connections. *Trends in Neuroscience, 5*, 345–350.

Warrington, E.K. (1975). The selective impairment of semantic memory. *Quarterly Journal of Experimental Psychology, 27*, 635–657.

Warrington, E.K. (1981). Neuropsychological studies of verbal semantic systems. *Philosophical Transactions of the Royal Society of London, B295*, 411–423.

Warrington, E.K., & McCarthy, R. (1983). Category-specific access dysphasia. *Brain, 106*, 859–878.

Warrington, E.K., & McCarthy, R. (1987). Categories of knowledge: Further fractionation and an attempted integration. *Brain, 110*, 1273–1296.

Warrington, E.K., & Shallice, T. (1984). Category-specific semantic impairment. *Brain, 107*, 829–854.

Wernicke, C. (1874/1908). *Der Aphasischen Symptomencomplex*. Breslau: Cohn and Weigert. [The Symptom-complex of aphasia. In A. Church (Ed.), *Disease of the nervous system*. New York; Appleton, 1908].

Zingeser, L.B., & Berndt, R.S. (1988). Grammatical class and context effects in a case of pure anomia: implications for models of language production. *Cognitive Neuropsychology, 5*, 473–516.

MEMORY, 1995, 3 (3/4), 265–307

Refractory Semantics in Global Aphasia: On Semantic Organisation and the Access–Storage Distinction in Neuropsychology

Emer Forde and Glyn W. Humphreys

University of Birmingham, UK

A single case study is reported of a global aphasic patient, JM, with impaired access to semantic information which was particularly severe for the class of proper names. JM's ability to perform matching tasks with printed words and pictures to auditory words deteriorated when items were repeated, especially when the response–stimulus interval was short. Performance was also inconsistent across items. The effect of repeated testing on items generalised to other, previously untested members of the same category. Despite this, JM was able to access general semantic information about stimuli from the affected categories (e.g. to categorise boys' and girls' names), and showed good ability to access an input lexicon concerning these stimuli. There was also a close relationship between the categories affected when he was tested with pictures and printed words. We propose that JM's deficit can be attributed to his semantic system entering an abnormal refractory state once semantic access for a particular item has been achieved, and with this stage being isolated from the procedures providing access to stored lexical knowledge. Furthermore, the representations affected seem common to pictures and printed words. We discuss the implications of the results for understanding the nature of semantic representations in general and for proper names in particular, and for the distinction between access and storage deficits in neuropsychology.

INTRODUCTION

Over the past 25 years there has been an increasing interest in aphasic patients with impairments in recognition and name retrieval for specific categories of object and word. For example, both group and single case studies have suggested differences in the representation of action names and object names

Requests for reprints should be sent to Emer Forde, Cognitive Science Research Centre, School of Psychology, University of Birmingham, Edgbaston, Birmingham B15 2TT, UK.

We are extremely grateful to JM and his wife for their hours of time and endless enthusiasm. This work was supported by a grant from the Department of Education in Northern Ireland to the first author and by grants from the Medical Research Council of Great Britain and the Human Frontier Science Programme awarded to the second author.

(Goodglass, Klein, Carey, & James, 1966; McCarthy & Warrington, 1985; Miceli, Silveri, Villa, & Caramazza, 1984). Other work suggests that there may be functionally separate representations for several further categories of item, including: concrete and abstract nouns (Warrington, 1975; Warrington & Shallice, 1984), colours and concrete objects (Goodglass et al., 1966), body parts and other classes of object (Yamadori & Albert, 1973), and living things and artefacts (Sartori, Miozzo, & Job, 1993; Sheridan & Humphreys, 1993; Warrington & Shallice, 1984). Of particular relevance to the present study are cases demonstrating dissociations between recognition and name retrieval for common objects and for proper names (i.e. names that function to denote individual instances in kinds).

Proper Names and Object Names

One particularly clear case of a deficit for the retrieval of proper names was reported by Semenza and Zettin (1988). Their patient, PC, could not name any famous personalities, cities, countries, mountains, or rivers, although he could access correct semantic information and match the name to the correct picture. PC also performed flawlessly at naming fruit, vegetables, body parts, colours, letters, vehicles, and furniture. Semenza and Zettin concluded that the impairment was at the level of the phonological output lexicon which they proposed was categorically organised (although see Burton & Bruce, 1993; see also the General Discussion here). McKenna and Warrington (1980) reported a fractionation within the class of proper names. They documented a patient with a selective impairment in the retrieval of the names of famous personalities along with preservation of place names (see also Lucchelli & De Renzi, 1992). One difficulty in interpreting such results, however, is that the retrieval of proper names may be more difficult than that of object (kind) names even for non-brain-damaged subjects. McKenna and Warrington, in a group study with both left-hemisphere lesioned patients and non-brain-damaged, age-matched controls, found no significant difference in the pattern of responding between the two groups, and that, for both groups, the retrieval of proper names was more difficult than that of object names. This suggests that deficits that are more pronounced for proper names could be due to task difficulty rather than selective representation of these different classes of lexical item.

Against the task difficulty account, McKenna and Warrington (1978), Cipolotti, McNeil, and Warrington (1993), Semenza and Sgaramella (1993) and Warrington and Clegg (1993) have all reported cases showing the opposite pattern of dissociation, namely preservation in the naming of proper nouns along with deficits in naming common objects. These last cases suggest that retrieval processes for proper names and for the names of common objects are doubly dissociable. The results pose problems for accounts of name retrieval that posit that proper names are typically difficult to retrieve because these names, unlike names for common objects, have a unique referent and so may be sparsely connected within the semantic or name representation systems (cf Bredart, 1993; Burton & Bruce, 1993; Cohen, 1990).

This distinction between proper names and common nouns is not a novel concept and indeed even in the last century philosophers such as Mill (1843) drew distinctions between the two. More recently, Wittgenstein (1922) and Kripke (1980) proposed that proper names are referential and not connotative. That is, proper names denote an individual but they do not imply any semantic properties relating to a particular person (see also Frege, 1892, for the distinction between ''sense'' and ''reference'' for meanings). The same distinction between proper names and nouns has been made by modern linguists (Jackendoff, 1983; Katz, 1972; Levelt, 1989) who differentiate between type and token. Stimuli can be classified as tokens (or individuals) of a general type (or category). Proper names have token and not type reference. Proper names refer to one person only, and names that happen to be shared by different people do not imply that these individuals have anything more in common. This is not true for common nouns such as teacher. Hence proper names and common names may differ not only in terms of the number of their semantic referents but perhaps even in the nature of their representations. We return to this point in the General Discussion.

Access and Representation Deficits

The form of the impairment in the recognition and naming of particular classes of stimulus can also vary across patients. For example, for many patients a consistent pattern of impairment is apparent, with the patient being poor at identifying the same stimuli on different occasions (Warrington & Shallice, 1984) and when tested across different modalities (e.g. Silveri & Gainotti, 1988). In other cases, however, performance can be inconsistent, with some items being identified correctly on one occasion but not on another, and vice versa for other items. An inconsistent pattern of performance has been attributed to a problem in gaining access to stored representations, whereas a consistent deficit across items on different test occasions has been attributed to the presence of degraded stored representations (e.g. Shallice, 1987; Warrington & McCarthy, 1983, 1987; Warrington & Shallice, 1979; although see Humphreys, Riddoch, & Quinlan, 1988; Rapp & Caramazza, 1993, for counter arguments). Warrington and Shallice outlined a number of criteria for distinguishing between an access and a storage disorder based on the patterns of performance of dyslexic patients, EM and AR (Coughlan & Warrington, 1981; Warrington & Shallice, 1979), and Shallice (1988) has suggested that the criteria are potentially applicable to all subsystems within a functional architecture. The criteria include: consistency of performance on items across time (inconsistent performance indicates an access problem); depth of processing (performance on tests of superordinate and specific attribute information should be equivalent for access disorders, but superordinate knowledge should be relatively well preserved compared with attribute information in a storage disorder); priming effects (important only for access disorders); frequency effects (important only for storage disorders); and rate of presentation (important only for access deficits).

However, there are a number of problems with these criteria. For example, Shallice (1988) has suggested that the variables of consistency and priming have the greatest validity, but there have been reports of patients with Alzheimer's disease who show consistent deficits, suggesting a storage impairment, but who demonstrate marked priming effects, characteristic of an access disorder (Chertkow & Bub, 1990). McNeil, Cipolotti, and Warrington (1994) question whether the criteria generalise across disorders, and in particular if they generalise to "access dysphasia". In patients reported with access dysphasia, performance is worse with sets of semantically related (dog, cat, horse), rather than unrelated (dog, chair, apple) items (Warrington & McCarthy, 1983, 1987). From this, McNeil et al. speculate that these patients may not show the positive priming effects that should be characteristic of access disorders.

Warrington and McCarthy (1987) reported a detailed case study of an "access dysphasic" patient (YOT) who showed the characteristic inconsistent pattern of performance. Interestingly, the impairment was most pronounced with certain classes of stimulus. Warrington and McCarthy found that YOT was better at matching tasks involving proper nouns with a unique referent (famous names, countries, cities) relative to tasks involving proper nouns without a specific referent (girls' names, boys' names, surnames). For example, on a written word–spoken word matching test YOT scored 100% correct when asked to point to written names of famous people and 88% correct for cities and countries; in contrast she was only 22% correct for surnames and 17% correct for boys' names (though the deficit was not confined to proper nouns without a unique referent; YOT also had difficulty in tasks involving "small, manipulable objects", such as book, pen, key etc.). YOT also showed an inconsistent pattern of performance. In tasks involving spoken word–picture matching, YOT would point correctly to a named picture on one occasion but not on another, with her level of performance decreasing with repeated testing. In addition, there were effects of the interval between her response and the presentation of the next stimulus, and of semantic similarity between target and distractor words. When asked to carry out spoken word–picture matching with a relatively long interval between her response and the next spoken stimulus (five seconds), YOT performed well (90% correct when asked repeatedly to point to one of a set of five objects). However, when the response–stimulus interval was reduced to two seconds, she made an increased number of errors (63% correct with the same set of items). Similarly, YOT's errors were increased when she was asked to point to a target picture surrounded by pictures corresponding to items that were semantically close to the target (e.g. to a target pen among the words key, pencil, book etc.), relative to when the same target was surrounded by words semantically distant to the target (pen among chair, door, foot, and hat).

From this pattern of results, Warrington and McCarthy suggest that YOT has a deficit in gaining access to specific classes of semantic information concerning proper nouns without a unique referent and small manipulative objects. This deficit increased with a short response–stimulus interval and with repeated testing for a given stimulus because YOT's ability to access her semantic system became "refractory" after initially being accessed (i.e. there was a reduction in the accessibility of the system for an abnormally prolonged period of time). Once in this refractory state, the semantic information that can be accessed fails to specify the unique referent for the picture or written word–spoken word matching test. Performance may be most impaired when discriminations are required between items from the same semantic category because there is a "spread" in the refractory state between the procedures for accessing stored knowledge about items within the same category. An alternative position would be to propose that there was a spreading hyperactivation to members of the same category so that discrimination between them became difficult. To maintain that there remains a deficit in access procedures rather than the semantic representations themselves, we must presume that the access procedures are categorically organised (see McNeil et al., 1994; Warrington & McCarthy, 1983, for this argument and for similar cases).

Recently, Smith and Klein (1990) have presented evidence for refractory states in tasks accessing semantic information for normal subjects. They had subjects repeat superordinate category words either 3 or 30 times, before carrying out a category decision task. Response times to the exemplars from the repeated category were reliably slower when the category name was repeated 30 times compared to 3 times. Following repetition of an incongruent category label there was no significant difference between 30 and 3 repetitions. They suggested that, following repeated naming of the words, semantic information became less accessible, slowing down performance in the category decision task.

To date, relatively few patients with apparent problems in accessing semantic information have been reported in the neuropsychological literature (see McNeil et al., 1994; Warrington & McCarthy, 1983, 1987, for examples). And, even in the cases reported, it is not clear that the inconsistent pattern of performance, the effects of the response–stimulus interval, and the deterioration in performance with repeated testing—variables held to indicate an access deficit (Warrington & McCarthy, 1983, 1987)—occur for all classes of impaired stimulus, and in particular, for proper nouns without a unique referent. For example, Warrington and McCarthy (1987) tested the effects of repetition and response–stimulus interval with food, animals, and inanimate objects, not proper nouns. In the present paper, we report the case of a patient, JM, who demonstrates problems very similar to those reported for other patients with apparent problems in accessing semantic information. The case analysis goes beyond those previously reported in several ways. Initially (Section A) we contrast JM's impaired ability to access semantic information with his relatively good performance on lexical decision and object decision tasks. We then show that his performance manifests the pattern found with other patients with an apparent "semantic access" problem (Section B); for example, performance deteriorates with repeated testing and is affected by the interval between the last response and the next stimulus. This pattern of performance holds for proper names as well as for other categories. In Section C we present new experimental results showing that (i) JM can gain access to superordinate semantic information about items that he cannot reliably identify in auditory–written word matching tasks, and (ii) the refractory state can spread to other items in the affected category. Section D re-analyses some of the earlier data to assess whether JM's performance is inconsistent across items. The data have implications for understanding the functional locus where a deficit in accessing information about proper nouns might arise, and for understanding the nature of the representations at this functional locus.

CASE REPORT

JM, a 72-year-old man, formerly Head of Languages at a grammar school, was admitted to hospital following a stroke on 12.2.92. Due to the stroke he had a right-sided hemiparesis which left his arm and leg weak. By the time that testing for the present paper was initiated (11.3.93), he had no voluntary control over his right arm although motor control over his leg had improved to the level that he was able to walk. A CAT scan (Fig. 1, p. 291) showed a hypodense area in the left temporo-parietal region. Prior to his stroke, JM was fluent in six languages (English, French, German, Italian, Spanish, and Russian). Subsequently, however, JM was globally aphasic, having no spoken output and only minimal written output (for some single letters but for no words). For example, he scored 15 and 13/26 when asked to write single letters to dictation; when asked to write the letters of the alphabet in order he scored 17 and 14/26 on two test occasions. He was unable to write any single word correctly. JM's spoken output was limited to a single repetitive utterance (da, da). On the Standard Progressive Raven's Matrices he scored a total of 27/60 which is intellectually average for his age. His auditory digit span, measured using a digit-matching test (test 13 in the PALPA test battery; Kay, Lesser, & Coltheart, 1992) was 4. He could point to up to three items in correct serial order when given their names auditorily. He showed no signs of unilateral neglect on line cancellation. The tests reported in this paper were conducted over a period of 11 months, during which time JM's level of performance remained stable.

Preliminary tests suggested that JM had relatively good access to stored lexical knowledge from vision and from audition. For example, in a visual lexical decision task requiring discrimination between regular words, exception words, pronounceable nonwords, and pseudohomophones (test 27 in PALPA; Kay et al., 1992), he scored 55/60 (92%) correct. He made one error with a regular word (out of 15), one with a pronounceable nonword (N = 15), and three with pseudohomophones (N = 15). He was below normal scores only in the pseudohomophone condition (mean for normals = 14.52, SD = 0.75). In an auditory lexical decision task involving regular and exception words and pronounceable nonwords, he scored 51/60 (85%) correct. He made four errors on regular words and four on exception words, and one error on nonwords. An age-matched control subject scored 58/60 (97%). JM performed these tasks by pointing either to a letter W (for a word) or a letter N (for a nonword) placed in front of him.

JM also performed well on tasks designed to test access to the structural description of objects from vision. For example, in an object-decision task, requiring discrimination between pictures of real objects and non-objects formed by interchanging the parts of real objects (test 10 from BORB; Riddoch & Humphreys, 1993), he scored 32/32. In a colour object-decision task, requiring discrimination between two instances of an object, one depicted in its correct colour and another in an incorrect colour, he scored 13/13. In these last two tests he pointed either to a letter C (for correct) or I (for incorrect).

In contrast to relatively good access to stored lexical information from visual and auditory input, JM had poor access to output phonology and only minimal ability to manipulate phonological representations internally. He scored 10 and 9/26 when asked to point to named letters, and 6/20 when required to point to a named nonword surrounded by other nonwords sharing letters but not pronunciations (e.g. vib, vit, vab). This was not due to a peripheral deficit in audition; JM performed relatively well at auditory lexical decision (see earlier text), and when given a name auditorily he could point to one of three pictures that were semantically dissimilar but whose names differed by one phoneme (e.g. goat, coat, goal). However, when asked to judge whether pairs of written words either rhymed or had the same pronunciation (i.e. with homophones), he again performed poorly. On the written-word rhyme matching task from PALPA (test 15), he scored 12/15 on rhyming words with similar spellings (town–gown) relative to 11/15 on non-rhyming spelling pattern controls (food–blood), and 7/11 for rhyming words with dissimilar spellings (ghost–roast) relative to 12/15 on non-rhyming spelling pattern controls (bond–hand). This overall level of performance (42/60; 70% correct) is significantly impaired compared to one age-matched control who scored 58/60, Fisher Exact Probability, $P < 0.05$. On the homophone matching task from PALPA (test 28), he scored 34/60 (57%) correct (14/20 with regular words, 12/20 with exception words and 8/20 with nonwords). His level of performance here does not differ from chance. One aged-matched control scored 57/60. He also failed to assemble phonology from nonwords. He was unable to point to which of three nonwords was pronounced with the same name as an object (e.g. nale, zalt, orse), scoring 8/20. When asked to tap the number of syllables in spoken words he scored 6/22 (27% correct) (words could have either one, two, or three syllables), chance level of performance. When asked to match pictures on the basis of whether their names rhymed, he scored 10/34 (29% correct) in a test requiring him to point to two out of four pictures that had rhyming names. Matching pairs either had similar or dissimilar spellings (boat–goal vs pear–chair). His performance was unaffected by this variable (6/19 on matching items with similar spellings vs 4/15 on matching items with dissimilar spellings). In a rhyme-decision task requiring discrimination between two pictures that either had or did not have rhyming names, he scored 30/70 (43%) correct. When given the picture names auditorily he scored 54/70 (77%) correct. His performance was better on the rhyme judgements with auditorily presented names than with picture names, χ^2 (1) = 15.74, $P < 0.001$, indicating that he understood the nature of the task; however, he was impaired at both versions of the task relative to normal subjects (non-brain-damaged age-matched controls perform at ceiling). He was also unable to judge whether the names of two pictures began with the same initial letter, scoring 7/33 (21%) correct. His performance on the last test was below chance, primarily because he tended to judge that stimuli did not have the same initial letter.

These preliminary tests indicated a dissociation between JM's ability to access different types of stored knowledge. Access to the input lexicon and to the structural description for words and objects respectively is relatively good; access to output phonology is poor. This was the case whether output phonology was accessed from pictures, printed words, or printed nonwords. To judge from JM's performance on auditory rhyme judgements, he was somewhat better (but still impaired) at accessing output phonology from audition. The data with printed words and nonwords indicate that JM's ability to use direct lexical and non-lexical reading routes to access output phonology was severely limited.

In the following experimental investigations, we examine JM's ability to access semantic information from words and pictures, and his ability to perform picture and written word–spoken word matching tests for particular types of stimuli. We also show a dissociation between JM's ability to match written to spoken words for certain stimuli and his ability to access lexical representations corresponding to the same stimuli from print. This dissociation indicates that, for JM, written word–spoken word matching is mediated by semantic representations; his performance is then impaired because of a deficit in accessing semantic information or in the semantic representations themselves.

EXPERIMENTAL INVESTIGATIONS: SECTION A: ACCESSING SEMANTIC INFORMATION

JM's ability to access semantic information was assessed in various ways. In the first case, he was asked to carry out tasks requiring him to match stimuli on the basis of whether they were semantically related or not (Experiments 1–3). He was also asked to categorise stimuli (Experiment 4) and to perform picture and written word–spoken word matching tasks where distractors were semantically related to target stimuli (Experiment 5).

Experiment 1: Matching Semantically Related Stimuli

Method

The test was devised by Raffaella Rumiati (Rumiati, Humphreys, Riddoch, & Bateman, 1994). JM was presented with a central picture surrounded by four pictures (Experiment 1a), or a central printed word surrounded by four printed words (Experiment 1b), and he was asked to point to the surrounding picture or word that was most closely semantically related to the central target item. The tests with pictures and with words were each presented on two different occasions, in an ABBA fashion. The test with printed words was also repeated after a period of two weeks. The stimuli surrounding the central target (e.g. sword) were either closely semantically related (shield), distantly semantically related (gun), visually related (in the pictorial condition, e.g. anchor), or unrelated (chain). These stimuli were taken from the picture–word matching task from PALPA (Kay et al., 1992; see Experiment 6), although in this test JM was required to match the target to the semantically most-close item, whereas in the picture–word match task he was required to discriminate between the target and semantic distractors. The position of the target was rotated across trials.

Results and Discussion

Experiment 1a: Picture–Picture Matching.   JM scored 31/40 on this test. He made six errors by pointing to the visually related distractor, two by pointing to the distractor that was distantly related to the target, and one by pointing to an unrelated distractor.

Experiment 1b: Matching Printed Words.   With printed words JM scored 28/40 on the first occasion and 19/40 on the second.[1] An age-matched control

---

[1] Although JM's performance was significantly worse on time 2, our impression is that his performance is stable. To confirm this view we repeated the test 12 months later and found that he scored 22/40 with words and 29/40 with pictures, which is comparable to his original performance.

scored 38/40 on both versions of the test. There was a tendency for his performance to be worse with words compared to pictures, and comparing his performance with pictures and words on time 2 there is a significant difference between the two modalities (McNemar test, $\chi^2 = 8.1$, $df = 1$, $P < 0.01$). There was no consistency across items for JM's performance with pictures and words on either test 1 (Fisher exact probability = 0.75) or test 2 (Fisher exact probability = 0.65), or across words on tests 1 and 2 (Fisher exact probability = 0.2). Note that the matching task used in Experiment 1 provides a stronger test for consistency across items than two-alternative forced-choice tests of access to semantics (e.g. Experiment 2), as discrimination is required between four items, lowering the probability of responses being correct by chance.

These data suggest that JM has a deficit in accessing semantic information from both pictures and printed words, and that there was little consistency in his performance across different items, both within and across modalities.

Experiment 2: Pyramids and Palm Trees

Method

In this test (Howard & Orchard-Lisle, 1984), JM was asked to match a target stimulus against an associatively related stimulus, and to ignore an unrelated distractor. He was given the task either in pictorial form (Experiment 2a) or with the stimuli presented as written words (Experiment 2b). These two versions were presented in ABBA order. Four months later, he was asked to perform the same task with the stimuli presented simply as auditory names (Experiment 2c).

Results and Discussion

Experiment 2a: Picture–Picture Matching.   JM scored 47/52.

Experiment 2b: Matching Printed Words.   JM scored 38/50.

Experiment 2c: Matching Auditory Words.   JM scored 44/52.

Howard and Orchard-Lisle (1984) report that control subjects make three errors or less on this test. JM performed below this normal level irrespective of how the stimuli were presented, although performance tended to be worst with printed words.

Experiment 3: Synonym Matching

JM was asked to judge whether two words had the same meaning or not. The stimuli were taken from tests 49 and 50 in PALPA (Kay et al., 1992), and were presented either auditorily (Experiment 3a) or in written form (Experiment 3b).

Method

There were 60 stimuli, 30 high-imageability words and 30 low-imageability words. JM was given each pair in sequence and asked to decide whether they had the same meaning.

Results and Discussion

Experiment 3a: Matching Auditory Words.   JM scored 50/60 (83%) correct. There was no difference between high- and low-imageability words (25/30 for each).

Experiment 3b: Matching Printed Words.   JM scored 45/60 (72% correct). His performance tended to be better with high- than with low-imageability words (25 vs 20/30) and with auditory words than with written words. An age-matched control subject scored 59/60 on both auditory and written versions (high imageability 30/30, low imageability 29/30). JM is worse than the control level for both auditory (Fisher Exact probability = 0.04) and printed word (Fisher Exact probability, $P < 0.001$) versions of the test.

Experiment 4: Categorisation

In this experiment JM was asked to sort either pictures (Experiment 4a) or printed words (Experiment 4b) into piles according to the categories to which the stimuli belonged. The study was also carried out with auditorily presented words (Experiment 4c), and in this case JM was given printed versions of the category labels that he was to point to. A first test required superordinate categorisation between animals (on the one hand) and fruits and vegetables (on the other). Following this, two finer-grained categorisation tasks were performed: English vs foreign animals, and fruits vs vegetables.

Method

For the superordinate categorisation task there were 20 animals and 20 fruits and vegetables. For the finer-grained categorisation tasks there were 18 animals (9 English, 9 foreign) and 11 fruits and vegetables (6 fruit, 5 vegetables). Categorisation with pictures was carried out nine months before categorisation with printed and auditory words. These last two tests were spaced one week apart (printed words first).

Results and Discussion

Experiment 4a: Picture Categorisation.   JM scored 40/40 on the super-ordinate categorisation (animals vs fruits and vegetables); 18/18 on categorising English vs foreign animals; 8/11 on categorising fruits vs vegetables. He misclassified a pepper, a mushroom, and an onion as fruit.

Experiment 4b: Categorising Printed Words. JM scored 40/40 on superordinate categorisation; 18/18 on English vs foreign animals; 10/11 on fruits vs vegetables. His only error was to misclassify a mushroom as a fruit.

Experiment 4c: Categorising Auditory Words. JM scored 40/40 on superordinate categorisation; 18/18 on English vs foreign animals; 10/11 on fruits vs vegetables. His error was the same as that made with printed words.

Overall JM performed relatively well on these categorising tasks, suggesting that he can gain access to general and to some finer-grained semantic information about stimuli, whether they are presented as pictures, or as visual or auditory words.

Experiment 5: Picture–Word Matching

In this test JM was required to point to a target picture presented along with four distractors, when he was presented with the target's name either auditorily (Experiment 5a) or in print (Experiment 5b). The target was surrounded either with a close semantic distractor, a distant semantic distractor, a visual distractor, or an unrelated distractor (the same items as were used in Experiment 1). The test was taken from PALPA (tests 47 and 48; Kay et al., 1992).

Method

The two versions of this test (Experiments 5a and 5b) were given in an ABBA design over two sessions conducted one week apart.

Results and Discussion

Experiment 5a: Auditory Word–Picture Matching. JM scored 39/40. His one error involved pointing to a close semantic distractor.

Experiment 5b: Printed Word–Picture Matching. JM scored 31/40. He made errors by pointing to five close semantic distractors, one distant semantic distractor, one visually similar distractor, and two unrelated distractors. Kay et al. (1992) report that control scores on this test average 39.5, with a standard deviation of 1. JM scored at the control level on picture matching to auditory words, but he was below average on matching pictures to printed words. His performance on matching with printed words was worse than that with auditory words (Fisher Exact probability = 0.007).

Summary

The tests suggest that JM has a problem in gaining access to semantic information. This problem is most pronounced when written words are used as input, but it is also present with both pictures and auditorily presented words. The deficit is also most apparent when relatively fine-grained semantic information must be accessed for adequate task performance (e.g. in matching semantically close items, in Experiment 1), rather than when broader semantic information is sufficient (Experiment 4, where categorisation was required). JM's problems in accessing semantic information contrast with his relatively good performance on lexical and object-decision tasks, which require access only to stored lexical knowledge and stored structural descriptions (see e.g. Riddoch & Humphreys, 1987a,b). We have also shown that JM's ability to access information is inconsistent across items, both when he is tested across time within the same modality (matching printed words) and when tested across different modalities (matching printed words and matching pictures). This last result has previously been used to argue for a deficit in gaining access to semantic knowledge, rather than there being a deficit within the semantic system itself (e.g. Shallice, 1987; Warrington & Shallice, 1979). In Section B we examine the nature of JM's performance in more detail, by assessing whether his performance (i) varies across different categories of item; and (ii) is sensitive to variables found to affect other patients with apparent problems in accessing semantic information, namely repeated testing, the response–stimulus interval, and the ''semantic distance'' between target and distractor stimuli.

SECTION B: EFFECTS OF CATEGORY, RESPONSE–STIMULUS INTERVAL AND SEMANTIC DISTANCE

To examine whether JM's performance was affected by factors such as the category of item tested, the response–stimulus interval, and the semantic distance between targets and distractors, we used (mainly) auditory word–printed word matching tests. JM was typically presented with six printed words in a random spatial order and asked to point to the word that matched the name given by the experimenter. Names were given in a pseudo-random temporal order. Once all six words had been prompted, the test was repeated by gathering the printed words together and re-randomising their positions. As previous work suggested that the response–stimulus interval might critically affect performance, this was strictly maintained at five seconds unless otherwise noted (see McNeil et al., 1994).

Experiment 6 examined JM's ability to perform printed word–auditory word matching across different categories of item, and the effects of repeated testing with those items. We also contrasted printed word–auditory word matching with picture–auditory word matching, to assess whether a similar pattern of breakdown across categories occurred for different modalities of test. A deficit with proper names was apparent in the results. Experiment 7 assessed whether this problem held for all proper names or only to names without specific referents. Experiment 8 tested whether JM's matching of printed words and pictures to auditory words was affected by the response–stimulus interval.

Experiments 9 and 10 evaluated the effects of the "semantic distance" between target and distractor words.

Experiment 6: Effects of Category and Stimulus Modality

Method

In Experiment 6a, JM was required to match a spoken word to one of six written words. The words on each trial were all exemplars from the same category, and one trial was completed when all the words in the category had been tested once (in pseudo-random order). The trial was then repeated a second time, using a different temporal order of testing and spatial layout for the written words. 28 categories were tested (see Table 1). Experiment 6b used the same procedure, but had line drawings of objects replace the written words for as many categories as possible. Both Experiments 6a and 6b were conducted twice, on tests separated by one month, using a different set of six exemplars for each category. This was done in order to ensure that any effects were not due simply to the exemplars chosen for particular categories, but generalised across category members. When Experiment 6b was first conducted 13 categories were tested; on the second test occasion, nine categories were tested (see Appendix 1 for a full list of stimuli). Fewer categories were tested with pictures than with words because of the difficulty in finding pictures for low imageability stimuli.

Results and Discussion

The scores for each category on each presentation are illustrated in Table 1. Adding together the data from the two sets of category exemplars, JM scored 252/336 (75% correct) on the first presentation of words, and 220/336 (66% correct) on the repeated presentation of words (Experiment 6a). He scored 123/132 (93% correct) on the first presentation of pictures and 109/132 (82.6% correct) on the repeated presentation (Experiment 6b). His performance was better on the first than on the repeated presentation of the stimuli, both with words, McNemar $(1) = 6.6$ $P < 0.05$, and with pictures, McNemar $(1) = 7.6$, $P < 0.05$. He also performed better with pictures than with words overall $(\chi^2 (1) = 31.6, P < 0.005.$[2]

---

[2] In the analyses conducted from repeated test sessions, it is possible that the data are non-independent due to serial dependency across trials. Serial dependency is shown by the decreased likelihood of JM responding correctly when tests are repeated, even though his performance on individual items is inconsistent (see Section D). Serial dependency violates the assumption of independence for Chi square analyses where data are added together across repetitions. However, for all the critical analyses, JM showed the same reliable effects of the variable in question (e.g. printed words vs pictures in Experiment 6) on the first trial as well as when first and repeated trials were combined. In addition, all the comparisons involved equal repetitions across the variables in question (e.g. printed words and pictures), and so did not confound effects of the variables of interest.

JM showed better matching for some categories of stimulus than for others (Table 1). In particular, across both pictures and words, and across the different category exemplars, he was relatively good at matching clothes, animals, transport, and office items to their names (178/192, 93% correct) and somewhat worse at matching geographical features, fruits, vegetables, and colours (135/192, 70% correct). Generally, his performance with pictures tended to mirror that with printed words. On the ''relatively poor'' categories fruits, vegetables, colours, and geographical features, JM scored 62/96 (65% correct) with printed

TABLE 1

Number of Correct Responses on Auditory—Written Word and Auditory–Picture Match, Experiment 6

Category	Written Word					Picture				
	Set 1		Set 2			Set 1		Set 2		
	P1	P2	P1	P2	t	P1	P2	P1	P2	t
Famous names	6	6	5	5	22					
Transport	6	5	5	6	22	6	5	6	6	23
Animals	6	6	5	4	21	6	6	6	6	24
Sport	6	6	5	4	21	6	6			(12)
Occupations	6	5	6	4	21					
Countries	6	6	5	3	20					
Cities	5	6	5	4	20					
Clothes	6	4	6	4	20	6	6	6	6	24
Office Items	6	6	4	4	20	6	6	6	6	24
Residences	4	5	4	6	19					
Weather	6	4	5	4	19					
Emotions	6	3	5	5	19					
Subjects	4	3	6	5	18					
Fruits	5	5	4	4	18	6	4	6	4	20
Body Parts	4	4	4	2	18	6	4			(10)
Instruments	5	6	3	3	17	6	6			(12)
Colours	3	3	6	5	17	5	3	4	4	16
Geographical	5	2	5	5	17	3	4	5	5	17
Kitchen Items	2	4	6	5	17			6	6	(12)
Materials	3	3	6	3	15					
Boys' names	2	3	5	5	15					
Vegetables	3	4	4	3	14	5	3	5	3	16
Furniture	4	0	5	4	13	6	5			(11)
Units of time	3	3	4	3	13					
Parts of a room	2	6	2	2	12	6	5			(11)
Surnames	1	1	5	4	11					
Girls' names	2	1	5	1	9					
Flowers	4	2	1	1	8					

Maximum score = 6, P1 is the first presentation of those items, P2 is the second. Set 1 refers to the first set of six exemplars, Set 2 to six new exemplars. t refers to the total correct for that modality.

words and 69/96 (72% correct) with pictures. On the "relatively good" categories clothes, animals, transport, and office items, he scored 81/96 (84% correct) with printed words and 95/96 (99% correct) with pictures.

JM also demonstrated an interesting dissociation within the general category of proper names. He was particularly good with famous names, cities, and countries (62/72, 86% correct) and very impaired with girls' names, boys' names, and surnames (35/72, 49% correct). Interestingly, this pattern of performance is similar to that shown by two patients previously reported with "access dysphasia": YOT (Warrington & McCarthy, 1987) and MED (McNeil et al., 1994). We return to this point in the General Discussion.

JM's uneven performance across the different categories of item cannot easily be attributed to co-variation in factors such as name frequency or visual familiarity. For instance, the similarity between his pattern of performance with printed words and pictures suggests that visual familiarity of the particular stimulus is relatively unimportant. In addition, we analysed for effects of the name frequency and familiarity of the stimuli on JM's performance, by determining the means for name frequency or familiarity of correct and incorrect items. To do this we applied the name-frequency counts given in the Kucera and Francis (1967), and familiarity ratings from Snodgrass and Vanderwart (1980)[3], to as many of the stimuli as possible. Analyses of the effects of familiarity were conducted only with pictures, as the visual familiarity measures collected do not apply to the visual forms of words (see also McNeil et al., 1994). There was no evidence that either name frequency or familiarity was an important factor, as the mean name-frequency and familiarity scores for the items matched correctly and for those matched incorrectly were very close (see Table 2). In Experiment 7 we provide a more direct test of whether such factors are important for JM's impairment with proper names. Experiment 6a showed that JM was somewhat better at pointing to famous names than at pointing to either forenames or surnames alone (Table 1). However, the individual names used were not matched (see Appendix 1). In Experiment 7 we compare his performance with the same names when they form a famous name (Jane Austen, Florence Nightingale) relative to when they form an unfamiliar name (Jane Nightingale, Florence Austen). Note that the frequency or familiarity of the famous name cannot be higher than the frequency or familiarity of the particular fore- and surname, as the fore- and surnames occur across many more individuals. JM's ability to point on verbal command to printed forenames and surnames is severely impaired (Experiment 6a; see also Experiment 7); any improvement with matched famous names cannot be due to the frequency or familiarity of the individual printed words used.

---

[3] The familiarity ratings derived by Snodgrass and Vanderwart (1980) were specific to their stimuli. Nevertheless, it seems likely that they may reflect the general visual familiarity of particular types of item and not just the familiarity of the tokens used by Snodgrass and Vanderwart.

TABLE 2
Mean Name Frequencies and Familiarity Ratings for Correct and Incorrect Responses,
Experiment 6

| | Name frequency | | Familiarity | |
	Correct	Incorrect	Correct	Incorrect
Words	33.94	40.20	—	—
Pictures	41.08	42.25	3.63	3.82

Frequency values are taken from Kucera and Francis (1967), familiarity values from Snodgrass and Vanderwart (1980).

The preliminary tests with JM indicated a deficit in accessing phonology from both pictures and printed stimuli. With printed stimuli, the problem was common to words and nonwords, suggesting that both the direct lexical and the non-lexical route to phonology was impaired (cf Morton & Patterson, 1980). If neither of these two routes can easily be utilised, then JM may be forced to match printed words to auditory words on the basis of common semantic information. The same may hold for picture–auditory word matching. The finding that JM's performance deteriorated when testing was repeated is consistent with him having problems in gaining access to semantic information. It is interesting in this respect that his pattern of performance with pictures closely mirrors that with printed words (Table 1). We return to discuss this point more fully in the General Discussion, but for now we note that a similar pattern of deficit across different categories suggests a common underlying impairment with pictures and words, rather than a deficit that is specific to the access route to semantics from these two types of stimulus.

Experiment 7: Pointing to Forenames and Surnames Embedded in Famous or Unfamiliar Full Names

Experiment 6a indicated that JM had a problem in pointing to named girls' and boys' forenames and to surnames. Such a problem might be due to several causes, including the paucity of semantic information that might be attached to individual proper names (e.g. because they have only referential meaning; see the Introduction). If such a factor is important, then JM might perform better at pointing to forenames and surnames embedded in a full name that can be attached to a specific person than at pointing to forenames or surnames either alone (as in Experiment 6a) or when embedded in an unfamiliar full name. Any improvement in performance would indicate that JM's deficit with forenames and surnames is not due to the frequency or familiarity of the individual stimulus, but due to the lack of associated semantic information for these stimuli.

Method

JM was presented with sets of famous and unfamiliar names of men and women. The famous and unfamiliar names were presented in an ABBA fashion, beginning first with women's names and then with the names of men. In each case he was presented with six names (e.g. Jane Austen, Florence Nightingale, or Jane Nightingale and Florence Austen) printed on individual cards and randomly arranged on a table. The test with forenames (Experiment 7a) was conducted prior to the test with surnames (Experiment 7b), and the tests were conducted on separate weeks. In Experiment 7a, a forename (e.g. Jane) was auditorily presented by the experimenter (EF) and the task was to point to the card with that name. A trial consisted of the presentation of each forename once (in pseudo-random order), and the entire set was repeated three times consecutively before the next condition commenced. The same procedure was followed in Experiment 7b, except that individual surnames were auditorily presented.

Results and Discussion

Experiment 7a: Forenames.   JM was significantly better at pointing to a forename when it was embedded in a famous full name (22/36) relative to when it was embedded in an unfamiliar full name (12/36), χ^2 (1) = 5.57, $P < 0.025$.

Experiment 7b: Surnames.   JM was significantly better at pointing to a surname when it was embedded in a famous name (23/36) than when it was embedded in an unfamiliar name (14/36) $\chi^2(1) = 4.5$, $P < 0.05$.

The advantage for forenames and surnames embedded in famous relative to unfamiliar full names occurred even on the first trial within each set (15/24 vs 7/24, for famous and unfamiliar names; χ^2 (1) = 5.37, $P < 0.05$).

These results show a clear advantage when JM was asked to point to either a forename or a surnamed embedded in a famous name, relative to when the same names were embedded in an unfamiliar name. As the individual names were the same in all cases, and as the frequency and familiarity of the full names cannot be higher than the frequency and familiarity of the individual fore- and surnames, the results demonstrate that JM's deficit with proper names is not simply due to familiarity or frequency. Rather the data suggest that JM's performance is dependent on whether the stimuli are associated with a specific referent; when stimuli are so associated, his performance is improved.

Experiment 8: Effects of the Response–Stimulus Interval

In previous studies with patients who have shown an inconsistent pattern of printed word–auditory word matching across items, and worse matching with repeated testing, experimenters have shown that the response–stimulus interval critically affects accuracy. We examined this variable in auditory word–written word matching in Experiment 8a and in auditory word–picture matching in Experiment 8b.

Experiment 8a

Method.   JM was tested with two categories of stimulus, one relatively intact (jobs) and one impaired (surnames). In each case he was given six cards, each with the printed name of a category exemplar on it, and on one trial he was asked to point to each of the six names in a random order. This procedure was then repeated. Each category was also tested with three intervals between his last response and the naming of the next item: 30 seconds, 10 seconds, and 2 seconds. Each category was tested, first with a 30-second response–stimulus interval (RSI), next with a 2-second interval and finally with a 10-second interval.

Results and Discussion.   The number of correct responses for each category at each response–stimulus interval are given in Table 3. The intact category, jobs, did not show any reliable effects of the response–stimulus interval; however, the impaired category, surnames, did (comparing data from the 2- and 30-second intervals, Fisher Exact probability = 0.02). Performance decreased when the response–stimulus interval was short (2 seconds) relative to when it was long (30 seconds). This pattern of performance matches that observed with other dysphasic patients with apparent problems in accessing semantic information (McNeil et al., 1994; Warrington & McCarthy, 1983, 1987).

Experiment 8b

Method.   JM was tested with four categories: colours, fruit, vegetables, and geographical features. He was presented with an array of six cards, each with a picture of a category exemplar on it, and on one trial he was asked to point to each of the six names in a random order. This procedure was then repeated

TABLE 3
Number of Correct Responses as a Function of the Response–Stimulus Interval,
Experiment 8

| Category | Response–Stimulus Interval | | |
	2 seconds	10 seconds	30 seconds
Impaired	1	2	7
Intact	11	12	12

Maximum score is 12.

twice. Each category was also tested with two intervals between his last response and the naming of the next item: 30 seconds and 2 seconds.

Results.   JM scored 54/72 with the 30-second RSI and 40/72 with the 2-second RSI. His performance was significantly influenced by rate, $\chi^2(1) = 6.0$, $P < 0.02$. This indicates that rate is an important variable when JM is required to match across both modalities of words and pictures.

Experiment 9: Effects of Semantic Distance (i)

Warrington and McCarthy (1987) reported that their patient, YOT, was worse at picture–auditory word matching when a target picture was surrounded by other items from the same semantic category relative to when targets were surrounded by stimuli from other categories. They suggested that there might be a "spread" of refractoriness within an access route, affecting other members of a probed category. This was examined for JM in Experiment 9.

Method

The stimuli were arrays of six printed words from six of JM's impaired categories (time, girls' names, boys' names, surnames, kitchen items, and flowers) and from six of his intact categories (clothes, animals, occupations, transport, office items, and countries). Each of the 36 items was tested under conditions of "close" and "distant" semantic similarity between targets and distractors. In the close condition all six items in an array were from the same category (e.g. aeroplane, van, car, train, ship, bus). In the distant condition the arrays consisted of one item from each of the six impaired categories or from each of the six preserved categories. A trial again consisted of each name in the array being given once, and each category was probed three times consecutively.

Results

The number of correct responses in each condition is given in Table 4. Overall, performance was better for the intact relative to the impaired categories, confirming the results from Experiment 6—this held both when the data from the repeated tests were included, $\chi^2(1) = 78.4$ $P < 0.01$, and when only the first trial was used, Fisher exact probability = 0.05. Most importantly, performance was better in the semantically distant relative to the semantically close condition—this held both when all trials were included, $\chi^2(1) = 36.56$, $P < 0.05$, and when only the first trial was included, $\chi^2(1) = 7.73$, $P < 0.05$. The improved performance with semantically distant distractors occurred for both the intact and the impaired categories; the effect was numerically larger for the impaired

TABLE 4
Number of Correct Responses in the Semantically Distant and Close Conditions,
Experiment 9

Category	Close	Distant
Intact	87	107
Impaired	42	78

Maximum score in each condition is 108.

categories (see Table 4), but further improvements in the intact categories may have been obscured by a ceiling effect.

The results again clearly showed that JM is affected by the category of the stimulus. In addition, he is affected by whether targets are surrounded by other items from the same category. This might be due to various factors. For example, there could be a "spread of refractoriness" from one item to other members of the same category. Alternatively it could be that the representation of one item, once tested, becomes refractory in such a way that only general semantic information may be retrieved from it; when this occurs to a number of stimuli from the same category, stimuli within that category become confusable. These possibilities are examined in Experiment 13, where we tested for "transfer" of the refractory state across items. Experiment 10 tests the specificity of the semantic distance effects apparent in Experiment 9. For example, within the impaired category of forenames, is there any distinction between boys' and girls' names for JM, suggesting some form of hierarchical breakdown in his performance within the general category of proper names?

Experiment 10: Effects of Semantic Distance (ii)

Method

JM was presented with six randomly positioned cards. In the close condition the stimuli were either all boys' or all girls' names. In the distant condition there were three names of girls and three of boys. On one trial JM was asked to point to each name, presented in a pseudo-random order. Each trial was repeated three times consecutively. JM was first presented with the boys' names (close condition), followed by the two sets of mixed boys' and girls' names (distant condition), followed by the girls' names (close condition).

Results and Discussion

When exemplars were all from the same category of boys' and girls' forenames (in the close condition) JM scored 11/36 (31% correct). When there were mixed boys' and girls' names (in the distant condition) he scored 23/36

(64% correct). Performance was better in the distant relative to the close condition—when all the trials were included, $\chi^2(1) = 8.0$, $P < 0.005$; when only the first trial for each condition was included, Fisher exact probability = 0.05.

In addition, in the distant condition, we assessed whether JM tended to make errors within or across categories (e.g. incorrectly pointing to a boy's name instead of a girl's name). Of JM's 13 errors, he made 10 within-category and 3 across-category. This differs from chance distribution of errors (Binomial probability = 0.007) indicating that he was more likely to make an error within rather than across categories.

JM's performance improved when he had to point to a boys' name among girls' names relative to when all the words present were boys' names (and vice versa for girls' names). Thus the effect of semantic distance does not just occur across widely different categories (as in Experiment 9; see also Warrington & McCarthy, 1987) but also within the general class of proper names. This conclusion is also supported by the error analysis, which indicates that, in the distant condition, JM was more likely to make a within-category pointing error than expected by chance. These results suggest some form of hierarchical breakdown in JM's performance, in which he gains access to general information about the category of a word but not to specific information associated with the word. This is examined in more detail in Experiment 11.

Summary

The results in Section B have shown that JM's pattern of performance closely mirrors that reported for other patients with apparent deficits in accessing semantic information (e.g. patient YOT, Warrington & McCarthy, 1987). Thus JM's performance varied widely across different categories of stimulus; it was affected by the interval between his response and the presentation of the next stimulus (at least in the impaired categories); and it was affected by the semantic distance between target and distractor stimuli (being worst when targets and distractors were semantically close). We have extended previous work by showing that the pattern of breakdown across categories is very similar both when printed words and pictures are presented as stimuli (Experiments 6a and 6b), and that effects of semantic distance extend within the general class of proper nouns (Experiment 10). JM performs worse when items are immediately repeated and when the response–stimulus interval is short—effects that are thought to be characteristic of a difficulty in accessing semantic information.

SECTION C: EXPERIMENTAL TESTS OF THE NATURE OF THE ACCESS DEFICIT

The experiments reported in Section A showed that JM was selectively poor at tasks requiring the retrieval of semantic information, and those reported in Section B indicated a pattern expected if the problem were one of accessing semantic knowledge according to the criteria proposed by Warrington and Shallice (1979). In Section C we report experimental tests designed to assess in more detail the nature of the difficulty in accessing semantic knowledge. In particular we ask: (i) what information can JM gain access to about the items that he finds difficult in written word–auditory word picture matching? (Experiment 11), and (ii) is there transfer of the apparent refractory state from tested to previously untested items within the same category? (Experiment 12). These experiments constrain our interpretation of where and how such refractory states arise.

Experiment 11: Categorising Stimuli from the Impaired Categories

Experiment 10 indicated that even when JM found it difficult to access semantic information to distinguish different boys' names and different girls' names, he was nevertheless able to differentiate between boys' names and girls' names. It is possible that the information distinguishing these two classes of names may have affected JM's performance implicitly; for example, if boys' names and girls' names are relatively widely separated within some form of semantic space, and there is a spread of a refractory state within this space, items within the same category of proper name may be more affected than items within different categories of proper name. In Experiment 11 we assessed whether JM had explicit access to categorical knowledge about stimuli within the classes that he found difficult in auditory–written word matching tasks, by requiring him to categorise stimuli. Note that if he performs well at this task, we may take it as given that JM also has good access to a stored visual lexical representation for printed words as that is a prerequisite for good categorisation.

Method

JM was required to perform several categorisation tasks with printed and auditory words. First he was asked to distinguish between printed famous and unfamiliar full names (24 stimuli; 12 famous and 12 unfamiliar). He was then asked to distinguish surnames from names referring to units of time (six stimuli per category), and between forenames for boys and for girls (six names for boys and six for girls, taken from Experiment 6a). The task requiring categorisation of boys' and girls' names was also performed with auditory presentation, some two months after the test with printed words. For the tests with printed words JM was asked to sort the cards into one of two piles using the categories indicated by the experimenter. For the test with auditory words, he was asked to point to a card with either a B (for boys) or G (for girls) on it.

Results and Discussion

JM performed at a high level on these tasks. He correctly categorised 21/24 of the famous and unfamiliar names from print; 11/12 of the surnames and units of time (he incorrectly categorised the surname Baxter as a unit of time); 12/12 of the girls' and boys' names from print, and 12/12 of the girls' and boys' names from audition.

In contrast to JM's poor ability to match the auditory name for these stimuli to their printed names, he generally performed well when required to sort the names into superordinate categories. He performed flawlessly at categorising boys' and girls' names both from audition and from print, suggesting that (a) access to an input lexicon for both types of stimulus is intact, and (b) that he can access superordinate information for items that he cannot identify. However, this general superordinate information is insufficient to support performance on an auditory–written word matching task, which requires more detailed information to distinguish between exemplars of the same category.

Experiment 12: Spreading the Refractory State

From the results presented hitherto, it is possible that the refractory state apparent in JM's cross-modality matching performance could arise for a number of reasons. First, the locus of the refractoriness could either be in the semantic representations of items, or in access processes to these representations. There may also be a spread of this state to either the semantic representations of related items or to the access procedures for related items, making performance worse when stimuli are drawn from the same semantic category (Experiments 9 and 10). Alternatively, the refractory state may be specific to the presented item, and the deterioration in performance with repeated testing may occur because, following presentation, that item only gains access to general semantic information.

In Experiment 12 we attempted to provide the first test cf whether there is any empirical support for the concept of a spreading refractory state. Cross-modality matching of printed and auditory words was required, but not all the items present on each trial were repeatedly probed. Half the items on a trial were repeatedly probed so they would become refractory and half the items were not probed until the fourth and final trial, when printed word–auditory word matching was then required for all items. Here we assess whether repeated cross-modality matching of items from the same category is sufficient to put other exemplars into a refractory state, measured by a drop in performance when the stimuli are probed for the first time on the fourth trial relative to when they are probed on a first trial.

Method

On each trial JM was presented with an array of six randomly positioned words which were all from the same category. This was repeated for nine categories; three categories were chosen from the set of intact categories in Experiment 6 (transport, occupations, and countries), three from intermediate categories (body parts, vegetables, and time) and three from impaired categories (surnames, girls' names, and boys' names). On each trial, JM was required to carry out printed word–auditory word matching for three of the six stimuli present. Following the probing of three of the items, the spatial positions of the six printed words were changed and repeated testing of the same three items was conducted. The three items were then probed a third time. On the fourth consecutive trial auditory names were presented for all six of the stimuli present (i.e. the three items that had been repeatedly probed [Rep] and the three items not probed hitherto [New]). To counterbalance the experiment, the three items that had been repeated became the new items on a separate occasion. This allowed comparisons to be made for the same items on trial 1, trial 4 (Rep), and trial 4 (New). This procedure is illustrated in Fig. 2.

We were also interested in whether the refractory state spread only to items that would be likely to be close in semantic space, or to all items within the category. There were three conditions in which the relations between the repeated and newly probed items were varied: (1) typical items were repeated on trials 1–4 and new typical items were probed on trial 4 (the typical-typical

Time 1		p1	p2	p3	p4
	France	*	*	*	*
	England	*	*	*	*
	Russia	*	*	*	*
	Germany				*
	Canada				*
	Italy				*
Time 2		p1	p2	p3	p4
	France				*
	England				*
	Russia				*
	Germany	*	*	*	*
	Canada	*	*	*	*
	Italy	*	*	*	*

Note: * indicates that this item was probed.

FIG. 2.   An illustration of the procedure in Experiment 13 using the category countries in the typical-typical condition.

condition) to see if there was any evidence for spreading refractoriness; (2) typical items were repeated on trials 1–4 and new atypical items were probed on trial 4 (the typical-atypical condition) to see if the refractoriness had spread to atypical members of the category which would presumably be further away in semantic space than the typical items; (3) atypical items were repeated on trials 1–4 and new typical items were probed on trial 4 (the atypical-typical condition). The same items were used in conditions 2 and 3 so that the repeatedly probed items in the typical-atypical condition became the newly probed items on trial 4 in the atypical-typical condition, and vice versa. Typicality was determined using the Battig and Montague (1969) norms.

The typical-typical, typical-atypical, and atypical-typical conditions also occurred with two response–stimulus intervals; 2 and 30 seconds (cf Experiment 8). The order of the response–stimulus intervals was randomly determined for each category.

Results

The numbers of correct printed word–auditory word matches made for each of the three conditions (typical-typical, typical-atypical, and atypical-typical stimuli), for each response–stimulus interval, are given in Table 5.

Condition 1: Typical-typical. Overall, performance was better when there was a slow response–stimulus interval than when there was fast interval, 205/270 vs 162/270 for a 30-second and a 2-second response–stimulus interval respectively, $\chi^2(1) = 16.9$, $P < 0.005$. For items repeatedly probed through trials

TABLE 5
Number of Correct Responses as a Function of the Response–Stimulus Interval, Condition, and Trial Number, Experiment 13

| Response–Stimulus interval | | Trial Number | | | |
	1	2	3	4 (R)	4 (N)
Typical-Typical					
2	43	29	32	27	31
30	44	42	38	38	43
Typical-Atypical	typ	typ	typ	typ	atyp
2	24	16	17	17	15
30	22	22	22	21	18
Atypical-Typical	atyp	atyp	atyp	atyp	typ
2	21	18	21	19	18
30	22	18	20	20	22

R = items repeated across trials 1–4, N = "new" items probed for the first time on the fourth trial.
Scores in the typical-typical condition are /54, and in the typical-atypical and atypical-typical /27.

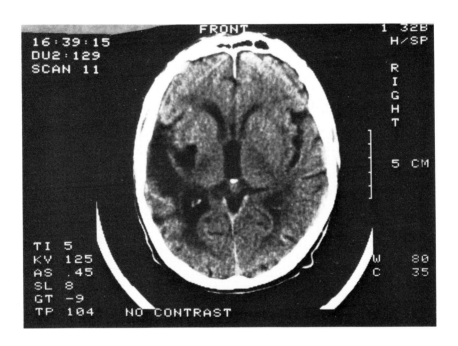

FIG. 1.   CT scan for JM indicating a hypodense area in the left tempero-parietal region.

291

1–4, and with a fast response–stimulus interval, performance was better on trial 1 than on trial 4, 43/54 vs 27/54, McNemar (1) = 10.2, $P < 0.005$. However there was no significant difference between the first (44/54) and fourth (38/54) presentation when the rate was slow, McNemar (1) = 2.1, $P < 0.2$. These results replicate the effects of repeated testing and of the response–stimulus interval reported in Experiments 6 and 8.

At the two-second response–stimulus interval, there was a significant transfer of performance from the repeatedly probed items to the newly probed items. When the items were newly probed on trial 4, JM scored 31/54; the difference relative to performance on trial 1 is reliable, 31/54 vs 43/54, McNemar (1) = 7.6, $P < 0.01$. The difference between repeatedly probed items and newly probed items on trial 4 was not significant (31/54 vs 27/54).

At the 30-second response–stimulus interval, there was no transfer from repeatedly probed (44/54 for newly probed items on trial 1) to new items (43/54 for newly probed items on trial 4).

Conditions 2 and 3. Again the results of Experiments 6 and 8 were replicated. The response–stimulus interval affected performance, and, with the fast response–stimulus interval, performance declined with repeated probing. With a response–stimulus interval of two seconds, JM scored 186/270 correct overall, relative to 207/270 with a response–stimulus interval of 30 seconds, $\chi^2(1) = 4.1$, $P < 0.05$.

At the two-second response–stimulus interval there was a significant decrease in performance on trial 4 for items repeatedly probed relative to performance on the same items on trial 1, 45/54 for trial 1 vs 36/54 for the same items on trial 4; McNemar (1) = 3.8, $P < 0.05$. This effect was not significant with a 30-second response–stimulus interval (44/54 on trial 1 vs 41/54 on trial 4).

Spreading from Typical to Atypical. There was a trend for transfer of interference from repeated typical exemplars to new atypical exemplars. With a two-second response–stimulus interval, JM scored 15/27 on new items on trial 4 (condition 2) relative to 21/27 on the same items on trial 1 (condition 3), McNemar(1) = 2.5, $P < 0.2$. With a 30-second interval there was also a trend in the same direction; he scored 18/27 on trial 4 compared with 22/27 on trial 1.

Spreading from Atypical to Typical. With a short response–stimulus interval (two seconds), there was a spread of interference from probed atypical to new typical items. JM scored 24/27 for typical exemplars on trial 1 relative to 18/27 on the same items when they were first probed on trial 4 following the repeated probing of atypical items (Fisher Exact probability = 0.05). There was no such trend with the longer 30-second response–stimulus interval (22/27 when typical items were presented on trial 1 vs 22/27 when they were presented on trial 4 following repeated probing of atypical items).

Overall Effects of Typicality.   Overall, JM showed relatively minor effects of typicality on his performance. On trial 1, he scored 67/81 (83% correct) on typical category exemplars, and 21/27 (78% correct) on atypical category exemplars with a short response–stimulus interval; with the longer 30-second interval he scored 66/81 (81% correct) with typical and 22/27 (81.5%) with atypical exemplars. These differences are not reliable. On trial 4 with new items, he scored 49/81 (61%) on typical and 15/27 (56% correct) on atypical exemplars, with the short response–stimulus interval; with the longer interval he scored 65/81 (80% correct) on typical and 18/27 (67%) correct on atypical. On trial 4 with repeated items, the scores were 44/81 (54%) for typical and 19/27 (70%) for atypical with the short response–stimulus interval; with the long response–stimulus interval he scored 59/81 (73%) for typical and 20/27 (74%) for atypical exemplars. These overall scores suggest that irrespective of the typicality of the items, performance tended to decrease on new items presented on trial 4 relative to when the same items were presented on trial 1 (although in the individual conditions, only the transfers onto typical new items with a two-second response–stimulus interval were reliable). The results are summarised in Table 6.

Discussion

The results from Experiment 12 provide the first direct demonstration that the refractory state induced by repeated probing of items can transfer to new items within the same category. The effect was strongest when typical category members were repeated and new typical exemplars were then probed, but the overall results suggest that typicality effects were at best only minor influences on performance.

Following repeated testing it is possible that the semantic representation for the presented item enters a refractory state in which only general semantic information can be retrieved. When a number of items from the same category

TABLE 6
Overall Effects of Typicality, Experiment 13

| | | Trial Number | |
	1	*4 (R)*	*4 (N)*
2-second response–stimulus interval			
Typical	83	54	61
Atypical	78	70	56
30-second response–stimulus interval			
Typical	81	73	80
Atypical	82	74	67

Scores are % correct in each condition.

are repeatedly tested, so that all their semantic representations enter a refractory state, discrimination between them may prove difficult, as they all access the same general semantic information. Performance then decreases when targets and distractors are from the same semantic field (cf Experiments 9 and 10 here). Were this the case, however, the performance on new items from the same category should remain relatively good, because their representations should not have entered the refractory state. The results contradict this, and suggest instead that the refractory state spreads from previously tested items to other items within the same category, perhaps reflecting spreading inhibition within the semantic system (cf Neumann, Cherau, Hood, & Steinnagel, 1993). This spread of the refractory state may be most pronounced between typical category members, perhaps because they are located closely together within a semantic field (see Valentine, 1991, for this argument in the domain of face recognition). One further possibility, which cannot be rejected from the present data, is that there is prolonged activation of semantic representations following the probing of a target stimulus, with this activation also spreading to other items within the same category (see also McNeil et al., 1994). This spread of activation decreases the signal-to-noise ratio for target relative to distractor representations at the semantic level, even when the target exemplars are newly probed following the earlier probing of exemplars from the same category. Though we will proceed to discuss the results in terms of the spreading of inhibitory processes, this alternative view of spreading activation should continue to be borne in mind.

SECTION D: ANALYSIS OF CONSISTENCY

In Section A, tests of consistency were carried out for Experiment 1 and indicated that JM was inconsistent in his responses both in tests using different input modalities and in tests using the same input modality at different times.

Further analyses of item consistency were carried out for Experiment 6 and Experiment 12. For Experiment 6 the analysis was performed on categories that were not at ceiling. Testing was also separated according to whether stimuli belonged to the first or second set of items tested in each category. This showed that JM's performance was inconsistent over time for words from set 1 ($\chi^2(1) = 2.7$, $P > 0.05$), set 2 ($\chi^2(1) = 0.006$), and pictures from set 2 (Fisher Exact probability = 0.99). For pictures from set 1 there were some effects of consistency (Fisher Exact probability = 0.01) although for three out of nine categories tested here he only made one error, which may have increased the consistency due to responses being near to ceiling.

To test the consistency of JM's performance in Experiment 12 we looked at his responses over the first four repetitions of items. In doing this, we assumed independence over trials and used a binomial expansion to estimate the performance levels expected by chance consistency (for justification of this technique applied to data from matching tasks, see McNeil et al., 1994). The data are shown in Table 7. Chi square tests between observed and expected (chance) values were not significant in any condition (typical-typical and typical-atypical, at 2-second and 30-second response–stimulus intervals).

GENERAL DISCUSSION

This paper has documented a case study of a global aphasic patient, JM, with: (i) a severe impairment in retrieving phonological information from printed words and pictures; (ii) good access to an input lexicon from words and to a structural description from pictures; (iii) impaired access to semantic information, particularly from printed words; and (iv) an impaired ability to match printed words, auditory words and pictures, where such matching is mediated by access to semantic information (see later section). JM's matching performance is (i) particularly poor for certain classes of stimuli, including the class of proper names without specific referents; and (ii) characterised by being inconsistent across time, worse with repeated testing, worse when stimuli are presented rapidly following a prior response, and worse when target stimuli are surrounded

TABLE 7
Consistency Between Items, Experiment 13

	✓✓✓✓	✓✓✓✗	✓✓✗✗	✓✗✗✗	✗✗✗✗
2-second response–stimulus interval					
Typical-Typical					
Expected	1.5	7.9	14.0	10.1	2.5
Observed	6	7	8	9	6
Typical (Typical-Atypical)					
Expected	1.3	5.4	7.2	3.6	0.5
Observed	2	4	8	3	1
Atypical (Typical-Atypical)					
Expected	2.5	6.5	6.5	2.5	0.4
Observed	2	7	6	3	0
30-second response–stimulus interval					
Typical-Typical					
Expected	6.8	14.4	10.8	3.6	0.4
Observed	14	9	5	4	4
Typical (Typical-Atypical)					
Expected	4.5	7.7	4.9	1.3	0.1
Observed	7	5	3	2	1
Atypical (Typical-Atypical)					
Expected	2.9	6.8	5.8	2.1	0.4
Observed	6	3	4	4	1

by distractors from the same semantic field. In addition, (i) the deficit across particular categories of stimulus is very similar whether printed words or pictures are presented; (ii) JM can access superordinate information about stimuli even when he fails to access specific semantic information, and (iii) the deterioration in accessing semantic information "spreads" from items initially probed to other members of the same category. There are interesting implications of these results for understanding: (i) the relations between lexical and semantic knowledge stores in human memory; (ii) the nature of semantic representations, and (iii) the relations between "access" and "storage" deficits following brain damage.

Presemantic Stores and Semantic Memory

JM's case supports the argument for the existence of a functionally separate structural description, input lexicon, and semantic (functional and associative) stores, specifying different types of information about objects, as has been argued from prior studies of both reading (e.g. Morton & Patterson, 1980) and visual object recognition (Riddoch & Humphreys, 1987a,b). JM performed normally on tests requiring judgements about the perceptual familiarity of a stimulus (e.g. visual and auditory lexical decision, object decision), and on tests requiring superordinate judgements about exemplars from impaired categories (e.g. distinguishing boys' names from girls' names, Experiment 11), but poorly on tests requiring access to specific semantic information (e.g. Experiment 1). His picture–word matching performance was also influenced by semantic similarity between targets and distractors (Experiments 5, 8, and 9), indicating impaired access to semantic information.

Across-modality Matching Based on Semantic Representations

JM had minimal access to output phonology, and also showed no evidence of explicit access to internal phonology. This held for written words (e.g. in rhyme and homophone judgement tasks), for nonwords (e.g. pointing to a named pseudohomophone), and for pictures (in rhyme judgement tasks). The lack of access to phonology from both words and nonwords suggests that there is impairment of direct routes to phonology for words. Models of visual word processing typically posit that there exist either two or three "routes" to word naming, involving both the direct mapping of orthography to phonology and an indirect semantically mediated route, involving visual recognition of the word's meaning (e.g. Seidenberg, 1992; Seidenberg & McClelland, 1989). The direct route may itself be sub-divided to create separate lexical and non-lexical routes (Coltheart, Curtis, Atkins, & Haller, 1993). Given impairments that prevent the direct route(s) from operating for JM, printed words may only be matched to stimuli presented via other modalities (such as auditory words) by means of access to semantic representations. Similarly, given his poor access to output phonology from pictures, his picture–word matching may be based on the activation of common semantic representations.

Category-specific Semantic Representations for Proper Names

JM showed a clear dissociation between good performance when matching names that have a clear referent in semantic memory, such as Jane Austen or Florence Nightingale, relative to his poor matching of the same fore- and surnames when presented with them either in isolation or in an unfamiliar combination (Jane Nightingale, Florence Austen; Experiment 7). We argued earlier that JM's poor performance on auditory–written word matching can be linked to impaired access to semantic information. It follows that the deficit for proper names without a specific referent must reflect something about the representation of these stimuli in the semantic system. Proper names with a specific referent will have individuating semantic information connected with them, such as, author, nurse, Crimean war etc. In contrast, the names Jane and Florence presented in isolation will tend not to have individuating semantic information associated with them, although general information, such as gender, could be associated with unfamiliar names. It follows that performance will be worst with proper names without a specific referent, relative to stimuli from other categories, because unfamiliar proper names have fewer connections to semantic attributes that may facilitate cross-modality matching in a patient such as JM, who is unable to perform such matching by non-semantic means. Interestingly, Young, McWeeny, Ellis, and Hay (1986) reported that non-brain-damaged subjects took longer to name unfamiliar (Jack Martin and Dean Nicholson) compared to familiar names (Jack Nicholson and Dean Martin), which suggests that proper-name reading is not completely based on lexical transcription, but influenced by the semantic system.

McNeil et al. (1994) offer an alternative explanation of the dissociation between familiar and unfamiliar proper names, built on prior proposals concerned with differences between common and proper nouns. It has been suggested that the crucial difference between common nouns and proper nouns reflects the mapping between the name and referent, which is many-to-one and one-to-one respectively (Burton & Bruce, 1992; Semenza & Zettin, 1988). The many-to-one mapping for common nouns may make their recall more robust for normal subjects (Brennen, Baguley, Bright, & Bruce, 1990; Burke, Mackay, Worthley, & Wade, 1991; Hanley & Cowell, 1988; Young, Hay, & Ellis, 1985). However, McNeil et al. suggest that, for patients affected by semantic interference between items, many-to-one mappings may prove problematic, because interference effects will then be increased relative to when stimuli have one-to-one mappings. Nonfamous names are shared, and so have many-to-one mappings from semantics to names, whereas famous names are linked to one reference within the semantic system. Hence famous names may be less prone to interference effects. McNeil et al.'s proposal concerning shared semantic representations for nonfamous proper names contrasts with our argument that nonfamous proper names have relatively impoverished semantic representations, although it should be noted that, within our scheme, the impoverished representations for nonfamous proper names may also be shared across many items from the same class (eg. gender is shared across the category of boys' names).

Related arguments have been made in the literature on the recall of common and proper names. For instance, Cohen (1990) suggested that proper names are meaningless and arbitrary, and demonstrated that proper-name recall is similar to recall of meaningless words for normal subjects. Other researchers have shown that proper-name anomia co-occurs with a difficulty in recall of arbitrarily paired associates (Hittmair-Delazer, Denes, Semenza, & Mantovan, 1994; Semenza & Zettin, 1988), consistent with proper names being difficult to retrieve because they are meaningless labels and have few semantic associates. However, the pattern of results with JM suggests that semantic associations for famous proper names must be relatively rich compared with those for nonfamous proper names, because we have argued that he relies on semantic activation for cross-modality matching.

It is also relevant to consider previous evidence reported on the reading of deep dyslexic patients. Similar to the arguments we have made concerning JM, it has been proposed that deep dyslexics must read via semantics because they have impaired direct lexical and non-lexical routes for reading print (Newcombe & Marshall, 1980a, b). Interestingly, Saffran, Schwartz, and Marin (1976) documented two deep dyslexic patients who were relatively good at reading words when they were incorporated into unfamiliar proper names. In their Experiment 1, Saffran et al. asked their patients to read two lists of words aloud. List 1 contained a series of words from various categories (e.g. Robin, Ruby), in list 2 the same words were used to create unfamiliar names (e.g. Robin Kelly, Ruby Clark). When reading list 1, the deep dyslexics made significantly more semantic errors, such as reading robin as bird and ruby as opal, than when reading list 2. They argued that performance was better with proper names because the words (e.g. Ruby) no longer activated the usual set of semantic alternatives (e.g. opal) and so competition for name selection was reduced. Here we must presume that the semantic representations the patients were able to access for the unfamiliar proper names were nevertheless sufficient for name retrieval to take place. We propose that, like deep dyslexic patients, JM reads via his semantic system, but he shows the opposite effect; words that are unfamiliar proper names cannot be read as easily as words that have richer semantic associations. We suggest that overlap among the activated semantic representations from the auditory and written modalities is used as the basis for JM's cross-modality matching, but such overlap might sometimes lead to competition for name selection in patients with access to output phonology. JM's access to output phonology is minimal, so that any effects of increased competition between items for name selection will not affect his performance.

Such results suggest that semantic overlap can either be beneficial or harmful to the performance of brain-damaged patients, perhaps according to the functional locus of the damage. In turn this might help to explain why some patients have been reported with selective preservation for proper nouns compared to common nouns (Cipolotti et al., 1993; Warrington & Clegg, 1993), which might be due to the patients being hyper-sensitive to competition between name alternatives rather than being impaired when semantic representations are impoverished. Models of name retrieval need to be able to account for both patterns of deficit, and not just the normal advantage for common nouns over proper names (cf Burke et al., 1991; Burton & Bruce, 1993; Cohen, 1990; Semenza & Zettin, 1988).

One final point is that, interestingly, JM performed poorly on cross-modality matching even when his own forename, or the forenames of relatives, were used. A priori one might have thought that one's own forename would have relatively rich semantic associations, and so might be treated more like a famous name than a proper name without semantic referent. The data contradict this. It would appear that even our own forenames are separately represented from full names having semantic (type) referents, whether the forenames are represented separately within semantic memory or within a separate lexical system.

For the other classes of stimulus for which JM either showed selective impairment or selectively preserved performance, it is difficult to find any single underlying dimension that would link together the impaired and the preserved categories, though we note that the items that JM matched correctly and those he did not were not distinguished in terms of either their name frequency or their familiarity (Experiment 6). It may be that a combination of factors was crucial, including the number of semantic referents (e.g. for proper names and units of time) and whether perceptual attributes are strongly weighted (e.g. for fruits, vegetables, flowers, and colours) (see Sheridan & Humphreys, 1993; Warrington & McCarthy, 1987; Warrington & Shallice, 1984).

The Underlying Semantic Representations

The categories that JM found either relatively difficult or easy to match were largely the same irrespective of whether auditory words had to be matched to printed words or to pictures. This suggests that performance with pictures and words was influenced by a common factor. Interestingly, a similar result was reported by Warrington and McCarthy (1987) with their patient YOT, for whom similar categories of stimulus were affected for cross-modality matching with both pictures and printed words (to auditory words). There are at least two ways that we can conceptualise the data. One is that there is a single impairment to a semantic system that is common to both pictures and printed words (e.g. Caramazza, Hillis, Rapp, & Romani, 1990; Riddoch, Humphreys, Coltheart, & Funnell, 1988). The other is that there are separate impairments to either (i) input procedures into a common semantic network, (ii) input procedures into semantic networks that are distinct from either the modalities of input (McCarthy & Warrington, 1988; Warrington, 1975), or for the nature of the information represented (Beauvois, 1982; Shallice, 1993); or (iii) the separate semantic networks selectively accessed by pictures and printed words. According to each of these last accounts, the fact that the same categories tended to be preserved or impaired irrespective of whether matching involved pictures or printed words is either coincidental or due to similarity in the underlying structure of either the separate semantic representations themselves or the modality-specific access procedures (e.g. because certain categories have sparser semantic representations, and so perhaps more sparsely connected transmission routes). The idea that there is a single deficit affecting both pictures and printed words, involving a common semantic network, is the more parsimonious. In further work with JM, we show that the refractory state induced by pictures generalises to when stimuli are subsequently presented as words (Forde & Humphreys, in preparation). Such a result is difficult to account for either in terms of separate deficits to independent access routes or to independent semantic networks.

Access and Storage Deficits

Previous neuropsychological case studies have made much of the distinction between deficits to underlying stored representations (storage deficits) and those to the procedures that access the representations (access deficits). As we discussed in the Introduction, this distinction has been grounded on contrasting patterns of performance across different patients. Some patients show a pattern of deficits that is consistent across items across time (e.g. Silveri & Gainotti, 1988; Warrington & Shallice, 1984). From this, it has been argued that the patients have degraded stored representations (Shallice, 1987; Warrington & Shallice, 1979). Other patients show a pattern of performance that is inconsistent across items, and, in other cases similar to JM, performance deteriorates with repeated testing and when a short response–stimulus interval is used (e.g. McNeil et al., 1994; Warrington & McCarthy, 1983, 1987). The deficits in these last patients have been attributed to problems in gaining access to intact stored representations. The distinction between access and storage deficits has also been linked to other correlated findings, such as whether patients show improved performance when primed (consistent with an access problem, with the stored representations being intact; Warrington & Shallice, 1979) and whether the patients show a hierarchical pattern of breakdown such that superordinate

302 FORDE AND HUMPHREYS

knowledge about items is preserved when subordinate knowledge is impaired (Warrington, 1975; Warrington & Shallice, 1979). In the present paper we have shown that JM demonstrated the typical pattern of performance found in patients with apparent access deficits, namely inconsistency across items across time, deterioration in performance with repeated testing, and large effects of the response–stimulus interval. Nevertheless, he also showed good access to superordinate knowledge about the categories with which he was impaired (Experiments 4 and 11), which is thought characteristic of a degraded store deficit.

In addition, on a theoretical level, we have proposed that the most parsimonious account of JM's deficit is that a semantic network accessed by both printed words and pictures becomes refractory after being accessed by a stimulus. Once in a refractory state, fine-grained semantic distinctions can no longer be made. Also, this refractory state spreads within the semantic network, affecting previously unprobed stimuli from the same category (Experiment 12). An alternative view is that there are correlated category-specific breakdowns in the semantic access procedures for pictures and words (McNeil et al., 1994). The proposal that deleterious effects of repeated presentation and short response–stimulus intervals necessarily reflect problems in semantic access may presuppose a particular theoretical position in which semantic representations are viewed as library or black box entries, which either contain or do not contain the requisite information about a stimulus. If the semantic representation is intact, then it should always be accessed unless there is some impairment for the access process. Within other frameworks, semantic representations may take the form of neuronal units entering a particular firing state, which may be affected by (among other things) levels of activation thresholds. Within such frameworks, it is quite plausible that refractory states could be brought about by, for example, abnormal threshold settings within the neuronal units themselves. We suggest that the notion that there are refractory semantic states provides a simpler and more parsimonious account of JM's performance than the proposal that there are problems within access procedures along with intact semantic representations. It further follows that evidence for inconsistent patterns of performance and deleterious effects of repeated testing and short response–stimulus intervals should not be taken as evidence for distinguishing access and storage deficits in neuropsychological cases.

REFERENCES

Battig, W.R., & Montague, W.E. (1969). Category norms for verbal items in 56 categories: A replication and extension of the Connecticut category norms. *Journal of Experimental Psychology, 80*, 1–45.

Beauvois, M-F. (1982). Optic aphasia: A process of interaction between vision and language. *Philosophical Transactions of the Royal Society, London, B298*, 35–47.

Bredart, S. (1993). Retrieval failures in face naming. *Memory, 1*, 351–366.

Brennen, T., Baguley, T., Bright, J., & Bruce, V. (1990). Resolving semantically induced tip-of-the-tongue states for proper nouns. *Memory & Cognition, 18*, 339–347.

Burke, D.M., Mackay, D.G., Worthley, J.S., & Wade, E. (1991). On the tip-of-the-tongue: What causes word finding failures in young and older adults. *Journal of Memory & Language, 30*, 542–579.

Burton, A.M., & Bruce, V. (1993). Naming faces and naming names: Exploring an interactive activation model of person recognition. *Memory, 1*, 457–480.

Caramazza, A., Hillis, A.E., Rapp, B.C., & Romani, C. (1990). The multiple semantics hypothesis: Multiple confusions? *Cognitive Neuropsychology, 7*, 161–189.

Chertkow, H., & Bub, D. (1990). Semantic memory loss in dementia of Alzheimer's type. *Brain, 113*, 397–417.

Cipolotti, L., McNeil, J.E., & Warrington, E.K. (1993). Spared written naming of proper nouns: A case report. *Memory, 1*, 289–311.

Cohen, G. (1990). Why is it difficult to put names to faces? *British Journal of Psychology, 81*, 287–297.

Coltheart, M., Curtis, B., Atkins, P., & Haller, M. (1993). Models of reading aloud: Dual route and parallel distributed processing approaches. *Psychological Review, 100*, 569–608.

Coughlan, A.K., & Warrington, E.K. (1981). The impairment of verbal semantic memory: A single case study. *Journal of Neurology, Neurosurgery and Psychiatry, 44*, 1079–1083.

Forde, E., & Humphreys, G.W. (in preparation). Access dysphasia: A semantic locus.

Frege, G. (1892). Über Sinn und Bedeutung [On sense and meaning]. In G. Patzig (Ed.), *Funktion, Begriff, Bedeutung*, (pp. 40–65). Gottingen: Vanderhoek und Ruprecht.

Goodglass, H., Klein, B., Carey, P., & James, K.J. (1966). Specific semantic word categories in aphasia. *Cortex, 2*, 74–89.

Goodglass, H., & Wingfield, A. (1993). Selective preservation of a lexical category in aphasia: Dissociations in comprehension of body parts and geographical place names following focal brain lesion. *Memory, 1*, 313–328.

Hanley, J.R., & Cowell, E.S. (1988). The effects of different types of retrieval cues on the recall of names of famous faces. *Memory & Cognition, 16*, 545–565.

Hittmair-Delazar, H., Denes, G., Semenza, C., & Mantovan, M.C. (1994). Anomia for people's names. *Neuropsychologia, 32*, 465–476.

Howard, D., & Orchard-Lisle, V.M. (1984). On the origin of semantic errors in naming: Evidence from the case of a global aphasic. *Cognitive Neuropsychology, 1*, 163–190.

Humphreys, G.W., Riddoch, M.J., & Quinlan, P.T. (1988). Cascade processes in picture identification. *Cognitive Neuropsychology, 5*, 67–103.

Jackendoff, R. (1983). *Semantics and cognition*. Cambridge, MA: MIT Press.

Kaplan, E., & Goodglass, H. (1976). *Boston Naming Test*, Boston: Boston University Press.

Katz, J. (1972). *Semantic theory*, New York: Harper & Row.

Kay, J., Lesser, R., & Coltheart, M. (1992). *PALPA*. London: Lawrence Erlbaum Associates Ltd.

Kripke, S. (1980). *Naming and necessity*. Oxford: Basil Blackwell.

Kucera, H., & Francis, W.N. (1967). *Computational analysis of present-day American English*. Providence, Rhode Island: Brown University Press.

Levelt, W.J.M. (1989). *Speaking: From intention to action*. Cambridge, MA: MIT Press.

Lucchelli, F., & De Renzi, E. (1992). Proper name anomia. *Cortex, 28*, 221–230.

McCarthy, R., & Warrington, E.K. (1985). Category specificity in an agrammatic patient: The relative impairment of verb retrieval and comprehension. *Neuropsychologia, 23*, 709–727.

McCarthy, R., & Warrington, E.K. (1988). Evidence for modality-specific meaning systems in the brain. *Nature, 334*, 428–430.

McKenna, P., & Warrington, E.K. (1978). Category-specific naming preservation: A single case study. *Journal of Neurology, Neurosurgery and Psychiatry, 43*, 781–788.

McKenna, P., & Warrington, E.K. (1980). Testing for nominal dysphasia. *Journal of Neurology, Neurosurgery and Psychiatry, 43*, 781–788.

McNeil, J.E., Cipolotti, L., & Warrington, E.K. (1994). The accessibility of proper names. *Neuropsychologia, 32*, 193–208.

Miceli, G., Silveri, M.C., Villa, G., & Caramazza, A. (1984). On the basis for the agrammatic's difficulty in producing main verbs. *Cortex, 20*, 207–220.

Mill, J.S. (1843). *A system of logic* [10th edn. ed. 1879]. London: Longmans.

Morton, J., & Patterson, K.E. (1980). A new attempt at an interpretation, or an attempt at a new interpretation. In M. Coltheart, K.E. Patterson, & J.C. Marshall (Eds.), *Deep dyslexia.* London: Routledge & Kegan Paul.

Neumann, E., Cherau, J.F., Hood, K.L., & Steinnagel, S.L. (1993). Does inhibition spread in a manner analogous to spreading activation? *Memory, 1*, 81–106.

Newcombe, F., & Marshall, J.C. (1980a). Response monitoring and response blocking in deep dyslexia. In M. Coltheart, K.E., Patterson, & J.C. Marshall (Eds.), *Deep dyslexia,* London: Routledge & Kegan Paul.

Newcombe, F., & Marshall, J.C. (1980b). Transcoding and lexical stabilization in deep dyslexia. In M. Coltheart, K.E. Patterson, & J.C. Marshall (Eds.), *Deep dyslexia,* London: Routledge & Kegan Paul.

Obler, L.K., & Albert, M.L. (1979). *Action Naming Test.* Unpublished.

Rapp, B.A., & Caramazza, A. (1993). On the distinction between deficits of access and deficits on storage. *Cognitive Neuropsychology, 10*, 113–142.

Riddoch, M.J., & Humphreys, G.W. (1987a). Visual object processing in optic aphasia: A case of semantic access agnosia. *Cognitive Neuropsychology, 4*, 131–185.

Riddoch, M.J., & Humphreys, G.W. (1987b). A case of integrative agnosia. *Brain, 110*, 1431–1462.

Riddoch, M.J., & Humphreys, G.W. (1993). *BORB: The Birmingham Object Recognition Battery,* London: Lawrence Erlbaum Associates Ltd.

Riddoch, M.J., Humphreys, G.W., Coltheart, M., & Funnell, E. (1988). Semantic systems or semantic system? Neuropsychological evidence re-examined. *Cognitive Neuropsychology, 5*, 3–25.

Rumiati, R., Humphreys, G.W., Riddoch, M.J., & Bateman, A. (1994). Pure visual agnosia without prosopagnosia or alexia: Evidence for hierarchical theories of visual recognition. *Visual Cognition, 1*, 181–225.

Saffran, E., Schwartz, M.F., & Marin, O.S.M. (1976). Semantic mechanisms in paralexia. *Brain and Language, 3*, 255–265.

Sartori, G., Miozzo, M., & Job, R. (1993). Category-specific naming impairments? Yes. *Quarterly Journal of Experimental Psychology, 46A*, 489–504.

Seidenberg, M.S. (1992). Beyond orthographic depth in reading: Equitable division of labour. In R. Frost & L. Katz (Eds.), *Orthography, phonology, morphology and meaning.* Amsterdam: North Holland.

Seidenberg, M.S., & McClelland, J.L. (1989). A distributed, developmental model of word recognition and naming. *Psychological Review, 96*, 523–568.

Semenza, C., & Sgaramella, T.M. (1993). Production of proper names: A clinical case study of the effects of phonemic cueing. *Memory, 1*, 265–280.

Semenza, C., & Zettin, M. (1988). Generating proper names: A case of selective inability. *Cognitive Neuropsychology, 5*, 711–721.

Shallice, T. (1987). Impairments of semantic processing: Multiple dissociations. In R. Job, G. Sartori, & M. Coltheart (Eds.), *The cognitive neuropsychology of language*. London: Lawrence Erlbaum Associates Ltd.

Shallice, T. (1988). *From neuropsychology to mental structure*. Cambridge, Cambridge University press.

Shallice, T. (1993). Multiple semantics: Whose confusions: *Cognitive Neuropsychology, 10*, 251–262.

Sheridan, J., & Humphreys, G.W. (1993). A verbal–semantic category-specific recognition impairment. *Cognitive Neuropsychology, 10*, 143–184.

Silveri, M.C., & Gainotti, G. (1988). Interaction between vision and language in category specific semantic impairment. *Cognitive Neuropsychology, 5*, 677–709.

Smith, L., & Klein, R. (1990). Evidence for semantic satiation: Repeating a category slows subsequent semantic processing. *Journal of Experimental Psychology: Learning, Memory and Cognition, 16*, 852–861.

Snodgrass, J.G., & Vanderwart, K. (1980). A standardised set of 260 pictures: Norms for name agreement, image agreement, familiarity and visual complexity. *Journal of Experimental Psychology: Human Perception and Performance, 6*, 174–215.

Valentine, T. (1991). A unified account of the effects of distinctiveness, inversion and race in face recognition. *Quarterly Journal of Experimental Psychology, 43A*, 161–204.

Valentine, T., Bredart, S., Lawson, R., & Ward, G. (1991). What's in a name? Access to information from people's names. *European Journal of Cognitive Psychology, 3*, 147–176.

Valentine, T., Moore, V., Flude, B., Young, A.W., & Ellis, A.W. (1993). Repetition priming and proper name processing: Do common names and proper names prime each other? *Memory, 1*, 329–349.

Warrington, E.K. (1975). The selective impairment of semantic memory. *Quarterly Journal of Experimental Psychology, 27*, 635–657.

Warrington, E.K., & Clegg, F. (1993). Selective preservation of place names in an aphasic patient: A short report. *Memory, 1*, 281–288.

Warrington, E.K., & McCarthy, R. (1983). Category specific access dysphasia. *Brain, 106*, 859–878.

Warrington, E.K., & McCarthy, R. (1984). Category specific semantic impairments. *Brain, 107*, 829–854.

Warrington, E.K., & McCarthy, R. (1987). Categories of knowledge: Further fractionations and an attempted integration. *Brain, 110*, 1273–1296.

Warrington, E.K., & Shallice, T. (1979). Semantic access dyslexia. *Brain, 102*, 43–63.

Warrington, E.K., & Shallice, T. (1984). Category specific semantic impairments. *Brain, 107*, 829–853.

Wittengenstin, L. (1922). *Tracticus logico-philosophicus* [trans. C.K. Ogden]. London.

Yamadori, A., & Albert, M.L. (1973). Word category aphasia. *Cortex, 9*, 112–125.

Young, A.W., Hay, D.C., & Ellis, A.W. (1985). The faces that launched a thousand slips: Everyday difficulties and errors in recognising people. *British Journal of Psychology, 76*, 495–523.

Young, A.W., Mcweeny, K.H., Ellis, A.W. & Hay, D.C. (1986). Naming and categorizing faces and written names. *Quarterly Journal of Experimental Psychology, 38A*, 297–318.

APPENDIX 1: STIMULI FOR EXPERIMENT 6

Set 1

GRAPE BANANA ORANGE CHERRY PEAR APPLE

JACKET SKIRT SOCKS CAP BLOUSE SCARF

HORSE TIGER CAT COW DOG PIG

WOOL COTTON LINEN NYLON VELVET SILK

BLUE YELLOW PURPLE GREEN BROWN RED

MOUNTAIN RIVER CAVE LAKE VALLEY CLIFF

TABLE RUG CHAIR BED BENCH STOOL

ELBOW MOUTH FOOT NOSE EYE ARMS

CARROT ONION TOMATO LETTUCE PEAS TURNIP

NURSE TEACHER DENTIST DOCTOR ENGINEER BAKER

AEROPLANE VAN CAR TRAIN SHIP BUS

COTTAGE PALACE CABIN HOUSE TENT HOTEL

SNOW GALE WIND DROUGHT RAIN THUNDER

DAISY TULIP ROSE VIOLET CROCUS POPPY

SAUCER PAN SPOON BOWL DISH KNIFE

ENVELOPE BRUSH PEN COIN BOOK SCISSORS

GERMANY RUSSIA CANADA ENGLAND FRANCE ITALY

DUBLIN GLASGOW HULL CARDIFF BRISTOL LONDON

CHURCHILL HITLER NAPOLEON PICASSO DICKENS MOZART

ANNE SUSAN SALLY JANE ELIZABETH MARY

DAVID PETER RICHARD JOHN STEVEN TOM

JONES THOMPSON WILLIAMS BAXTER SMITH JACKSON

HISTORY GEOGRAPHY CHEMISTRY BIOLOGY MATHS PHYSICS

BOXING GOLF SWIMMING FOOTBALL SKIING TENNIS

CEILING DOOR WALL WINDOW ROOF FLOOR

HAPPY TIRED GREEDY AFRAID ANGRY SAD

DAY MINUTE MONTH SECOND YEAR HOUR

PIANO DRUM FLUTE TRUMPET GUITAR VIOLIN

Set 2

LEMON PEACH APRICOT RASPBERRY PLUM MELON

TIE HAT DRESS COAT GLOVE SHOE

RAT DONKEY BEAR CAMEL SHEEP GOAT

SATIN DENIM CANVAS CORDUROY RAYON TWEED

BLACK WHITE ORANGE GREY PINK BEIGE

HILL ISLAND OCEAN BEACH FOREST DESERT

LAMP CARPET SOFA DESK WARDROBE CURTAINS

EAR KNEE SHOULDERS CHIN FINGER LEG

POTATO SPINACH SPROUTS CUCUMBER LEEKS CABBAGE

LAWYER GROCER TYPIST SALESMAN CARPENTER PLUMBER

TAXI MOTORBIKE BOAT HELICOPTER TRUCK COACH

FLAT CARAVAN CASTLE BUNGALOW MANSION HUT

FLOOD FOG LIGHTNING SUNSHINE SHOWER STORM

DAFFODIL IRIS LILY ORCHID CARNATION GERANIUM

FORK WHISK JUG GLASS CUP PLATE

RUBBER ASHTRAY PAPERS CLOCK RULER PURSE

SCOTLAND AMERICA PERU AUSTRIA NORWAY IRELAND

LEEDS BIRMINGHAM EDINBURGH PARIS LYON LIVERPOOL

MONET REAGAN GANDHI SHAKESPEARE KENNEDY BACH

MOLLY KATE RUTH EMMA RACHEL JOANNE

CLIVE ALEX JAMES PAUL IAN BILL

FORDE MANSFIELD HUGHES CRAWFORD HUMPHREYS COOKE

PSYCHOLOGY ENGLISH ART MUSIC FRENCH GEOLOGY

RUGBY RUNNING CRICKET POLO SQUASH WRESTLING

CHIMNEY FIREPLACE STAIRS LOUNGE HALL KITCHEN

JEALOUS FRIGHTENED MERRY CALM EXCITED EXHAUSTED

WEEK FORTNIGHT DECADE MILLISECOND CENTURY WEEKEND

BANJO ORGAN VIOLA RECORDER TRIANGLE CYMBALS

MEMORY, 1995, 3 (3/4), 309–332

Towards a Unitary Account of Access Dysphasia: A Single Case Study

Lisa Cipolotti and Elizabeth K. Warrington

National Hospital for Neurology and Neurosurgery, London, UK

We report the case of a patient, H.E.C., with a profound verbal comprehension impairment. His comprehension impairment involved both common names (animal and inanimate items) and proper names. Within the proper name category, his comprehension of country and famous peoples' names was better than his comprehension of common forenames. By using matching to sample techniques, H.E.C.'s impairment was found to be affected by presentation rate and by semantic relatedness, but not by word frequency. An analysis of his responses showed marked inconsistency and serial position effects (i.e. a decrement of performance on subsequent presentations of the same items). H.E.C.'s comprehension deficit was interpreted in terms of an ''access'' impairment within the word-meaning system. A unitary account of this impairment in terms of a deficit that delays the return, following activation, of the set of representations underlying a word, to a ''ready state'' is proposed.

INTRODUCTION

In the last 15 years an increasing number of studies describing specific breakdowns of categories of semantic memory have been reported. These studies addressed the issues of the organisation of representations within semantic memory. In addition impairments in accessing semantic representations have been differentiated from those in which there has been loss (or degradation) of the stored representations (Warrington, 1975; Warrington & McCarthy, 1983, 1987; Warrington & Shallice, 1979). Impairments in accessing semantic information would result in its temporary unavailability. Impairments in the stored information would result in its permanent inaccessibility. Warrington and colleagues have proposed a specific set of empirical criteria to distinguish between deficits of ''access'' and deficits of ''storage''. These are: consistency, frequency, rate of presentation, priming or cueing and depth of

Requests for reprints should be sent to Lisa Cipolotti, National Hospital for Neurology and Neurosurgery, Queen Square, London WC1N 3BG, UK.

We wish to thank Dr. A. Thompson for his permission to investigate H.E.C., a patient under his care, and to report our findings. We also wish to thank Dr. D.W. Langdon for her assistance and Dr. A. McClelland for advice on statistics.

processing. These criteria are open to criticism and indeed their validity has recently been questioned (see Rapp & Caramazza, 1993).

We do not intend to argue whether or not the proposed distinction between impairments of "access" or "storage" is empirically and theoretically valid (however, see Warrington & Cipolotti, submitted, for a discussion of this point). We rather wish to discuss and attempt a unitary account of the remarkable empirical similarities observed in the three dysphasic patients (V.E.R., Y.O.T., and M.E.D.) who all presented the core features of an "access" dysphasic disorder (McNeil, Cipolotti, & Warrington, 1994; Warrington & McCarthy, 1983, 1987). All three patients had a severe global aphasia. They all presented with: (1) a significant rate of presentation effect, (2) inconsistencies in their responses to individual items, and (3) a semantic relatedness effect.

Furthermore, remarkably similar selective impairments and selective preservation of specific categories of semantic knowledge were found. Specifically, the comprehension of inanimate items for all three patients was, in general, significantly more impaired than for animate items. This contrasted with the more frequently reported pattern of impairment—degraded knowledge of animate items with preserved knowledge of inanimate items, often reported in patients with semantic memory impairments (e.g. Laiacona, Barbarotto, & Capitani, 1993; Sartori & Job, 1988; Silveri & Gainotti, 1988; Warrington & Shallice, 1984). In addition, superior performance with proper names when compared with common names has been observed in two of our three access dysphasic cases in whom this particular category was assessed (Y.O.T. and M.E.D.). Remarkably, within their proper name vocabulary there was a significant dissociation between their good comprehension of country and famous people's names, and impaired comprehension of common forenames. The general pattern of impairment in these three patients was so similar that McNeil et al. (1994) raised the possibility that there might be a coherent syndrome common to dysphasic patients showing the hallmarks of an "access" syndrome.

We have recently had the opportunity to study a patient (H.E.C.) with a severe global dysphasia whose performance showed the characteristics of an "access" deficit. Our aim was twofold: first to explore whether there is an invariant pattern of preserved and impaired categories in a patient with an access dysphasic syndrome, and second to explore the properties of an access deficit in more detail.

CASE REPORT

H.E.C. is a 52-year-old, right-handed man who had been an accountant. In January 1993, he was admitted to a district general hospital following the sudden onset of an occipital migraine and language difficulties. Over the next 48 hours he presented an increased speech loss resulting in a global aphasia and a dense right hemiplegia. A CT scan showed a low-density left-hemisphere lesion compatible with an extensive cerebral infarction. Doppler ultrasound of the carotid showed a 40–60% stenosis of the right internal carotid and 60–80% stenosis of the left internal carotid. The patient was admitted to the Neuro-Rehabilitation Unit of the National Hospital in February 1993 to receive intensive physiotherapy and, in addition, speech therapy.

Neuropsychological Assessment

H.E.C. was referred on the 12th of February 1993 to the Psychology Department for an assessment of his dysphasia and other cognitive deficits. He was unable to attempt any of the verbal or performance subtests of the WAIS-R. On the Raven Coloured Progressive Matrices, he scored below the normal range (22/36). On the visual version of the Recognition Memory Test (Warrington, 1984) he obtained an average score (Faces 46/50). On the Object decision test of perception and on the Dot centre test of visuo-perception (from the VOSP, Warrington & James, 1991), his performance was satisfactory (19/20 and 19/20, respectively).

Language Functions

His spontaneous speech was mainly restricted to a few simple stereotyped sentences. He was unable to repeat any single phonemes, words or number names. He was unable to name any item from the Oldfield naming test or from the graded naming test (GNT, McKenna & Warrington, 1980). He was also unable to name any proper nouns from the GNT. On the Peabody Picture Vocabulary test (Form B), in which he was required to match a spoken word to a picture, he scored 36 correct on the first 50 items, and by submitting the patient to all the 150 items, his score was 90/150 (the strict scoring criterion was not applied). His literacy skills were also severely compromised. He was unable to read aloud or write single digits, letters, and simple high-frequency words.

EXPERIMENTAL INVESTIGATION

General Procedures

In the following experiments, H.E.C.'s residual comprehension skills were investigated using matching to sample techniques. He was required to match either a spoken word or a picture to an item (written word or picture) in an array displayed on a desk. The arrays comprised four, five, or six items and each stimulus was probed three or four times in a pseudorandom order, without changing the array. Thus, he was assessed in blocks consisting of a total of 12 or 18 trials for the four- and six-item arrays probed three times, and in 20 trials for the five items arrays probed four times. The response–stimulus intervals (RSIs, i.e. the time between H.E.C.'s response and the presentation of the next stimulus in any block of trials) were timed. Unless otherwise stated the RSIs were two seconds. The patient was not given knowledge of results.

Experiment 1: Spoken Word–Picture Matching Task; Foods, Animals and Objects

Our aim in this experiment was to establish first whether H.E.C.'s comprehension of the categories, objects, animals, and foods were differentially impaired, and second whether he was sensitive to the duration of the RSI, as were the previous three access dysphasics.

Procedure.   The stimuli in this spoken word to picture matching task consisted of coloured pictures of 15 very common objects, 15 animals, and 15 foods (for details see Warrington & Shallice, 1984). The pictures were arranged in arrays of five items and each item was probed four times. The three categories were tested in a latin square design on two separate occasions. First using a standard RSI of two seconds, and second using a slower RSI of five seconds.

Results.   The number and percentage score for each category for each RSI is given in Table 1. The overall effect of category was not significant at the fast rate ($\chi^2 d.f.$ 2 = 1.95, n.s.), however it was significant at the slower rate, with the category of foods being the most impaired (χ^2 $d.f.$ 2 = 9.43, $P < 0.01$; in this and in the following experiments we made the assumption of independence of each response to each stimulus). The overall effect of presentation rate was significant (McNemar's Test $d.f.$ 1 = 8.11, $P < 0.01$).

Error Analysis.   The results obtained in this experiment using an RSI of two seconds have been analysed in terms of the *serial position effect* and in terms of *consistency*. Previous studies on access dysphasic patients suggested that they tended to respond correctly on the first administration of a particular item, but on

TABLE 1
Experiment 1

	Food	Animals	Objects	Total
2 sec. RSI	36/60	43/60	41/60	120/180
%	60	72	68	67
5 sec. RSI	41/60	50/60	54/60	145/180
%	68	83	90	80

Number and percentage of correct responses on the spoken word–picture matching task: foods, animals, and objects. Effect of presentation rate.

subsequent trials they would make an error (e.g. McNeil et al., 1994; Warrington & McCarthy, 1983, 1987). This was formally assessed in our patient by analysing his responses to the first and second probe on the same items. There were 19 instances of his responses being correct on the first probe and incorrect on the second probe; there were only six instances of the converse pattern (incorrect on the first probe and correct on the second probe). This is a significant difference (McNemar's test $d.f.$ $1 = 5.76$, $P < 0.02$).

His response consistency was computed (assuming independency over trials) using the binomial expansion to generate the expected distribution for chance variation in response consistency using p = proportion correct = 0.67 and q = 1–p. The expected and observed distributions of responses with no errors, 1 error, 2 errors, and 3 errors are given in Table 2. It was found that the distribution of H.E.C.'s correct responses did not significantly differ from that expected by the binomial expansion (χ^2 $d.f$ $3 = 2.48$, $P < 0.5$).

Comment. On this very easy spoken word to picture matching task (normal subjects perform at ceiling) our patient's performance was clearly impaired and this impairment, like the previously reported patients, was subject to a rate effect. However, in contrast with the earlier access dysphasic patients who have been tested with the same stimuli, no clear evidence of an animate/inanimate category effect was present at either speed. The only suggestion of a category effect was H.E.C.'s slightly inferior comprehension of foods at the slow rate. In addition, as was observed in the previously reported cases, the patient's incorrect responses were characterised by a serial position effect and by inconsistency.

Experiment 2: Picture–Picture Matching Task; Animals and Objects

In the first experiment it was demonstrated that H.E.C.'s performance in a word–picture matching task was impaired. This deficit could arise either through a failure to comprehend the spoken words, or to identify the pictures, or both. In this experiment our aim was to establish whether in a purely visual task his performance would also be impaired.

TABLE 2
Experiment 1

	No Errors ✓✓✓✓	1 Error ✓✓✓✗	2 Errors ✓✓✗✗	3 Errors ✓✗✗✗	4 Errors ✗✗✗✗
Expected	8.9	17.8	13.3	4.4	0.6
Observed	7	18	17	3	0

Consistency analysis: Expected and observed distribution of each combination of correct and incorrect responses.

Procedure. The stimuli consisted of 25 pairs of pictures of objects and 25 pairs of pictures of animals. For each object and each animal there were two visually different representations. The object pictures were coloured; the animal pictures were black and white line drawings. The pictures were arranged such that each five-item array consisted of stimuli that were semantically related. Each item was probed three times. The two categories were tested on two different days. The patient was asked to match one picture stimulus with its pair.

Results. H.E.C's performance on this picture–picture matching task was fairly intact; his percentage correct responses for the object category was 96% and for the animal category was 95%.

Comment. This result of intact visual–visual matching performance indicates that the identification of visual objects required for these experiments is adequate. It has been previously established that the semantic relatedness of the arrays is a significant parameter in determining the level of performance in a matching to sample task (McNeil et al., 1994; Warrington & McCarthy, 1987). For this experiment, by selecting arrays that were semantically close, we would claim that this was a fairly stringent test of the integrity of our patient's visual domain, in so far as the demands of visual–visual matching tasks include processing up to the level of meaning (e.g. De Renzi, Scotti, & Spinnler, 1969; Warrington & McCarthy, 1994; Warrington & Taylor, 1978). Indeed, we have observed patients with a category-specific visual semantic memory deficit failing this task (Warrington & Cipolotti, submitted). We would therefore infer that his impairment in the word–picture matching test arose entirely within the verbal domain.

Experiment 3: Spoken Word–Picture Matching Task; Rate Effect

In the first experiment, comparing a two-second with a five-second presentation rate we found a significant effect of rate. Our aim in this experiment was to manipulate more adequately the effect of rate by using both a shorter and a longer interstimulus interval in a word–picture matching task.

Procedure. The stimuli in this spoken word–picture matching task consisted of eight coloured pictures of animals and eight coloured pictures of objects. The pictures were arranged in arrays of four items and each item was probed three times. Two RSIs were used for each array, a fast one-second rate and a slower rate of 15 seconds, using an ABBA design.

Results. The number and percentage correct score for each category for each RSI is given in Table 3. The overall effect of presentation rate was highly

TABLE 3
Experiment 3

	RSI = 1 sec	*RSI = 15 secs*
Animal	38/48	45/48
%	79	94
Object	34/48	43/48
%	71	89
Total	72/96	88/96
%	75	92

Number of correct responses on the spoken word–picture matching task: animals and objects. Effect of presentation rate.

significant for both types of array (McNemar's test $d.f.$ 1 = 8.6, $P < 0.01$). The small difference in scores between animate and inanimate items was not significant at either the fast or the slow rate of presentation (χ^2 $d.f.$ 1 = 0.88 n.s. and χ^2 $d.f.$ 1 = 0.54 n.s. respectively).

Comment.   By contrasting a fast rate with a much slower rate we have corroborated the result of Experiment 1. Indeed with our 15-second RSI H.E.C.'s performance was nearly at ceiling. It is clear that it was possible to optimalise his spoken-word comprehension.

Experiment 4: Spoken Word–Picture and Spoken Word–Written Word Matching Task: Objects. Effect of Semantic Relatedness

The category of inanimate objects is very broad indeed. Within this broad category there are what we shall term subcategories in which items to some extent share common usage (e.g. clothes, tools, vehicles, etc). Semantic relatedness effects have been described in previously reported cases of "access dysphasia" within the broad inanimate-object category. Thus, there is a decrement in performance with semantically "close" arrays as compared with semantically "distant" arrays. Our aim in this experiment was to investigate the semantic relatedness effect for both spoken and written words.

Procedure.   The stimuli consisted of 36 black and white line pictures of common objects, which included six from each of the following subcategories: office stationery, clothes, household, kitchen utensils, furniture, and vehicles (for details see Warrington & McCarthy, 1987; vehicles being substituted for body parts). The pictures were arranged in six-item arrays. There were a total of 12 arrays: six *close* arrays in which all six items of the array were semantically close (e.g. trousers, shirt, dress, skirt, jumper, and coat), and six *distant* arrays consisting of one item from each of the six subcategories (e.g. trousers, sofa, pencil, kettle, key, and car). Each item was probed three times. There were two conditions assessed on two different days: (1) spoken word to picture matching; (2) spoken word to written word matching. In this condition written words were substituted for the pictures.

Results. The number and percentage correct score for the close and distant arrays for each condition are given in Table 4. The effect of semantic relatedness is significant in both the spoken word–picture and the spoken word-written word matching condition (χ^2 *d.f.* 1 = 21.69, $P < 0.001$, and χ^2 *d.f.* 1 = 9.94, $P < 0.001$ respectively). In addition, H.E.C.'s performance on the spoken word–picture matching task was significantly superior to his performance on the spoken word–written word matching task (binomial expansion $z = 4.57$, $P < 0.0001$). However, even for the most impaired condition his performance was well above chance.

Comment. The effect of semantic relatedness appears to be very clear-cut for both conditions. Qualitatively our patient's performance was very similar to previous descriptions of patients with access dysphasia (e.g. patients Y.O.T. and M.E.D).

Experiment 5: Spoken Word–Picture Matching Task: Foods, Animals, and Objects. Effect of Semantic Relatedness and Frequency

It is well established that word frequency is an important variable in word comprehension tasks in aphasic patients (Poeck, Hartje, & Kerschensteiner, 1973; Poeck & Stachowiack, 1975; Schuell, Jenkins, & Landis, 1961). The frequency variable was considered in one previous investigation of access dysphasia (patient M.E.D). Somewhat unexpectedly there was no good evidence that low-frequency items were more difficult to comprehend than high-frequency items. Our aim in this experiment was to explore the effect of both

TABLE 4
Experiment 4

	Close	Distant	Total
Word–picture	65/108	95/108	160/216
%	60	88	74
Word–word	49/108	72/108	121/216
%	45	67	56

Number and percentage of correct responses on spoken word–picture and spoken word–written word matching tasks: objects. Effect of semantic relatedness.

semantic relatedness and frequency in the context of the major animate/inanimate distinction.

Procedure. The patient was asked to match a spoken name to the corresponding picture. The stimuli consisted of coloured pictures of 16 objects, 16 animals, and 16 foods. There was a total of 12 four-item arrays: six *close* arrays in which all four items of the array were semantically close, and six *distant* arrays consisting of items sharing the same superordinate but less semantically associated. The whole experiment was replicated a second time in the same testing session.

Independent semantic-relatedness ratings were obtained from 18 subjects (all professional graduates). The subjects were required to rate each array according to how conceptually similar they perceived the items to be to one another (i.e. their semantic relatedness) on a 5-point scale where 1 corresponded to "very distant", 2 corresponded to "distant", 3 corresponded to "fairly close", 4 corresponded to "close" and 5 corresponded to "very close". The mean semantic-relatedness ratings for each array and their standard deviations are given in Appendix 1. The overall mean semantic-relatedness ratings for all the close and all the distant arrays and their standard deviations were 4.4 (S.D. = 0.68) and 2.4 (S.D. = 0.8) respectively.

Half of the close and half of the distant arrays comprised *high-frequency* names (e.g. close: pear, banana, orange, apple; distant: hat, teapot, glasses, key). Half of the close (e.g. octopus, lobster, starfish, crab) and half of the distant (e.g. koala, shrimp, bison, walrus) arrays comprised *low-frequency* names. The frequency count of each word using the Carroll, Davies and Richman (1971) norms is given in Appendix 1. These norms are based on *written* word-frequency counts and therefore do not necessarily correspond to their *spoken* word frequency. For example, *teapot*, an obvious high-frequency word in English spoken language has a low written-frequency count. In addition, the word-frequency counts are contaminated by the polysemous meanings of some words. For example, *dates*, referring to the fruit, a relatively infrequent word in spoken language, has a high written-frequency count. This resulted in some of the words used in this experiment (and in the next one) having somewhat anomalous frequency ratings. Consequently, some words with a low-frequency count were included in a high-frequency array and some words with a high-frequency count were included in a low-frequency array. We therefore obtained subjective *spoken* word frequency ratings from 17 subjects (all professional graduates). The subjects were required to rate each word according to their subjective estimate of the frequency of their usage in their spoken language on a 7-point scale where 1 corresponded to "unknown", 2 to "very infrequent", up to 7 which corresponded to "very frequent". The mean subjective-frequency ratings of each word and their standard divisions are given in Appendix 1. The overall mean subjective-frequency ratings for all the high- and all the low-frequent items and their standard deviations were 5.69 (S.D. = 1.31) and 3.75 (S.D. = 1.38) respectively.

Thus, each of the four possible combinations of frequency and semantic relatedness (close high-frequency, close low-frequency, distant high-frequency and distant low-frequency) for each category was tested. For all of the high and low, close and distant arrays the overall Carroll et al. (1971) mean frequency norms and our obtained subjective frequencies and semantic relatedness ratings are reported in Appendix 3. A series of frequency and semantic-relatedness contrasts were computed using the Mann-Whitney U test. The values of U and Z and their significance levels are given in Appendix 4. All the frequency and semantic-relatedness contrasts were highly significant. There was no suggestion of any interaction between frequency and semantic relatedness (see Appendix 4).

Results. The number and percentage correct score for each category, for each frequency level, and for each semantic-relatedness level is given in Table 5. H.E.C.'s overall performance on objects, animals, and foods summing across close and distant arrays and high- and low-frequency arrays was at a very similar level (χ^2 *d.f.* 2 = 1.533, n.s.). Similarly, again summing across categories and close and distant arrays there was no significant difference in his performance on the high- and low-frequency words (χ^2 *d.f.* 1 = 0.07, n.s.). By contrast his performance on the semantically distant arrays was significantly better than his performance on the semantically close arrays (χ^2 *d.f.* 1 = 6.36, $P < 0.01$).

Comment. First, this experiment replicates the absence of a category effect along the animate/inanimate dimension that was reported in Experiment 1. Second, using arrays for which we have obtained an independent index of

TABLE 5
Experiment 5

	Objects		*Animals*		*Foods*	
	High	Low	High	Low	High	Low
Close	15/24	16/24	17/24	21/24	17/24	16/24
%	62	67	71	87	71	67
Distant	19/24	23/24	23/24	17/24	19/24	19/24
%	79	96	96	71	79	79

	High	*Low*	*Close*	*Distant*	*Objects*	*Animals*	*Foods*
Total	110/144	112/144	102/144	120/144	73/96	78/96	71/96
%	76	78	71	83	76	81	74

Effect of category, word frequency, and semantic relatedness on the spoken word–picture matching task: food, animals and objects. Number and percentage of correct responses.

semantic relatedness, we have found a clear effect of semantic distance. This replicates the semantic-relatedness effect observed in Experiment 4. Third, we have failed to find a frequency effect. There is no suggestion from this finding that low-frequency stimuli are more vulnerable as is commonly the case in patients with brain damage. Therefore we can be confident that the semantic-relatedness effect is not confounded by interaction with frequency.

Experiment 6: Spoken Word–Picture Matching Task; Foods and Animals: Effect of Semantic Relatedness and Frequency.

In our Experiment 5 we obtained a result not directly predicted from previous investigations of patients with dysphasia. Although in many types of language disorders, frequency is a powerful determinant of performance, this appeared not to be so in our patient. Our aim in this experiment was to obtain further evidence to support this essentially negative effect of frequency in the context of semantic relatedness.

Procedure. The patient was asked to match a spoken name to the corresponding picture. The stimuli were 16 coloured pictures of 16 animals and 16 foods. The pictures were arranged in eight four-item arrays: four *close* arrays in which all the items of the array were semantically close, and four *distant* arrays where the items were less semantically associated although they shared the same superordinate. The whole experiment was replicated a second time in the same testing session.

In order to obtain independent semantic-relatedness ratings an identical procedure, as in Experiment 5, was adopted. The mean semantic-relatedness ratings for each array and their standard deviations are given in Appendix 2. The overall mean semantic-relatedness ratings for the close and the distant arrays and their standard deviations were 4.25 (S.D. = 0.76) and 2.48 (S.D. = 0.82) respectively.

As in the previous experiment, half of the close and half of the distant arrays comprised *high-frequency* names while half of the close and half of the distant arrays comprised *low-frequency* names. As in Experiment 5, each of the four possible combinations were used for each category (close high, close low, distant high, and distant low). The frequency count of each word using the Carroll et al. (1971) norms and the subjective-frequency ratings obtained using the same procedure adopted in Experiment 5, are given in Appendix 2. The mean overall subjective-frequency ratings for all of the high-and all of the low-frequency items and their standard deviations were 5.64 (S.D. = 1.28) and 3.66 (S.D. = 1.34) respectively. For all of the high and low, close and distant arrays the overall Carroll et al. (1971) mean frequency norms and our obtained subjective frequencies and semantic-relatedness ratings are reported in

Appendix 3. As in Experiment 5 a series of frequency and semantic-relatedness contrasts were computed using the Mann-Whitney U test. The values of U and z and their significance levels are given in Appendix 4. As in the case of Experiment 5, all the frequency and semantic-relatedness contrasts were highly significant (see Appendix 4).

Results.   The number and percentage correct scores for each category for each condition are given in Table 6. There was a significant effect of semantic relatedness (χ^2 *d.f.* 1 = 10.63, $P < 0.001$) and a non-significant effect of category and frequency (χ^2 *d.f.* 1 = 1.18, n.s., and χ^2 *d.f.* 1 = 2.1, n.s. respectively).

Comment.   This experiment replicates the findings of Experiment 5. The effects of frequency and category are negligible, whereas the effect of semantic relatedness is again significant. The absence of any effect of frequency and category along the animate/inanimate distinction cannot be attributed to a trivial consequence of inappropriate task sensitivity, as the manipulation of semantic relatedness using the same stimuli gives a highly significant effect.

Experiment 7: Spoken Word–Written Word Matching Task: Proper Names

In two previously studied access dysphasics (patients Y.O.T. and M.E.D.) the comprehension of country and famous people's names was relatively well preserved as compared with inanimate items and common forenames. Our aim in this experiment was to assess whether H.E.C.'s comprehension of proper names was a preserved category.

TABLE 6
Experiment 6

	Foods		Animals	
	High	*Low*	*High*	*Low*
Close	17/24	15/24	19/24	17/24
%	71	62	79	71
Distant	22/24	20/24	23/24	21/24
%	92	83	96	87

	High	*Low*	*Close*	*Distant*	*Animals*	*Foods*
Total	81/96	73/96	68/96	86/96	80/96	74/96
%	84	76	71	89	83	77

Effect of category, word frequency, and semantic relatedness on the spoken word–picture matching task: foods and animals. Number and percentage of correct responses.

Procedure. The test stimuli were selected from four categories of proper names: countries, cities, names of famous people (e.g. Stalin), and common forenames (e.g. Tom, see Appendix 4). There were four five-item arrays for each category. The four categories were tested in a latin square design. Each item was presented four times using a spoken name to written name matching procedure. No attempt was made to control semantic relatedness, frequency, or familiarity.

Results. The number and percentage correct scores for each category is given in Table 7. First it is clear that our patient's performance was not at ceiling on any of the proper nouns categories, and certainly not superior to his performance with common nouns. Although his comprehension of city and country names is at an almost equivalent level (χ^2 *d.f.* 1 = 1.08, n.s.), his comprehension of famous people's names is significantly worse than countries although not cities (χ^2 *d.f.* 1 = 5.54, $P < 0.02$, and χ^2 *d.f.* 1 = 1.77, n.s., respectively). His comprehension of common forenames was significantly worse than his comprehension of famous people's names (χ^2 *d.f.* 1 = 6.56, $P < 0.01$).

Comment. H.E.C's overall comprehension of proper names does not mirror exactly the pattern of performance observed in two previous access dysphasic patients (Y.O.T. and M.E.D.); although in one respect his performance is similar. He shows the same dissociation between famous proper names and common forenames. However, his performance with the famous proper names could not be interpreted as a preserved category and indeed his performance was not so dissimilar from the level of performance observed with objects tested at speed. We note also that there was evidence of superior comprehension of country names as compared with famous people's names, but these too could not be regarded as an intact category.

TABLE 7
Experiment 7

Countries	47/60
%	78
Cities	42/60
%	70
Famous people	35/60
%	58
Common forenames	21/60
%	35
Total	145/240
%	60

Number and percentage of correct responses on the spoken word–written word matching task: proper nouns.

DISCUSSION

In this study we investigated the residual comprehension skills of a patient with a severe global aphasia. On a series of word–picture matching tasks his performance was gravely impaired. However, his visual perceptual processing was intact and on the visual–visual matching task his performance was at ceiling. This observed dissociation would suggest that our patient's deficit lay within the verbal domain.

Our patient's verbal comprehension impairment was characterised both by a marked semantic-relatedness effect and a minor category effect. Semantically distant item arrays were comprehended far better than semantically close item arrays. Clearly this contrast would be inexplicable in terms of a phonological input deficit. Indeed, there is no suggestion whatever that semantically close arrays are also phonologically confusable. Famous proper names were understood better than common forenames. Again, this effect is unlikely to arise as a result of poor phonological processing. These two effects imply that the locus of H.E.C.'s impairment is within the semantic component of the word-processing system. If the locus of his impairment was in processing phonological input, or was due to added noise to, or loss of capacity of, the transmission route feeding the semantic system, these two effects would be inexplicable unless, of course, the unmotivated assumption is made that semantic information is available at presemantic levels of information processing.

H.E.C.'s performance was sensitive to the rate of presentation; decreasing the rate of presentation significantly improved his performance. Indeed, it is possible that if the rate of presentation had been decreased sufficiently it might have been possible to find an almost intact vocabulary in this patient. In addition, his performance in verbal comprehension tasks was characterised by a highly inconsistent pattern of responding; given multiple presentations of the same stimuli, he did not consistently fail the same items. More crucially his inconsistent pattern of responses from trial to trial demonstrated a striking serial position effect. An analysis of his first and second responses in matching spoken words to pictures showed that the probability of his responding correctly on the first trial and incorrectly on the second trial was significantly higher than the converse, namely responding incorrectly on the first trial and correctly on the second trial. Finally, H.E.C.'s verbal comprehension was not affected by overall written word frequency as applied to individual arrays (Carroll et al., 1971 norms). Additional evidence is provided by our subjective spoken word frequency ratings in which we were able to establish virtually no overlap in the individual items between designated high- and low-frequency arrays. This is in contrast to those results in the literature showing that patients with auditory comprehension difficulties understand high-frequency words better than low-frequency words (e.g. Poeck et al., 1973; Poeck & Stachowiack, 1975; Schuell et al., 1961; however, see,

Franklin, Howard, & Patterson, 1994, for a lack of frequency effect in a patient with a word comprehension impairment). These three effects, the rate of presentation, the inconsistency in responding demonstrating a serial position effect, and the lack of a frequency effect, meet the criteria of an "access" disorder (Shallice, 1988; Warrington & McCarthy, 1983, 1987).

In the following discussion these three effects found in H.E.C.'s pattern of comprehension performance will be interpreted as reflecting an "access" impairment, a temporary unavailability of the stored representations. However, Rapp and Caramazza (1993) have recently criticised such an interpretation, proposing that a storage disorder (i.e. a degradation of the stored representations) could also account for each of these effects. Although each of their individual arguments has brought to light a potential weakness of the original account, nonetheless the authors have failed to challenge those formulations that attempt to integrate the various features that characterise "access" and "storage" disorders. In fact, they have not provided a unitary account of the entire empirical pattern either as a form of storage deficit or as a function of some other class of deficit. In contrast, we will attempt to articulate a provisional, unitary account of our patient's comprehension impairment in terms of an "access" disorder.

Access disorders within the word-meaning system could reflect different types of impairments. However, not all access disorders would result in the pattern of response effects observed in H.E.C. For example, could H.E.C.'s comprehension impairment be due to random added noise resulting in a generalised reduction in the activation levels of the underlying set of semantic properties of a word? (from now on the "activation" hypothesis). Within this account, the rate of presentation effect would be seen an index of the altered level at which the system can achieve activation. However, the lack of a frequency effect, the serial position effect, and the semantic relatedness effect are less easily explicable in terms of the "activation" hypothesis. Considering first the frequency effect. According to many models of language processing, high-frequency words are assumed to have either lower thresholds or higher resting levels of activation than low-frequency words (e.g. Dell, 1986, 1989; Harley & MacAndrew, 1992; Morton, 1970). The accessibility of high-frequency words would thus be expected to be less affected than that of low-frequency words if there had been an overall reduction of the activation levels (see also Rapp & Caramazza, 1993 for a similar argument). However, H.E.C. did not show a frequency effect. Second, a reduction of the activation of the system could result in an inconsistent pattern of responding; according to the achieved activation levels of the representations, sometimes the correct response would reach threshold and sometimes not. However, the serial position effect would not be predicted. Indeed, it seems likely that this account would predict that previous activation of a word might actually facilitate it following reactivation. Third, this account would seem to predict that words semantically close to previous targets should also be advantaged. If semantically close words share a set of properties, or a semantic space, then previous semantically similar targets should, if anything, increase the probability of the representations reaching threshold. We wish to stress here that we do not have any specific commitment with regard to those properties that might underpin semantic similarity or the defining features of a semantic space. On the basis of these considerations we would therefore reject the "activation" hypothesis of the access dysphasic impairment in our patient H.E.C.

We would suggest that the concept of "refractoriness" provides a better basis for a preliminary unitary account of the access disorder we have observed in H.E.C. By this we mean that the nature of H.E.C.'s access impairment might involve damage that delays the return, following activation, to a "ready state" of a set of representations underpinning a word. This change is assumed to be temporary, and perhaps even sporadic, and will result in the reduction of the efficiency of the system for some time following activation. The implications of the "refractoriness" for the representation's "ready states" might be of, at least, two forms: the impairment to the semantic system might decrease the rate at which the activation levels of the representations return to a "ready state", or the impairment might delay the response recovery (i.e. decrease the probability that the representations can be reactivated following previous activation). In purely operational terms, the predictions of these two specifications are very similar; H.E.C.'s comprehension impairments can be accommodated by either account. Therefore, in the following discussion, we will use the term "refractoriness" without commitment to a more precise specification of the deficit in returning to a "ready state".

The "refractoriness" hypothesis (as with the "activation" hypothesis) clearly would predict a rate-of-presentation effect because at slower rates of presentation there would be a greater probability that the activation levels would have returned back to a "ready state". This would obviously improve the overall performance enhancing the likelihood of accessing the set of properties underlying a word. The rate-of-presentation effect would therefore provide an index of the rate at which the representations return to a "ready state".

The semantic-relatedness effect can be explained if one assumes that semantically similar words are represented in terms of shared underlying semantic properties or shared semantic space (again without any commitment to the basis of this similarity). Then, the deleterious effect of the activation of a particular set of representations would be expected to extend also to those that are semantically related. The presentation of semantically related words would maintain high levels of activation for all of the representations belonging to a particular semantic space and further delay the return to a "ready state". This would result in a decreased likelihood that semantically similar items would be correctly identified.

Two points could be adduced to incorporate the lack of a frequency effect into our unitary account of the access disorder. As there is no reason to believe that high- and low-frequency words differ in their rates of return to a "ready state", there would also be no reason to expect that high-frequency words would be less affected than low-frequency words by the rate of decay of activation impairment; hence the lack of a word-frequency effect in H.E.C.'s impairment. In addition, following the argument that low-frequency words are more likely to have "circumscribed crystalised" semantic representations, we would suggest that low-frequency words should be less exposed to the semantic relatedness effect than high-frequency words (Cipolotti, McNeil, & Warrington, 1993). The lack of a frequency effect could then be interpreted as reflecting an additional difficulty that high-frequency words encounter by having a higher number of share representations, thus cancelling out their normal gain.

Finally, the inconsistency of responding is explained as a consequence of the fact that the response elicited would be, at least in part, a consequence of the prior levels of "readiness" of the semantic representations for activation. Subsequent presentation of the same words would result in a further delay of the return of the representations to their "ready states", particularly after the first series of trials. This would decrease the probability that the correct item would be chosen. The serial position effect could be thought of as a refractory process reaching asymptote after a single activating event. Thus, H.E.C. would be more likely to make errors on subsequent presentation of the same items.

The access impairment described here in terms of "refractoriness" seems to present a good fit not only with the effects found in the comprehension pattern presented by H.E.C., but also with the effects present in the comprehension performance of the access dysphasic patients that have been previously described (McNeil et al., 1994; Warrington & McCarthy, 1983, 1987). However, there is an important caveat. We would not wish to claim that all access disorders would conform to the pattern of impairments observed in H.E.C. and in the other previously reported patients. For example, it would not seem appropriate to extend these speculations to access dyslexia (e.g. Warrington & Shallice, 1979).

One further aspect of H.E.C.'s verbal comprehension merits discussion; the differences in his performance as a function of category. Considering first the inanimate category: the previously reported access dysphasic patients (V.E.R., Y.O.T., and M.E.D.) were similar in that they were both significantly poorer in comprehending inanimate names as opposed to animate ones. The question arises whether this pattern is artefactual or whether it is a meaningful category effect. Parameters such as frequency, familiarity, visual complexity, or visual similarity have all been evoked to explain a particular category vulnerability (e.g. Funnell & Sheridan, 1992; Humphreys, Riddoch, & Quinlan, 1988; Stewart, Parkin, & Hunkin, 1992). The category impairment for inanimate items in the access dysphasics described so far could perhaps be accounted for in terms of a semantic-relatedness effect. The category of objects includes not only many highly familiar items but also many items that might be functionally related. Thus, it could be predicted that this category might be more vulnerable in patients with access dysphasia. Paradoxically, the absence of a category effect along the animate/inanimate distinction in H.E.C. would suggest that the vulnerability of the inanimate category cannot be dismissed in this way. H.E.C. shows a strong semantic-similarity effect yet, unlike the previously reported access dysphasic patients, his performance was no more impaired for the inanimate than the animate category. This clearly demonstrates that a semantic-relatedness effect and the category effect for the inanimate should be regarded as orthogonal dimensions, with the previously reported impairments for the inanimate not being reducible to the semantic-relatedness effect.

We would propose that a similar argument applies with regard to H.E.C.'s comprehension of proper names. Two previously reported access dysphasic patients (Y.O.T. and M.E.D.) showed the selective preservation of proper names. Both patients' comprehension of common forenames (e.g. Anne) was very impaired, yet their comprehension of country and famous people's names (e.g. Gandhi) was almost at ceiling. Again it could be questioned whether the sparing of country and famous people's names could have been explained in terms of an artefact (see McNeil et al., 1994 for further discussion on this point). H.E.C.'s comprehension of common forenames was also more impaired than his comprehension of famous people's names. In contrast with the previous two cases, his comprehension of country names was actually slightly better than his comprehension of famous people's names. However, his comprehension of both these categories could hardly be regarded as intact. The selective sparing of country and famous peoples name's present in the previous two patients was therefore unlikely to be an artefact of semantic similarity, because in H.E.C. the pattern of performance was somewhat different. Given the scanty data available up to now, we would be inclined to interpret the observed dissociations in H.E.C.'s performance between country and famous people's names as a product of semantic categorical organisation. Whether his impairment with common forenames reflects a deficit within the semantic system or within the lexical system (as has been suggested by Burton & Bruce, 1993) cannot be determined from present evidence.

In conclusion, we would claim that H.E.C. is a clear example of an access dysphasia. We would agree that our account of this syndrome is not, in the words of Rapp and Caramazza (1993, p. 137), presented in "the context of a theory that is sufficiently detailed to support the distinction one is trying to make and the observations one is attempting to account for". However, we do not agree that the "relevant scientific audience cannot evaluate and understand this proposal" because of this. We consider that the phenomenon we have described is a strong empirical pattern which has the potential of furthering our understanding of the nature of the cognitive processing and representations of the semantic system. Indeed, we believe that this evidence might provide constraints for developing a more fully realised theoretical framework regarding the nature of access mechanisms.

REFERENCES

Burton, A.M., & Bruce, V. (1993). Naming faces and naming names: Exploring an interactive activation model of person recognition. *Memory, 1*(4), 457–480.

Carroll, J.B., Davies, P., & Richman, B. (1971). *Word frequency book.* Boston: Houghton Mifflin Co.

Cipolotti, L., McNeil, J., & Warrington, E.K. (1993). Spared written naming of proper nouns: A case report. *Memory, 1*(4), 289–311.

Dell, G.S. (1986). A spreading activation theory of retrieval in sentence production. *Psychological Review, 93*, 283–321.

Dell, G.S. (1989). The retrieval of phonological forms in production: Tests of predictions from a connectionist model. In W. Marslen-Wilson (Ed.), *Lexical representation and process.* Cambridge, MA: MIT Press.

De Renzi, E., Scotti, G. & Spinnler, H. (1969). Perceptual and associative disorders of visual recognition: Relationship to the site of lesion. *Neurology, 19*, 634–642.

Franklin, S., Howard, D., & Patterson, K. (1994). Abstract word meaning deafness. *Cognitive Neuropsychology, 11*, 1–34.

Funnell, E., & Sheridan, J. (1992). Categories of knowledge? Unfamiliar aspects of living and nonliving things. *Cognitive Neuropsychology, 9*, 135–153.

Harley, T.A., & MacAndrew, S.B.G. (1992). Modelling paraphasias in normal and aphasic speech. *Proceedings of the 14th Annual Conference of the Cognitive Science Society*, pp. 378–383. Bloomington, IL.

Humphreys, G.W., Riddoch, M.J., & Quinlan, P.T. (1988). Cascade processes in picture identification. *Cognitive Neuropsychology, 5*, 67–103.

Laiacona, M., Barbarotto, R., & Capitani, E. (1993). Perceptual and associative knowledge in category specific impairment of semantic memory: a study of two cases. *Cortex, 29*, 727–740.

McKenna, P., & Warrington, E.K. (1980). Testing for nominal dysphasia. *Journal of Neurology, Neurosurgery and Psychiatry, 43*, 781–788.

McNeil, J., Cipolotti, L., & Warrington, E.K. (1994). Accessibility of proper names. *Neuropsychologia, 32*, 193–208.

Morton, J. (1970). A functional model for memory. In D.A. Norman (Ed.), *Models of human memory.* New York: Academic Press.

Poeck, K., Hartjie, W., & Kerschensteiner, M. (1973). Sprachverstandnisstorungen bei aphasischen und nichtaphasischen Hirnkranken. *Deutsche Medizinische Wochenschrift, 98*, 139–147.

Poeck, K., & Stachowiack, F.G. (1975). Farbennennungsstorungen bei aphasischen und nicht aphasischen Hirnkranken. *Journal of Neurology, 209*, 95–102.

Rapp, B., & Caramazza, A. (1993). On the distinction between deficits of access and deficit of storage: a question of theory. *Cognitive Neuropsychology, 10*, 113–141.

Sartori, G., & Job, R. (1988). The oyster with four legs: A neuropsychological study on the interaction of visual and semantic information. *Cognitive Neuropsychology, 5*, 105–132.

Schuell, H., Jenkins, J., & Landis, L. (1961). Relationship between auditory comprehension and word frequency in aphasia. *Journal of Speech and Hearing Research, 4*, 30–36.

Shallice, T. (1988). *From neuropsychology to mental structure.* Cambridge: Cambridge University Press.

Silveri, M.C., & Gainotti, G. (1988). Interaction between vision and language in category specific semantic impairment. *Cognitive Neuropsychology, 5*, 677–709.

Stewart, F., Parkin, A.J., & Hunkin, N.M. (1992). Naming impairments following recovery from herpes simplex encephalitis: Category-specific? *Quarterly Journal of Experimental Psychology, 44A*, 261–284.

Warrington, E.K. (1975). The selective impairment of semantic memory. *Quarterly Journal of Experimental Psychology, 27*, 635–657.

Warrington, E.K. (1984). *Recognition Memory Test.* Windsor: NFER-Nelson.

Warrington, E.K., & Cipolotti, L. (submitted). Word comprehension impairments: The distinction between access and storage.

Warrington, E.K., & James, M. (1991). *The Visual Object and Space Perception Battery.* Bury St Edmunds, UK: Thames Valley Test Company.

Warrington, E.K., & McCarthy, R. (1983). Category-specific access dysphasia. *Brain, 106*, 859–878.

Warrington, E.K., & McCarthy, R. (1987). Categories of knowledge. *Brain, 110*, 1273–1296.

Warrington, E.K., & McCarthy, R. (1994). Multiple meaning systems in the brain: A case for visual semantics. *Neuropsychologia, 32*, 1465–1473.

Warrington, E.K., & Shallice, T. (1979). Semantic access dyslexia. *Brain, 102*, 43–63.

Warrington, E.K., & Shallice, T. (1984). Category-specific semantic impairments. *Brain, 107*, 829–853.

Warrington, E.K., & Taylor, A.M. (1978). Contribution of the right parietal lobe to object recognition. *Cortex, 9*, 152–164.

APPENDIX 1

EXPERIMENT 5

Animals

	High Frequency				
	Close SRI (X = 4.08; s.d.0.8)			Distant SRI (X = 2.4; s.d. = 0.8)	
Freq.	CDR	SF X (s.d.)	Freq.	CDR	SF X (s.d.)
rabbit	209	5.40 (1.1)	bee	128	5.05 (1)
donkey	156	4.50 (1.3)	dog	1380	6.50 (0.8)
cow	263	5.10 (1.4)	horse	1263	5.52 (1.1)
lamb	94	5.10 (0.9)	swan	29	4.82 (1.23)
X (s.d.)	180.50 (72.3)	5.04 (1.2)	X (s.d.)	700 (720.3)	5.40 (1.2)

	Low Frequency				
	Close SRI (X = 4.2; s.d.0.7)			Distant SRI (X = 2; s.d. = 0.7)	
Freq.	CDR	SF X (s.d.)	Freq.	CDR	SF X (s.d.)
starfish	46	3.10 (1.2)	koala	3	3.20 (1.2)
lobster	9	3.80 (1.1)	shrimp	29	3.60 (1.2)
crab	62	3.80 (1.4)	bison	18	2.70 (1)
octopus	19	3.10 (0.9)	walrus	21	2.80 (0.8)
X (s.d.)	34 (24.3)	3.40 (1.1)	X (s.d.)	17.7 (10.8)	3.10 (1.1)

Objects

		High Frequency			
	Close SRI (X = 4.5; s.d.0.6)			Distant SRI (X = 2.05; s.d. = 0.8)	
Freq.	*CDR*	*SF* X (s.d.)	*Freq.*	*CDR*	*SF* X (s.d.)
trousers	60	6.35 (1.1)	teapot	21	5.8 (1.5)
blouse	64	5.52 (1.3)	key	652	6.3 (1)
dress	396	6.05 (1.4)	hat	511	6.0 (0.8)
jacket	143	6.20 (0.8)	glasses	150	6.2 (0.9)
X (s.d.)	165.70 (158.1)	6.05 (1.1)	X (s.d.)	333.5 (296.8)	6.1 (1)

		Low Frequency			
	Close SRI (X = 4.2; s.d.0.6)			Distant SRI (X = 2.05; s.d. = 0.7)	
Freq.	*CDR*	*SF* X (s.d.)	*Freq.*	*CDR*	*SF* X (s.d.)
pliers	14	4.2 (1.2)	funnel	73	4.0 (1)
hoe	33	3.6 (1.4)	earphones	13	3.4 (1.4)
axe	27	4.2 (1.3)	barometer	42	2.8 (1)
rake	37	3.6 (1.3)	piano	418	4.8 (1.2)
X (s.d.)	27.7 (10)	3.8 (1.3)	X (s.d.)	136.5 (189.2)	3.7 (1.4)

Foods

		High Frequency			
	Close SRI (X = 4.7; s.d.0.4)			Distant SRI (X = 3.05; s.d. = 0.7)	
Freq.	*CDR*	*SF* X (s.d.)	*Freq.*	*CDR*	*SF* X (s.d.)
apple	294	6.5 (0.7)	grapes	88	5.1 (1.2)
bananas	113	5.9 (1.5)	potatoes	274	6.3 (0.7)
orange	221	6.0 (1.4)	cabbage	139	5.0 (1.45)
pear	32	5.2 (1.4)	cherries	71	5.2 (1.3)
X (s.d.)	165 (115.7)	5.9 (1.3)	X (s.d.)	143 (91.9)	5.3 (1.3)

		Low Frequency			
	Close SRI (X = 4.8; s.d.0.3)			Distant SRI (X = 3.1; s.d. = 0.7)	
Freq.	*CDR*	*SF* X (s.d.)	*Freq.*	*CDR*	*SF* X (s.d.)
raspberries	14	4.8 (1.5)	rhubarb	3	3.8 (1.3)
blackberries	9	4.5 (1.4)	peach	76	4.8 (1.2)
gooseberries	3	3.7 (1.6)	dates	109	3.6 (1.5)
blueberries	16	3.8 (1.6)	olives	42	4.2 (1.2)
X (s.d.)	10.5 (5.8)	4.2 (1.5)	X (s.d.)	57.5 (45.4)	4.0 (1.3)

Freq. refers to frequency.
SRI refers to the semantic–relatedness index derived from 18 subjects.
CDR refers to the Carroll et al. (1971) word–frequency count.
SF refers to the subjective frequency count derived from 17 subjects.
X (s.d.) = mean and standard deviation.

APPENDIX 2

EXPERIMENT 6

Animals

	High Frequency					
	Close SRI (X = 3.8; s.d.0.8)			Distant SRI (X = 2.2; s.d. = 0.9)		
Freq.	CDR	SF X (s.d.)		Freq.	CDR	SF X (s.d.)
squirrel	88	4.7 (1.5)		goat	130	4.6 (1.3)
cat	620	6.4 (0.7)		goldfish	45	4.9 (1.3)
mouse	207	5.2 (1.4)		robin	57	4.7 (1.3)
puppy	87	5.0 (1.5)		lion	264	5.2 (1.4)
X (s.d.)	250.5 (252.9)	5.4 (1.4)		X (s.d.)	124 (100)	4.9 (1.3)

	Low Frequency					
	Close SRI (X = 4.3; s.d.0.7)			Distant SRI (X = 2.5; s.d. = 0.9)		
Freq.	CDR	SF X (s.d.)		Freq.	CDR	SF X (s.d.)
caterpillar	66	3.6 (1.2)		otter	29	3.4 (0.9)
grasshopper	46	3.1 (1.3)		owl	21	4.1 (1.3)
beetle	41	4.1 (1.3)		koala	3	3.2 (1.2)
ladybird	2	3.8 (1.2)		hyena	8	3.1 (1.3)
X (s.d.)	38.7 (26.7)	3.6 (1.3)		X (s.d.)	15.2 (11.8)	3.4 (1.2)

Foods

	High Frequency					
	Close SRI (X = 4.1; s.d.0.7)			Distant SRI (X = 2.4; s.d. = 0.6)		
Freq.	CDR	SF X (s.d.)		Freq.	CDR	SF X (s.d.)
bread	515	6.7 (0.5)		tomato	45	6.1 (1.0)
sweets (candies)	256	5.8 (0.9)		onions	52	5.6 (1.1)
biscuits (cookies)	168	6.2 (0.9)		ice-cream	33	5.9 (0.8)
cakes	133	5.8 (1.1)		eggs	379	6.3 (0.9)
X (s.d.)	268 (172)	6.2 (0.9)		X (s.d.)	127.2 (168)	6.0 (1)

	Low Frequency					
	Close SRI (X = 4.6; s.d.0.6)			Distant SRI (X = 2.7; s.d. = 0.7)		
Freq.	CDR	SF X (s.d.)		Freq.	CDR	SF X (s.d.)
parsnip	2	3.9 (1.3)		pepper	45	4.0 (1.5)
beetroot	0	3.9 (1.3)		figs	13	3.1 (1.4)
turnip	16	3.9 (1.1)		beansprouts	0	3.7 (1.4)
radish	14	3.4 (1.2)		blackcurrant	0	3.8 (1.5)
X (s.d.)	8 (8.1)	3.8 (1.3)		X (s.d.)	14.5	3.6 (21.2)

APPENDIX 3

The overall mean and standard deviation of frequency and semantic–relatedness ratings for all the high and low, close and distant arrays.

Experiment 5

	SRI X (s.d.)	CDR X (s.d.)	SF X (s.d.)
CHF	4.0 (0.09)	170.40 (109.3)	5.6 (1.3)
CLF	4.4 (0.6)	23.03 (17.4)	3.8 (1.3)
DHF	2.5 (0.8)	392.10 (475.5)	6.0 (1.2)
DLF	2.4 (0.9)	70.50 (114.1)	3.6 (1.3)

Experiment 6

	SRI X (s.d.)	CDR X (s.d.)	SF X (s.d.)
CHF	4.0 (0.7)	259.20 (200.0)	5.8 (1.26)
CLF	4.4 (0.6)	23.37 (24.6)	3.75 (1.3)
DHF	2.3 (0.7)	125.60 (128.0)	5.4 (1.2)
DLF	2.6 (0.8)	14.80 (15.9)	3.5 (1.3)

APPENDIX 4

Comparison of frequency contrasts (Mann-Whitney U).

Experiment 5

	CDR	SF
HF vs LF	$z = 4.66, P < 0.0001$	$z = 5.86, P < 0.0001$
CHF vs DHF	$z = 0.46, P < 0.32$	$z = 0.20, P < 0.42$
CLF vs DLF	$z = 1.21, P < 0.11$	$z = 0.89, P < 0.18$

Experiment 6

	CDR	SF
HF vs LF	$z = 4.41, P < 0.0001$	$z = 4.83, P < 0.0001$
CHF vs DHF	$U = 14, P < 0.03$	$U = 23, P < 0.19$
CLF vs DLF	$U = 26, P < 0.28$	$U = 24.5, P < 0.22$

Comparison of semantic relatedness contrasts (Mann-Whitney U)

	Experiment 5 SRI	Experiment 6 SRI
C vs D	$U = 0, P < 0.001$	$U = 0, P < 0.014$

APPENDIX 5

Experiment 7

Countries

France
Holland
Spain
Chile
Hungary
Germany
Russia
Canada
Mexico
Italy
Ireland
India
Australia
Japan
Cuba
England
Greece
Africa
Austria
Brazil

Famous People

Hitler
Dickens
Mozart
Napoleon
Montgomery
Churchill
Lenin
Freud
Lincoln
Shakespeare
Stalin
Einstein
Franco
Gandhi
Beethoven
Mussolini
Picasso
Marx
Cromwell
Castro

Cities

Paris
Rome
London
Delhi
Madrid
Edinburgh
Berlin
Tokyo
New York
Vienna
York
Athens
Cairo
Miami
Munich
Moscow
Zurich
Venice
Chicago
Dublin

Common Forenames

Diana
Susan
Sally
Mary
Elizabeth
Helen
Sarah
Jane
Margaret
Anne
David
Peter
John
Richard
Steve
Tom
James
Brian
Anthony
Paul

MEMORY, 1995, *3* (3/4), 333–358

The Compositionality of Lexical Semantic Representations: Clues from Semantic Errors in Object Naming

Argye E. Hillis

Johns Hopkins University, Baltimore, USA

Alfonso Caramazza

Dartmouth College, Hanover, USA

We present evidence that semantic errors in object naming can arise not only from impairment to the semantic system but also from damage to input and output processes. Although each of these levels of disruption can result in similar types of semantic errors in object naming, they have different types of consequences for performance on other lexical tasks, such as comprehension and naming to definition. We show that the analysis of the co-occurrence of semantic errors in naming with different patterns of performance in other lexical processing tasks can be used to localise the source of semantic errors in the naming process. Finally, we argue that the similarity of semantic errors in object naming, resulting from damage to different components of the naming process, reflects the compositional nature of lexical semantic representations, and the processes by which they are activated by visual input, as well as the processes by which they activate output representations.

INTRODUCTION

The analysis of error types has played an important role in the development of cognitive models. For example, the analysis of speech errors (from both normal and brain-damaged subjects) has been the most important source of data for developing models of speech production (Brown & McNeil, 1966; Butterworth, 1981, 1983; Dell, 1989; Garrett, 1980, 1992; Levelt, 1989). Similarly, the analysis of spelling errors by neurologically impaired subjects has played a crucial role in the development of models of the spelling process (Beauvois &

Requests for reprints should be sent to Alfonso Caramazza, Department of Psychology, William James Hall, Harvard University, 33 Kirkand Street, Cambridge, MA 02138, USA.

A version of this paper was presented at the Twelfth European Workshop on Cognitive Neuropsychology in Bressanone, Italy, January 1994. The authors are grateful to Roz McCarthy, Andy Ellis, and an anonymous reviewer for helpful comments on an earlier version of the paper. The research reported here was supported in part by NIH grant (NINCD) RO1 19330 to Alfonso Caramazza.

Derouesné, 1981; Caramazza & Miceli, 1990; Ellis, 1988; Goodman & Caramazza, 1986). However, the link between the type of error that is produced and the source of the error is not always straightforward. Semantic errors are a case in point. Where do semantic errors come from?

Different answers have been given to this question. The most common answer is that semantic errors in naming (or reading or writing) come from damage to the semantic component of the language processing system (Butterworth, Howard, & McLoughlin, 1984; Coltheart, 1980; Howard & Orchard-Lisle, 1984; Kay & Ellis, 1987). But it has also been argued that semantic errors can come from damage at other levels of representation or processing, such as damage at the level of the phonological or orthographic output lexicon (Caramazza & Hillis, 1990; see also Barry & Newton, 1994; Levelt, 1983). Recently it has been argued that semantic errors (as well as visual errors) in reading can come from damage to almost any level of processing in the reading task (Hinton & Shallice, 1991; Plaut & Shallice, 1993). This claim is based on the finding that both semantic and visual errors arise as a consequence of "lesioning" any component of an implemented connectionist network developed to provide a model of normal as well as impaired reading performance. Thus, the mere observation of semantic errors in the performance of brain-damaged patients is insufficient to identify the locus of damage to the lexical processing system.

In this paper we argue that even though the production of semantic errors on its own has little value in determining the source of errors, the pattern of semantic errors across various lexical tasks can support the proposal of damage to a specific component of the lexical system. We present evidence that semantic errors in object naming can arise from impairment to any one of several levels in the naming process—including input, semantic, and output levels. Although each of these levels of disruption can result in similar types of semantic errors in object naming, they have different types of consequence for performance on other lexical tasks, such as comprehension and naming to definition. We show that the analysis of the co-occurrence of semantic errors in naming with different patterns of performance in other lexical processing tasks can be used to localise the source of semantic errors in the naming process. Finally, we argue that the similarity of semantic errors in object naming, resulting from damage to different components of the naming process, reflects the compositional nature of lexical semantic representations, and the processes by which they are activated by visual input, as well as the processes by which they activate output representations.

We compare the performance of three neurologically impaired patients (KE: Hillis, Rapp, Romani, & Caramazza, 1990; DHY: Hillis & Caramazza, 1995; and RGB: Caramazza & Hillis, 1990) who make semantic errors in object naming, but whose distinct patterns of performance across lexical tasks can only be accounted for by assuming damage to a different component of the naming process in each case. Semantically related responses constitute the vast majority of the errors in each case (92% of errors by KE; 83% of errors by DHY; and

TABLE 1
Examples of Semantic Errors in Picture Naming

STIMULUS → RESPONSE		
KE	DHY	RGB
nose → ear	nose → finger	toe → finger
tiger → lion	giraffe → raccoon	giraffe → racoon
onion → carrot	celery → lettuce	celery → lettuce
peach → banana	strawberry → cucumber	banana → apple
frog → turtle	frog → cricket	goose → turkey
sock → gloves	button → button hole	mittens → socks
jacket → belt	dress → scarf	berry → flower
lobster → shrimp	beetle → caterpillar	clam → octopus
fork → knife	frying pan → cup	apple → peach
sofa → chair	iron → sewing machine	stool → bench
bear → fox	bear → hippopotamus	kangaroo → racoon

100% of errors by RGB). Among these errors were "definitions" or circumlocutions, which constituted 50% of RGB's errors and 50.9% of DHY's errors (but none of KE's responses, as he was severely nonfluent and produced mostly single-word utterances). DHY also produced a large number of perseverative responses (16% of her total errors). Nevertheless, the semantically related single-word errors in the three cases were indistinguishable (Table 1). There were no significant differences in the distribution of types of semantically related word error (coordinate, superordinate, and associative errors; by chi square) nor in terms of the frequency or familiarity score of these error responses (by unpaired t-tests), as shown in Table 2.

TABLE 2
Analysis of Error Responses

	KE	DHY	RGB
Number of semantically related word errors	17	12	12
Distribution of semantically related word error types:			
% coordinate errors	76.5%	67%	67%
% superordinate errors	11.8%	17%	17%
% associative errors	11.8%	15%	17%
Mean word frequency of error responses	22.6	23.4	21.1
Mean frequency of the stimuli that elicited the errors	19.5	18.8	16.9
Mean length (in letters) of error responses	4.9	5.2	5.3
Mean familiarity scores of error responses	4.0	3.9	3.5

Analysis of semantically related word errors in oral picture naming by KE, DHY, and RGB for the same set of 47 stimuli.

Despite the similarity of the three patients' performance on object naming tasks, there are striking differences among them in their performance on other tasks (Table 3). For example, in naming objects presented for tactile exploration, KE and RGB make semantic errors at the same rate as in picture-naming tasks, whereas DHY makes no semantic errors. By contrast, in word/picture matching tasks, DHY and KE make mostly semantic errors as they do in picture naming, but RGB makes no semantic errors at all. In this paper we account for the differences and similarities among these patients by proposing that the semantic errors in each patient come from damage to a different component of the naming process. As the analysis of performance in each case is reported in detail elsewhere, only those aspects of performance that are crucial for the proposals in this paper will be summarised here. Following the summary of each case we present a model of object naming that can account for the production of the identical type of semantic error as a result of damage to different levels of processing.

THE SOURCE OF SEMANTIC ERRORS IN EACH PATIENT

Patient KE

KE, a 52-year-old, right-handed corporate executive, sustained a left frontoparietal stroke six months prior to testing. His spontaneous speech was agrammatic and nonfluent, consisting mostly of single content words, with frequent semantic errors. In oral reading and spelling to dictation he only responded to concrete nouns, to which he made frequent semantic errors (as described later). He did not attempt to respond to most abstract words nor to virtually any pseudoword (e.g. hannee) or even consonant–vowel syllables (e.g.

TABLE 3
Rate of Total Errors and Semantically Related Errors Across Tasks

| | KE | | DHY | | RGB | |
	total	semantic	total	semantic	total	semantic
Oral Picture Naming	40.4	38.3	71.5	67.5	31.9	31.9
Oral Tactile Naming	46.8	44.7	0	0	36.2	36.2
Spoken Word/Picture Verification*	40.4	40.4	31.2	31.2	0	0

Rate as a % of total responses; N = 47
* In this task, each object name is presented once with a picture of a corresponding object, once with a picture of a semantically related object, and once with a picture of an unrelated object (in separate sessions). To be scored "correct" for a given word, the patient must respond accurately on each of the three trials in which the word is presented. Thus, if the patient responded purely randomly, the rate of total errors would approximate 87.5% and the rate of semantic errors would approximate 50%. As shown, nearly all of our three patients' errors constituted acceptance of the semantically related picture (as well as the correct, corresponding picture) and rejection of the unrelated picture.

ba). Detailed analyses of his errors in a variety of lexical and nonlexical tasks have been previously reported (Hillis et al., 1990).

Performance Across Lexical Tasks. On a list of 144 objects (or their names) administered for each lexical task (in counterbalanced order), KE made the identical types of errors, at approximately the same rates, in written and spoken word comprehension (word/picture verification), written and oral naming, oral reading, and writing to dictation (Table 4).

His similar rates of semantic errors across all lexical tasks indicates that a single underlying deficit is the most likely source of his semantic errors in all of the tasks. The only alternative account is that he has damage to separate input and output components—phonological and orthographic and picture input and/ or phonological and orthographic output—and that the damage to each component is quantitatively and qualitatively equal. Even if such an alternative account were plausible, it is ruled out by the results of the analysis of item-by-item consistency across the various tasks and the analysis of semantic category effects to be reported shortly.

All the tasks (except word/picture verification tasks) were repeated, and item-by-item consistency across administrations of the same task was compared to item-by-item consistency across tasks. KE did not consistently make semantic errors in comprehension on items that elicited semantic errors in oral naming. However, his item-by-item consistency across tasks was essentially the same as his consistency across administrations of the same task (Table 5). In other words, the production of a semantic error in one task (say, naming) could predict the production of a semantic error in another task (say, comprehension), just as well as it could predict the production of a semantic error in a repeated oral naming task with the same item. This result provides strong evidence that a single underlying deficit was the source of his semantic errors in all lexical tasks.

If we are correct in proposing a single underlying impairment as the basis for KE's semantic errors in all lexical tasks, then the types of items most likely to be affected in one task should also be the items most likely to be affected in other

TABLE 4
KE's Error Rates Across Tasks

Task	Total Errors	Semantic Errors
Spoken Word/Picture Verification	42.4	42.4
Written Word/Picture Verification	36.8	36.1
Oral Picture Naming	44.4	41.0
Written Picture Naming	46.5	34.7
Oral Reading	41.7	36.1
Writing to Dictation	41.7	27.8

Rate as a % of total responses; N = 144.

TABLE 5
Intra-task and Inter-task Item Consistency for Same Accuracy

	Test-Retest Consistency*	Mean Intertask Consistency**
Oral Picture Naming	66.7	74.8
Written Picture Naming	74.3	75.2
Oral Reading	71.5	66.2
Writing to Dictation	71.5	69.4
Spoken Word/Picture Verification	—	75.2
Written Word/Picture Verification	—	73.4

* Number of stimuli correct on both trials or incorrect on both trials divided by the total number of stimuli.

** The arithmetic mean of the task–task consistency (measured in the same way as test–retest consistency) for each pair of tasks.

tasks. This prediction was confirmed by analysing KE's accuracy across semantic categories (e.g. animals vs. clothing), matched for frequency and length in letters and syllables. The category differences were essentially the same across lexical tasks; that is, categories in which he made the most (semantic) errors in naming, such as body parts and furniture, also elicited the most (semantic) errors in reading, comprehension, and writing tasks (Fig. 1).

Conclusions from KE. The central feature of KE's performance is the co-occurrence of semantic errors in all input and output tasks tested—oral and written naming in response to visually and tactilely presented stimuli, reading and writing to dictation, auditory and visual word/picture matching tasks. Two other important features of KE's performance are that he made roughly the same proportion of semantic errors in all tasks and that he showed the same hierarchy of difficulty for different semantic categories in all tasks. It is extremely difficult to account for this pattern of results by proposing separate impairments to different input and output components of the lexical processing system. Such an account would have to argue that the quantitatively and qualitatively similar performance across the various tasks just happened by accident. Thus, for example, the proposal of separate impairments affecting different modalities would have to argue that damage just happened to affect semantic categories in the same way in each separate component of processing. A far more plausible explanation for these results is that a single damaged component—the lexical semantic component—common to the tasks of reading, writing, naming, and comprehension, accounts for the production of semantic errors in all the tasks[1].

---

[1] Note that damage to the semantic system does not necessarily result in semantic errors in oral reading and writing to dictation, as these tasks can be supported by non-lexical mechanisms for converting print to sound or sound to print. However, KE's profoundly impaired performance in reading and spelling pseudowords indicates that these mechanisms were not available to him.

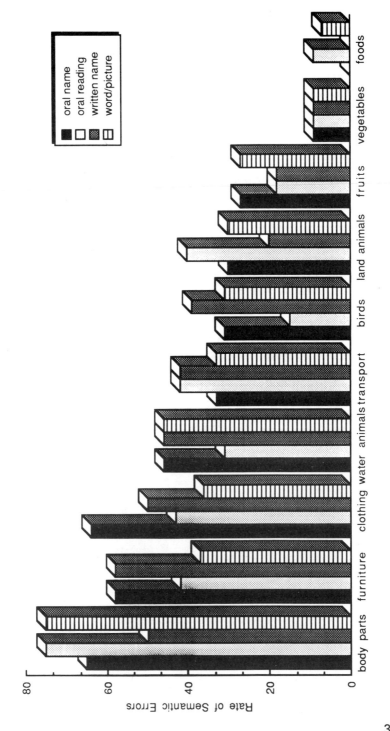

FIG. 1. KE's percentage of semantic errors (semantic errors/total responses) across tasks with different input and output modalities.

339

We have noted that patient DHY also made semantic errors in picture naming. And, like KE, she made quantitatively and qualitatively comparable errors in picture/word matching or verification tasks. However, her performance in tasks with tactile and auditory input demonstrated that her semantic errors could not come from damage at the level of the semantic component because she did not make any errors in these tasks.

Patient DHY

DHY is a right-handed retired nurse, who had been an avid reader prior to her neurological damage. This investigation began when she was 64 years old, 17 months after a stroke involving the left periventricular white matter at the level of the lateral ventricle and the thalamus and six months after an infarct in the left occipital lobe and splenium (by MRI). Her spontaneous speech was fluent and grammatical without any obvious language errors in social conversations or in relating stories about her personal history. She was very mildly dysarthric, but completely intelligible. Her oral reading was severely impaired, and was characterised by attempts to read letter-by-letter with frequent letter identification errors. However, she easily recognised words spelled aloud to her. In written spelling she showed substantial difficulty in forming letters, but her oral spelling of dictated words was quite accurate. Her naming performance in response to a variety of stimuli is described here and reported in detail in a separate paper (Hillis & Caramazza, in press).

Performance Across Lexical Tasks.   In naming the set of 260 pictures in Snodgrass and Vanderwart (1980), DHY produced the correct name of 25% of the pictures (after self-correction). The majority (162/195, or 83%) of her errors could be classified as "semantic errors", of the types shown in Table 6. Only

TABLE 6
DHY's Errors in Picture Naming

Coordinate semantic errors	*Superordinate semantic errors*
axe → wrench	ant → creepy crawler
foot → leg	ball → child's toy
jacket → dress	camel → animal
motorcycle → car	caterpillar → insect
nail → screw	cherry → food
frying pan → cup	*Associative semantic errors*
giraffe → raccoon	button → button hole
helicopter → motorcycle	fly → bird
iron → sewing machine	ring → diamond

Descriptions
apple → food that you eat. Green, usually, or you can have white ones.
skunk → You see those in the wild. They smell bad. Everybody avoids them.

two items elicited names of visually similar objects that are not semantically related. The remaining 31 responses indicated perseveration on a concept (not necessarily the identical word given before). Many of her descriptive responses or semantic errors were also related to earlier responses.

Like KE, DHY also made errors in word/picture verification tasks, all of which involved acceptance of a semantically related picture as the referent of the word. However, as already noted, in naming objects presented to tactile exploration, DHY made almost no errors, whereas KE's performance was essentially identical to his performance in picture-naming tasks (Fig. 2). DHY's accuracy in tactile naming was within the range we have found for non brain-damaged controls, and her occasional errors were similar to those made by the controls (e.g. plastic pill bottle—"a plastic salt shaker"). In contrast, her errors in naming the same objects presented visually or depicted in pictures were semantic and perseverative in nature, equivalent to those described for the larger set of pictures. Furthermore, when asked to name in response to definitions a subset of 84 of the 260 items from Snodgrass and Vanderwart (1980), DHY's accuracy in naming was identical to that of control subjects— 80/84 correct. It seems, therefore, that DHY's semantic errors are specific to the visual modality.

DHY's errors in the visual modality were not due to low-level perceptual deficits, as she performed perfectly normally on tasks designed to evaluate the

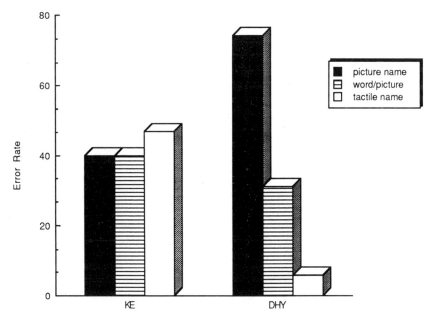

FIG. 2. Percentage of total errors (total errors/total responses) across tasks with different input modalities, by KE and DHY.

veridical representation of the visual stimulus (delayed copying, matching identical pictures, identifying the "different figure" among abstract shapes). She also performed normally on tasks that have been used to evaluate access to a stored 3-D model (Marr, 1982) or structural description (Riddoch & Humphreys, 1987) of a visual stimulus: (1) matching objects depicted in different views; (2) performance in an object decision task; (3) drawing an object in a different rotation from that depicted in a stimulus picture; and (4) drawing objects in response to their name (see Appendix for examples from these tasks). She made no frank errors in pantomiming the use of visually presented objects, although more than half of her gestures were somewhat ambiguous (i.e. could not be distinguished from semantically related objects). DHY also showed 95% accuracy in verifying colour/object correspondences using the Snodgrass and Vanderwart pictures coloured in with crayons. Her only errors consisted of incorrectly accepting objects with a colour that would be appropriate for another item in the same class. For example, she accepted a lemon coloured bluish purple (a colour that would be appropriate for other fruits, such as a plum or a blueberry). However, she was quite poor (59% correct, where chance level is 33% correct) in deciding which two of three objects (depicted in black and white drawings) in the same category have the same colour. For example, she identified a pineapple and a strawberry as having the same colour, rather than a strawberry and an apple.

On visual tasks DHY had no difficulty in distinguishing between semantically unrelated (but visually similar) pictures, but had a great deal of difficulty when she had to distinguish between semantically related pictures (Table 7). In one task DHY was asked to identify which of two visually presented items was most closely related to a third picture. When the foil was a semantically unrelated but visually similar object (e.g. a pear presented with a light bulb and a light switch; Fig. 3, top) her performance was 100% accurate in identifying the associated pictures. But when she was given the same pairs of associated pictures one week later with a semantically related foil, she could not choose which of the two semantically related objects (e.g. a light bulb or a traffic light) was more closely related to the third (a light switch in this example; Fig. 3, bottom). These results suggest that she was able to access only partial semantic information from pictures. Nevertheless, DHY had no trouble accessing complete semantic information in the auditory modality. For instance, when she was given the object association task just described with the same items, but in the auditory-verbal modality (e.g. asked, "Which is more closely related to a light switch: a traffic light or a light bulb?") her performance was 100% accurate, even with semantically related foils, indicating that she could access complete (or at least more complete) semantic information about objects from spoken words[2].

---

[2] Two age and education matched control subjects were 100% accurate on both forms of this task.

TABLE 7
DHY's Performance on Various Types of Semantic Tasks

| Task | % Correct | |
	Foils: semantic coordinates/ complete information	Foils: unrelated words/ partial information
Auditory–Verbal Tasks:		
Naming to Definition	95%	100% (naming the category)
Identifying Associated Words	100%	100%
Visual–Verbal Tasks:		
Naming Pictures	25%	100% (naming the category)
Word/picture Matching	69%	100%
Visual–Nonverbal Tasks:		
Identifying Associated Pictures	58%	100%
Matching Pictures to Photographs	60%	100%

FIG. 3.   An example of each of the associative picture-matching tasks.

343

Conclusions from DHY.   The general pattern of performance shown by DHY—frequent semantic errors in picture naming, in the face of (1) accurate naming of the same objects from spoken description or tactile exploration, and (2) accurate "recognition" of pictures—corresponds to the pattern labelled "optic aphasia" (Beauvois, 1982; Beauvois & Saillant, 1985; Coslett & Saffran, 1989, 1992; Lhermitte & Beauvois, 1973; Manning & Campbell, 1992; Peña-Casanova et al., 1985). However, by administering tasks that probe for detailed semantic knowledge from vision we discovered that despite her intact visual perception[3], DHY is unable to access complete semantic information from visual stimuli, even though she is able to access complete semantic information from auditory and tactile stimuli. Together with evidence from the visual processing tasks, which indicate relatively spared access to stored "structural descriptions" of objects, these data are consistent with the hypothesis that DHY's object-naming deficit occurs at a level of processing located after a structural description is computed and before a complete semantic representation is activated (see Riddoch & Humphreys, 1987, for a similar case). In short, it seems that DHY's semantic errors in picture naming (and other visual semantic tasks) come from impaired access to intact semantic information from an intact "structural description" of a visual stimulus.

Thus far we have shown that the semantic errors by KE and those by DHY, although superficially similar, arise at different levels of processing in the naming task. Now we turn to RGB, and argue that his semantic errors arise from yet another different level of processing in the naming task.

Patient RGB

At the time of testing, RGB, a right-handed, retired Personnel Manager was 62 years old and four years post-onset of a left frontoparietal infarct. His speech was fluent and grammatical, and showed no evidence of articulation difficulty. However, he made frequent semantic errors and circumlocutions in spontaneous speech (see Caramazza & Hillis, 1990, for details).

Performance Across Lexical Tasks.   RGB was presented with the 144 stimuli, which were also used in testing KE, in various lexical tasks (in counterbalanced order). As reported for KE, RGB made quantitatively and qualitatively comparable semantic errors in oral reading and in oral naming. However, unlike KE and DHY who made errors in word/picture verification tasks that were similar to those made in oral naming, RGB made no errors in the comprehension tasks, as shown in Table 8. This pattern of performance suggests that RGB is able to process information normally up through the semantic component but is impaired at some stage of lexical output. In the following experiments we: (1) obtained additional evidence that RGB's processing is

---

[3] Or, more accurately, sufficiently spared to permit good performance in basic perceptual tasks.

TABLE 8
Error Rates Across Tasks for KE and RGB (N = 47)

| | KE | | RGB | |
Task	total	semantic	total	semantic
Oral Picture Naming	40.4	38.3	31.9	31.9
Oral Tactile Naming	46.8	44.7	36.2	36.2
Oral Reading	41.7	36.1	30.6	30.6
Spoken Word/Picture Verification	40.4	40.4	0	0
Written Word/Picture Verification	36.8	36.1	0	0

unimpaired through the level of activating a complete semantic representation, irrespective of the modality of input; and (2) obtained direct evidence that his semantic errors arise at the level of the phonological output lexicon.

RGB was asked to read a list of 100 words, and then to immediately define the printed word. Although he made semantic errors in reading about 30% of the words, he correctly defined 100% of the same words, even when he had just misread them. As illustrated in Table 9, RGB clearly understood the words that he misread as semantic errors. It should be noted that the seemingly paradoxical dissociation between good performance in producing definitions versus oral reading simply reflects the fact that the definition task allows the patient to select words whose phonological representations are easily accessible, whereas reading requires selection of a specific phonological representation which may be inaccessible. Nevertheless, some of RGB's definitions, like other samples of his spontaneous speech, did contain semantic errors. For example, he defined *table* as "what you sleep on, no *eat* on.' However, in such an unconstrained task it is difficult to evaluate the occurrence of semantic errors unless they are self-corrected.

TABLE 9
RGB's Definitions of Words, Following Semantic Errors

Stimulus	Response in Oral Reading	Definition of the Printed Word
records	radio	You play 'em on a phonograph ... can also mean notes you take and keep.
dollar	money	A bill ... a hundred cents.
pharmacist	drugs	He gives you your prescriptions.
rubber	tires	What erasers are made of, and rubberbands.
pleasure	sadness	If you like something, and you're happy.
leopard	rhinoceros	It's a kind of cat with spots.
eagerness	generous	You're thinking about things and you want to do them.
red	yellow	The colour of blood ... and the flag has it in it.
six	seven	Half a dozen.

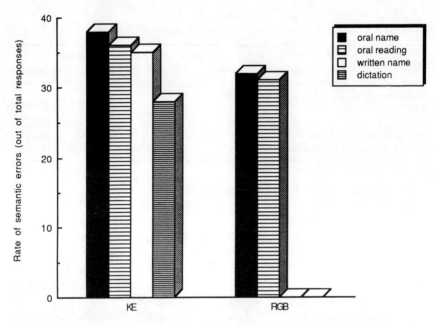

FIG. 4. Percentage of semantic errors (semantic errors/total responses) across tasks with oral or written output by KE and RGB.

Further evidence that RGB's deficit was not at the level of semantic representation, was the fact that his impairment did not affect all forms of output, but only spoken production. In writing the names of the items in the set of 144 stimuli, both in response to pictures and to dictation, he made only 6% errors, compared to about 30% errors in oral production tasks (Fig. 4). More importantly, and in contrast to KE who made frequent semantic errors in written naming and spelling to dictation, RGB made no semantic errors at all in these writing tasks. His errors in writing were limited to minor spelling errors (Table 10).

TABLE 10
Examples of Responses across Output Tasks

Stimulus	Oral Name	Written Name	Dictation
lemon	sour	+	+
celery	lettuce	celey	celry
clam	octopus	+	+
beet	you eat them pickled	+	+
goose	turkey	+	+
banana	apple	banna	+
pear	apple	+	+
sponge	table cloth	+	spoge

+ = correct response

Conclusions from RGB.   The semantic errors produced by RGB could not have arisen at the level of the semantic component, as was proposed for KE, because he apparently activated intact semantic representations in the comprehension and writing tasks. Instead, the reported pattern of performance indicates that RGB's semantic errors arise in a component specific to oral production—either in activating phonological representations (in the phonological output lexicon) or in articulatory processes. RGB's fluent, rapid speech, with no phonemic or articulatory errors, speaks against a deficit in motor planning or execution. Instead, his errors seem to arise in the course of activating or selecting a lexical phonological representation[4].

One possible difficulty with our account of RGB's errors has been raised by Garrett (1992). In Caramazza and Hillis (1990) we reported that RGB was more impaired in naming pictures and words in categories of "living things" relative to artefacts. This finding would not be predicted by damage at the level of the phonological output lexicon, as there is no theoretical reason for assuming that the output lexicon would be organised by semantic category. Garrett proposed an alternative account of RGB's semantic errors which, he argued, could account for the observed semantic category effects. He hypothesised that RGB's disruption in lexical processing is at the level of lemma representations—a level of representation between semantic/conceptual representations and orthographic and phonological lexical representation (see also Butterworth, 1989; Kempen & Huijbers, 1983; Nickels & Howard, 1994). Presumably, lemmas might be organised by semantic category. However, impairment at the level of the lemma cannot account for RGB's spared written naming of items that elicit errors in oral naming, as the lemma activates both phonological and orthographic lexical representations for output. Garrett offered two possible explanations of RGB's production of semantic errors in oral naming but not in written naming. One account—that written naming exceeded spoken naming because written naming is slower (and perhaps more often self-corrected) than oral naming—cannot explain RGB's performance, as RGB often produced an incorrect spoken name even after having produced it correctly in writing. Garrett's second account is that RGB's difficulty arises in the "linkage" between the lemma representations and phonological representations. Although we have no data that would allow us to reject this hypothesis, it is unclear what is gained by proposing damage to a link between an intermediate, lemma representation and the phonological representation, over proposing damage to a direct link between a lexical semantic representation and a phonological representation (which might also account for semantic category effects). Moreover, an alternative to our account

---

[4] Note that like KE, RGB was profoundly impaired in converting print to sound using sublexical orthography-to-phonology conversion (OPC) procedures. If he were not, we would have expected fewer errors (and especially fewer semantic errors) in oral reading tasks, as these mechanisms could have been employed in activating phonological representations for output in reading (see Hillis & Caramazza, 1991, 1995, for detailed discussion).

that RGB's semantic errors in oral production arise from damage at the level of the lexical–phonological representation is only necessary if the effect of living things versus nonliving things in naming performance truly reflects the variable of "semantic category" and not some other variable that might affect processing at the level of the phonological output lexicon.

One such account of the category effects in RGB's naming is that living things and nonliving things vary with respect to processing complexity as predicted by such variables as familiarity, frequency, and visual complexity (Funnell & Sheridan, 1992; Riddoch & Humphreys, 1987; Stewart, Parkin, & Hunkin, 1992). In our original analysis we tested for frequency effects and found that although RGB's performance was affected by this variable, frequency alone did not account for the category effects, as they persisted when frequency was controlled. A second variable that could also give rise to spurious category-specific effects is familiarity (Funnell & Sheridan, 1992; Stewart et al., 1992). A post-hoc analysis of RGB's naming performance as a function of familiarity was carried out for all items for which familiarity norms were available. RGB was far more accurate in naming items with "high familiarity" than "low familiarity" scores (24/29 *vs.* 12/35; $\chi^2 = 15.24$ $P < 0.0001$). More importantly, there were no significant differences between living things versus nonliving things, when frequency and familiarity were controlled (Table 11). On a subset of items, in which living things were closely matched to nonliving things in both frequency and familiarity, performance on living and nonliving things was identical (9/14, or 64% correct for each). It would appear, then, that our earlier report of a "semantic category" effect in RGB's naming performance is an artefact of differences in familiarity between the items included in the living and nonliving things categories. This result removes a potential obstacle to the explanation we offered for RGB's production of semantic errors as arising from selective damage to the phonological output lexicon.

TABLE 11
RGB's Accuracy in Naming Living and Nonliving Things

	Living Things		Nonliving Things	
High Familiarity				
medium frequency	4/4	(100)	14/16	(88)
low frequency	2/5	(40)	4/4	(100)
Low Familiarity				
medium frequency	3/9	(33)	0/1	(0)
low frequency	7/20	(33)	2/5	(40)

GENERAL DISCUSSION

We have shown that the semantic errors produced by KE, DHY, and RGB in each case come from damage to a different component of the naming process. However, the similar quality of their errors is unlikely to be a chance phenomenon, despite the fact that they arise from damage at different levels of the lexical processing system. Indeed, we will argue that the similar quality of errors probably reflects the structure of semantic representations (KE), the way in which they are activated by visual input (DHY), and how they serve to activate lexical representations for output (RGB). We discuss these claims in the context of a model of the cognitive processes underlying picture naming. A schematic representation of this model is depicted in Fig. 4.

Following Marr (1982) we assume that visual processing of an object (or picture of an object) requires computation of a series of representations of the visual stimulus, beginning with a retinotopically organised representation of the variations in light intensities and culminating with a 3-D model of the object that is independent of both the location of the object in the visual field and the rotation of the object in space. Accurate computation of a 3-D model requires access to stored information—a "structural description" of familiar objects. We assume that the structural description specifies colour, size, and other visual features of familiar instances of objects. For example, the structural description of toothbrush might include features specifying [bristles], [handle], [6–8 inches long], and so on. By hypothesis, computation of a 3-D model that matches a stored structural description would support "recognition" of a stimulus as a familiar object[5].

We further propose that the structural description "as a whole" (just like lexical orthographic or phonological representations) activates a semantic representation—the set of functional, perceptual, and other features that jointly constitute the meaning of the name of an object. For example, the semantic representation of toothbrush might include features like <for brushing>, <for cleaning>, <for teeth>, , <hand-held>, and so on. It is this level of representation that specifies which individual instances correspond to a specific semantic category. That is, at the level of the semantic representation, but not at the level of the structural description, there would be information for determining that

---

[5] As we can recognise "my toothbrush" versus "my daughter's toothbrush", we must also have stored structural descriptions of individual instances of objects. In this example, the stored, structural description of "my toothbrush" might include information like colour that does not pertain to all toothbrushes. It is unclear whether the structural descriptions of individual, familiar instances need to be encoded independently in the brain. As many structural features of "my toothbrush" and "my daughter's toothbrush" and many other visually similar items would overlap, the activation of the structural description of an individual toothbrush might well constitute activation of the collection of structural features (some of which would also be activated in recognising any other toothbrush or other visually similar item, whereas other features would be specific to that instance of toothbrush).

350

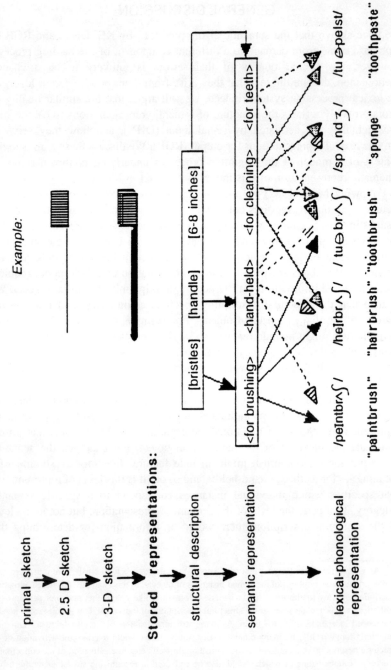

FIG. 5.   A model of the cognitive processes underlying visual object naming.

"my toothbrush" and "my daughter's toothbrush" are both instances of the concept "toothbrush". In the case of toothbrush, a feature specifying a particular colour would not be stored in the semantic representation, as a particular colour is not a general property of toothbrushes (but would be specified at the level of the structural description of an individual toothbrush). However, colour information would be specified in the semantic representation of those items that have a characteristic colour. For instance, <yellow> would be a component of the semantic representation of "lemon", as the colour is important in differentiating a lemon from a semantically related item, "lime".

A further assumption of the model is that in addition to the whole access procedure (in which the complete semantic representation is accessed from the complete structural description), we propose that the individual features of a structural description activate individual semantic features of the semantic representation of a lexical item (see Caramazza, Hillis, Rapp, & Romani, 1990, for detailed discussion of the Organised Unitary Content Hypothesis—OUCH). For example, the feature [bristles] in the structural description of toothbrush might activate the features of the semantic representation <bristles> and <for brushing>. Although "bristles" are a part of both the structural description and the semantic representation, the structural feature [bristles] is quite different from the semantic feature . The former simply specifies what the feature looks like (e.g. stiff, cylindrical appendages with a tiny diameter), whereas the latter specifies *also* a common use. Thus, the structural feature [bristles] would not in itself support a gesture or action (such as scrubbing or brushing), but might serve to activate a semantic feature that would support such a gesture or action (even if the complete semantic representation of the object was not accessible).

Certain forms of brain damage, as in the case of DHY, might interfere with the activation of the complete semantic representation from the structural description. (Furthermore, such a lesion might also interfere with activation of some of individual semantic features directly from features of the structural description). To illustrate, in response to a pictured toothbrush, DHY might be able to correctly compute a complete structural description but fail to access the complete semantic representation. However, some of the features of the structural description (say, the structural feature corresponding to the bristles) might still activate their associated semantic features (in this case, <bristles> and <for brushing>). In this way, DHY would only have accessed an incomplete semantic representation. This incomplete set of semantic features, say, <bristles> and <for brushing> might be equally compatible with the responses "hairbrush", "paintbrush", "pastry brush", "clothes brush", and so on, if the distinguishing feature of toothbrush—<for teeth>—could not be activated from the structural description. KE, on the other hand, might also only have access to incomplete semantic information, but as a consequence of damage at the level of the semantic representation itself. Thus, for both DHY and KE, a visually presented object (say, toothbrush) might lead to the activation of an incomplete semantic representation with the consequence that a semantically related word (say, "paintbrush") would be incorrectly accepted as the name of that object.

Continuing with this model, the individual features of the semantic representation, in turn, activate every phonological representation with which they are associated. In our example <for brushing> would normally activate phonological representations such as "toothbrush", "hairbrush", 'clothes brush" and so on; <hand-held> would activate phonological representations such as "toothbrush", "fork", and "razor"; <for teeth> would activate phonological representations like "toothbrush", "toothpaste", "dental floss"; <for cleaning> would activate phonological representations such as "tooth-brush", "sponge", "broom"; and <plastic> would activate "toothbrush" and a host of other phonological representations. Assuming that all is well with the neural mechanism responsible for this processing, the phonological representa-tion "toothbrush" would receive the greatest activation from the set of semantic features of toothbrush. So, normally a toothbrush is called "toothbrush". But in the case where brain damage affects activation of a subset of the semantic features either because they are damaged (as proposed for KE) or because they cannot be accessed from vision (as proposed for DHY), several phonological representations consistent with the spared features might be activated roughly equally. For example, if DHY or KE failed to activate the feature <for teeth>, but did activate features like <for brushing>, <hand held>, and <plastic>, the phonological representations of "toothbrush", "hairbrush", and "pastry brush" would be equally activated. This situation would account for the inconsistent production of correct names and various semantically related names in response to the same items in object naming by both patients.

But suppose that brain damage were to affect not the activation of semantic features but the activation of phonological representations for output (as proposed for RGB). In this case, processing of a picture would be spared through the level of activation of a complete semantic representation, and so performance on comprehension tasks such as word/picture verification would be unimpaired. Furthermore, each semantic feature would activate to some degree its corresponding phonological representations. So, again, <for brushing>, <for cleaning>, <for teeth>, and so on would at least partially activate phonological representations of "toothbrush", "hairbrush", "sponge", "toothpaste", etc., but of these, only the phonological representation of "toothbrush" would be activated by all of the semantic features of toothbrush. If the target phonological representation of "toothbrush" were unavailable (or had an excessively high "threshold of activation" or excessively low "resting state of activation") a more readily available phonological representation that received partial activation (say, "hairbrush"), might be selected for further processing and produced as a response. In this way, we can account for the production of semantic errors by patients like RGB who demonstrate unimpaired comprehension with both words and picture stimuli (Caramazza & Hillis, 1990).

Another feature of the three patients' patterns of errors can be neatly accounted for by this model. KE, DHY, and RGB all tended to produce names of objects as semantic errors that were of relatively higher frequency than the target (see Table 2). Our model predicts this response pattern for each patient, for different reasons. KE and DHY would be expected to access impoverished semantic representations, due to impairment at the level of the semantic system (in the case of KE) or impairment in access to the semantic system from the structural description (in the case of DHY). Such an incomplete semantic representation would equally activate a number of phonological representations consistent with the residual semantic features. The phonological representation that is selected for further processing might well be the highest-frequency representation among those that are activated. Thus, both KE and DHY would tend to produce relatively high-frequency names as semantic errors. RGB, on the other hand, would be expected to access a complete semantic representation, which in turn would activate a number of phonological representations. Even though the target phonological representation would receive the greatest activation from the semantic representation in his case, it might not be selected for further processing due to damage (e.g. raised thresholds of activation) at this level of processing. He would instead select a more available phonological representation, which might well be the highest-frequency representation that was activated, even partially, by the complete semantic information. Thus, RGB, too, would be expected to produce relatively high-frequency semantic errors.

Although the model we have outlined here is still very poorly developed and speculative in many respects it can account for the production of semantic errors as a result of damage to input processes (activation of semantic representations from structural descriptions in visual processing, as proposed for DHY), damage at the level of semantic representations (as in KE), or damage to the level of output representations (as in RGB). Furthermore, the multi-component model proposed here has important advantages over those models that propose a unitary account of the production of semantic errors. Specifically, our model can account for the differences between patterns of performance across lexical tasks in patients who all make seemingly identical types of errors. To illustrate, KE and RGB might both be classified as "deep dyslexics" by virtue of the fact that they both made semantic errors in reading, failed to read pseudowords, and showed effects of grammatical word class and frequency in reading accuracy. But we have shown that different loci of impairment in the lexical system must be proposed to account for their semantic errors in reading. Models that attempt to provide a unitary account of "deep dyslexia" (e.g. Plaut & Shallice, 1993) fail to explain the contrast between RGB's accurate comprehension of words he reads as semantic errors versus KE's impaired comprehension (quantitatively equivalent to his impaired production) of words he reads as semantic errors.

In summary, the model of object naming we have described, an elaboration of the OUCH hypothesis (Caramazza et al., 1990), remains grossly underdeveloped. Nevertheless, the proposals that (1) a lexical semantic representation consists of a set of features that overlap with features of other semantic representations, and (2) features of a "structural description" individually access corresponding features of a semantic representation, which in turn individually activate corresponding lexical phonological representations for output, provide the basis for explaining the production of semantic errors as a consequence of damage at any of these three levels of representation. That is, this model can account for the production of semantic errors as a result of damage to input processes (as proposed for DHY), damage at the level of semantic representation (as in KE), or damage to the level of output representations (as in RGB). Furthermore, our proposal can account for the homogeneity in the quality of semantic errors that arise from different sources of damage. And, in contrast to unitary accounts of the production of semantic errors, this model also provides a principled account not only for the similarities, but also the differences, in patterns of semantic errors resulting from brain damage.

REFERENCES

Barry, C., & Newton, P. (1994). *Concreteness effects in the production of semantic errors in reading.* Paper presented at the Twelfth European Workshop on Cognitive Neuropsychology, Bressanone, Italy.

Beauvois, M.F. (1982). Optic aphasia: A process of interaction between vision and language. *Philosophical Transactions of the Royal Society of London, B 289,* 35–47.

Beauvois, M.F., & Derouesné, J. (1981). Lexical or orthographic agraphia. *Brain, 104,* 21–49.

Beauvois, M.F., & Saillant, B. (1985). Optic aphasia for colours and colour agnosia: A distinction between visual and visuo-verbal impairments in the processing of colours. *Cognitive Neuropsychology, 2,* 1–48.

Brown, R., & McNeil, D. (1966). The "tip of the tongue" phenomenon. *Journal of Verbal Learning and Verbal Behavior, 5,* 325–337.

Butterworth, B. (1981). Speech errors: old data in search of new theories. *Linguistics, 19,* 627–662.

Butterworth, B. (1983). Lexical representation. In B. Butterworth (Ed.), *Language production, Vol. 2.* (pp. 257–294). London: Academic Press.

Butterworth, B. (1989). Lexical access in speech production. In W. Marslen-Wilson (Ed.), *Lexical representation and process.* Cambridge, MA: MIT Press.

Butterworth, B., Howard, D., & McLoughlin, P. (1984). The semantic deficit in aphasia: The relationship between semantic errors in auditory comprehension and picture naming. *Neuropsychologia, 22,* 409–426.

Caramazza, A., & Hillis, A.E. (1990). Where do semantic errors come from? *Cortex, 26,* 95–122.

Caramazza, A., Hillis, A.E., Rapp, B.C., & Romani, C. (1990). The multiple semantics hypothesis: Multiple confusions? *Cognitive Neuropsychology, 7,* 161–190.

Caramazza, A., & Miceli, G. (1990). The structure of orthographic representations. *Cognition, 37,* 243–297.

Coltheart, M. (1980). The semantic error: Types and theories. In M. Coltheart, K.E. Patterson, & J.C. Marshall (Eds.), *Deep dyslexia.* London: Routledge & Kegan Paul.

Coslett, H.B., & Saffran, E.M. (1989). Preserved object recognition and reading comprehension in optic aphasia. *Brain, 112,* 1091–1110.

Coslett, H.B., & Saffran, E.M. (1992). Optic aphasia and the right hemisphere: a replication and extension *Brain and Language*, *43*, 148–161.

Dell, G.S. (1989). The retrieval of phonological forms in production: Tests of predictions from a connectionist model. In W. Marslen-Wilson (Ed.), *Lexical representation and process*. Cambridge, MA: MIT Press.

Ellis, A. (1988). Normal writing processes and peripheral acquired dysgraphias. *Language and Cognitive Processes*, *3*, 99–127.

Funnel, E. & Sheridan, J. (1992). Categories of knowledge? Unfamiliar aspects of living and nonliving things. *Cognitive Neuropsychology*, *9*, 135–153.

Garrett, M.F. (1980). Levels of processing in sentence production. In B. Butterworth (Ed.), *Language production, Vol. 1*. (pp. 177–210). London: Academic Press.

Garrett, M.F. (1992). Disorders of lexical selection. *Cognition*, *42*, 143–180.

Goodman, R.A., & Caramazza, A. (1986). Phonologically plausible errors: Implications for a model of the phoneme–grapheme conversion mechanism in the spelling process. In G. Augst (Ed.), *Proceedings of the International Colloquium on Graphemics & Orthography*, pp. 300–325.

Hillis, A.E., & Caramazza, A. (1991). Mechanisms for accessing lexical representations for output: Evidence from a category specific semantic deficit. *Brain and Language*, *40*, 106–144.

Hillis, A.E., & Caramazza, A. (1995). Converging evidence for the interaction of semantic and phonological information in accessing lexical information for spoken output. *Cognitive Neuropsychology*, *12*, 187–227.

Hillis, A.E., & Caramazza, A. (in press). Cognitive and neural mechanisms underlying visual and semantic processing: Implications from "Optic Aphasia". *Journal of Cognitive Neuroscience*.

Hillis, A.E., Rapp, B.C., & Caramazza, A. (1995). Constraining claims about theories of semantic memory: More on unitar⟍ s. multiple semantics. *Cognitive Neuropsychology*, *12*, 175–186.

Hillis, A.E., Rapp, B., Romani, C., & Caramazza, A. (1990). Selective impairments of semantics in lexical processing. *Cognitive Neuropsychology*, *7*, 191–243.

Hinton, G.E., & Shallice, T. (1991). Lesioning an attractor network: Investigations of acquired dyslexia. *Psychological Review*, *98*, 74–95.

Howard, D., & Orchard-Lisle, V. (1984). On the origin of semantic errors in naming: Evidence from a case of a global aphasic. *Cognitive Neuropsychology*, *1*, 163–190.

Kay, J., & Ellis, A.W. (1987). A cognitive neuropsychological case study of anomia: Implications for psychological models of word retrieval. *Brain*, *110*, 613–629.

Kempen, G., & Huijbers, P. (1983). The lexicalisation process in sentence production and naming: Indirect selection of words. *Cognition*, *14*, 185–209.

Levelt, W.J.M. (1983). Monitoring and self-repair in speech. *Cognition*, *14*, 41–104.

Levelt, W.J.M. (1989). *Speaking: From intention to articulation*. Cambridge, M.A.: MIT Press.

Lhermitte, E., & Beauvois, M.F. (1973). A visual–speech disconnexion syndrome: report of a case with optic aphasia, agnosic alexia and colour agnosia. *Brain*, *96*, 695–714.

Manning, L., & Campbell, R. (1992). Optic aphasia with spared action naming: a description and possible loci of impairment. *Neuropsychologia*, *30*, 587–592.

Marr, D. (1982). *Vision*. New York: W.H. Freeman & Co.

Nickels, L., & Howard, D. (1994). A frequent occurrence? Factors affecting the production of semantic errors in aphasic naming. *Cognitive Neuropsychology*, *11* (3), 289–320.

Peña-Casanova, J., Roig-Rovira, T., Bermudez, A., & Toloso-Sarro, E. (1985). Optic aphasia, optic apraxia, and loss of dreaming. *Brain and Language*, *26*, 63–71.

Plaut, D., & Shallice, T. (1993). Deep dyslexia: A case study of connectionist neuropsychology. *Cognitive Neuropsychology*, *10*, 377–500.

Riddoch, M.J., & Humphreys, G.W. (1987). Visual optic processing in optic aphasia: A case of semantic access agnosia. *Cognitive Neuropsychology*, *4*, 131–185.

Snodgrass, J.G., & Vanderwart, M. (1980). A standardised set of 260 pictures: Norms for name agreement, image agreement, familiarity and visual complexity. *Journal of experimental psychology: Human learning and memory, 6,* 174–214.

Stewart, F., Parkin, A.J., & Hunkin, N.M. (1992). Naming impairments following recovery from herpes simplex encephalitis: category specific? *Quarterly Journal of Experimental Psychology, 44A,* 261–284.

APPENDIX

Examples of Nonobjects in Object Decision Task

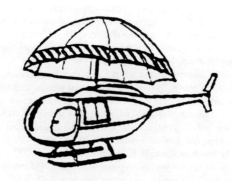

Example of DHY's Copy of an Upside Down Object

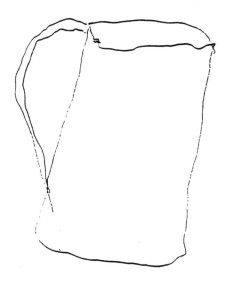

Examples of DHY's Drawings, in Response to the
Name of the Object

cat:

ashtray:

car:

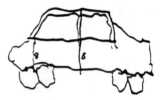

camel:

MEMORY, 1995, 3 (3/4), 359–395

Investigating Semantic Memory Impairments: The Contribution of Semantic Priming

Helen E. Moss and Lorraine K. Tyler

Birkbeck College, London

The semantic priming task is a valuable tool in the investigation of semantic memory impairments in patients with acquired disorders of language. This is because priming performance reflects automatic or implicit access to semantic information, unlike most other tests of semantic knowledge, which rely on explicit, voluntary access. Priming results are important for two main reasons: First, normal priming results may be observed in patients who perform poorly on other semantic memory tests, enabling us to distinguish between loss of, or damage to, information in semantic memory, and voluntary access to that information. Second, we can investigate the detailed pattern of loss and preservation of different types of semantic information, by charting the priming effects for different kinds of words, and different kinds of semantic relations between primes and targets.

We discuss the use of the priming task in this context, and address some of the theoretical and methodological criticisms that have been raised in connection with use of the priming task to address these issues. We then describe two recent studies in which we have employed semantic priming tasks, along with other more traditional methods, to investigate specific questions about the semantic memory deficits of three patients.

INTRODUCTION

Impairments of semantic memory—our long-term store of conceptual knowledge about the meanings of words, as well as about objects and events in the world—have been reported for patients with a variety of acquired disorders of language. Semantic memory impairments are commonly accompanied by other linguistic deficits, as in aphasia (e.g. Howard & Franklin, 1988; Zurif, Caramazza, Myerson, & Galvin, 1974), and cognitive deficits, as in dementia of the Alzheimer's type (Chertkow & Bub, 1990; Hodges, Salmon, & Butters,

Requests for reprints should be sent to Helen Moss, Department of Psychology, Birkbeck College, University of London, Malet Street, London WC1E 7HX, UK. E-mail: ubjta42@bbk.ac.uk

This research was partly supported by a Medical Research Council programme grant to Lorraine K. Tyler and William Marslen-Wilson, a Medical Research Council project grant to John Hodges and Lorraine K. Tyler, and a British Academy research fellowship to Helen Moss. We are grateful to Mary Cooke, Naida Graham, and Frances Jennings for their assistance with this research, and to Karalyn Patterson and John Hodges for their collaboration on the first study.

1992; Huff, Corkin, & Growden, 1986). In other cases, semantic memory can be affected with relatively little damage to other linguistic and cognitive functions, most notably in patients with semantic dementia (Hodges, Patterson, Oxbury, & Funnell, 1992; Schwartz, Marin, & Saffran, 1979; Snowden, Goulding, & Neary, 1989; Warrington, 1975).

Semantic memory impairments have generated a great deal of interest in cognitive neuropsychology because of the light that the nature of impairments may shed on the organisation of the semantic store, and on the content and structure of semantic representations. For example, the apparent existence of selective impairments of knowledge about specific semantic categories, such as living things, artifacts, or even just fruit and vegetables, has been seen as evidence that semantic memory is highly structured according to these different content domains (e.g. Sachett & Humphreys, 1992; Warrington & McCarthy, 1987; Warrington & Shallice, 1984), and modality-specific semantic impairments have been taken as evidence for multiple semantic systems (Shallice, 1988a, b; Warrington, 1975). These kinds of claims continue to generate lively debate, and several alternative accounts have been put forward (e.g. Funnell & Sheridan, 1992; Riddoch, Humphreys, Coltheart, & Funnell, 1988).

A central problem in the interpretation of semantic memory impairments is that it is often difficult to be certain that a patient's performance reflects a true disorder of semantic memory—that is, loss or disruption of stored representations—rather than problems involving the access or retrieval of this information. Most tasks designed to probe the nature of semantic memory cannot distinguish between central semantic storage impairments and disorders of voluntary access to semantic information. This is because, as well as involving stored semantic knowledge, such tasks require an additional element—voluntary access or retrieval of that knowledge. For example, in order to sort pictures into category groups, a person must not only know which pictured objects belong to the same category, but they must also be able to retrieve the appropriate information, under voluntary control, when required to do so by the experimenter. The possibility that patients may have problems with the voluntary access of semantic information makes it more difficult to draw inferences about the loss or sparing of underlying semantic representations.

Our aim in this paper is to demonstrate that the appropriate use of on-line tasks, in particular semantic priming, can provide insights into the nature of semantic memory impairments that cannot be garnered from the use of traditional off-line tasks alone. The reason for this is that semantic priming taps automatic or implicit access to semantic representations, rather than voluntary access. It is possible for stored semantic information to be intact and accessible in an implicit, automatic task like priming, but for that same information to be inaccessible to voluntary access processes which have been disrupted in some way. Thus, we can compare priming data with data from off-line tasks in order to discriminate between problems of storage and problems of voluntary access. Moreover, we can investigate the detailed pattern of loss and preservation of different types of semantic information, by charting the priming effects for different kinds of words, and different kinds of semantic relations between primes and targets.

This is not to claim that the priming task is without pitfalls (although most of these can be avoided, as we argue later), or that it should replace other tasks entirely—indeed we will suggest that the most fruitful approach is to make use of both kinds of task in concert—but rather that data from priming can make a unique contribution to our understanding of semantic memory, both in characterising the functional impairments of different patients and in understanding the normal system.

The remainder of the paper is organised as follows: in the first section we discuss in more detail the issue of distinguishing impairments of semantic representation and access. We then examine the use of the semantic priming task in this context, identifying a number of theoretical and methodological issues that need to be addressed. Finally, we describe two of our recent studies, which illustrate the use of the priming paradigm in exploring semantic memory. The first investigates the nature of the ''loss of semantic memory'' in a patient with semantic dementia, and the second concerns knowledge of abstract and concrete word meanings in two non-fluent aphasic, deep dyslexic patients. In each study we discuss the implications of the findings for accounts of representation and processing in the normal semantic system as well as the functional impairments of the individual patients.

IMPAIRMENTS OF ACCESS AND STORAGE

The difficulty associated with distinguishing between storage and access deficits of semantic memory has led to discussions of how we might discriminate between them (Shallice, 1988a, b; Warrington & Shallice, 1979). On the one hand, it is relatively straightforward to identify access deficits that are specific to one modality of input (and similarly, to identify modality-specific production deficits, which could also be a confounding factor). This requires the testing of patients with a range of different tasks that probe semantic knowledge via different input and output modalities—typically picture matching to a written or spoken word, naming to a picture or written or spoken word, relatedness judgments, picture sorting, and so on. An example of a modality-specific access problem identified on this basis is provided by Franklin, Howard, and Patterson (1994) in a study of a patient with abstract word deafness. Where a patient has a problem across the range of tasks, a modality-specific access problem can be ruled out, as for example, for the semantic dementia patients studied by Hodges et al. (1992a).

We should note here that we are referring to modality-specificity *within* the verbal domain, e.g. to written versus spoken words, rather than to the distinction between verbal and visual inputs in general. When patients have shown dissociations between recognition of objects/pictures and understanding of the corresponding verbal labels, this has sometimes been interpreted as a modality-specific access deficit (e.g. Riddoch et al., 1988), but other researchers have claimed that there is a storage impairment to one or other of multiple semantic systems, suggesting that there are separate visual and verbal (and possibly other) semantic stores (e.g. Shallice 1988b; Warrington, 1975). Our current discussions concern only verbal inputs. We believe that it is implausible to attribute a deficit in, say, comprehension of spoken words but not written words, to an impairment in the semantic store for spoken language, while the meanings of the same words are preserved in a separate semantic store for written language, and we also believe that modality-specific deficits within the verbal domain can be interpreted as clear evidence that the impairment is one of access rather than storage.

Generalised modality-*independent* access deficits are not so straightforwardly isolated. Where a patient shows a semantic deficit across different input and output modalities, the possibility remains that this does not reveal loss or degradation of information in semantic memory, but rather a modality-independent problem with accessing that information under voluntary control. The distinction between voluntary or effortful and automatic access is an important one in memory research (Hasher & Zacks, 1979) and has been valuable in studies of acquired language disorders (Chenery, Ingram, & Murdoch, 1990; Tyler, 1992). All the tasks standardly used to investigate memory impairments (picture-pointing, sorting, category fluency, and so on) involve voluntary access to, and reflection on, semantic representations. One approach to disentangling disorders of storage and access was provided by Warrington and Shallice (1979) who suggested a number of criteria for identifying the two kinds of impairment. They argued that a patient with a central storage disorder would show consistency of errors on individual items across tasks and testing sessions, relative preservation of superordinate over feature-level knowledge, and a frequency effect, but no effect of semantic priming (or more correctly, cueing). Warrington and McCarthy (1983) added the additional criterion that such patients would also show no effect of rate of presentation of materials. An access disorder would be revealed by the opposite pattern of performance. These criteria have been widely applied, although often only a subset of the criteria have been tested for individual patients (e.g. Butterworth, Howard, & McLoughlin, 1984; Chertkow & Bub, 1990; Hillis, Rapp, Romani, & Caramazza, 1990; Warrington & Shallice, 1984). However, the validity of this approach has recently been questioned, most notably by Rapp and Caramazza (1993) (see also Riddoch et al., 1988). The central problem is that, depending on the specific model of semantic representation and access adopted, the supposedly distinguishing patterns of performance may be consistent with either storage or access deficits.

Although we agree with many of the points made by Rapp and Caramazza (1993), we believe that semantic priming performance is less vulnerable to their critique than the other criteria. Moreover, because the semantic priming task reflects automatic rather than voluntary access to semantic information, it enables us to tap into semantic representation in a different way from other tasks. In this paper we focus only on this on-line version of semantic priming. In some studies, the term semantic priming has been used synonymously with semantic cueing, in which subjects are prompted with a related cue word when they are unable to name a picture, for example. Although this has some properties in common with priming, it is not an on-line task, as subjects are still required to access information under voluntary control, and the relation between the cue and the target is explicit. The patterns of performance in cueing and priming tasks have been shown to differ (Chertkow & Bub, 1990). In the following section we discuss the priming task as a probe of semantic memory impairment in more detail, and address potential theoretical and methodological problems, including those raised by Rapp and Caramazza.

SEMANTIC PRIMING AND AUTOMATIC ACCESS

Semantic priming involves automatic, implicit access to semantic information, rather than voluntary, explicit retrieval. Subjects are asked to make a timed response, such as lexical decision or naming, to a target word. The latency and accuracy of this response are measured as a function of the preceding prime word. It has frequently been demonstrated that when the prime word is semantically or associatively related (e.g. *cat–DOG*), responses to the target are facilitated compared to the baseline condition in which the preceding word is unrelated (e.g. *pen–DOG*), both for young (e.g. Meyer & Schvaneveldt, 1971; Moss, Ostrin, Tyler, & Marslen-Wilson, in press; for a review see Neely, 1991) and older adult subjects (Burke, White, & Diaz, 1987; Ostrin & Tyler, 1993). Priming is believed to tap implicit, automatic access because subjects are not instructed to pay attention to the relation between prime and target—in fact, pains are taken to try to obscure the relation by the use of unrelated filler items. Facilitation of the target by the preceding prime appears to stem from automatic processes, of which the subject may be completely unaware. Thus priming can be used to assess the nature of underlying semantic representations without involving controlled access processes.

Several different accounts have been put forward to explain the priming effects found in the normal system (for a review see Neely, 1991). These include spread of activation between related concepts in a semantic network (Collins & Loftus, 1975), perseveration of activation of overlapping microfeatures in a distributed memory system (Masson, 1991), and the use of prime and target to form a compound cue to search semantic memory (McKoon & Ratcliff, 1992). On all such accounts (and it is beyond the current scope to try to distinguish between them) priming is based on automatic, non-conscious processes. We should note here that several non-automatic components of priming have been suggested, such as generation of expectancy sets and semantic matching (see Neely, 1991 for a review). However, it is clear that these account for only a part of the facilitation found in most cases, (e.g. Fischler, 1977a; Posner & Snyder, 1975) and also that the contribution of "strategic effects" can be reduced in various ways, such as having a low proportion of related items in the list (e.g. de Groot, 1984; Tweedy, Lapinski, & Schvaneveldt, 1977) and a short delay between prime and target (de Groot, 1984).[1]

Therefore we can use the priming task to provide evidence as to whether a patient's impairment in off-line tests of semantic knowledge results from loss or damage to representations in semantic memory, or a disruption in the process of accessing those representations under voluntary control. If the disorder is one of representation, we would not expect to find normal semantic priming effects, as information that is lost or damaged will be inaccessible (or difficult to access) to automatic access as well as to voluntary access. On the other hand, if the impairment is one of voluntary access to intact underlying representations, then normal priming is predicted, supported by automatic access. This rationale has now been applied in several studies of semantic impairment, in which performance in a priming task has been compared with that in off-line tasks, most frequently for patients with Alzheimer's dementia (e.g. Chertkow, Bub, & Seidenberg, 1989; Glosser & Friedman, 1991; Nebes, Martin, & Horn, 1984).

However, it is important to note that a lack of priming effects for a patient in a particular task does not, by itself, necessarily implicate a central semantic storage deficit. In certain cases it could be that the lack of priming stems from a disruption of the automatic access processes that underpin priming effects. This claim has been made by Milberg and Blumstein and colleagues for a group of nonfluent aphasic patients (Blumstein, Milberg, & Shrier, 1982; Milberg & Blumstein, 1981). These patients did not show significant semantic priming effects in a visual lexical decision study. Rather than interpreting this as a semantic storage deficit, the authors argued that nonfluent aphasics have problems with the automatic activation of lexical information. One variant of this claim is that the activation processes are abnormally slow, so that priming is not observed at short delays. The basis of the claim that the lack of priming stems from disruption of automatic access rather than loss of information within semantic memory, is that the nonfluent patients performed well in a semantic relatedness judgment task on the same word-pairs as used in the priming task, demonstrating that they were able to access the meanings of the words in a task where speed of automatic activation was not a crucial factor.

---

[1] One of the suggested strategic priming mechanisms is post-lexical semantic matching—that is, trying to integrate the target with the prime to give a coherent meaning. It is arguable that this is in fact an automatic rather than strategic process, and reflects the normal processes of language comprehension, i.e. integrating the successive words of an utterance (Hodgson, 1991).

Although we have argued against this particular version of the automaticity hypothesis (Tyler, Ostrin, Cooke, & Moss, 1995), it highlights the point that an absence of semantic priming can be due to a disruption of automatic access processes as well as to loss or damage to semantic representations. For this reason, it is vital that priming studies are carried out, not in isolation, but in conjunction with a range of tasks that reflect voluntary access, and which do not rely on real-time automatic activation processes being completely unimpaired. If a patient does not show priming, but performs well in off-line tasks, disruption of automatic access may be the correct account. However, if there is no priming and a patient also performs poorly in off-line tasks, then it is more likely that there has been damage to the underlying semantic representations.

Both sets of priming studies mentioned here—those of semantic memory loss in DAT and of automatic access in nonfluent aphasics—have produced apparently conflicting results and interpretations. However, we believe that this does not reflect a problem inherent in the use of the priming task. One source of the problem is that many of the studies have averaged results over groups of patients classified in different ways, such that different deficits or combinations of deficits in the representation and access of semantic information may be confounded both within and across studies (cf Badecker & Caramazza, 1985). For this reason, our approach is to investigate the priming performance of single patients in detail. In addition, most studies have paid little attention to the types of semantic relation tested, and strength of semantic relation between primes and target, factors that we have found to be crucial to the pattern of results obtained with normal subjects. We return to these points in more detail in the later sections.

THEORETICAL ISSUES IN THE USE OF PRIMING TO PROBE SEMANTIC MEMORY IMPAIRMENTS

Two main kinds of objection have been raised to the use of priming to probe the nature of semantic memory impairments. The first is that priming may reflect ''low-level'' intra-lexical connections rather than access to information within semantic memory (Shallice, 1988a,c, cited in Rapp & Caramazza, 1993). The other is that priming may be supported by semantic representations that are partially degraded, and so may not distinguish a disorder of storage from one of access (Chertkow et al., 1989; Rapp & Caramazza, 1993). We believe that although these are valid concerns, both can be addressed.

The first point is that the priming criterion may conflict with other indices of storage/access disorders because priming could stem from low-level ''pre-semantic'' connections (Shallice, 1988c).This claim rests on the assumption that, in addition to conceptual/semantic representations of the meanings of words, there are also lexical-level representations, encoding the form of the words. This distinction between lexical form and semantic representations is clearly drawn in most models of language comprehension, including the kind of spreading activation network models that have been widely adopted in the priming literature (Collins & Loftus, 1975; McNamara, 1992). On this kind of model, activation may spread between nodes at either the semantic level or at the lexical-form level. It is possible that a patient with loss or damage to semantic representations would still show a normal priming effect, supported by intra-lexical spread of activation rather than activation of representations in semantic memory, and as such the usefulness of priming as a probe of semantic knowledge would be seriously undermined.

Our reply to this point is that this may be true of priming based on associative strength between words, but it cannot account for priming between non-associated semantically related words. Associated word pairs can be identified by the frequency with which the target is given as a response to the prime in association norms (e.g. Moss & Older, in prep.). For example, over 50% of subjects give *dog* as the first word they think of in response to *cat*. Several researchers have argued that association strength reflects the frequent co-occurrence of words in the language, over and above any semantic relation between them (Glosser & Friedman, 1991; Moss, Ostrin, Tyler, & Marslen-Wilson, in press; Shelton & Martin, 1992) and this is supported by findings of correlations between associative strength and co-occurrence of words in large language corpora (Rapp & Wettler, 1991; Spence & Owens, 1990). Thus, it is plausible that priming between strongly associated word stems from spreading activation between lexical representations, with the activation links built up by frequency of co-occurrence.

However, it has also been shown that words that are semantically related in various ways, but share no associative strength, support priming (e.g. Chiarello, Burgess, Richard, & Pollock, 1990; Fischler, 1977b; Moss, Ostrin, Tyler, & Marslen-Wilson, in press). For example, word pairs like *pig–horse*, *broom–floor*, *stick–cane*, which are semantically related in one way or another, but not associated, produce reliable priming effects. We have also demonstrated that priming for associated words differs both quantitatively and qualitatively from priming for words that are purely semantically related, for normal subjects; associative priming is usually greater in magnitude (Moss, Ostrin, Tyler, & Marslen-Wilson, in press), and is less affected by contextual semantic influences (Moss & Marslen-Wilson, 1993; see also Tanenhaus & Lucas, 1987)[2]. It is unlikely that priming for words that are semantically related but share no degree

---

[2] It has recently been claimed that a further distinction can be drawn between semantic and associative priming; that associative priming is automatic, whereas purely semantic priming is based on post-lexical strategic mechanisms (Shelton & Martin, 1992). This was based on a finding of significant priming for associated category co-ordinates (e.g. *cat-dog*) but not purely semantic related co-ordinates (e.g. *pig-horse*) in a visual single-word lexical decision experiment. However, we have recently questioned this claim, and shown that purely semantic priming is obtained in this paradigm for at least some types of semantic relation (Moss, Ostrin, Tyler, & Marslen-Wilson, in press).

of associative strength is underpinned by low-level intra-lexical connections. Therefore, when priming is used to probe the nature of representations in semantic memory, it is essential to separate associated and purely semantically related materials. If significant priming is found for associated conditions only, there are grounds for suggesting that there has been loss or damage within the semantic system, but that lexical-level representations and connections are intact. However, if a patient shows significant priming effects for purely semantically related pairs (as well as associated words) this suggests that priming is tapping truly semantic-level knowledge. Although it is theoretically possible that there is some small degree of lexical co-occurrence for semantically related words, which is too weak to be picked up in association norms, such weak connections are unlikely to contribute greatly to any priming effects observed for such word pairs.

On these grounds, it is possible that intact lexical-level associative connections may be the correct account of the priming results for patients with DAT. Glosser and Friedman (1991) reported a group of patients with DAT who showed associative but not purely semantic priming. Most studies of priming for DAT patients have used strongly associated word pairs (e.g. Nebes et al., 1984) so it is possible that associative links are responsible for these effects. In the one study where non-associated semantically related word pairs were tested, an abnormal pattern of *hyper-priming* was found (for some words at least), suggesting impaired semantic representations (Chertkow et al., 1989).

The second kind of objection to the priming task as a probe of semantic memory, is that priming may be supported even though the semantic representations involved have been impaired in some way: that is, that the presence of priming in a patient may be consistent with a semantic storage impairment rather than an access impairment, as long as we accept that an impairment of storage does not necessarily entail all-or-none loss of semantic representations, but can also be due to partial degradation of some kind.

This point has been made by Rapp and Caramazza (1993). They suggest that a storage deficit may be based on the raising of activation thresholds for the nodes encoding some or all of the features making up a semantic representation. To use their example, the semantic representation for *stool* will include the features (*three legs, for sitting, wooden, no back*), all of which nodes are activated when the word *stool* is heard. On this kind of model, some of the same features will also be activated by semantically similar words (e.g. *table* will include *four legs* and *wooden*) and this is the basis for priming. One account of damage to stored representations in this model is that the activation thresholds for some feature nodes are elevated, such that, when for example *stool* is heard, its features will not be ''recognised''. But the prior presentation of a related prime will provide additional activation to the feature nodes it shares with the target. This additional activation may be sufficient to push the node over the elevated threshold, speeding word recognition, and thus facilitation will be seen. Given this kind of distributed activation model, this is a possibility that seems plausible. Indeed, models of this kind tend to blur the distinction between disorders of representation and access generally.

Chertkow et al., (1989) make a similar claim. They found a pattern of *hyper-priming* for six patients with DAT: that is, very long lexical-decision reaction times and exaggerated priming effects, particularly for those target words that earlier testing had shown to be unknown to the patient, as determined in off-line tasks. The explanation is that damage to a semantic representation led to a long baseline reaction time for a word, and thus it would "stand more to gain" from spreading activation provided by the prime. Similarly, if we adopt the framework that priming in lexical decision is post-lexical, the following account could hold: subjects consult semantic memory before making a decision, with reaction times being slower when the item to be checked has an impaired semantic representation. The presence of the prime word may facilitate this checking (focusing attention on the correct superordinate category)—giving the observed pattern of long reaction times with large priming effects. Although there are other possible accounts of hyper-priming that do not involve degraded semantic representations (for example, there might be difficulties at some point in the word-recognition process, or in the decision making required for lexical decision), Chertkow et al.'s account, like that of Rapp and Caramazza, suggests ways in which partially degraded semantic representations *could* support priming.

If impaired representations can support priming, then performance in the priming paradigm may not be able to distinguish between intact and degraded semantic representations. This would reduce its usefulness as an index of semantic memory impairment or preservation. However, it is possible to distinguish "normal" priming effects based on intact semantic representations, and abnormal priming effects, which may be based on partial, damaged semantic representations. There are two ways in which we can do this. The first rests on the fact that the accounts of priming by partial semantic representations, discussed earlier, all predict abnormally long reaction times to target words in the baseline or control condition (i.e. when they are not preceded by the related primes). It is clear from priming studies with unimpaired subjects, that semantic information is involved at a very early stage in reaction-time tasks such as lexical decision and naming (Balota, Ferraro, & Connor, 1991; James, 1975).[3]

---

[3] There are various possible accounts of the influence of semantic factors in lexical decision. It may be a direct effect in that subjects consult semantic information in order to make their decision; or indirect, because semantic representations are automatically accessed as a by-product of accessing form-representations, and activation from the semantic level feeds back to increase activation level of the form representation (as in an interactive activation model, McClelland & Elman, 1986).

Therefore, degraded semantic representations will make word recognition more difficult, and lexical decision latencies longer, allowing for disproportionately large priming effects when the semantic information is supplemented by the prime. This is the basis of the "stands more to gain" account of the hyper-priming pattern reported by Chertkow et al. We would argue, then, that if a patient shows baseline reaction times and priming effects well *within* the normal range, this indicates "normal" priming based on intact semantic representations, rather than hyper-priming based on degraded representations.

It should be noted that, in spite of the evidence of semantic involvement in lexical decision in normal subjects, access to semantic information is not *necessary* for lexical decision: it would be possible to make the decision as a result of accessing (or failing to access) a lexical form representation only. It is possible that some patients are making lexical decisions in this way, and thus that degraded semantic representations would have no effect on lexical decision latencies. Specifically, degraded semantic representations would not result in the abnormally long baseline reaction times predicted on the hyper-priming account. However, if this were the case, we would not expect to see a semantic priming effect at all in such patients. If semantic information is not involved at any point in the lexical decision response, then it would not be possible for prior access to related semantic information (i.e. the prime) to facilitate that response. A patient performing lexical decision without reference to semantics might be expected to show a similar pattern to normal subjects who have been encouraged to process words very shallowly, by doing a letter search on the visually presented prime. This manipulation appears to eliminate semantic priming, presumably because the meaning of the prime has not been accessed (Henik, Fredrich, & Kellog, 1982).

Therefore, although it is possible that a given patient could be making lexical decisions without accessing semantic information, this would tend to lead to a pattern of no priming, rather than a pattern of hyper-priming. Thus, this possibility does not affect the interpretation of hyper-priming as a possible indicator of degraded semantic representations. What it does highlight, however, is that a finding of an across-the-board absence of semantic priming for a patient does not necessarily indicate loss of semantic information. The lack of priming could result from the patient performing lexical decision without reference to semantic information.

A second way to determine whether priming is based on intact rather than partial semantic representations is to establish that a normal priming effect holds up for a range of different kinds of semantic relationship. For example, if *cat* primes *whiskers*, *kitten*, *pet*, and *black*, as well as *dog*, then this would be strong evidence that there has been no extensive loss of the semantic properties of *cat*, even if the patient is unable to access these kinds of information under voluntary control in an off-line task. On the other hand, we might find a pattern of priming for certain types of semantic information and not others, which would be consistent with an account in terms of partial degradation (extending to the relations that fail to prime) and partial preservation of information (for those relations that support priming). It is important to note that a lack of priming for specific types of semantic information is different from an across-the-board absence of priming. As we discussed in the previous paragraph, a general lack of priming is difficult to interpret because of the possibility of lexical decision without semantic access. However, a lack of priming for specific types of semantic information, in the face of normal priming for other types of semantic information could not be accounted for in this way. Distinguishing between these two patterns is an additional motivation for examining priming for a range of semantic relations.

METHODOLOGICAL ISSUES IN THE USE OF PRIMING TO PROBE SEMANTIC MEMORY

A second set of potential objections to the priming task involve methodological considerations; certain patients may not be able to perform the priming task well enough for reliable results to be obtained. First, many patients with semantic memory impairments will have accompanying reading difficulties (whether these are independent or connected deficits may vary over different patients), and therefore auditory presentation of stimuli will sometimes be necessary. Although the vast majority of priming studies with the unimpaired population have been conducted in the visual domain (see Neely, 1991 for a review), we have found that semantic and associative priming are reliably obtained in the auditory modality for both young (Moss, Ostrin, Tyler, & Marslen-Wilson, in press), and elderly (Tyler, Ostrin, Cooke, & Moss, 1995) normal populations.

However, even when materials are spoken rather than written, some patients find it difficult to perform the standard reaction-time tasks with sufficient speed or accuracy for results to be meaningful. In several studies we have used a lexical decision task. Both fluent and non-fluent aphasic subjects have performed well in this task, with reaction times within or close to the range for age-matched controls. However, high error rates can be a problem, seriously reducing the amount of data left for analysis (for example, in the study of Blumstein et al., 1982, patients in some groups were performing with error rates over 30%). Where this is a problem, several measures can be taken. One is to lengthen the interval between prime and target (ISI) to allow patients more time to process the primes. This can be useful to a certain point, but at longer ISIs the possible contribution of strategic priming effects (in the control population if not the patients themselves) must be considered and controlled for where possible. Another approach is to simplify the task by using a single word presentation procedure rather than the standard prime–target pair task. (Shelton & Martin, 1989; 1992). In this version of the task, all the primes, targets, and fillers are presented in a list and the subject makes a lexical decision to every word, rather than just to the targets. The advantage of this task is that patients do not have to distinguish between the primes to which no response is made, and the targets to which they should make a response. An independent advantage of this task is also that it is thought to minimise strategic priming effects, which is helpful when priming is being used with the express goal of tapping into automatic access. On the other hand, the disadvantage is that the inter-stimulus interval must be long enough to allow for the lexical decision response to be completed, which can necessitate long delays between primes and targets.

For subjects who have difficulty with a lexical decision task, even in the simplified single word presentation task, we have developed a *primed monitoring task*, which we have found to be suitable for use with various patients. In this task, subjects are asked to monitor for a target in a list of words and to press a response button when they hear it. In the primed condition the target is preceded by a related word, and in the control condition the prime is replaced with an unrelated word. Priming is measured as the difference in reaction time to the target in the two conditions, in the standard way. So for example, if the target were DOG, subjects might hear DOOR ... STROLL ... CARROT ... FULL ... CAT ... *DOG* in the primed condition and DOOR ... STROLL ... CARROT ... FULL ... PEN ... *DOG* in the control condition. Studies with control subjects have shown that the priming effects in this task are comparable with those from a lexical decision task. We have also found that many patients with aphasia and semantic dementia are able to perform the task fast and accurately (Moss, Tyler, Hodges, & Patterson, 1995). Moreover, the primed monitoring task provides a means of testing semantic priming in patients with severe semantic impairments who would not be testable under more standard conditions.

In order to provide a suitable estimate of the normal priming effects against which to evaluate the performance of a patient it is, of course, necessary to establish that the priming effects of interest are reliable for a group of age-matched control subjects. Effects should reach significance in analyses of mean reaction times calculated over both subjects and materials. It is also important to establish whether or not patients' responses in both test and control conditions are within the normal range (especially to identify possible hyper-priming effects).

Although the priming effects we report are always highly significant for control groups, it is occasionally the case that an individual control subject shows no priming. A failure to show priming can arise for a variety of reasons; in lexical decision, a subject could possibly adopt a strategy of making lexical decisions without reference to semantic information (as discussed earlier), he or she could have difficulties with the attentional demands of the task, or the decision components of lexical decision. Other factors can arise in different paradigms. For example, in the prime monitoring task, we have found that a few subjects respond so rapidly in the unrelated condition, that there is little room for any speeding-up of reaction times in the related condition. Whatever the cause, this kind of general lack of priming, which occurs for a minority of control subjects, is not problematic for our interpretation of patient data. As we argued earlier, we would not make any claims about the nature of semantic representation and processing only on the basis of an overall lack of priming, exactly because this lack of priming could have numerous causes other than semantic impairment. In cases where we are claiming that there is a semantic impairment, this is based on differential patterns of priming across conditions. In these cases it is always necessary to examine individual control subjects' data to ensure that no control shows the same pattern as a patient; i.e. that the pattern of priming could not be considered normal.

To summarise, priming is a valuable task for probing the nature of semantic memory impairment as it reflects automatic rather than controlled access to semantic representations. If measures are taken to ensure that priming is reflecting more than intra-lexical associations, and to distinguish possible hyper-priming from normal priming, priming experiments can be an important part of neuropsychological study of semantic memory. In the following sections we describe two studies that illustrate some of the ways in which the priming paradigm (in conjunction with other tasks) can contribute to our understanding of the representation and access of semantic information. These examples also show how we have implemented the measures that we have argued to be necessary to address specific theoretical and methodological issues.

1. EXPLORING THE LOSS OF SEMANTIC MEMORY IN SEMANTIC DEMENTIA

Our first example of the use of priming to probe semantic memory impairment concerns a patient, PP, with profound semantic dementia. This study was carried out in collaboration with John Hodges and Karalyn Patterson (Moss, Tyler, Hodges, & Patterson, 1995). Because PP has been described in detail elsewhere (Hodges, Patterson, Oxbury, & Funnell, 1992; Hodges, Patterson, & Tyler, 1994) we give only a brief summary here. See Table 1 for case details.

Semantic dementia refers to a form of progressive aphasia with selective deterioration of semantic memory, accompanied by relative sparing of other linguistic and cognitive abilities (Snowden et al., 1989). A series of studies by Hodges and Patterson and colleagues has charted the extent of PP's semantic memory impairment in detail (Hodges, Patterson, Oxbury, & Funnell, 1992; Hodges et al., 1994). Table 2 shows PP's performance on a battery of tasks designed to probe knowledge of object and word meanings via different input and output modalities, administered in August, 1990. Her performance was at floor on most of the tasks. For example, she was unable to produce any exemplars of six categories in a fluency task, or to name any picture or object presented to her. There was some ability to sort at the highest level of living

TABLE 1
Details of Patient PP

Date of birth: 1921
Date of onset: 1988
Occupation: Former clerical officer and secretary

General Details:
Digit span: Forwards, 9: Backwards, 6
WAIS tests, age-scaled scores (administered August, 1990)
Information: 1
Vocabulary: 4
Similarities: 0
Block design: 12
Digit symbol: 8

Token test: good performance on modified version with reduced vocabulary

BDAE: repetition. Good repetition of words and phrases

Spontaneous speech: Fluent and well-articulated, but with severe word-finding difficulties and frequent semantic paraphasias.

TABLE 2
Performance of PP and Normal Controls on a Battery of Tests Designed to Probe Semantic Knowledge (August, 1990)

	PP	*Controls*	
	Number	*Mean*	*(SD)*
Category fluency			
Living	0	46.8	(12.6)
Non-living	0	47.7	(14.3)
	% Correct	*Mean %*	*(SD)*
Naming (line drawings)	0	96.7	(2.2)
Generation of definition	0	97.9	(1.5)
Word to picture matching	27	99.8	(0.1)
(chance = 17%)			
Sorting of pictures			
(chance = 50%)			
Living vs man-made	100	100.0	(0.1)
Superordinate category	72	95.6	(2.5)
Subordinate category	42	96.5	(3.9)

For further details see Hodges, Patterson, Oxbury, and Funnell (1992) and Hodges, Patterson, and Tyler (1994).

versus man-made object, but this too declined over the testing period. In contrast, PP's autobiographical and episodic memory remained relatively intact (she was able to remember appointments and keep track of family events). Also visuo-spatial abilities and working memory were unimpaired, as demonstrated, for example, by her digit span (9 forward, 6 backward) and performance on the Rey figure copy (32/36) and Raven's coloured matrices (35/36).

PP's inability to perform any task requiring semantic knowledge extended to all input and output modalities tested. There seemed to be no difference whether objects were presented as pictures or as spoken words or definitions, or whether she was required to name, sort, or describe objects. This pattern of performance would suggest a central deficit to stored semantic knowledge rather than a problem with access to that information. Consistent with this hypothesis, one of the last tasks that she could perform above chance was sorting at superordinate level. It has been claimed that preserved knowledge of superordinate category in the face of loss of more fine-grained semantic attributes stems from loss of information within the semantic system (Shallice, 1988a; Warrington & Shallice, 1979).

However, as discussed earlier, all the tasks used to assess PP's semantic knowledge involved voluntary access to semantic representations, and so it is possible that what seems to be a clear disorder of storage could in fact be a profound disturbance in the processes of accessing semantic information under voluntary control. The relative preservation of superordinate sorting is inconclusive on this question for two reasons: (1) it may be possible to perform at an elevated level in the high-level sorting task by exploiting general visual similarities between pictures in the living versus non-living categories (PP's good performance on visuo-spatial problem-solving tasks suggests that this is plausible), and (2) an advantage for superordinate information does not necessarily implicate loss of underlying semantic information but could also be consistent with a range of access disorders (Rapp & Caramazza, 1993). It was not possible to apply other standard diagnostics of a storage disorder—consistency of correct and incorrect responses over the same items on different tasks and testing sessions, or the presence of a frequency effect—as there were too few correct answers to analyse Therefore, this was an ideal situation in which to employ semantic priming as a probe of semantic memory impairment. This study is reported in more detail in Moss, Tyler, Hodges, and Patterson (1995).

The basic predictions for the priming task were as outlined earlier: if PP has suffered extensive loss of semantic information, then we would expect her to show little or no normal priming effects, or, if the loss of information is partial rather than complete, to show abnormally long reaction times and large priming effects. On the other hand, if PP's impairment is one of voluntary access to intact underlying representations, then normal priming is predicted. In order to ensure that priming was supported by relations within the semantic system, and not just intra-lexical connections, we contrasted conditions in which primes and targets were strongly associated (greater than 20% association strength) and conditions in which prime and target shared the same kind of semantic relation but were not normatively associated in either forward or backward direction. We tested two main kinds of semantic relation. The first was common category membership (e.g. *pig–horse*, *gold–silver*), and the second was a functional relation between the referent of the prime and target, e.g. *broom–floor*, where you use a *broom* to sweep the *floor*, or *theatre–play*, where you go to the *theatre* to see a *play*. The motivation for including these types of relation was that the category relation could be supported by the kind of superordinate knowledge that is thought to be relatively preserved in semantic memory disorder, while the functional relations are an example of the kind of detailed attribute knowledge which is expected to be more vulnerable to semantic deficits. In addition, both these relations have been found to support robust priming for unimpaired subjects in previous priming studies (Moss, Ostrin, Tyler, & Marslen-Wilson, in press).

The three variables—type of semantic relation (category co-ordinate or functionally related), association (strongly associated or non-associated), and prime type (related or unrelated)—were fully crossed, so that there were 12 prime–target pairs in each of the four conditions: associated category co-ordinates (e.g. *dog–cat*), non-associated category co-ordinates (e.g. *pig–horse*), associated functional relations (*e.g. hammer–nail*), and non-associated functional relations (e.g. *broom-floor*). Each target word was also paired with an unrelated ''prime'' to give the corresponding control conditions (e.g. *boat–cat, chair–horse, oven–nail, pump–floor* etc.). Length and frequency of words in each condition were matched, as was the strength of semantic relation between prime and target. To determine strength of semantic relation, all prime–target pairs were presented to a group of 12–15 young control subjects, who were asked to rate how related the two words were in meaning on a scale of 1–9. In order to control for possible natural kind/artifact category differences, half of the pairs in the category co-ordinate conditions came from natural kind categories, such as animals, vegetables, and metals, and half from artifact categories such as tools and vehicles. All the words in the functional conditions referred to artifacts.

We established in pilot studies that PP was unable to perform a lexical decision task with any accuracy, and so the primed monitoring task described earlier was used. We also determined for PP that the optimum interval between items in the list was 1500ms. Because this long inter-stimulus interval (ISI) could allow for strategic priming effects, we ran a preliminary study with two groups of control subjects; one group with the 1500ms ISI and the other with the same materials at a 200ms ISI. This established that the pattern of results at the short and long delay were identical. Primes and targets (or unrelated controls and targets) were embedded in lists of between four and ten words. Items were counterbalanced over two versions to avoid repetition of items within subjects. In order to increase the reliability of the priming results, PP was tested on two occasions about two months apart (November, 1991 and January, 1992). The procedure and design were identical in the two sessions, but two different sets of items were used, which met all the criteria described earlier.

The results for PP and the seven age-matched control subjects are shown in Table 3. As associative strength had no effect in any analysis, the results are collapsed over this factor. The control group showed a consistent priming effect for all conditions, with no interactions with degree of association or with type of semantic relation—50ms priming for category co-ordinates and 55ms for functionally related items: $F1(1,6) = 15.5$, $P < 0.01$; $F2(1,40) = 151$, $P < 0.001$. PP, however, showed a different pattern, with a significant interaction between priming and type of semantic relation, $F2(1,88) = 6.8$, $P < 0.01$. This was due to there being a significant facilitation effect for the functional condition, 50ms, $F2(1,40) = 10.7$, $P < 0.01$, but not for the category coordinates, −11ms, $F < 1$. Further examination of the category co-ordinate condition confirmed that PP showed no priming for either the natural kind category members (−5ms) or the artifact category members (−17ms). It may be noted from the range data in Table 3 that one control subject shows no priming for the category co-ordinate condition. However, the same control subjects shows no priming for the functionally related items either, and thus the pattern is not the same as that for PP, where the crucial result is the difference between the priming effect for category co-ordinates and functionally related items, rather than being the absence of priming *per se*.

It is clear that PP is not showing hyper-priming, as her overall reaction times, as well as the size of the facilitation effect in the functional condition, are well within the range for her age group. In addition, she made almost no errors. The

TABLE 3
Mean Reaction Times (Msec) in Each Condition for Control Subjects and PP in the Primed Monitoring Study

	Related	Unrelated	Priming (U–R)	Percentage Priming[a] (and Range)
Age-matched Controls				
Category co-ordinates	337	387	50**	9.2 (−5.9–20)
Functionally related	362	417	55**	9.4 (0.4–22)
PP[b]				
Category co-ordinates	403	392	−11	−2.8
Functionally related	344	394	50**	12.7

** $P < 0.01$

[a] Priming effect as a proportion of the unrelated baseline reaction time.

[b] Combined data for original study and replication on new set of items, Nov. 1991–Jan. 1992.

fact that priming (in the functional condition) was as great for non-associated as associated items shows that she was not relying solely on lexical level connections. These results suggest that although information relating members of a common semantic category is lost from PP's semantic memory, knowledge of detailed functional properties of objects is not lost, but is inaccessible to voluntary access. The fact that relations between words such as *broom–floor* and *restaurant–wine* reliably supported priming indicates that this kind of functional semantic relation was still represented and accessible to automatic access. This was in spite of the fact that PP had no conscious awareness of this information and was unable to use it explicitly. PP's inability to use functional semantic information in an explicit task was shown in a number of the tasks reported by Hodges et al. (1992, 1994). For example, even as early as 1990, she was unable to sort pictures according to functional properties such as electrical *vs* non-electrical, or to answer feature probe questions about functional properties of objects. Moreover, in February, 1991, she could not group real household objects according to their functional relatedness (e.g. candle and matches, needle and sewing thread), and she was able to mime the use of only 8 out of 25 objects (Hodges, Patterson, & Tyler, 1994). It was not possible to carry out a task such as semantic relatedness judgments on the same set of items as used in the priming task, as PP was unable to understand a judgment task by the time of testing. However, the kinds of items used in the earlier semantic battery tasks were very similar to those used in the priming task. Thus the comparison between the on and off-line results provides a clear dissociation in performance.[4]

It is perhaps surprising that the information that is retained concerns detailed functional attributes of the words' referents, rather than superordinate information which would support priming between members of a common category. This is inconsistent with the view that superordinate information is preferentially preserved in the face of semantic memory impairment. However, the ability to access functional information automatically is consistent with an observation that has been made about patients with semantic dementia by several researchers; that is, that they are often able to use objects in appropriate ways, in spite of being unable to demonstrate knowledge of the semantic properties of those objects in any other way (Saffran & Schwartz, 1992; Snowden, Griffiths, & Neary, 1994; this volume). PP could also use objects in everyday life to some extent, being able to dress herself and use cutlery appropriately to eat, even late into the progression of the semantic dementia, when she performed very poorly in off-line tests of semantic knowledge of all

---

[4] It will be noted that the off-line tasks were carried out some time before our priming study. By the time we were testing PP with the primed monitoring she could not understand the instructions for off-line tasks. It seems reasonable to assume that her performance would have deteriorated further, if anything, by the time we carried out the priming study. Thus her ability to do the monitoring task and show significant priming is even more striking.

kinds. What priming and everyday object use have in common is that access to the semantic information necessary to support them is implicit and automatic. There is no requirement to retrieve certain representations under voluntary control and to reflect on them in any way. Priming demonstrates that this information was also available at a linguistic level when accessed under the right conditions; knowledge about what you do with a broom or a hammer could be accessed by hearing the words *broom* and *hammer* as well as by needing to sweep the floor or knock in a nail.

Elsewhere we have discussed in detail the possible bases for the dissociation between category and functional information (Moss, Tyler, Hodges, & Patterson, 1995). These include loss of certain kinds of semantic feature (similar in some ways to the account of category-specific deficits given by Farah & McClelland, 1991) or preservation of script-type representations of event structure. Although we do not yet have a complete account for the basis of the pattern of impairments, the important point is that it was only by using the priming task that we were unable to uncover the distinction between category and functional information at all. In all tasks that tapped voluntary access, PP was equally impaired for all kinds of information tested.

The implication of this study for our understanding of semantic memory in general is that there may be representational distinctions among different types of semantic information about the meanings of words/concepts that cut across different content domains, such as living things and artifacts. This kind of distinction between different kinds of semantic information has been hypothesised as a potential basis for category-specific deficits, the claim being that the semantic representations of living things have a higher weighting of perceptual features over functional features than do the representations of artifacts (Farah & McClelland, 1991; Warrington & McCarthy, 1987). We are not suggesting here that PP has a category-specific deficit for natural kinds, as she showed no priming for either artifact or natural-kind category co-ordinates, and no evidence of a selective deficit in the range of semantic tasks reported by Hodges and colleagues, but rather that there could be a similar kind of account in terms of damage to specific types of semantic property.

The priming data for PP advances previous accounts of representational differences for different kinds of information in two ways: First, it provides direct evidence of a difference in impairment for two different kinds of information, rather than indirect evidence on the basis of category differences; and second, it suggests a division between functional properties and taxonomic or category-based information, which has not previously been demonstrated. A final observation is that the apparent loss of category information did not lead to abnormally long reaction times and disproportionately large priming effects for PP, even though she could be described as having partially degraded semantic representation (i.e. loss of taxonomic information but intact functional information). This also suggests independent representations of the two kinds of information, as loss of one kind does not adversely affect priming for the other.

An important question is whether the distinction between preserved priming for functional but not category priming will be found for other patients who have semantic dementia or similar forms of progressive aphasia. We have recently started to see evidence of this pattern emerging in a second patient, in a study that we are carrying out in collaboration with John Hodges and Karalyn Patterson (Tyler, Moss, Patterson, & Hodges, 1994). FM is a 57-year-old woman who was originally reported as having semantic dementia by Hodges, Patterson, Oxbury and Funnell (1992), although subsequent testing has revealed that she is not a typical case of semantic dementia. Her semantic impairment is mild relative to the degree of anomia, and syntactic as well as semantic deficits have developed (Patterson, Hodges, Graham, & Coot, 1994; Tyler, Moss, Patterson, & Hodges, 1994). Nevertheless, she can still be compared to PP under the more general notion of fluent progressive aphasia.

We have tested FM in a priming study which probes a range of semantic relationships, including the category and functional relations tested in our study of PP. In this experiment the same prime word was tested across all semantic relations. The category co-ordinate condition was similar to that in the previous study (e.g. *squirrel–rabbit, aeroplane–train*). In the functional condition, the target word described a functional (i.e. non-perceptual property) of the prime, as established in a property listing pre-test (e.g. *squirrel–tree, aeroplane–pilot*). In all cases, prime and target were not normatively associated.

Unlike PP, FM is able to perform a lexical decision task with few errors and with reaction times not greatly slower than the normal range. Therefore we used a paired auditory lexical decision paradigm with an ISI of 200ms. A group of six age-matched control subjects showed robust priming for both category co-ordinates, 69ms; $F1(1,5) = 387$, $P < 0.001$; $F2(1,40) = 63$, $P < 0.001$, and functionally related items, 58ms; $F1(1,5) = 31$, $P < 0.01$; $F1(1,40) = 33$, $P < 0.001$, in this experiment. When we tested FM in December 1993, she showed a similar pattern with significant priming in both the category co-ordinate condition, 176ms; $F1(1,35) = 10.8$, $P < 0.01$, and in the functional condition, 111ms; $F2(1,30) = 6.4$, $P < 0.05$. However, when we tested her again in August, 1994, the pattern had changed. Although functionally related items continued to prime, 103ms, $F2(1,32) = 9.2$, $P < 0.01$, the effect for category was no longer significant, 63ms; $F2(1,33) = 1.9$, $P > 0.1$. Results for FM and the control group are shown in Table 4.

This suggests that during this period there has been some further degradation of representations in FM's semantic memory, such that category co-ordinate relations are no longer automatically activated, giving a pattern very similar to the one we observed for PP. In an explicit semantic-relatedness judgment task on the same pairs of items as used in the priming study, FM performed very poorly in all conditions, with a strong bias to respond positively to both related

TABLE 4
Mean Reaction Times (Msec) in Each Condition for Control Subjects and FM in the
Lexical Decision Study

	Related	Unrelated (and range)	Priming (U–R)	Percentage priming[a] (and range)
Age-matched Controls				
Category co-ordinates	708	777 (625–857)	69**	8.5 (6.7–10.7)
Functionally related	730	787 (655–857)	57**	7 (3.1–11.5)
FM (December 1993)				
Category co-ordinates	928	1104	176**	15.9
Functionally related	1029	1140	111*	9.7
FM (August 1994)				
Category co-ordinates	843	906	63	6.9
Functionally related	746	849	103*	12.1

* $P < 0.05$
** $P < 0.01$
[a] Priming effect as a proportion of the unrelated baseline reaction time.

and unrelated trials. The data in Table 4 show that in the first time slice, FM's reaction times in the control conditions are rather slow compared to the control subjects, and that the size of the priming effect is also very large, especially for the category co-ordinates. However, in the second time slice, her reaction times are on the borders on the normal range, and the priming effect for functionally related items is no greater than for some control subjects. This pattern of change over time is consistent with some degree of loss of category information at the earlier time, resulting in hyper-priming, followed by further loss of category information over the subsequent months to the second testing period, by which time priming for category co-ordinates has ceased to be significant at all. This change for category co-ordinates is taking place while priming for functionally related information remains relatively stable. Close observation of the pattern of priming in future testing sessions is required to determine whether this is the correct interpretation.

To summarise, the results of the priming study for FM support those for PP, in suggesting relative preservation of functional properties rather than category structure in progressive aphasia. Theses studies also highlight the value of priming studies in revealing distinctions in performance that are not picked up in off-line tasks.

2. REPRESENTATION AND ACCESS OF ABSTRACT WORDS

Many patients with acquired language disorders have greater difficulty processing abstract words, such as *truth, risk,* and *luck*[5] than concrete words such as *table, building,* and *cat.* Abstract words are those whose referents cannot be directly experienced through the senses. Patients have been reported who have problems with repeating abstract words (Franklin et al., 1994; Howard & Franklin, 1988), understanding abstract words (Franklin, 1989; Franklin et al., 1994), and perhaps most well known, with reading abstract words (Coltheart, Patterson, & Marshall, 1980). Indeed, a greater difficulty in reading abstract than concrete words is seen as one of the key characteristics of deep dyslexia. There have been a few reports of patients who seem to have a greater difficulty for concrete words, either in reading (Warrington, 1981), or more generally (Breedin, Saffran, & Coslett, 1994; Warrington, 1975; Warrington & Shallice, 1984), but this seems to be much rarer. What gives rise to the problem with abstract words for individual patients, and what is it about abstract words that seems to make them particularly vulnerable to disruption? These are important questions, as they may lead to identification of a fundamental distinction in semantic memory between the representation of abstract and concrete word meanings.

We have investigated knowledge of the meanings of concrete and abstract words for two aphasic patients in a series of semantic priming studies (Tyler, Ostrin, Cooke, & Moss, 1995; Tyler, Moss, & Jennings, in press). DE and JG are both non-fluent (agrammatic) aphasics who have also been classified as deep dyslexic, and both have extensive left-hemisphere lesions (see Table 5 for patient details). Our question was whether their apparent difficulties with abstract words stemmed from a central loss of stored semantic information for abstract words, or whether it could be traced to impairments in accessing intact underlying semantic representations. Both kinds of account have been put forward to explain the deficit of different deep dyslexic patients (Shallice, 1988a). In order to address this question, we have used priming tasks alongside a range of off-line procedures to tap into automatic and voluntary access of the words' semantic representations.

Our first test confirmed that both DE and JG clearly have greater difficulty in reading abstract than concrete words. For a matched set of 20 abstract and 20 concrete words, DE read 100% of the concrete words accurately, but only 55% of the abstract words, whereas JG read 90% of the concrete words correctly but only 45% of the abstract words. We then carried out a word-to-picture matching

---

[5] Abstractness is highly (negatively) correlated with the imageability of a word—in that highly abstract words are difficult to picture. Abstractness and imageability have often been used interchangeably and we do not attempt to distinguish between them here.

TABLE 5
Details of Patients, DE and JG

DE

Date of birth: 1954
Date of onset: 11.6.70
Occupation: Storekeeper

General Details:
Hearing loss: 7.0dB
Digit span: 3
Digit matching task: 6/6 correct on 4 and 5 digits; 4/6 correct on 6 digits
Simple RT: 121ms

Standard Aphasia Tests:
Trail making test: 39 seconds
Token Test: 24/36 (moderate impairment)
BDAE (administered June, 1983)[a]
 a) Auditory comprehension: $z = +0.75$
 b) Repetition: good repetition of single words, poor repetition of phrases
 c) Spontaneous speech: slow and hesitant. He rarely produces more than single word utterances, which primarily consist of content words.

JG

Date of birth: 1929
Date of onset: 22.11.80
Previous occupation: Groundsman

General Details:
Hearing loss: 22.1dB
Digit span: 3
Digit matching task: 5/6 correct on 4 digits; 6/6 correct on 5 digits; 3/6 correct on 6 digits
Simple RT: 185ms

Standard Aphasia Tests:
Trail making test: 67 seconds
Token Test: 10/36 (severe impairment)
BDAE (administered October, 1981)[a]
 a) Auditory comprehension: $z = -0.75$
 b) Repetition: normal repetition of single words, poor repetition of phrases
 c) Spontaneous speech: produces short utterances, consisting of one or two words. His speech is hesitant and effortful.

---

[a] Although these tests were administered several years ago, the scores remain valid, because neither DE nor JG have shown any significant change in their language-processing profiles over the last 10 years.

study to determine whether the same problem with abstract words would be manifest when the input modality was auditory rather than visual, and a spoken response was not required. This is one of the standard ways to distinguish between a modality-specific access problem and a central semantic (storage) impairment.

We used the word-to-picture matching task devised by Shallice and McGill (unpublished), in which subjects are asked to indicate the picture corresponding to a word spoken by the experimenter, from an array of four alternatives. The test set includes 30 concrete and 30 abstract words. In this task, both DE and JG performed considerably more poorly on the abstract than concrete words (DE: concrete 3% errors, abstract 33% errors; JG: concrete 10% errors, abstract 50% errors). Although this seems to support the view that the deficit for abstract words is a central one, the picture is not so clear when we examine the range of performance by control subjects in this task. We tested six elderly control subjects who had a similar level of education to DE and JG (in that they left school at 16 years or earlier). Although the mean error rates were lower than for the patients (0.6% for concrete words and 21% errors for abstract words) some subjects found the abstract words very difficult: the range of error rates was 0–3.3% for concrete words but 10–33% for abstract words. This means that DE was actually within the normal range of performance for abstract words, and slightly above the range for concrete words. JG, on the other hand, made more errors than the controls on both sets of words. Thus it is not clear that either are showing a selective deficit for abstract words in this task, and therefore we cannot answer the question of whether the reading difficulty for abstract words reflects a semantic memory impairment or a modality-specific access deficit.

Therefore we designed an auditory semantic priming task to compare priming for abstract and concrete words for JG and DE. In an earlier set of studies we have found both patients show normal semantic priming in a lexical decision task for concrete nouns sharing various different kinds of semantic relation, including the category co-ordinate and functional relations described earlier in the study of PP (Ostrin & Tyler, 1993; Tyler, Ostrin, Cooke, & Moss, 1995).[6] Would DE and JG show similar normal priming for abstract words, or would they show a pattern of no priming, or hyper-priming suggesting damage to the underlying semantic representations?

We selected a set of 44 pairs of abstract words which were strongly semantically related according to rating pre-tests completed by a group of subjects from our subject pool. These were mostly near-synonyms such as *courage–bravery* and *risk–danger*, but also included a few antonyms such as

---

[6] Our finding of semantic priming for agrammatic patients conflicts with the claims made by Blumstein and colleagues (Blumstein et al., 1982; Milberg & Blumstein, 1981) that these patients do not show normal automatic access of lexical representations (see Tyler, Ostrin, Cooke, & Moss, 1995 for details of this point).

forget–remember. As a control for low-level intra-lexical priming, we ensured that half of the pairs were strongly normatively associated (e.g. *courage–bravery*) and that the other half were purely semantically related with no association in either forward or backward direction (e.g. *doubt–suspicion*). All of the words in the abstract condition had a concreteness rating of less than 3.5 on a scale of 1–7 (mean 2.9). A set of 44 near-synonym pairs of concrete words were also selected (concreteness ratings over 3.5, mean 4.9). Again, half of these were strongly associated (e.g. *street–road*) and half were not associated (e.g. *stick–cane*). Targets in the concrete and abstract conditions were matched for length and familiarity, and the strength of semantic relation to the prime (for further details see Tyler, Moss, & Jennings, in press).

The priming task was paired auditory lexical decision with a 200ms inter-stimulus interval. Each target was preceded either by the related prime or an unrelated control word, and these were counterbalanced over two versions, carried out a month apart, to avoid repetition effects. The results for DE and JG are shown in Table 6, alongside those for seven elderly control subjects.

Control subjects showed significant priming in all conditions, $F1(1,6) = 110.76$, $P < 0.001$; $F2(1,80) = 74.9$, $P < 0.001$. There was an interaction between priming and concreteness, with a tendency for a larger priming effect for concrete items (91ms) than for abstract items (52ms), $F(1,6) = 4.9$, $P = 0.069$; $F2(1,80) = 5.6$, $P < 0.0$ (although the priming effect was robust for the abstract words by themselves). The degree of associative strength between prime and target had no effect on priming ($F1$ and $F2 < 1$).

JG and DE both performed the lexical decision task reasonably well. DE made errors on 13.6% of the real-word targets, and his reaction times were within the normal range (mean 937ms; normal range 799–992ms). JG made errors on 5.7% of the real-word targets and his overall reaction times were slightly faster than the normal range (mean 796ms). JG showed a significant priming effect of 127ms overall, $F2(1,71) = 50$, $P < 0.001$. Like the control subjects he also showed more priming for concrete than abstract words; 176ms and 76ms respectively, $F2(1,71) = 7.5$, $P < 0.01$—although, again like the controls, the priming effect for the abstract words was still significant.

However, JG's pattern of priming did appear to differ from that of the control subjects in one striking way: there was significantly less priming for associated than non-associated word pairs, in both concrete and abstract conditions, $F2(1,71) = 5.8$, $P < 0.05$. In our previous studies we have generally found an increase rather than a decrease in priming when associative strength is added to any kind of semantic relation; an effect we have called the *associative boost* (Moss, Ostrin, Tyler, & Marslen-Wilson, in press; Moss, Hare, Day, & Tyler, 1994). However, in the present study, the group of elderly control subjects showed very little difference in the mean priming effects for pairs of words with and without association, in spite of the fact that young control subjects showed the expected significant associative boost for the same materials (Moss, Hare,

TABLE 6
Mean Reaction Times (msec) for Elderly Controls, DE, and JG in the Lexical
Decision Task

	Related	Unrelated (and range)	Priming (U–R)	Percentage priming[a] (and range)
Controls				
Concrete words				
+ association	832	924 (812–1126)	92*	10 (5–12)
– association	875	965 (889–1122)	90*	9 (1–14)
Abstract words				
+ association	846	903 (815–1093)	57*	6 (1–12)
– association	908	955 (852–1156)	47*	5 (–2–11)
DE				
Concrete words				
+ association	858	882	24*	3
– association	901	1068	167*	16
Abstract words				
+ association	854	957	103*	11
– association	933	1055	123*	12
JG				
Concrete words				
+ association	676	804	128*	16
– association	729	946	218*	23
Abstract words				
+ association	733	767	34*	4
– association	794	913	119*	13

* = $P < 0.05$
[a] Priming effect as a proportion of the unrelated baseline reaction time

Day, & Tyler, 1994). We attribute this reduction in the associative boost for the older subject group to the fact that the association norms, from which we selected the stimulus pairs, were collected from a young population. It is possible that the associative relations among some words differ across the younger and older generations tested, such that the manipulation of associated and non-associated items in the experiment is not as accurate for the elderly control group (examples such as the change in association from *glue–stick* to *glue–sniff* are readily apparent). JG does not only show a lack of associative boost, he slows a marked reduction in priming for associated pairs. It is not, however, clear to what extent this is an abnormal effect. Although the mean priming effects for the elderly control group are similar for associated and non-associated conditions, individual subjects differ considerably in the relative size of priming effect for the two conditions, ranging from an advantage of 88ms for associated items to an advantage of 63ms for non-associated items. Thus, although JG's reduction in priming for associated items (90 and 85ms in concrete and abstract conditions respectively) is outside the normal range, the general pattern of less priming for associated prime–target pairs is not as abnormal as it might first appear. The crucial point for our current purpose is that the effect of association for JG was identical for concrete and abstract words, and that even with this effect, there was still significant priming in all conditions.

DE also showed a significant priming effect, 105ms, $F2(1,57) = 11.5$, $P < 0.001$. There were no other main effects or interactions. He showed robust priming for abstract words (113ms) as well as for concrete words (96ms). However, an examination of the priming effects in the associated and non-associated conditions reveals a similar pattern to that of JG, with more priming for non-associated items than associated items in both concrete and abstract conditions (although not giving rise to a significant interaction). The reduction in priming for associated items in the abstract condition (23ms) was within the normal range, but the reduction of 143ms for the concrete condition was greater than that shown by any control subject.

Thus, both JG and DE showed reliable priming effects for abstract words. Moreover, there was little evidence of hyper-priming effects to indicate damage to the underlying semantic representations. Neither JG nor DE showed a baseline reaction time for lexical decision that was longer than the control range for any condition, including the abstract word conditions. This is clearly not the pattern predicted if priming were based on degraded semantic representations giving rise to abnormally long reaction times in the baseline condition. The magnitude of priming effects for the two patients were generally at the top of or just above the range for control subjects, with one exception: JG's 218ms (23%) priming effect for the non-associated concrete items is well above the control range (1–14%). However, this does not indicate a hyper-priming effect, according to the Chertkow et al. (1989) account. This is because the large facilitation effect is caused by exceptionally fast RTs in the related condition rather than exceptionally slow reaction times in the unrelated condition (see Table 6).

We can also conclude from these results that the priming effects for DE and JG in the abstract word condition were not mediated by lexical-level associative links rather than relations within the semantic system. This is because significant priming was found for pairs of word that were semantically related, but shared no associative connection in forward or backward direction. In fact, both DE and JG were adversely affected by associative connections between prime and target, although it is not clear to what extent this differs from the normal pattern for the elderly control group (we return to this issue in the Discussion).

The priming data indicate that there is no selective deficit in the semantic representation of abstract words for DE and JG. They are both capable of accessing those representations rapidly and automatically in order to support semantic priming. As a follow-up to the priming study we have carried out a definition-generation task for a subset of the abstract and concrete words, in order to compare JG and DE's ability to automatically access the meanings of abstract words as demonstrated in the priming task, with their ability to access those meanings under voluntary control in an explicit, metalinguistic task. The word to be defined was read to the subject by the experimenter, so that auditory comprehension could be tapped. We needed to do this because the word-to-picture matching task had not provided clear evidence as to the ability to access abstract words under voluntary control from an auditory input.

Asking someone to provide a definition of a word is an intuitively straightforward way of assessing their knowledge of the meaning of the word, although it is a highly metalinguistic task, requiring controlled access to semantic information and careful reflection on that information to produce a response. The advantage over the word-to-picture matching task is that it does not require a pictorial representation to be devised for abstract words which, almost by definition, are difficult to picture (this may have been an important factor in the difficulty of the task). On the other hand, it does require a spoken response from patients whose production is non-fluent; therefore we are interested solely in the semantic content of the definition, ignoring production style.

DE and JG were asked to give definitions for 22 of the abstract words from the priming experiment and 24 highly concrete words taken from this and earlier studies. The word to be defined was spoken by the experimenter in each case, and the patient gave a verbal definition which we recorded. A group of 11 elderly control subjects also completed the definition task. Control subjects read each word and wrote down a definition in a booklet.[7]

For both DE and JG, the ability to define abstract and concrete words was remarkably good. Both were able to give an adequate definition of all the concrete words. JG missed only one abstract word and DE only three. The definitions were such that it was clear that both patients had a good deal of knowledge about the meaning of the words and were able to access those meaning representations under the highly controlled, metalinguistic demands of the definition task. In general, DE and JG gave definitions that differed from those of control subjects in two main ways (1) they rarely gave a superordinate, although controls very often did, and (2) they generated more context-specific, personally relevant information about what the word meant to them, rather than general information. Importantly, however, these differences were the same for concrete and abstract words; there seemed to be no special difficulty with abstract word definitions. Examples of the definitions given by the controls and patients are shown in Table 7.

---

[7] We have compared the content of definitions for control subjects when they are asked to give written and spoken responses, and find no difference between the two versions of the task.

TABLE 7

Examples of Definitions to Concrete and Abstract Words Given by DE and JG

ABSTRACT WORDS

DE

temper:	very angry, half and half at work, temper sometimes
courage:	on telly, accident and things like that, courage, ring up 999, accident, conscious one side and leave it and ring up
kind:	generous, hope so, like children
dash:	time, dash along, very quickly, on the move all the time
dispatch:	all done finish, location, dispatch away to London something, sign it and away
mood:	children, very moody sometimes, phases, comb your hair, mood—ooh!
crave:	me, chocolate biscuits, different people, different things

JG

temper:	anger
courage:	medal, valiant, not in England, Rommel
kind:	my old mum
dash:	hurry
dispatch:	motor bike, in the war, and after there is dispatch and then come dispatch also
risk:	a gamble
crave:	I used to—an ounce of *Golden Virginia*—but given up

CONCRETE WORDS

DE

lettuce:	in garden, grow, green outside, very soft, salad
king:	hope so later on, king—Prince Charles, Queen
collar:	vicars use, church, things like that
oven:	at home, inside oven, bottom oven lift out, all black inside. Roast pork, beef, chicken, Yorkshire pudding
cow:	big, different colours, bull-horns, cow-underneath the, can't say, food, milk
bed:	night-time, things like that, mattress—sleep—hope so
queen:	throne, queen

JG

lettuce:	in the garden, grows and big and cut it off and eat, I grow them
king:	the grandest, and the beautiful crown
collar:	coat and smart uniform
oven:	the meat and all that, all lovely and bubbly
cow:	OK, but the dung is ughh!
bed:	sleep and wake up
queen:	the most highest in the land

The ability to define abstract words reinforces the priming results in showing that the abstract word deficit for DE and JG is not one of damage to the underlying semantic representations of abstract words. It also shows that the problem is not a general one of voluntary access to those representations either, but rather it seems to be specific to visual input. We are now in the process of conducting the priming studies with materials presented in the *visual* modality to determine the nature of the reading deficit. Is there a general problem with accessing the semantic representations of abstract words from visual inputs, in which case we would expect little priming in the visual modality, in contrast to the normal priming in the auditory modality? Or is the problem caused by some aspect unique to the reading task? For example, Marcel and Patterson (1978) suggested that the difficulty arose from the need to have a conscious representation of the phonological form of the word for reading aloud. If this kind of account is correct, visual priming effects may be normal for abstract words in spite of the reading impairment.

What are the implications of this study for the representation of abstract words in semantic memory? Although many more studies need to be carried out, our current hypothesis is that the difficulty with abstract words often experienced after brain damage is not due to a selective damage of the representations of abstract words themselves, but is more likely to be the result of disruption of access processes for a particular modality of input. The consequences of such access impairments generally affect abstract words more severely than concrete words, because of the nature of abstract word representations in semantic memory. Several authors have suggested that representations of abstract words are less "rich" than those of concrete words, in that they are made up of fewer semantic predicates or features (Jones, 1985; Plaut & Shallice, 1993), and also that there are less stable, context-independent correlations among the component features for abstract words (Plaut & Shallice, 1993). Such claims are supported by the fact that subjects generate fewer predicates, and rate it more difficult to think of a context for abstract words (Jones, 1985; Schwanenflugel, Harnishfeger, & Stowe, 1988).

Several studies have demonstrated that abstract words are more difficult to process for normal adult subjects (Schwanenflugel, 1992). This difficulty was also confirmed across the range of tasks in our study for our elderly control subjects; they showed less priming, more errors in word-to-picture matching, and found it more difficult to define abstract than concrete words. A similar pattern was found in a semantic relatedness judgment task for the word pairs used in the priming task; some control subjects made up to 34% errors for the abstract word pairs compared to a maximum of 16% errors for concrete words. Given these indications that abstract words are more difficult to access in the normal system, then it is plausible that damage to access routines will cause greater problems for abstract words. Thus damage to the auditory access process may result in abstract word deafness as in DRB (Franklin et al., 1994) whereas problems in the visual access route may be the basis of the abstract word effect in deep dyslexia, as modelled in a connectionist network by Plaut and Shallice (1993).

In spite of the plausibility of the claim that problems for abstract words for patients with language disorders are an exaggeration of the increased difficulty in processing abstract words in the normal system, there is one important challenge for this kind of account. As mentioned at the beginning of this section, there have been reports, albeit rare, of patients who seem to have a selective problem for concrete words rather than abstract words. This finding is clearly problematic. However, it is possible that such cases can be accounted for within the framework described here.

For example, Plaut and Shallice have shown how a specific deficit to concrete words can arise in the connectionist model in which they demonstrated the more common abstract word-reading problems of deep dyslexia. A deficit for concrete words resulted from lesioning the model at the level of semantic clean-up units, whose function is to facilitate the model in settling into a stable pattern corresponding to a known word meaning. This kind of lesion had a more detrimental effect for concrete words, because they have many more correlations among features, and so develop more effective clean-up routines during learning. For example, there is a strong correlation between *having eyes, having ears, being alive* and so on. Activation of just a few of these features would lead to strong activation of the correlated features via the clean-up units. These correlations are not present for abstract words, and thus there is little dependence on clean-up units (Plaut & Shallice, 1993). Although this account is somewhat speculative, it demonstrates that a pattern of selective deficit for concrete words does not necessitate the claim that there are separate semantic-memory stores for concrete and abstract words. This account also makes the interesting and testable claim that although abstract word deficits result from disrupted access processes, concrete word deficits result from problems within the central semantic system. Thus if a patient has difficulty with concrete words, the problem should extend to all modalities.

Finally, we return to the associative interference effect on priming that was shown by both JG and DE. In both concrete and abstract word conditions, there was considerably greater priming for pairs of words that were semantically related but not associated according to association norms (e.g. *doubt–suspicion, stick–cane*) than for those that were semantically related and also strongly associated (e.g. *courage–bravery, street–road*). Although this pattern was shown by some of the control subjects to a lesser degree, it remains a possibility that this finding does reflect a real deficit for the patients. This interpretation is also supported by our previous experiments in which DE and JG failed to show an advantage for associated prime–target pairs for a set of concrete words, where the elderly control subjects *were* showing a consistent associative boost (Moss & Tyler, 1993; Tyler, Ostrin, Cooke, & Moss, 1995).

One possibility we have investigated is that there has been a disruption at the level of intra-lexical links between associated words for DE and JG (while semantic connections remain intact). We tested this in a priming experiment in which we measured priming for pairs of words that are strongly associated but are not semantically related (e.g. *pillar–society, elbow–grease*). Control subjects show robust priming for such word pairs (66ms; range 24–126ms). If DE and JG had an impairment at this level, we might expect them to show abnormal effects for these items. However, their priming effects were exactly the same as for control subjects (DE, 69ms; JG, 69ms). This shows that any reduction in priming for semantically related words that are also associatively related is not caused by a disruption at the level of intra-lexical associative connections *per se*. If we continue to find a pattern of associative interference, above the normal range, it will be necessary to investigate this effect further.

GENERAL DISCUSSION

The studies of category and functional information for PP, and of abstract word meanings for DE and JG, are two examples of how the priming task can be used, along with a range of other more traditional methods, to investigate the nature of semantic memory impairments. The unique contribution of the priming task is that it taps into automatic rather than controlled access to semantic information, thus helping us to discriminate between disorders of access and storage.

In the first study described, use of the priming task indicated a relative preservation of functional information compared to category information for a patient with semantic dementia, which had not been revealed in an extensive battery of off-line tasks. The loss of information from PP's semantic memory was, thus, not as complete as might have been thought, although she was clearly unable to access even functional information under voluntary control. The difference in priming between functional and category information suggests that there may be representational distinctions between these two types of information in semantic memory.

In the second study, the priming results indicated that there was no selective impairment of the semantic representations for abstract words in two non-fluent, deep dyslexic patients. This finding reinforced the results of the definition task in which JG and DE were able to define abstract words as well as concrete words. By using a range of different tasks we were able to rule out a "category-specific" semantic impairment for abstract words, and hypothesised that the problem was a disruption of the visual access route, which exaggerated the "normal" difficulty of processing abstract words.

In these two studies we have demonstrated how the theoretical and methodological objections to the semantic priming task can be addressed. On the theoretical level we have controlled for intra-lexical priming effects by contrasting semantically related word pairs that are highly associated with those that are non-associated, and we have distinguished between normal and hyper-priming effects, in order to determine whether priming is supported by intact or partially degraded semantic representations. In the Introduction we suggested a second way of establishing that priming was based on intact semantic representations: to examine priming for a range of different targets for a prime word (e.g. *cat–dog*, *cat–whiskers*, *cat–pet*, *cat–animal*). Although we have not reported such an experiment here, a large-scale study of this kind with a group of patients with progressive aphasia is now under way.

In spite of the important results that we have already obtained with the semantic priming task, it is nevertheless the case that both of the studies described here are only the first stages of more extensive studies currently in progress. Both studies raise as many questions as they answer. For the study of semantic dementia, the pressing questions that have emerged are: Is the distinction between category and functional information one that is generally found in progressive semantic deficits, or is it specific to PP? What is the basis of the distinction in terms of representation? To what extent does the preserved functional knowledge rely on autobiographical knowledge? Our study of abstract word meanings raises a number of questions, such as: Is the problem for abstract words one of visual access or is it specific to the reading task? To what extent does the apparent effect of abstractness interact with the form class of the word? How can abstract words be understood by patients with extensive left-hemisphere lesions when studies of unimpaired subjects suggest that only concrete words can be processed in the right hemisphere? These are just a small sample of the issues that have been raised by our research to date. Many of these questions have become apparent only as a direct result of our findings from the various priming tasks we have carried out. In future work, the semantic priming task will have an equally vital part to play in answering these, and other, fundamental questions about the nature of semantic memory.

REFERENCES

Badecker, W., & Caramazza, A. (1985). On consideration of method and theory governing the use of clinical categories in neurolinguistics and cognitive neuropsychology: The case against agrammatism. *Cognition, 20*, 97–125.

Balota, D.A., Ferraro, F.R., & Connor, L.T. (1991). On the early influence of meaning in word recognition: A review of the literature. In P.J. Schwanenflugel (Ed.), *The psychology of word meanings*. Hillsdale, NJ: Lawrence Erlbaum Associates Inc.

Blumstein, S., Milberg, W., & Shrier, R. (1982). Semantic processing in aphasia: Evidence from an auditory lexical decision task. *Brain and Language, 17*, 301–316.

Breedin, S., Saffran, E., & Coslett, H.B. (1994). Reversal of the concreteness effect in a patient with semantic dementia. *Cognitive Neuropsychology, 11*, 617–660.

Burke, D.M., White, H., & Diaz, D.L. (1987). Semantic priming in young and older adults: Evidence for age constancy in automatic and attentional processes. *Journal of Experimental Psychology: Human Perception and Performance, 13*, 79–88.

Butterworth, B., Howard, D., & McLoughlin, P. (1984). The semantic deficit in aphasia: The relationship between semantic errors in auditory comprehension and picture naming. *Neuropsychologia, 22*, 409–426.

Chenery, H.J., Ingram, J.C.L., & Murdoch, B.E. (1990). Automatic and volitional semantic processing in aphasia. *Brain and Language, 38*, 215–232.

Chertkow, H., & Bub, D. (1990). Semantic memory loss in dementia of Alzheimer's type: What do various measures measure? *Brain, 113*, 397–417.

Chertkow, H., Bub, D., & Seidenberg, M. (1989). Priming and semantic memory loss in Alzheimer's disease. *Brain and Language, 36*, 420–446.

Chiarello, C., Burgess, C., Richard, L., & Pollock, A. (1990). Semantic and associative priming in the cerebral hemispheres: Some words do, some words don't ... sometimes, some places. *Brain and Language, 38,* 75–104.

Collins, A.M., & Loftus, E.F. (1975). A spreading activation theory of semantic processing. *Psychological Review, 82,* 407–428.

Coltheart, M., Patterson, K., & Marshall, J. (1980). *Deep dyslexia.* London: Routledge.

de Groot, A.M.B. (1984). Primed lexical decision: Combined effects of the proportion of related prime–target pairs and the stimulus–onset asynchrony of prime and target. *Quarterly Journal of Experimental Psychology, 36,* 253–280.

Farah, M.J., & McClelland, J.L. (1991). A computational model of semantic memory impairment: Modality specificity and emergent category specificity. *Journal of Experimental Psychology: General, 120,* 339–357.

Fischler, I. (1977a). Associative facilitation without expectancy in a lexical decision task. *Journal of Experimental Psychology: Human Perception and Performance. 3,* 18–26.

Fischler, I. (1977b). Semantic facilitation without association in a lexical decision task. *Memory and Cognition, 5,* 335–339.

Franklin, S. (1989). Dissociations in auditory word comprehension: Evidence from nine "fluent" aphasic patients. *Aphasiology, 3,* 189–207.

Franklin, S., Howard, D., & Patterson, K. (1994). Abstract word meaning deafness. *Cognitive Neuropsychology, 11,* 1–34.

Funnell, E., & Sheridan, J. (1992). Categories of knowledge? Unfamiliar aspects of living and nonliving things. *Cognitive Neuropsychology, 9,* 135–153.

Glosser, G., & Friedman, R.B. (1991). Lexical but not semantic priming in Alzheimer's disease. *Psychology and Aging, 6,* 522–527.

Hasher, L., & Zachs, R.T. (1979). Automatic and effortful processes in memory. *Journal of Experimental Psychology: General, 108,* 356–368.

Henik, A., Fredrich, F., & Kellog, W. (1982). The dependence of semantic relatedness effects on prime processing. *Memory and Cognition, 11,* 366–373.

Hillis, A., Rapp, B., Romani, C., & Caramazza, A. (1990). Selective impairment of semantics in lexical processing. *Cognitive Neuropsychology, 7,* 191–243.

Hodges, J.R., Patterson, K., Oxbury, S., & Funnell, E. (1992a). Semantic dementia: Progressive fluent aphasia with temporal lobe atrophy. *Brain, 115,* 1783–1806.

Hodges, J.R., Patterson, K., & Tyler, L.K. (1994). Loss of semantic memory: Implications for the modularity of mind. *Cognitive Neuropsychology, 11,* 505–542.

Hodges, J.R., Salmon, D.P., & Butters, N. (1992b). Semantic memory impairment in Alzheimer's disease: Failure of access or degraded knowledge? *Neuropsychologia, 30,* 301–314.

Hodgson, J. (1991). Information constraints on pre-lexical priming. *Language and Cognitive Processes, 6,* 169–205.

Howard, D., & Franklin, S. (1988). *Missing the meaning?* Cambridge, MA: MIT Press.

Huff, F.J., Corkin, S., & Growden, J.H. (1986). Semantic impairment and anomia in Alzheimer's disease. *Brain and Language, 28,* 235–249.

James, C.T. (1975). The role of semantic information in lexical decisions. *Journal of Experimental Psychology: Human Perception and Performance, 1,* 130–136.

Jones, G.V. (1985). Deep dyslexia, imageability and ease of predication. *Brain and Language, 24,* 1–19.

Marcel, A., & Patterson, K. (1978). Word recognition and production: Reciprocity in clinical and normal studies. In J. Requin (Ed.), *Attention and performance, VII.* Hillsdale, NJ: Lawrence Erlbaum Associates Inc.

Masson, M. (1991). A distributed memory model of context effects in word recognition. In D. Besner & G. Humphreys (Eds.), *Basic processes in reading: Visual word recognition.* Hillsdale, NJ: Lawrence Erlbaum Associates Inc.

McClelland, J., & Elman, G. (1986). The TRACE model of speech perception. In J.L. McClelland & D.E. Rumelhart (Eds.), *Parallel distributed processing: Explorations in the microstructure of cognition*, Vol. 2. Cambridge, MA: MIT Press.

McKoon, G., & Ratcliff, R. (1992). Spreading activation versus compound cue accounts of priming: Mediated priming revisited. *Journal of Experimental Psychology: Learning, Memory and Cognition*, 18, 1155–1172.

McNamara, T.P. (1992). Priming and the constraints it places on theories of memory and retrieval. *Psychological Review*, 99, 650–663.

Meyer, D.E., & Schvaneveldt, R.W. (1971). Facilitation in recognising pairs of words: Evidence of a dependence between retrieval operations, *Journal of Experimental Psychology*, 80, 227–235.

Milberg, W., & Blumstein, S. (1981). Lexical decision and aphasia: Evidence for semantic processing. *Brain and Language*, 14, 371–386.

Moss, H.E., Hare, M.L., Day, P., & Tyler, L.K. (1994). A distributed memory model of the associative boost in semantic priming. *Connection Science*, 6, 413–427.

Moss, H.E., & Marslen-Wilson, W.D. (1993). Access to word meanings during spoken language comprehension: The role of sentential context. *Journal of Experimental Psychology: Learning, Memory and Cognition*, 19, 1254–1276.

Moss, H.E., & Older, L.J. (in press). *Birkbeck Word Association Norms*. Hove, UK: Lawrence Erlbaum Associates Ltd.

Moss, H.E., Ostrin, R.K., Tyler, L.K., & Marslen-Wilson, W.D. (in press). Accessing different types of lexical semantic information. Evidence from priming. *Journal of Experimental Psychology: Learning, Memory and Cognition*.

Moss, H.E., & Tyler, L.K. (1993, October). *Semantic priming without an associative boost in aphasia*. Paper presented to the American Academy of Aphasia, Tucson, AZ.

Moss, H.E., Tyler, L.K., Hodges, J., & Patterson, K. (1995). Exploring the loss of semantic memory in semantic dementia: Evidence from a primed monitoring study. *Neuropsychology*, 9, 16–26.

Nebes, R.D., Martin, D.C., & Horn, L.C. (1984). Sparing semantic memory in Alzheimer's disease. *Journal of Abnormal Psychology*, 93, 321–330.

Neely, J.H. (1991). Semantic priming in visual word recognition: A selective review of current theories and findings. In D. Besner & G. Humphreys (Eds.), *Basic processes in reading: Visual word recognition*. Hillsdale, NJ: Lawrence Erlbaum Associates Inc.

Ostrin, R.K., & Tyler, L.K. (1993). Automatic access to lexical semantics in aphasia: Evidence from semantic and associative priming. *Brain & Language*, 45, 147–159.

Ostrin, R.K., & Tyler, L.K. (in press). Dissociations of lexical function: Syntax, semantics and morphology. *Cognitive Neuropsychology*.

Patterson, K., Hodges, J., Graham, K., & Croot, K. (1994). *Varieties of progressive anomia*. Paper presented to the British Neuropsychological Society, London.

Plaut, D., & Shallice, T. (1993). Deep dyslexia: A case study of connectionist neuropsychology. *Cognitive Neuropsychology*, 10, 377–500.

Posner, M.I., & Snyder, C.R.R. (1975). Attention and cognitive control. In R. Solso (Ed.), *Information processing and cognition: The Loyola Symposium*. Hillsdale, NJ: Lawrence Erlbaum Associates Inc.

Rapp, B., & Caramazza, A. (1993). On the distinction between deficits of access and deficits of storage: A question of theory. *Cognitive Neuropsychology*, 10, 113–141.

Rapp, R., & Wettler, M. (1991). *Production of free association norms based on Hebbian learning*. Paper presented at the International Joint Conference on Neural Networks, Singapore.

Riddoch, M.J., Humphreys, G.W., Coltheart, M., & Funnell, E. (1988). Semantic systems or system? Neuropsychological evidence re-examined. *Cognitive Neuropsychology*, 5, 3–25.

Sachett, C., & Humphreys, G. (1992). Calling a squirrel a squirrel but a canoe a wigwam: A category-specific deficit for artefactual objects and body parts. *Cognitive Neuropsychology*, 9, 73–86.

Saffran, E.J., & Schwartz, M.F. (1994). Of cabbages and things: Semantic memory from a neuropsychological point of view—A tutorial review. In *Attention and Performance, XV,* 507–536.

Schwanenflugel, P.J. (1992). Why are abstract words hard to understand? In P.J. Schwanenflugel (Ed.), *The psychology of word meanings.* Hillsdale, NJ: Lawrence Erlbaum Associates Inc.

Schwanenflugel, P.J., Harnishfeger, K.K., & Stowe, R.W. (1988). Context availability and lexical decision for abstract and concrete words. *Journal of Memory and Language, 27,* 499–520.

Schwartz, M.F., Marin, O.S.M., & Saffran, E.M. (1979). Dissociation of language function in dementia: A case study, *Brain and Language, 7,* 277–306.

Shallice, T. (1988a). *From neuropsychology to mental structure.* Cambridge, UK: Cambridge University Press.

Shallice, T. (1988b). Specialisation within the semantic system. *Cognitive Neuropsychology, 5,* 133–142.

Shallice, T. (1988c). *Access and storage disorders in semantic memory.* Paper presented at workshop on Semantic Memory, Orta (cited in Rapp, B.C., & Caramazza, A., 1993).

Shelton, J.R., & Martin, R.C. (1989). *A methodology for investigating automatic semantic priming and evidence for limited spreading activation for two aphasic patients.* Paper presented to the Academy of Aphasia, Santa Fe, New Mexico.

Shelton, J.R., & Martin, R.C. (1992). How automatic is automatic semantic priming? *Journal of Experimental Psychology: Learning, Memory and Cognition, 18,* 1191–1210.

Snowden, J.S., Goulding, P.J., & Neary, D. (1989). Semantic dementia: A form of circumscribed cerebral atrophy. *Behavioural Neurology, 2,* 167–182.

Snowden, J., Griffiths, H., & Neary, D. (1994). Semantic dementia: Autobiographical contribution to preservation of meaning. *Cognitive Neuropsychology, 11,* 265–288.

Spence, D.P., & Owens, K.C. (1990). Lexical co-occurrence and association strength. *Psycholinguistic Research, 19,* 317–330.

Tanenhaus, M.K., & Lucas, M.M. (1987). Context effects in lexical processing. *Cognition, 25,* 213–234.

Tweedy, J., Lapinski, R., & Schvaneveldt, R. (1977). Semantic context effects on word recognition: Influence of varying t proportion of items presented in an appropriate context. *Memory and Cognition, 5,* 84–89.

Tyler, L.K. (1992). *Spoken language comprehension: An experimental approach to normal and disordered processing.* Cambridge, MA: MIT Press.

Tyler, L.K., Moss, H.E., & Jennings, F. (in press). Abstract word deficits in aphasia: Evidence from semantic priming. *Neuropsychology.*

Tyler, L.K., Moss, H.E., Patterson, K., & Hodges, J. (1994). *Progressive aphasia: Impairment of syntactic processing in a fluent patient.* Presented to the American Academy of Aphasia, Boston, MA.

Tyler, L.K., Ostrin, R.K., Cooke, M., & Moss, H.E. (1995). The automatic access of lexical information: Against the automaticity hypothesis. *Brain and Language, 48,* 131–162.

Warrington, E.K. (1975). The selective impairment of semantic memory. *Quarterly Journal of Experimental Psychology, 27,* 635–657.

Warrington, E.K. (1981). Concrete word dyslexia. *British Journal of Psychology, 72,* 175–196.

Warrington, E.K., & McCarthy, R. (1987). Categories of knowledge: Further fractionation and an attempted integration. *Brain, 110,* 1273–1296.

Warrington, E.K., & Shallice, T. (1979). Semantic access dyslexia. *Brain, 102,* 43–63.

Warrington, E.K., & Shallice, T. (1984). Category-specific semantic impairment. *Brain, 107,* 829–853.

Zurif, E.B., Caramazza, A., Myerson, R., & Galvin, J. (1974). Semantic feature representations for normal and aphasic language. *Brain and Language, 1,* 167–187.

MEMORY, 1995, *3* (3/4), 397–408

Probing Sensory and Associative Semantics for Animals and Objects in Normal Subjects

Keith R. Laws, Sarah A. Humber, Deborah J.C. Ramsey, and Rosaleen A. McCarthy

University of Cambridge, UK

Neuropsychological studies of patients with "category-specific" semantic memory disorders have fuelled a debate concerning the organisation of knowledge. In particular it has been suggested that the reported double dissociation between knowledge of animals and living things on the one hand, and objects on the other, reflects a more fundamental division of semantic representation into functional-associative and sensory-visual domains. The present study attempted to investigate whether there were systematic differences along these dimensions in normal subjects using a sentence-verification technique. It was found that response times were significantly longer for verification of statements concerning the sensory attributes of objects than for statements about their associative attributes. In the case of animals, there were no differences in response latency to associative or sensory statements. In the light of this previously unreported fractionation within verbal semantics, the possible consequences for models of semantic memory are discussed.

INTRODUCTION

Inherent in the concept of semantic memory is the notion that knowledge or representations of the world are organised in some way. Such organisation is evident in the way that people (and their dictionaries) define concepts. Two main classes of information are typically employed; sensory and associative knowledge. The sensory properties of a concept encompass how it looks, sounds, smells, or feels: its concrete or imageable attributes. By contrast, associative knowledge subsumes the more abstract attributes of a concept, such as the context in which it is typically found, what it is used for, and what we

Requests for reprints should be sent to Keith R. Laws, Cognitive Neuropsychology Unit, Department of Experimental Psychology, University of Cambridge, Downing Street, Cambridge CB2 3EB, UK.

Keith R. Laws is supported by a MRC studentship. Sarah Humber & Deborah Ramsey carried out these experiments as a component of their University of Cambridge PtII MVST degree 1992. Rosaleen A. McCarthy's work was partially supported by a grant from the Leverhulme Trust to King's College, Cambridge.

have learned about its formal relationships to other concepts (see Table 1). Such a distinction is reflected in the differing importance that is given to these two broad classes of attribute information in defining different semantic categories of item.

When asked to describe an elephant, a typical response might relate various pieces of knowledge drawn from semantic memory including: that it is a very large animal, it has a trunk, it is grey in colour, it is a mammal, it lives in Africa and India, and eats vegetation. If we examine dictionary definitions of animals and living things, it is notable that priority is given to sensory and in particular, visual information rather than associative information. Compare this to a typical definition or description a person might give for a computer: it is a machine that stores, manipulates, and presents information, usually it consists of a keyboard and a rectangular screen. In this case, those components of the definition that relate to any sensory properties of the object are given less priority than associative information concerning how the object is used: i.e. to associative and functional knowledge. Such associative qualities are possibly given priority because several other objects have sensory properties in common with a computer (e.g. a television) but they are regarded as different because they serve different functions. It has been argued that, in the case of objects, associative attributes are more central or carry a greater weighting than sensory attributes. Indeed, perceptually salient features may themselves serve as pointers to object function (Tversky & Hemenway, 1984).

It is clearly critical to establish whether such claims concerning the different salience of sensory and associative attributes for different categories of information have any psychological validity. The systematic investigation of these variables in the normal population has only just begun, mostly in the context of control studies for neurological patients with semantic memory deficits. Many of these studies have drawbacks with regard to their precise experimental control of the frequency, complexity, and familiarity of items (cf Funnell & Sheridan, 1992; Stewart, Parkin, & Hunkin, 1992). Nevertheless, some interesting trends are apparent. Farah, Hammond, Mehta, and Ratcliff (1989) collected control data on a series of statements (devised by Warrington &

TABLE 1
Examples of Sensory and Associative Knowledge Types

Sensory knowledge		Associative knowledge	
Visual	Camels have humps	Contextual	Camels live in deserts
Auditory	Camels snort	Biological	Camels store water
Olfactory	Camels are odorous	Functional	Camels are used as transport
Visual	Cups have handles	Contextual	Cups are found in houses
Auditory	Cups clink when touching	Biological	Cups are inanimate
Olfactory	Cups have no smell	Functional	Cups are used for drinking

Shallice, 1984) describing true and false sensory (visual) and associative attributes for living and non-living things. A *post hoc* analysis of their data carried out by the present authors, indicates differences between visual and associative attributes for different categories[1]. Sartori and Job (1988) asked their normal control subjects to generate crucial differences between pairs of closely related items within the categories of animals, vegetables, and objects. Subjects generated more sensory (perceptual) features for animals and vegetables, and more associative attributes for objects. Powell and Davidoff (this issue) found that normal controls were significantly slower to verify visual than associative properties for both animals and objects; however, their animal stimuli were lower in frequency than the objects. Farah and McClelland (1991) asked subjects to rate the content of dictionary definitions for animals and objects. They found evidence for priority being given to visual characteristics in the case of animals. However, in the case of objects there was no significant difference between visual and associative attributes.

Perhaps the most widely cited evidence for the importance of these subtypes of attribute information has been based on neuropsychological case-studies of brain-injured patients with selective impairment (or preservation) of their semantic knowledge for particular categories: category-specific semantic deficits. It has been argued that differences between semantic categories can be traced back to the relative salience of particular classes of attribute knowledge. For example, the most commonly observed dissociation has been one between living and non-living things (e.g. Hart & Gordon, 1992; McCarthy & Warrington, 1988; Sartori & Job, 1988; Silveri & Gainotti, 1988; Warrington & McCarthy, 1983, 1987; Warrington & Shallice, 1984). Impaired knowledge of living things has been attributed to a disorder within that region of semantic knowledge in which information about sensory properties is represented. By contrast, patients with loss of object knowledge have been viewed as instances of disruption to associative (and especially to the functional) knowledge within semantic memory (e.g. Sacchett & Humphreys, 1992).

These dissociations have been accounted for within two theories of semantic organisation. Riddoch et al. (1988) have argued that associative knowledge is stored in an amodal semantic system that is common to visual and verbal input (see also Humphreys, Lamotte, & Lloyd-Jones, this issue). Sensory information is primarily held in an independent "structural description" subsystem. For example, in order to answer the question "do goats have hooves" the subject must interrogate visual information held in their structural description sub-

---

[1] Control subjects made significantly more errors in verifying: (a) the visual than non-visual attributes of living things (t = 6.62, $P = 0.001$); (b) the visual attributes of living than non-living things (t = 7.63, $P = 0.001$); and (c) more visual than non-visual attribute errors for non-living things (t = 3.19, $P = 0.01$).

system. By contrast, Warrington and her colleagues have argued for subregions within semantic memory, specialised for sensory or associative knowledge (e.g. Warrington & McCarthy, 1983; Warrington & Shallice, 1984). Farah and McClelland (1991) have proposed a parallel distributed processing (PDP) model of semantic memory with some similarities to the views advanced by Warrington and Shallice (1984). Farah and McClelland subdivide semantic knowledge into dichotomous visual and associative attribute domains, which are accessed in parallel by lexical input. Living things and manmade objects are primarily differentiated in terms of their relative weightings within locally specialised components of semantic memory. Farah and McClelland have demonstrated that a "lesion" confined to associative attributes primarily impairs naming of non-living things, whereas damage to the visual subsystem will *also* disproportionately impair retrieval of associative knowledge for living things, suggesting a certain lack of independence between the domains.

The verbal probing of sensory and associative knowledge in normal subjects could offer an opportunity to separate predictions derived from these contrasting views on the organisation of semantic knowledge. The Riddoch et al. (1988) model suggests that if sensory (visual) attribute knowledge were probed by asking a person to verify the statement "Tigers have claws" or "Chairs have legs", this would require knowledge that was *only* available in the structural description system. This predicts that, in the case of lexical input, judgement of visual attributes should be generally slower than associative attributes for *both* objects and animals. The alternative viewpoint makes no such prediction because visual and associative attributes are accessed in parallel from verbal input. Any difference between visual and associative attributes should reflect the centrality of these components in the composition of lexical semantic representations. The visual properties of animals should be relatively easy to judge by comparison with the visual properties of objects; similarly, functional and associative properties of objects should be more central, and therefore more rapidly verified than their visual attributes.

The relevance of sensory and associative types of attribute in verbal knowledge can be investigated by using a sentence verification technique (e.g. Collins & Quillian, 1969). In this procedure subjects are asked to judge the truth or falsity of statements of the form "*An X is a Y*" such as "A canary is a bird", and their reaction times (RT) are measured (e.g. Smith, Shoben, & Rips, 1974). It was hypothesised that, for any concept (x), the centrality of an attribute (y) would be reflected in the relative speed with which decisions to sentences of the form "*x has a y*" or "*xs are ys*" could be made.

EXPERIMENTAL INVESTIGATION

Materials

Statements were constructed that expressed subject–attribute relationships of the form *"An X has a Y"* or *"An X is a Y"* (see Fig. 1). The variables of interest concerned the subject type (animal and object) and attribute type (visual or associative). For true statements, the attributes were chosen to reflect specific characteristic qualities of the animals and objects (e.g. Snails have shells). Word frequency of subject nouns was balanced across categories for both means and standard deviation (Thorndike-Lorge ratings of 37.5 [sd = 27.9] for animals and 37.2 [sd = 30.2] for objects). Combinations of subject and attribute were balanced so that each animal or object subject appeared combined in different statements with a visual and an associative attribute, producing four statement categories: animal visual attributes (AVA), animal associative attributes (AAA), object visual attributes (OVA) and object associative attributes (OAA). Half of the statements were constructed to express true and false propositions; false statements were generated by mis-assigning attributes within subject category (see Fig. 1). Sentence length was matched across conditions.

I. Stimulus Preparation

A number of rating-based analyses were conducted to develop a stimulus pool that was matched for its agreed truth or falsity; its visual or associative content, and conceptual difficulty.

Procedure IA

Seven undergraduate subjects were presented with a pool of 80 statements and asked to rate them (a) for their truth/falsity (on a two-point scale—true or false) and (b) the extent to which they had to visualise the content of the statement in order to verify the sentence (on a five point scale—1 = entirely or predominantly associative; 2 = mostly associative; 3 = not sure or approximately an equal mixture; 4 = mostly visual; 5 = entirely or predominantly visual).

(1) *Animal visual* (AVA)	(3) *Object visual* (OVA)
Snails have shells (true)	Forks have prongs (true)
Snails have hair (false)	Forks have windows (false)
(2) *Animal associative* (AAA)	(4) *Object associative* (OAA)
Horses are mammals (true)	Pins are sharp (true)
Horses produce calves (false)	Pins are cutlery (false)

FIG. 1.   Examples of statements used in the sentence verification task.

Results

There was complete (100%) agreement on the truth/falsity of the 28 true and 28 false statements. These statements were analysed for their visual content. The mean of the median ratings for "visual/associative" weighting were: AAA (mean = 1.5 [sd = 0.50]); AVA (mean = 4.4 [sd = 0.49]); OAA (mean = 1.6 [SD = 0.49]) and; OVA (mean = 4.2 [sd = 0.40]). Wilcoxon rank sum tests revealed significant visual rating differences between AVA and AAA (W = 0, $P < 0.01$) and between OVA and OAA (W = 0, $P < 0.01$). Mann Whitney U-tests revealed no differences between OVA and AVA in their visual ratings ($U = 40$, $P > 0.05$) or between OAA and AAA in their associative ratings ($U = 45$, $P > 0.05$. The AVA and OVA statements were rated as containing significantly greater visual information, and the AAA and OAA statements as containing significantly greater associative content. In addition, the AVA and OVA statements did not differ in visual content, whereas the AAA and OAA statements did not differ in associative content.

Procedure IB

The critical 56 statements were rated by an independent group of six student subjects for their perceived difficulty. They were asked to rate the statements on a three-point scale comprising: "easy" (3), "average" (2), or "difficult" (1) to answer.

Results

The mean of the median ratings for perceived statement difficulty were: AAA (2.05 [sd = 0.43]); AVA (2.35 [sd = 0.41]); OAA (2.15 [sd = 0.47]); and OVA (2.45 [sd = 0.57[). Wilcoxon rank sum tests revealed no differences between AAA and AVA (W = 4.5, $P > 0.05$) or OAA and OVA (W = 9, $P > 0.05$). Mann Whitney U-tests revealed no differences between AAA and OAA ($U = 35.5$, $P > 0.05$) or AVA and OVA ($U = 43.5$, $P > 0.05$). Thus, the four statement categories were rated as having comparable levels of "perceived" difficulty-to-answer.

II. Sentence Verification

Subjects

Fifty-one Cambridge undergraduates participated in the verification task (23 males and 28 females). These subjects had not participated in "Part I" of the investigation.

Procedure

Each of the 56 critical stimuli (28 true and 28 false), were presented to each subject, three times in separate blocks together with 24 filler items. The order of stimuli was pseudo-randomised with the constraint that no two statements concerning the same subject should follow consecutively. Subjects were required to decide if each statement was true or false by pressing one of two designated buttons on the keyboard. Statements were presented in lower-case Geneva font (24 point size) on an Apple Macintosh SE computer and Psychlab^{TM} software was used to control timing and recording of responses. Each trial commenced with a blank screen for 500msec, which was replaced by a sentence in the centre of the screen. The sentence remained on display until response, and was replaced again by a blank screen for 500msec before presentation of the next trial.

Results

In analysing the response-time data for each subject, only correct true responses were used. Incorrect responses to true statements and extreme response times (RTs) of more than three standard deviations were removed from each individual's RT data. The errors made by subjects occurred randomly across all categories and their removal, along with extreme latency responses, did not reduce the set of items in any specific category. Five subjects (three males and two females) with an error rate of 10% or more (across true and false statements combined) were eliminated from the analyses. Another male subject was removed because his overall mean RT was more than three standard deviations above the group mean.

Latency. Mean reaction times for each of the variables of interest are shown in Fig. 2. *r* two-way repeated measures ANOVA revealed a significant main effect for attribute type [visual vs associative: $F(1,44) = 4.06, P = 0.05$], but no effect of semantic category [animal vs object: $F(1,44) = 0.1, P = 0.76$]. There was also a significant interaction between category and attribute type: $F(1,44) = 6.31, P = 0.02$. One-tailed post-hoc t-tests revealed that OVA statement RTs were significantly longer than OAA ($t = 3.18, P = 0.001$) and AVA statements ($t = 1.66, P = 0.05$).

These ANOVA findings were replicated when the data was analysed by statement, again revealing a significant interaction between category and attribute type: $F(1,12) = 4.611, P = 0.05$. Post-hoc t-tests gave the same results as the subject analyses, with OVA taking longer than OAA ($t = -5.563, P < 0.001$) and AVA ($t = 4.424, P = 0.025$).

Accuracy. The mean percentage error rate for each statement is shown in Table 2. Error rates across the different categories were examined with a three-

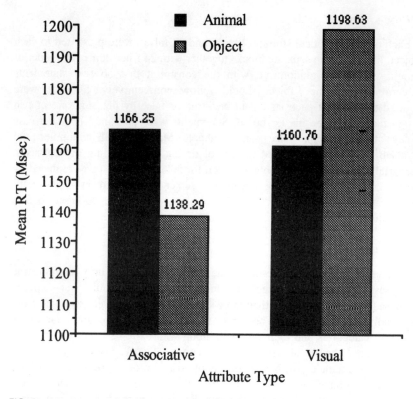

FIG. 2. Mean reaction time of normal subjects (n = 45) to verify true statements.

way repeated measures ANOVA, and no significant main or interaction effects
were found. These findings are consistent with the difficulty ratings obtained at
the start of the study and indicate that the statements can be considered to have
equivalent levels of difficulty for the normal subjects. Errors were also
examined as a function of RT for each subject and were not significantly

TABLE 2
Mean Percentage Error in Each Category

Category	True	False	T+F Mean
Animal associative	2.43	7.72	5.07
Object associative	4.65	3.17	3.91
Animal visual	7.09	3.91	5.50
Object visual	5.93	8.15	7.04
Total mean error	5.02	5.73	5.37

correlated ($r = 0.24$, $P > 0.05$), indicating that there was no important speed/ accuracy trade-off.

Homogeneity. To investigate if the overall mean RT pattern was individually represented among the 45 subjects, the number of subjects showing the fastest and slowest RTs in each category were noted (see Table 3). The individual patterns revealed a significant difference between the number of longest and shortest RTs in each category ($\chi^2 = 9.261$, $P = 0.02$) that reflected the general group pattern.

Summary

Response times for the OVA statements were significantly longer than those for OAA and AVA statements and this occurred for analyses by both subject and statement. Preliminary analyses eliminated an explanation in terms of differences in the category items related to perceived difficulty, visual/ associative content, word frequency, or sentence length. Analysis of the error data revealed no differences among categories and no evidence of a significant RT–error trade off.

General Discussion

The central findings of this study are that normal subjects are slower in verifying statements about the visual attributes of man-made objects than in verifying their associative attributes. There were no differences in verifying the visual and associative attributes of animals. This basic pattern was replicated at group, subject, and statement levels of analysis, and control measures ensured that the results were unlikely to be a consequence of differences in difficulty, degree of visual/associative content, sentence-length, or name frequency. These findings support an account of semantic organisation in which object and animal semantic categories have differential weighting on visual and associative attribute dimensions within the verbal domain. In effect, when confronted with a

TABLE 3
Number of Individual Subjects with Various Individual RT Patterns

Category	Shortest RT	Longest RT
Animal associative	10	12
Object associative	19	8
Animal visual	10	9
Object visual	6	16
Total	45	45

verbal statement, it is easier to access associative knowledge about objects than knowledge of their visual properties.

The ordering of verification latencies that we have documented is difficult to accommodate within the model of semantic organisation proposed by Riddoch, Humphreys, and their colleagues (e.g. Humphreys, Lamotte, & Lloyd-Jones, this issue; Humphreys & Riddoch, 1993; Riddoch et al. 1988). Their model proposes that visual information is stored in a quasi-independent structural description system, which is addressed via the semantic system (at least, in the case of verbal input). As this framework proposes that access to visual attributes requires an extra stage of processing, RTs to visual attributes should be generally slowed in comparison to associative attributes. Verification of visual statements did take longer in this experiment—but *only* in the case of object statements. The interaction between attribute and category appears to be at odds with the Humphreys and Riddoch position.

The alternative position proposes that latency reflects the salience of attributes (in sensory and associative sub-domains) and that they are accessed in parallel by lexical input. The present study indicates that associative attributes may be as accessible or prominent as visual attributes in lexical access to animal knowledge. Although these findings are broadly consistent with the Farah and McClelland (1991) position, they do suggest that some elaboration may be required. Although the data support the hypotheses that the names of objects have a more rapid or efficient access to associative than visual information, the lack of difference in RTs to visual and associative attributes for animals appears to undermine any simplistic model in which the "visual/associative" semantic division exactly reflects a partition between the categories of animals and objects. Such effects could conceivably be incorporated within the Farah and McClelland account by adopting weights derived from experimental tasks, rather than counts of dictionary entries.

Is such a dichotomous account sufficient? Associative attribute knowledge may be considerably more complex in its organisation than has hitherto been suggested. For example, it may be necessary to argue for a distinction between object and animal associative knowledge. Clearly, animals do not subserve or perform functions in the same way as objects; neither do objects entail the same kinds of associations as animals. It could be argued that the object-associative and animal-associative attributes encompass qualitatively different kinds of knowledge. Animal-associative knowledge might be closer to something like "general knowledge" or "facts" whereas object knowledge might be more immediately tied to functional goals. For example, the concept of "washing machine" necessarily incorporates the function of this object, however the concept of "cow" would be expected to, but need not, incorporate "chews the cud" or "provides leather". A person could still recognise a pictorial representation of a cow and retrieve visual information abut a cow (e.g. it has hooves) without necessarily having access to associative knowledge (see Laws, Evans, Hodges, & McCarthy, this issue).

Further case studies of brain-injured patients with semantic deficits complimented by converging evidence from normal subjects will be needed in order to clarify the complex interrelationships between attributes and semantic categories. The present evidence is consistent with a multi-dimensional code (incorporating sensory and associative attribute knowledge) being accessed on the basis of lexical input (e.g. Warrington & McCarthy, 1987). In the case of man-made objects, we have demonstrated that associative attributes tend to predominate over sensory (visual) attributes, at least in the verification task. However, the relative status of sensory and associative information in lexical semantics, and the further partitioning of sensory and associative knowledge within the semantic system remains somewhat underspecified and needs to be established by further research.

REFERENCES

Collins, A.M., & Quillian, M.R. (1969). Retrieval time from semantic memory. *Journal of Verbal Learning and Verbal Behavior, 8*, 240–247.

Farah, M.J., Hammond, K.H., Mehta, Z., & Ratcliff, G. (1989). Category-specificity and modality-specificity in semantic memory. *Neuropsychologia, 27*, 193–200.

Farah, M.J., & McClelland, J. (1991). A computational model of semantic memory impairment: Modality specificity and emergent category specificity. *Journal of Experimental Psychology: General, 120*, 339–357.

Funnell, E., & Sheridan, J. (1992). Categories of knowledge: Unfamiliar aspects of living and non-living things. *Cognitive Neuropsychology, 9*, 135–154.

Hart, J., & Gordon, B. (1992). Neural subsystems for object knowledge. *Nature, 359*, 60–64.

Humphreys, G.W., Lamotte, C., & Lloyd-Jones, T. (this issue). An interactive activation approach to object processing: Effects of structural similarity, name frequency and task in normality and pathology. *Memory, 3*(3/4).

Humphreys, G.W., & Riddoch, M.J. (1993). Object agnosias. In C. Kennard (Ed.), *Balliere's clinical neurology: Visual perceptual deficits*. London: Balliere Tindall.

Laws, K.R., Evans, J.J., Hodges, J.R.H., & McCarthy, R.A. (this issue). Naming without knowing and appearance without associations: Evidence for constructive processes in semantic memory? *Memory, 3*(3/4).

McCarthy, R.A., & Warrington, E.K. (1988). Evidence for modality-specific meaning systems in the brain. *Nature, 334*, 428–430.

McCarthy, R.A., & Warrington, E.K. (1994). Disorders of semantic memory. *Philosophical Transactions of the Royal Society B, 346*, 89–96.

Powell, J., & Davidoff, J. (this issue). Selective impairments of object-knowledge in a case of acquired cortical blindness. *Memory, 3*(3/4).

Riddoch, M.J., Humphreys, G.W., Coltheart, M., & Funnell, E. (1988). Semantic system or systems? Neuropsychological evidence re-examined. *Cognitive Neuropsychology, 5*, 3–25.

Sacchett, C., & Humphreys, G.W. (1992). Calling a squirrel a squirrel but a canoe a wigwam: a category specific deficit for artefactual objects and body parts. *Cognitive Neuropsychology, 9*, 73–86.

Sartori, G., & Job, R. (1988). The oyster with four legs: A neuropsychological study on the interaction between vision and semantic information. *Cognitive Neuropsychology, 5*, 105–132.

Stewart, F., Parkin, A.J., & Hunkin, N.M. (1992). Naming impairments following recovery from herpes simplex encephalitis: Category-specific? *Quarterly Journal of Experimental Psychology*, *44*a, 261–284.

Silveri, M.C., & Gainotti, G. (1988). Interaction between vision and language in category-specific semantic impairment. *Cognitive Neuropsychology*, *5*, 677–709.

Smith, E.E., Shoben, E.J., & Tips, L.J. (1974). Structure and process in semantic memory: A featural model for semantic decision. *Psychological Review*, *81*, 214–241.

Tversky, B., & Hemenway, K. (1984). Objects, parts and categories. *Journal of Experimental Psychology: General*, *113*, 169–191.

Warrington, W.K., & McCarthy, R.A. (1983). Category-specific access dysphasia. *Brain*, *106*, 859–878.

Warrington, E.K., & McCarthy, R.A. (1987). Categories of knowledge: Further fractionation and an attempted integration. *Brain*, *100*, 1273–1296.

Warrington, E.K., & Shallice, T. (1984). Category-specific semantic impairments. *Brain*, *107*, 829–853.

MEMORY, 1995, 3 (3/4), 409–433

Naming Without Knowing and Appearance Without Associations: Evidence for Constructive Processes in Semantic Memory?

Keith R. Laws

University of Cambridge, UK

Jonathan J. Evans

MRC Applied Psychology Unit, Cambridge, UK

John R. Hodges

Neurology Unit, Addenbrooke's Hospital, Cambridge, UK

Rosaleen A. McCarthy

University of Cambridge, UK

This study describes a patient (SE) with temporal lobe injury resulting from Herpes Simplex Encephalitis, who displayed a previously unreported impairment in which his knowledge of associative and functional attributes of animals was disproportionately impaired by comparison with his knowledge of their sensory attributes (including their visual properties and characteristic sounds). His knowledge of man-made objects was preserved. A striking aspect of the present case was that the patient remained able to name many animals from their pictures, despite making gross errors in generating associative information about these same animals. This suggests that a semantic representation incorporating stored sensory knowledge may be sufficient for naming (at least for biological categories) and associative information may be unnecessary. Semantic knowledge may normally incorporate more information than is necessary for identification. SE's errors were found to be confabulatory and reconstructive in nature and it is argued that this aspect of his performance challenges passive conceptions of semantic memory couched in terms of a catalogue of stored representations. It is proposed that the patient's disorder affects a dynamic, constructive, and inferential component of his knowledge base, and that this component is sensitive to semantic category.

Requests for reprints should be sent to Keith R. Laws, Cognitive Neuropsychology Unit, Department of Experimental Psychology, University of Cambridge, Downing Street, Cambridge CB2 3EB, UK.

We are grateful to John Piling for making the original referral, and to SE and his wife for their continuing assistance. To Naida Graham (who is supported by an MRC grant to John R. Hodges) who collected and scored much of the clinical interview material. Keith Laws is supported by a MRC studentship. Rosaleen McCarthy's work was partially supported by a grant from the Leverhulme Trust to King's College, Cambridge. We would also like to thank Elaine Funnell and an anonymous reviewer for their helpful comments on an earlier draft of this paper.

INTRODUCTION

Patients with category-specific semantic disorders have received considerable interest in the past few years because they have implications for the structure of stored knowledge. Most of the published cases concern patients who are impaired in their comprehension of biological things such as animals, fruit, and vegetables (e.g. Hart & Gordon, 1992; McCarthy & Warrington, 1988; Sartori & Job, 1988; Sheridan & Humphreys, 1993; Silveri & Gainotti, 1988; Warrington & Shallice, 1984). It has been suggested that the impairment of animate category knowledge might partly reflect a confounding of the frequency, complexity, and familiarity of items (cf Funnell, & Sheridan, 1992; Stewart, Parkin, & Hunkin, 1992). However, such an explanation would not account for the cases who, in contrast, experience more difficulty with man-made objects than living things (Hillis & Caramazza, 1991; Sachett & Humphreys, 1992; Warrington & McCarthy, 1983, 1987, 1994). One possible explanation for category-specific semantic impairments relates to differences in the weighting of different attributes in the process of acquiring semantic knowledge. Thus, Warrington and McCarthy (1983), and Warrington and Shallice (1984) have suggested that sensory attributes may be weighted more heavily than functional attributes in acquiring knowledge of living things, whereas the reverse could be true for man-made objects.

Using a parallel distributed processing (PDP) model of semantics, Farah and McClelland (1991) explored some possible relationships between visual and associative/functional attribute knowledge for living and non-living things. Their model showed how category-specific effects could arise from a semantic system that was subdivided by attribute modality (visual and functional) rather than category. They demonstrated that lesioning visual attributes primarily impaired living things, whereas damage to functional attributes primarily impaired man-made things. The model also showed that lesioning visual attributes necessarily impaired the retrieval of associative semantics for living things, because the latter failed to reach the "critical mass" needed for retrieval.

Riddoch, Humphreys, Coltheart, and Funnell (1988), and Sheridan and Humphreys (1993) have argued for the existence of a single amodal semantic system that contains associative/functional attribute knowledge, and a pre-semantic structural description system that is, according to Sheridan and Humphreys (1993, p.167): "The store of perceptual knowledge of object structures used to mediate visual object recognition". Sheridan and Humphreys (1993, p.171) also suggest that "Damage to the functional/semantic knowledge level may impair categories with functionally similar exemplars (e.g. foodstuffs) or items used in similar ways (e.g. small manipulable objects)". In contrast, the structural description system is thought to be particularly crucial in the recognition of living things because animals, fruits, and plants have greater structural overlap than objects.

The notion that sensory semantic attributes carry greater weighting than associative/functional attributes in the adult's capacity for identifying animals has received some support from studies of patients with category-specific semantic disorders. Silveri and Gainotti's (1988) patient (LA) was significantly more impaired at naming animals from definition when the definition stressed visual rather than associative attributes[1]; Sartori and Job (1988) found that their patient (Michaelangelo) made more visual errors when defining living things than non-living things; Farah, Hammond, Mehta, and Ratcliff (1989) found that their patient (LH) was significantly impaired on questions probing the visual characteristics of living things. Most recently, Hart and Gordon (1992) described a patient (KR) with a selective loss of knowledge of the visual attributes of animals. In contrast, his associative attribute knowledge for animals was intact.

Studies such as those outlined appear to show that deficits affecting living things are typically associated with a significant impairment of knowledge of their sensory attributes. Indeed, it has been proposed that such attribute-processing deficits are at the basis of category effects (Farah, Hammond, Mehta, & Ratcliff, 1989; Hart & Gordon, 1992; Sartori & Job, 1988; Sheridan & Humphreys, 1993; Silveri & Gainotti, 1988). However, most of these patients have also displayed some impairment of their associative attribute knowledge for animals. Some patients show limited or insignificant losses (Hart & Gordon, 1992; Farah, Hammond, Mehta, & Ratcliff, 1989), "equivalent" loss (Sheridan & Humphreys, 1993), or a milder loss (Sartori & Job, 1988; Silveri & Gainotti, 1988). Although the tests vary from study to study, the results appear to support the hypothesis that a disorder of sensory attribute knowledge is more fundamental in the category-specific impairment of living things.

However, there are inherent problems in interpreting co-occurring deficits—such as a semantic attribute deficit and a semantic category deficit. The possibility that visual attribute knowledge may just be more vulnerable than associative attribute knowledge has not been seriously considered, but such a pattern of selective loss could locally arise for reasons that are quite independent of "category-specific" effects. For example, visual attributes may be more difficult to recall, or they may require better-preserved semantic knowledge than associative attributes. Indeed, normal subjects find the visual attributes of objects more difficult to verify than their associative attributes (Laws, Humber, Ramsey, & McCarthy, this issue). Such potential performance–resource confounding are a serious limitation. Until a patient with disproportionate impairment of associative attribute knowledge is documented, it is not possible

---

[1] However, it is unclear whether this was a category or an attribute effect, as they did not include object definitions. Furthermore, some of their stimuli appeared to include mixed visual and associative attribute content (e.g. "*A domestic animal with whiskers that catches mice*" was classified as visual).

to deduce anything conclusive about the relative status of sensory or associative attribute knowledge in semantic memory organisation.

The present study reports a patient (SE) who was "functionally" recovering from Herpes Simplex Encephalitis. He was a patient with a highly atypical category-specific semantic disorder involving a severe and selective disruption of his associative knowledge for animals, together with relative sparing of his ability to name animals and to retrieve sensory knowledge about them.

CASE REPORT

SE was a 60-year-old left-handed ex-railwayman who was admitted to Addenbrooke's Hospital in Cambridge, for assessment of his complaints of "poor memory". Five years previously he had been admitted to hospital with a three-day history of headache, nausea, confusion, and disorientation. A provisional diagnosis of viral encephalitis due to Herpes Simplex was made, and at that time CT scans showed low density areas in the right temporal lobe. He was discharged from hospital three weeks later, described as being better-oriented, but having significant memory impairments particularly affecting his memory for people and places. Due to problems in recognising buildings and places he had difficulty in navigating in previously familiar environments and tended to get lost; he also mis-recognised some faces although most of his close family were recognised (a fully account of SE's topographical amnesia and prosopagnosia is given in McCarthy, Evans, & Hodges, in press).

Brain Imaging

Magnetic resonance imaging (MRI) was carried out in 1993 in Addenbrooke's Hospital radiology department using axial multiecho and 3-D SPGR with coronal reconstructions. The scans revealed gross destruction of the right temporal pole, uncus, hippocampus, parahippocampal gyrus, and inferior and lateral temporal gyri to the level of the insula with compensatory dilatation of the temporal horn of the right lateral ventricle. The left side was normal with the exception of a small region of high signal on the T2 weighted sequence in the region of the uncus and amygdala.

Neuropsychological Assessment

SE was assessed on a range of standard neuropsychological tests. The results are presented in Table 1. He had well-preserved general intellectual skills, with his current IQ, as measured by the Wechsler Adult Intelligence Scale–Revised (Wechsler, 1981) being no different from his predicted pre-morbid IQ, based on his performance on the National Adult Reading Test (Nelson & O'Connell, 1978). His performance on tests of perception, memory, and language were satisfactory. On tests of executive functioning (Wisconsin Card Sorting;

TABLE 1
SE's Performance on Standard Neuropsychological Tests

Test	Score
General Intellectual	
WAIS-R Performance IQ	101
WAIS-R Verbal IQ	99
WAIS-R Full scale IQ	100
National Adult Reading Test (NART) Estimated pre-morbid IQ	100
Perception	
Fragmented Letters	20/20
Cube Analysis	10/10
Position Discrimination	19/20
Benton Face Matching Test	44/54
Benton Line Orientation	39/40
Memory	
Wechsler Memory Scale—Revised (Index Score)	
General	94
Visual	100
Verbal	92
Delayed	76
Warrington Recognition Memory Test: Faces	33/50
Warrington Recognition Memory Test: Words	38/50
Rey-Osterrieth Complex Figure: Copy	34/36
Rey-Osterrieth Complex Figure: Recall	9/36
Executive	
Wisconsin Card Sorting Test	6 Categories
Verbal Fluency (FAS 60s each)	41
Trail Making Test A	22.5s
Trail Making Test B	76s
Cognitive Estimates Test	7 Errors
Language	
Token Test	36/36
Test for the Reception of Grammar (TROG)	76/80
Boston Naming Test	46/60

Cognitive Estimates) his performance was normal (see Table 1). On tests of category fluency, his ability to retrieve items in one minute was within the normal range: Animals (16), Birds (15), Water creatures (15), Body parts (22), Fruit (13), Vegetables (14). On FAS verbal fluency, his scores were: F (16), A (12), S (13), giving an overall score of 41, again within the normal range. He showed no tendency to perseverate and there were no intrusion errors. He appeared to have a moderate degree of naming difficulty on the Boston

Naming Test (46/60), with 50% of his errors consisting of an inability to name low-frequency animals (Octopus, Seahorse, Beaver, Pelican) and buildings or monuments (Igloo, Pyramid, and Sphinx).

SE was also required to name 258 items of the Snodgrass and Vanderwart (1980) line drawings. His naming across categories is presented in Table 2. He was generally poorer at naming items from animate categories, whereas his naming of inanimate items was perfect in most categories. An examination of the "familiarity", "visual complexity" (Snodgrass & Vanderwart, 1980) and word frequency (Francis & Kučera, 1982) ratings for named and un-named items, revealed that the items that SE was unable to name were also higher in visual complexity (2.91 vs 3.32) and lower in familiarity (3.3 vs 2.6) and word frequency (41.56 vs 6.04). The pattern of preserved and impaired categories is very similar to other published cases of naming impairments following Herpes Simplex Encephalitis. His similarity to these other cases extends to the relative sparing of body-parts in the "animate" category and the relative impairment of musical instruments in the "inanimate" category. However, his overall level of naming performance is superior to most reported cases of semantic memory dysfunction.

In order to further assess the status of his visual knowledge he was given the object decision test of Riddoch and Humphreys (1987), (kindly made available to JRH by Glyn Humphreys). The test consists of 64 line drawings of real and chimeric (composite) animals and objects, which were derived by exchanging parts of one item with another (e.g. the body of a rabbit and the head of a lion). The task requires the subject to state whether a single item is real or not. There were 32 real items (animals and objects) and 32 chimeras. A pre-test of 16 items was presented to make sure that SE understood the nature of the task. He scored 55/64 correct, which is within the range of normal controls (mean 58.7, sd = 2.4).

TABLE 2
Category-specific Naming Deficits on the Snodgrass and Vanderwart (1980) Picture Set

Animate categories	Named (%)	Inanimate categories	Named (%)
Animals	26/39 (67)	Vehicles	10/10 (100
Birds	7/8 (87)	Furniture	14/14 (100)
Insects	4/8 (50)	Tools	37/37 (100)
Fruit	8/11 (73)	Kitchen utensils	13/14 (93)
Vegetables	9/12 (75)	Buildings	4/4 (100)
Food	6/7 (86)	Clothing	26/27 (96)
Plants	3/3 (100)	Toys	11/11 (100)
Body parts	12/12 (100)	Containers	14/14 (100
		Musical instruments	7/9 (78)
		Miscellaneous	16/18 (89)
Total Animate	75/100 (75)	Total Inanimate	152/158 (96)

All of SE's errors were for animal items (he rejected three real animals and accepted six chimeric animals).

Clinical Investigations of Semantic Knowledge

SE was initially investigated to establish the status of his semantic knowledge using the naming component of the Hodges, Salmon, and Butters (1992) semantic battery (which is designed to compare knowledge of animals with man-made objects). In November, 1991 he named 27/48 items (11 living *vs* 16 man-made); in January, 1992 his score was 32/48 (14 living *vs* 18 man-made: normal controls score 43.5, sd = 1.1). Errors were made on both object and animal stimuli although there was a moderate category effect on both occasions.

SE was also asked to provide definitions of these same animals and objects when presented with their names (Hodges et al., 1992). On both testing occasions his definitions for animals were considered to be generally poorer than his definitions of objects. On the first testing session, two independent raters (who were blind to the hypotheses under investigation) considered that he conveyed the "core concept" for 10/24 of the animal stimuli and 20/24 of the objects (χ^2, 1 df = 8.88 P < 0.01). On the second occasion he was credited with conveying the core concept of 11/24 animals and 21/24 objects χ^2, 1 df = 9.375 P < 0.01). He was largely consistent in the items he could or could not define: 21/24 animal names and 20/24 object names were given the same or very similar definitions. By contrast, there was a relatively low concordance between naming and definition tasks on both testing sessions. For example, of the 18 items he was *unable* to define adequately on the first testing session, six could be named (five animals and one object). On the second occasion, he was able to name three animals and two objects that he could not define. This pattern of dissociation between definition and naming is clinically unusual.

SE's definitions were further examined by an independent rater and scored according to the type and quality of the information that he generated. His responses were categorised according to whether (a) the superordinate concept was mentioned, and (b) whether critical physical features or (c) critical associative properties were cited; (d) according to whether he produced intrusions or confabulatory information; and (e) whether some of the content was vague and non-specific. The results are shown in Fig. 1. SE was able to produce a considerable amount of correct and specific sensory/perceptual or associative information for the majority of animals and objects. The inadequacy of his definitions appeared to consist principally in his fluent confabulation of incorrect semantic information. On both testing occasions, two thirds of these confabulatory errors pertained to associative, non-sensory information. Only one object (Spinning Wheel) elicited such errors whereas 11 animal stimuli did so.

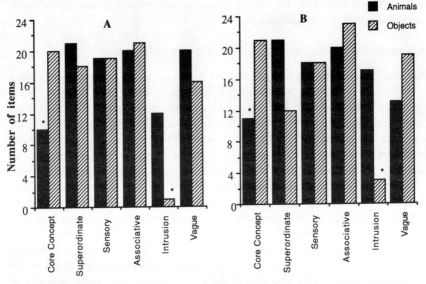

FIG. 1.   Classification of SE's definitions to the Hodges et al. (1992) test stimuli. SE's definitions to each item were scored according to their adequacy and content. The histographs illustrate the numbers of individual items in animal and object categories to which specific classes of response were given (max = 24). Graph A = test session 1; graph B = test session 2. * indicates significant differences between animal and object categories.

TEST 1: SEMANTIC KNOWLEDGE OF PICTURES AND WORDS

Test 1 comprised a series of tasks designed to assess the status of SE's semantic knowledge using a set of materials that were systematically matched on potential confounding or "nuisance" variables (cf Funnell & Sheridan, 1992; Stewart, Parkin, & Hunkin, 1992). The test was designed so that a comprehensive data set was produced which documented SE's ability to name, generate definitions, and answer probe questions in response to pictures and names drawn from living and non-living semantic categories. The semantic probe questions were devised so as to examine his ability to access sensory and associative attributes of the target stimuli.

Materials

This test made use of a set of frequency, familiarity, and visual complexity matched animal and object stimuli from the Snodgrass and Vanderwart (1980) set. The animal items consisted of 10 non-domestic and 8 domestic animals and the objects consisted of items drawn from various categories including transport, buildings, containers, and tools (see Appendix 1). Both animal and object sets consisted of items rated as below the 25th percentile on familiarity and above the 75th percentile on visual complexity. Thus, the animals (mean familiarity = 2.09, sd = 0.52; mean visual complexity = 3.77, sd = 0.45) and objects (mean familiarity = 2.15, sd = 0.52; mean visual complexity = 3.68, sd = 0.54) did not differ significantly in mean ratings of familiarity ($t = 0.36$, $P = 0.75$) or visual complexity ($t = 0.50$, $P = 0.62$). In addition, the animal and object items did not differ significantly in mean Thorndike and Lorge word frequency (animals = 25.16, sd = 24.74; objects = 27.9, sd = 25.85; $t = 0.31$, $P = 0.75$).

Procedure

Presentation. The line drawings were subdivided into two arbitrary subsets of 18 items (nine animal and nine object stimuli). SE was presented with one set of 18 randomly ordered drawings and asked to name them. For the remaining subset, SE heard the spoken name and was probed for his sensory and associative knowledge. On a subsequent occasion (three months later), the procedure was reversed, with the previously pictured subset of 18 items being probed from their names and the remaining stimuli being presented as pictures for naming. On a third and separate testing session, SE was asked to generate definitions to each of the named object and animal stimuli. On test session four, SE was presented with the entire set in picture format and probed for his sensory and associative knowledge of each item. Finally after one year, SE was re-examined on the picture-naming and definitions tasks.

Probes. The probe questions were developed so that the same questions were used for each of the animals and for each of the objects. The animal items were probed with the following forced-choice questions to assess sensory knowledge: "Does this animal have hooves or claws?" and "Is this animal bigger or smaller than a man?". (For the picture condition, the hooves or claws of each animal were occluded by a small rectangle.) The matched probes of sensory knowledge for objects were: "Does this item have any visible moving parts?" and "Is this item bigger or smaller than a man?". The associative probes for animals were: "Does this animal live in the forest, jungle, desert, open plains, or somewhere else?" and "Does this animal eat meat, vegetation, meat and vegetation, or something else?". The associative probes for objects were: "Is this object usually found indoors, outdoors, indoors and outdoors, or somewhere else?" and "Is this object a form of transport, a container, a building, a tool, or something else?". Although the associative semantic probes were unavoidably more complex than the sensory semantic probes, the frequency, familiarity, and complexity-matched object items serve as a direct control for the animal items. To summarise, the probe component of this test contrasted sensory and associative knowledge of animals and objects in response to name or picture stimuli.

Results

Naming.   SE made only two naming errors on the animal stimuli and both were for birds; one was a superordinate error (Owl → Bird) and one was a visual/semantic error (Ostrich → Swan). The single object error made by SE was a circumlocution and appeared to reflect a name-retrieval difficulty rather than lack of recognition (Spinning Wheel → "Thing for spinning cotton"). One year later, SE failed to name "Zebra", "Goat", "Ostrich", and "Spinning Wheel". The consistency of his naming across time was examined using the "two parameter stochastic model" suggested by Faglioni and Botti (1993). This provides two measures: the first (s), is a probability that a name is stored and the second (r), a probability that a stored name will be retrieved. For SE, the values of (s) and (r) were 0.96 and 0.90 respectively (neither was significantly different from an ideal naming probability of 1). The high storage and retrieval probabilities here (approaching 1) show that SE had intact and accessible name representations for the majority of stimuli in the set.

Definitions in Response to Names.   Once again his animal definitions were poor and often contained unusual semantic errors appertaining to associative attribute knowledge; his sensory attribute knowledge (and in particular his visual knowledge) seemed largely intact. On more detailed content analysis, it was noted that there were 16 examples of confabulatory errors distributed over 12/18 animals. Three confabulatory errors related to sensory information but 13 concerned associative knowledge. Table 3 shows some examples of SE's definitions. His errors were highly consistent over time: the same items elicited qualitatively similar responses over a 12-month testing interval.

Semantic Probes.   The results of the name condition are presented in Table 4 and an item-by-item tabulation appears in Appendix 1. In response to spoken names, SE made significantly more animal-associative than object-associative errors ($\chi^2 = 23.166$, $P = 0.0001$). There was no significant difference between animals and objects in his accuracy to sensory probes, indeed both scores were at or near ceiling (Fisher exact test: $P > 0.05$).

The results for the picture condition are presented in Table 4. There were no errors on objects. SE's scores on the sensory probes for animals were also near ceiling and non-significantly different from the objects (Fisher exact test: $P > 0.05$). However, once again he made significantly more animal-associative errors than object-associative errors ($\chi^2 = 26.891$, $P = 0.0001$). Comparing across picture and word input modalities there was no evidence of any major discontinuity or discrepancy. He was highly consistent, thus the same items that elicited associative errors in the verbal condition also elicited associative errors when presented as pictures (coefficient of concordance: C = 0.667 [maximum = 0.707]).

TABLE 3
Examples of SE's Definitions Given to the Names and Pictures of Animals and Objects

Animal definitions (1st testing)	Animal defintions (2nd testing—1 year later)	Object definitions
Zebra (N) "A striped type of animal, about the same size as a tiger, a forest animal, lives in South America, a member of the cat family."	*Zebra* (N) "An animal, think it's striped, lives in Africa. Thought to be very fast, yellow and black stripes. Related to the bear family."	*Television* (N) "A media used to see and hear artists, politicians or people who are in 'public-life'. A means for conveying to a person's home, visual contact with the world. Rectangular type of thing, consists of a screen and a number of buttons, has provision for an aerial and video units."
Penguin (N) "A bird that stands on two legs upright, black and white in colour, a sharp beak, I can't locate it geographically but it would be in a hot place."	*Penguin* (N) "Bird-like animal that lives in the jungle. It is black and white in colour, it stands on two legs and can fly, might be the same family as deer."	*Hand-cuffs* (N) "A means of security, they are placed on a prisoner's wrists, they have a chain linking them together, can be used with one on the prisoner and one on the arresting officer or both on the prisoner."
Kangaroo (P) "A kangaroo, a jungle animal, quite fast, it hops and it has a pocket for carrying their young in their belly, lives in the woodland areas of Africa."	*Kangaroo* (N) "Animal that lives in the jungle, also runs in Australia, fast moving animal. Brown in colour, long nose."	*Stethoscope* (P) "A stethoscope, used to test a patient's heart-beat, used by doctors."
Deer (P) "A deer, found in desert areas, places like North Africa in the desert, they eat anything, meat, vegetation, about the size of a donkey."	*Deer* (N) "An animal, extremely attractive to the eye, commonly known as one of the more docile animals for its size, it's fast in its movements. Slowly becoming very extinct. Better known in countries of Africa or South America, but not in this country. Related to a small horse."	*Camera* (P) "A camera, a 35mm camera. This is used to take pictures or slides, some can be automatic."

(N) = definition given to name; (P) = definition given to picture

419

TABLE 4
Test 1: SE's Percentage Error Rate on Probes for Names and Pictures of
Animals and Objects

	Name (% error)	Picture (% error)		Name (% error)	Picture (% error)
Animal Visual			*Object Visual*		
Hooves/claws	11.0	11.0	Moving parts	0	0
Size	11.0	11.0	Size	0	0
Mean Total	11.0	11.0	Mean Total	0	0
Animal Associative			*Object Associative*		
Environment	33.0	44.0	Indoor/outdoor	0	0
Food	72.0	72.0	Classification	0	0
Mean Total	52.5	58.0	Mean Total	0	0

Comment

The findings from this test are consistent with the clinical assessment in demonstrating that SE has marked distortions in his knowledge of the associative attributes of animals. SE demonstrated relatively intact naming for both animals and objects. However, this preserved naming occurred in the context of a significant impairment of semantic knowledge. He was inclined to generate confabulatory information about the associative attributes of animals. Both name and picture stimuli elicited comparable profiles of response and the deficit was stable over a 12-month test–retest interval. Moreover, the deficit did not appear to be limited to information generation; SE made substantially more efforts on probe recognition tasks evaluating his associative attribute knowledge of animals than on tasks evaluating his sensory knowledge.

In a further exploration of SE's confabulatory errors, he was asked to judge a set of statements including his own associative confabulations; true associative statements; false sensory information (e.g. zebras are red and white); and true sensory information. He rejected only 3/12 of his own associative confabulatory errors. With the exception of two statements concerning sensory properties, the remaining statements were judged correctly (34/36). It therefore appears that the processes underlying SE's confabulations are not merely random noise in the recall process. Rather, the errors are evidence of a semantic disorder that is also apparent in recognition tasks. They appear to be the product of a systematic and constrained distortion of his knowledge base.

The absence of errors (whether of omission or commission) in response to matched-difficulty semantic probes of object knowledge provides strong evidence for a category-specific disorder of associative knowledge rather than some more general difficulty with associative information.

TEST 2: SORTING ANIMALS BY SEMANTIC ATTRIBUTES

In order to examine further the status of SE's associative and sensory knowledge of animals, sorting tasks based on the attributes examined in Test 1 were administered. Such tasks allow us to assess SE's ability to assign specific animals to pre-determined sensory and associative attributes. (These tasks were conducted one year after the test of probed knowledge reported in Test 1 had been administered.)

Method and Procedure

Six sorting tasks were designed, in which SE was required to sort the names of the 18 animals (outlined in Test 1) into associative and sensory groupings. Two sets of visual/sensory and two sets of functional/associative sorting tasks were used. Three categories were chosen for each task, and the category labels were written on cards and presented to SE across the desk. The application and scope of each category was clearly explained and defined to SE prior to testing and he was given the opportunity to ask any further questions. He was handed a pack of 18 cards, each of which contained the name of one animal in clear print. He was instructed to read the name of each animal aloud and also to say the name of the category to which he was assigning the item (e.g. saying "Cat" and "Claws" as he sorted the appropriate card into the category of having claws). After each complete sort of 18 items, SE was allowed to move any items with which he was uncertain. The following three-category sorts were used:

A. *Sensory Attributes*
   (i) Hooves, Claws, something else
   (ii) Bigger than a man, smaller than a man, same size
B. *Associative Attributes*
   (iii) Eats meat, eats vegetation, eats both
   (iv) Lives in a hot climate, lives in a cold climate, lives in both

Results

SE scored 31/36 (86%) correct for sensory attributes (Hooves/Claws: 14/18; Size 17/18) compared with 20/36 (55%) correct for associative attributes (Diet: 5/18; Climate: 15/18). SE again made striking errors, particularly when sorting animals into the associative categories of "Diet". For example, he sorted "Owl" and "Crocodile" as vegetation eaters; "Camel" and "Rhino" as meat eaters; "Deer", "Zebra", and "Elephant" as eating both meat and vegetation.

Comment

SE was able to sort animal names by their sensory attributes at well above chance levels. However, his performance with associative attributes was more erratic. Further exploratory testing indicated that SE's knowledge of the countries and environments associated with particular animals was gravely distorted, despite his seeming adequacy on the "climates" test. For example he classified "Penguin" and "Swan" as living in the desert; "Fox" as living in the jungle; and "Ostrich" and "Zebra" as living in North America.

TEST 3: ASSOCIATIVE KNOWLEDGE
(I) ANIMAL PRODUCTS

Test 2 showed that SE could not access accurate associative information in response to the names of animals. Test 3 was designed to see if he could access animal names on the basis of one particular type of important associative information about animals, i.e. the products with which they are typically identified. This task was designed to be of such simplicity that normal subjects would be very unlikely to make any errors.

Method

SE was presented with the spoken names of 12 animal products and asked to name the animal from which the product was derived. The seven domestic and five non-domestic animals all had well-known products associated with them (e.g. Wool–Sheep; Pork–Pig). Over six months later, the task was reversed, so that SE was provided with the animal names and had to retrieve the names of the animal products.

Results

SE correctly named only 5/12 animals when given the associated product; these included not knowing from which animal we derive leather, and stating that pork came from deer. When the experimental stimuli were reversed (i.e. SE was given the animal name and had to retrieve the product), he obtained 7/12 correct. A qualitative impression of the extent of SE's problems can be conveyed in one example from the testing session: he offered his own suggestion for an animal product—"Olive oil". However he stated that he could not recall the name of the animal from which it came.

TEST 3: ASSOCIATIVE KNOWLEDGE
(II) NAMES OF ANIMAL OFFSPRING

In this test we examined SE's ability to access a further type of animal associative knowledge on the basis of an animal name, i.e. the well-known names of young animals.

Method

The names of 12 animals (9 domestic and 3 non-domestic) were presented; SE's task was to generate the name of the young of each species. The target names were those of animals for whom the names of their offspring are very well-known (e.g. Frog–Tadpole; Dog–Puppy; Cat–Kitten; Lion–Cub). The procedure was reversed six months later, and SE was provided with the name of the offspring and had to provide the name of the adult animal—this was done to control for the possibility that his poor performance could be impaired as a consequence of his naming problem[2].

Results

SE only managed to produce names of 5/12 of the offspring. His errors included some notable failures (e.g. Frog→"Froglet"; Swan→"Swanlet"; Cat→"Baby Cat"; Bird→"pass"). When the task was reversed, SE produced the names of 8/12 adults when given the name of the offspring. Again, he made some notable errors (e.g. Cub→"Pig").

TEST 4: SENSORY KNOWLEDGE
(I) ANIMAL SOUNDS

This test was designed to examine another sensory aspect of SE's semantics for animals. Most of the previous evidence for preserved knowledge of sensory attributes has concerned visual information. We wished to establish whether the integrity of his sensory knowledge extended beyond the visual-attribute domain. We therefore assessed his ability to generate animal names in response to the names of sounds distinctively associated with particular animals. The names were a mixture of formal and onomatopoeic labels.

METHOD

The names of 10 sounds associated with particular animals were read aloud to SE (e.g. which animal barks; which animal neighs; which animal hoots).

Results

SE performed well on this task, identifying 9/10 animals from which the sounds were derived (failing only "Snorts"→Pig).

TEST 4: SENSORY KNOWLEDGE
(II) ANIMAL AND OBJECT SIZE

SE's knowledge of animal and object size was examined using a reaction-time task that has previously been reported for normal subjects by Paivio (1975). In

---

[2] We are grateful to Elaine Funnell for this suggestion.

this task, subjects are required to compare two exemplars by their size. Previous work has shown that subjects are sensitive to the "real life" differences in size between comparison stimuli. Those stimulus pairs with a bigger size difference are judged more rapidly and more accurately than those that are closer together in real life. The aim of this test was to establish whether SE would show comparable sensitivity to size differences between animals and objects. It serves as a stringent measure of his ability to evoke sensory properties on the basis of pictorial and verbal input.

Method and Procedure

SE was presented with 20 pairs of pictures of animals or objects and the same 20 pairs of animals and objects presented as names. The task was to press one of two pre-identified keys to indicate whether the item on the left or right was larger in real life. The real-life size differences between the items were graded according to the scale devised by Paivio (1975)—this provided size differences ranging from a "small" size difference (= 1), to large (= 3), and very large (= 5). In the picture phase of the test, he was presented with the same animal and object pairs twice; on one occasion, the item on the left was larger and on another occasion the item on the right was larger (this gave a total set of 40 animal and 40 object pairs). The physical size of the pictures was varied in order to preclude SE's judgements being based on variables such as surface area. In the verbal condition, the printed names of the animals and objects were substituted for the pictures.

Results

Pictures. SE made seven errors (five animals [12.5%] and two objects [5%]). Four of his five animal errors were for closest size pairs (i.e. a value = 1). Overall, he was slower to respond to animal (mean RT = 1416.47) than to object pairs (mean RT = 1297.98). The important finding here was that SE showed a gradient in his RTs that reflected the size difference between pairs of items (animals and objects) and therefore the difficulty of the judgement. The mean reaction times for animals and objects at three different size disparities are shown in Table 5, along with R^2 values for RT plotted against size difference.

Words. SE made no errors for animals, and two errors (5%) for objects. There was no apparent RT difference for his animal (mean RT = 1054.11) and object (mean RT = 1063) judgements. However, once again SE showed an RT gradient relating to the size difference between pairs of items (see Table 5). The effect was strongest in the case of objects, but was also evident for the animal stimuli.

TABLE 5
RT's by Size Difference for Size Judgement Task

	RT			R^2
Size difference	1	3	5	—
Picture Object	1385.27	1263.58	1245.10	0.847
Picture Animal	1537.66	1472.00	1239.75	0.906
Word Object	1237.00	1103.40	848.60	0.969
Word Animal	1255.81	933.90	972.62	0.703

(1 = small size difference, 3 = medium and 5 = large size difference)

Comment

This test provides direct evidence of the efficacy of SE's ability to access a major sensory property on the basis of pictorial or verbal input. In the picture condition, SE made a small number of erroneous size judgements for animals, however, 4/5 of these were from the closest size category and were therefore the most difficult. For the word condition, he made no errors of size judgement for animals. Overall, SE showed a direct relationship in his RTs and the real-life size differences between animals and objects in the picture and in the word pairs. In this demanding task, SE seems able to access intact representations of animal and object size, and to use this knowledge to make judgements concerning the relative size of pairs of animals and pairs of objects.

TEST 5: SENTENCE VERIFICATION

Tests 1 and 2, along with the clinical assessment phase of this investigation documented that SE frequently generated inaccurate associative information about animals. This test directly contrasted his ability to verify sensory and associative attributes of animals and objects in a timed-response task. The task was based on a sentence verification technique (e.g. Collins & Quillian, 1969) and examined SE's speed and accuracy in deciding the truth or falsity of statements predicating sensory and associative attributes of various animals and objects. Essentially this task examines SE's ability to recognise item–attribute relations.

Materials and Procedure

The materials and procedure were the same as those outlined in Laws et al. (1995). Statements expressing subject–attribute relationships of the form "An X has a Y" or "An X is a Y" were constructed. The variables of interest were the subject type (animal or object) and attribute type (sensory or associative). Word frequency of subject nouns was balanced across categories (Thorndike-Lorge ratings of 37.5 [sd = 27.9] for animals, and 37.2 [sd = 30.2] for objects). Factorial combinations of subject and attribute were constructed so that each animal or object subject appeared combined in different statements with visual and associative attributes producing four statement categories: animal visual attributes (AVA), animal associative attributes (AAA), object visual attributes (OVA), and object associative attributes (OAA). Half of the statements were constructed to express true propositions; false statements were generated by mis-assigning attributes within subject category. Sentence length was matched across conditions. Statement items were matched by normal control subject ratings on perceived difficulty, their sensory and associative content, word frequency and sentence length (for details of ratings, see Laws et al., this issue).

Results

Following standard procedure in sentence verification tests, parametric analyses of SE's judgements were confined to "true" statements. A Spearman rank correlation revealed no significant relationship between RTs and errors ($r = 0.22$), thus ensuring no speed–accuracy trade-off.

Accuracy. There was no evidence of a response bias towards true/false judgements affecting any subject or attribute type; SE's error rate on "false" judgements was within the range of 45 normal control subjects. On "true" judgements, SE was substantially and differentially impaired in his judgements of animal associative attribute questions; his errors on other statements were not significantly different from controls. The mean percentage error rate for SE on same judgements, for each statement category, is shown in Table 6 together with the mean number of errors made by controls. A two-way repeated measures ANOVA was carried out on SE's data and revealed a significant main effect of category (animal/object), $F = 26.016$ (1,12), $P = 0.002$.

Latency (Exploratory Analysis). Only response time (RT) data for correct "true" responses were analysed. Incorrect responses and those more than three standard deviations from the mean were discarded. Mean RTs for SE and 45

TABLE 6
Mean Percentage Error for SE and Normal Control Subjects (n = 45)

Category	SE	Controls
AAA true	30.9	2.43
AVA true	9.5	7.09
OAA true	0	4.65
OVA true	2.4	5.93
Total mean percentage error	10.7	5.37

young subjects (from Laws et al., this issue) are shown in Table 7. SE's correct RTs were examined using a two-way repeated measures ANOVA with stimulus as a repeated variable, revealing a significant main effect of category (animal/object) $F(1,59) = 16.49$, $P = 0.0001$, but not for attribute type (visual/associative), $F(1,59) = 0.867$, $P = 0.355$. However, there was a significant interaction between category and attribute type, $F(1,59) = 16.39$, $P = 0.0002$. Post-hoc t-tests showed that animal associative attribute (AAA) judgement RTs were significantly longer than animal visual attribute (AVA) RTs ($t = -2.864$, $P = 0.004$) and object associative attribute (OAA) RTs ($t = 4.293$, $P = 0.0002$). In addition, object visual attribute (OVA) RTs were significantly longer than object associative attribute (OAA) RTs ($t = -2.855$, $P = 0.007$): a finding similar to that documented in young control subjects.

Comment

SE had slower RTs to AAA than AVA and OAA statements, indicating a selective difficulty with responding to questions concerning the associative attributes for animals. It is of note that his performance on "false" judgements was comparable to controls, thereby ruling out any response bias. In the error analysis, SE showed a significant effect of category that was entirely a consequence of his poor AAA performance. This pattern of task difficulty contrasts directly with that observed in control subjects, who actually found visual attribute statements concerning objects the most difficult to verify (Laws et al., this issue). SE's error rates in the other categories were commensurate with those of normal controls.

DISCUSSION

In this study we have documented a selective impairment of associative knowledge of animals in a patient 'functionally'' recovering from Herpes Simplex Encephalitis. The deficit was selective to the animals category and was observed to affect both visual (i.e. pictorial) and verbal modalities of stimulus presentation. The patient retained his knowledge of the sensory attributes of animals and also remained able to name animals from their pictures. These

TABLE 7
Mean RTs for SE and Normal Controls (n = 45)

Category	SE	Controls
AAA true	1567.25	1166.25
AVA true	1363.96	1160.76
OAA true	1097.35	1138.29
OVA true	1325.27	1198.63

findings indicate that associative and sensory information are cognitively dissociable. Our results suggest a degree of independence between the effects of category specificity and of attribute specificity.

The pattern of performance demonstrated by SE is unique in the growing literature on category-specific semantic disorders. SE's performance shows that disturbance to animal associative semantics can leave sensory knowledge about animals unaffected. He contrasts very strikingly with case KR described by Hart and Gordon (1992). KR showed a selective loss of visual attribute knowledge for animals in the presence of preserved animal associative semantics. Considered together, these findings indicate that attributional sub-components of animal semantics can be doubly dissociated. More importantly, the complementary performance of KR and SE suggests that intact sensory attribute knowledge might be necessary for naming to occur. This dissociation supports a more crucial role for visual than associative knowledge in the *identification* of animals (cf McCarthy & Warrington, 1994; Warrington & Shallice, 1984).

The category-specific aspects of SE's disorder, i.e. the *combination* of intact object functional/associative knowledge together with impaired animal associative knowledge cannot be accommodated easily within an account placing the locus of impairment within a unitary semantic system, at the level of structural descriptions—or in the operations of mapping between structural and semantic knowledge bases (e.g. Riddoch et al., 1988; Humphreys, Lamotte, & Lloyd-Jones, this issue). However, the present findings are broadly compatible with models that posit a greater role for sensory than for associative knowledge in the initial acquisition of animal concepts (e.g. McCarthy & Warrington, 1994). Although the specific dual semantic system model proposed by Farah and McClelland (1991) has difficulty explaining a selective loss of associative semantics for animals, it is conceivable that suitable refinements could be incorporated. One possibility is that the relatively lower weighting given to associative knowledge of animals in concept acquisition might lead to qualitative differences in the way that such knowledge is stored and addressed by the adult.

We would suggest that models of semantic memory need elaboration in order to incorporate multiple dimensions of "associative" or "functional" knowledge (see also Laws et al., this issue). Associative knowledge, like sensory knowledge, is almost certainly heterogeneous. The associative knowledge that is involved in the semantic representation of objects has far closer links to skilled actions than the associative knowledge pertinent to animals and living things. For example, knowing where an animal lives may be reliant on different types of information from knowing where an object is typically found. Such an elaborated account of associative knowledge might predict further dissociations such as the loss of functional object information (Morlaas, 1928) co-occurring with preserved animal associative information.

We have established that deficits of animal associative semantic knowledge are not necessarily a consequence of a primary deficit of animal sensory knowledge: the two levels of representation can be dissociated. The present case demonstrates that a failure of associative information does not invariably affect the subject's knowledge of man-made objects. Category-specific effects, such as those affecting biological categories, cannot be reduced to a core disorder of sensory or "associative" semantics *per se*. Such a pattern of differential impairment directly challenges those theories that propose deficits at the level of attribute knowledge as total explanations of category-specific dysfunction (e.g. Sartori & Job, 1988; Silveri & Gainotti, 1988). As had been widely argued, different weightings of sensory and associative knowledge may be necessary for establishing a differentiated semantic knowledge base. However, this does not entail that a disorder of attribute knowledge will necessarily result in loss of an *established* semantic category or semantic field.

However, the data gathered from SE strongly supports the notion that the semantic knowledge base incorporates far more information than is strictly necessary for *identification*. This argument has been proposed in similar formats by various authors (e.g. Chertkow, Bub, & Caplan, 1992; Smith, 1989; Smith & Medin, 1981; Smith, Medin, & Rips, 1984). Edward Smith and his colleagues have distinguished between the "*identification procedure*" and the "*core*" of a concept. The former are considered useful for so-called "quick and dirty" identification and categorisation of objects, and consist of salient properties, however they are not diagnostic of category membership. In contrast, core properties are diagnostic of category membership, tend to be relatively "hidden", and are therefore less useful for rapid categorisation. Similarly, Chertkow et al. (1992) make a distinction between those aspects of a concept that allow the recognition of a visual instantiation of an object and the sum of what is generally known about the object (e.g. to recognise a picture of a kangaroo, it is not necessary to know that it comes from Australia). Moreover, Chertkow et al. (1992, p.359) speculate that "... the fact that a patient proved unable to answer foreign/local questions about animals would consequently have no bearing on the status of semantic knowledge required for naming visual instances". In many regards, SE's performance fits well with this theoretical speculation, because he shows impaired associative attribute knowledge for animals but remains able to name pictures of those animals[3].

Models of semantic memory have typically presented a "library" type metaphor in accounting for the storage and access of "knowledge". Network (Anderson, 1983; Collins & Quillian, 1969; Norman & Rumelhart, 1975), feature (Smith, Shoben, & Rips, 1974), and PDP models (Farah & McClelland, 1991) assume that items of information stored in the brain can be directly "addressed" when required. However, some aspects of SE's performance

---

[3] Chertkow et al. have sought to establish identity between pictorial processing tasks and the "identification routine" component of semantic knowledge. We are using the two-level account here without any such commitment.

suggest a more "dynamic" or compiled aspect to semantic memory; perhaps more in accord with those cognitive models of memory that emphasise the activities of "reconstruction" in retrieval (e.g. Bartlett, 1932). We are led to speculate along these lines because of the qualitative characteristics of SE's responses.

Explanations invoking a deficit in a passive stored knowledge base account well for the typical performance of many patients with semantic disorders (e.g. they tend to produce "don't know" or superordinate-level responses in definition tasks: see e.g. Hodges et al., this issue). However, an account simply couched in terms of addressing stored representations seems quite inadequate to explain the *confabulatory* nature of SE's associative semantic errors. This confabulatory profile occurred in the context of well-preserved reasoning skills (see Table 1) and therefore cannot be attributed to a more general failure of executive function such as a failure to monitor. One previous report of a similar form of semantic confabulation has been documented in the literature by Sandson, Albert, and Alexander (1986). Their patient, a fluent aphasic who had suffered a left temporal intracerebral haematoma, produced confabulations in response to gaps in his semantic knowledge (Sandson et al., 1986, p.624): "confabulations were obtained in response to questions about the attributes of common objects *in particular of animals*. He confidently stated ... that dogs can fly and that elephants are taller than giraffes" [our italics]. Sandson et al. emphasised that their patient's disorder was primarily for questions of semantic content rather than autobiographical knowledge. The dissociation between autobiographical and semantic confabulation has also been documented by Dalla Barba (1993). The present study, together with those of Sandson et al. (1986) and Dalla Barba (1993), suggests that domain-specific constructive processes may be important in the assembly of attributes pertinent to specific concepts. And furthermore, that the specific procedures required for *associative* attribute knowledge are impaired in SE.

SE's confabulatory errors were not random but were consistently evoked by the same stimulus items. Their quality suggests an inability to access the appropriate point on relevant and important semantic dimensions (e.g. climate, diet, skin pattern). For example, he produced associative attribute information that included antonyms (e.g. penguins live in hot places), errors of conceptual overlap (e.g. there are two types of Camel—the one-humped type found in India and two-humped type found in Africa), confusion of coordinate concepts (e.g. goats provide pork; rats eat carrots), and associative attribute errors based on visual similarity (e.g. zebras, like tigers, have stripes and are therefore also members of the cat family). One possibility is that SE's difficulty might lie in those active operations of "mapping" that are required by the associative knowledge task. Perhaps active cognitive operations are required when attempting to assemble information beyond that which is required for a simple differentiation between exemplars. Within the "two level" framework of semantic processing outlined earlier, we might speculate that SE's deficit lies in the active process of co-ordinating routine differentiation or identification processes with more abstract—or core—associative knowledge of concepts.

Such a dynamic view of semantic memory operation echoes the importance of "economy" of representation in semantic memory that was incorporated by earlier network models (e.g. Collins & Quillian, 1969). Information common to several exemplars may be shared (e.g. flying is a property of most birds and therefore can be generalised as an attribute of eagles, sparrows, and parrots). Exceptions may be coded as such. Indeed, some attributes may not be directly "stored" but might be constructed as and when needed (e.g. whether hamsters suckle their young; whether frogs have blood). It seems plausible to suggest that this information can be computed by domain-specific mapping operations spanning "identification" and "core" levels of knowledge. A multiple-level mode of operation seems likely to be a characteristic mode of normal semantic processing.

In summary, then, we wish to claim that SE's semantic memory disorder affects the constructive and inferential component of his semantic knowledge base. It is remarkable that the operations of this component can be compromised while identification and even naming are spared. Moreover, the evidence appears to be consistent with a partitioning of such associative or inferential procedures along category-specific and even attribute-specific lines. Our findings indicate that disorders of semantic memory are clearly far more complex, and far more interesting, than a simple "look-up table" or library metaphor would suggest. SE provides us with a glimpse into those dynamic and problem-solving aspects of knowledge processing that are characteristic of applying semantics to the real world.

REFERENCES

Anderson, J.R. (1983). *The architecture of cognition.* Cambridge, MA: Harvard University Press.

Bartlett, F.C. (1932). *Remembering: A study in experimental and social psychology.* Cambridge: The University Press.

Chertkow, H., Bub, D., & Caplan, D. (1992). Constraining theories of semantic memory processing: evidence from dementia. *Cognitive Neuropsychology, 9,* 327–365.

Collins, A.M., & Quillian, M.R. (1969). Retrieval time from semantic memory. *Journal of Verbal Learning and Verbal Behavior, 8,* 240–247.

Dalla Barba, G. (1993). Different patterns of confabulation. *Cortex, 29,* 567–581.

Faglioni, P., & Botti, C. (1993). How to differentiate retrieval from storage deficit: a stochastic approach to semantic memory modeling. *Cortex, 30,* 301.

Farah, M.J., Hammond, K.H., Mehta, Z., & Ratcliff, G. (1989). Category-specificity and modality-specificity in semantic memory. *Neuropsychologia, 27,* 193–200.

Farah, M.J., & McClelland, J. (1991). A computational model of semantic memory impairment: Modality specificity and emergent category specificity. *Journal of Experimental Psychology: General, 120,* 339–357.

Francis, W.N., & Kučera, H. (1982). *Frequency analysis of English Usage: Lexicon and grammar.* Boston, MA.

Funnell, E., & Sheridan, J. (1992). Categories of knowledge: Unfamiliar aspects of living and non-living things. *Cognitive Neuropsychology*, 9, 135–154.

Hart, J., & Gordon, B. (1992). Neural subsystems for object knowledge. *Nature*, 359, 60–64.

Hillis, A.E., & Caramazza, A. (1991). Category-specific naming and comprehension impairment—A double dissociation. *Brain*, 114, 2081–2094.

Hodges, J.R., Graham, N., & Patterson, K. (this issue). Charting the progression in semantic dementia: Implications for the organisation of semantic memory. *Memory*, 3(3/4).

Hodges, J.R., Salmon, D.P., & Butters, N. (1992). Semantic memory impairment in Alzheimer's disease: failure of access or degraded knowledge? *Neuropsychologia*, 30, 301–314.

Humphreys, G.W., Lamotte, C., & Lloyd-Jones, T.J. (this issue). An interactive activation approach to object processing: Effects of structural similarity, name frequency, and task in normality and pathology. *Memory*, 3(3/4).

Laws, K.R., Humber, S., Ramsey, D., & McCarthy, R.A. (this issue). Probing sensory and associative semantics for animals and objects in normal subjects. *Memory*, 3(3/4).

McCarthy, R.A., Evans, J.J., & Hodges, J.R. (in press). Topographic amnesia: Spatial memory disorder, building agnosia or category-specific semantic memory impairment?

McCarthy, R.A., & Warrington, E.K. (1988). Evidence for modality-specific meaning systems in the brain. *Nature*, 334, 428–430.

McCarthy, R.A., & Warrington, E.K. (1994). Disorders of semantic memory. *Philosophical Transactions of the Royal Society B*, 346, 89–96.

Morlaas, J. (1928). *Contribution à l'étude de l'apraxie*. Paris: Amedée Legrand.

Nelson, H.E., & O'Connell, A. (1978). Dementia: the estimation of premorbid intelligence levels using the New Adult Reading Test. *Cortex*, 14, 234–244.

Norman, D.A., & Rumelhart, D.E. (1975). *Explorations in cognition*. San Francisco: Freeman.

Paivio, A. (1975). Perceptual comparisons through the mind's eye. *Memory & Cognition*, 3, 635–637.

Riddoch, M.J., & Humphreys, G.W. (1987). Visual object processing in optic aphasia: A case of semantic access agnosia. *Cognitive Neuropsychology*, 4, 131–185.

Riddoch, M.J., Humphreys, G.W., Coltheart, M., & Funnell, E. (1988). Semantic system or systems? Neuropsychological evidence re-examined. *Cognitive Neuropsychology*, 5, 3–25.

Sacchett, C., & Humphreys, G.W. (1992). Calling a squirrel a squirrel but a canoe a wig-wam: A category-specific deficit for artefactual objects and body parts. *Cognitive Neuropsychology*, 9, 73–86.

Sandson, J., Albert, M.L., & Alexander, M.P. (1986). Confabulation in aphasia. *Cortex*, 22, 621–626.

Sartori, G., & Job, R. (1988). The oyster with four legs: A neuropsychological study on the interaction between vision and semantic information. *Cognitive Neuropsychology*, 5, 105–132.

Sheridan, J., & Humphreys, G.W. (1993). A verbal–semantic category-specific recognition impairment. *Cognitive Neuropsychology*, 10, 143–184.

Silveri, M.C., & Gainotti, G. (1988). Interaction between vision and language in category-specific semantic impairment. *Cognitive Neuropsychology*, 5, 677–709.

Smith, E.E. (1989). Concepts and induction. In M. Posner (Ed.), *Foundations of cognitive science*. Cambridge, MA: MIT Press.

Smith, E.E., & Medin, D.L. (1981). *Categories and concepts*. Cambridge, MA: Harvard University Press.

Smith, E.E., Medin, D.L., & Rips, L.J. (1984). A psychological approach to concepts: Comments on Rey's "Concepts and stereotypes". *Cognition*, 17, 265–274.

Smith, E.E., Shoben, E.J., & Rips, L.J. (1974). Structure and process in semantic memory: A featural model for semantic decision. *Psychological Review*, 81, 214–241.

Snodgrass, J., & Vanderwart, M. (1980). A standardized set of 260 pictures: Norms for name agreement, familiarity, and visual complexity. *Journal of Experimental Psychology: General*, 6, 174–215.

Stewart, F., Parkin, A.J., & Hunkin, N.M. (1992). Naming impairments following recovery from herpes simplex encephalitis: Category-specific? *Quarterly Journal of Experimental Psychology,* *44a*, 261–284.

Warrington, E.K. (1984). *Recognition Memory Test.* Windsor, UK: NFER-Nelson.

Warrington, E.K., & James, M. (1991). *The Visual Object and Space Perception Battery.* Bury St. Edmunds, UK: Thames Valley Test Company.

Warrington, E.K., & McCarthy, R.A. (1983). Category-specific access dysphasia. *Brain, 106,* 859–878.

Warrington, E.K., & McCarthy, R.A. (1987). Categories of knowledge: Further fractionation and an attempted integration. *Brain, 100,* 1273–1296.

Warrington, E.K., & McCarthy, R.A. (1994). Category-specific visual agnosia: a case for visual semantics. *Neuropsychologia, 32,* 1465–1473.

Warrington, E.K., & Shallice, T. (1984). Category-specific semantic impairments. *Brain, 107,* 829–853.

Wechsler, D. (1981). *Manual for the Wechsler Adult Intelligence Scale–Revised.* New York: Psychological Corporation.

Wechsler, D., & Stone, C.P. (1945). *Wechsler Memory Scale* [Manual]. New York: Psychological Corporation.

APPENDIX

Item-by-item Details of SE's Naming and Attribute Errors for Animals

The 18 "object" items were: Anchor, Well, Axe, Barn, Basket, Cannon, Peg, Cigar, Yacht, Chisel, Helicopter, Spinning wheel, Revolver, Windmill, Pram, Barrel, Crown, Rollerskate.

Animal	Naming	Visual Attribute Errors	Associative Attribute Errors
Zebra	✓	0	1
Gorilla	✓	0	2
Ostrich	✗	2	2
Deer	✓	2	4
Squirrel	✓	0	3
Camel	✓	1	4
Goat	✓	0	2
Penguin	✓	0	4
Fox	✓	0	1
Owl	✗	0	2
Kangaroo	✓	0	2
Eagle	✓	0	1
Pig	✓	1	1
Frog	✓	0	1
Elephant	✓	0	2
Bear	✓	1	2
Crocodile	✓	0	4
Rhinoceros	✓	1	2
Total		8	40

MEMORY, 1995, 3 (3/4), 435–461

Selective Impairments of Object Knowledge in a Case of Acquired Cortical Blindness

Jennie Powell

*University Department of Geriatric Medicine, Llandough Hospital,
South Glamorgan, UK*

Jules Davidoff

University of Essex, UK

A patient (N.B.) is described, who displays distinct deficits of object knowledge related to knowledge type (Functional/Associative *vs* Visual) and also to knowledge category (Animate *vs* Inanimate). The patient was first given an orally presented forced-choice test devised to assess orthogonal combinations of knowledge type and knowledge category. In the production of this test it was found that normals took longer to respond to Visual questions than to Functional/Associative questions; therefore, sets of questions were compiled that were matched for both accuracy and latency. There were two main findings concerning N.B.'s semantic memory. First, with careful matching of difficulty level, the patient showed selective preservation of Functional/Associative knowledge of Animate objects compared with Visual knowledge of Animate objects and also compared with Functional/Associative knowledge of Inanimate objects. Second, there was a qualitative difference in patterns of knowledge retrieval for Visual compared with Functional/Associative knowledge. Retrieval of Visual knowledge, both Animate and Inanimate, was inconsistent and, in a word-pair recall test, a high degree of connection of a Visual property to an object did not promote paired-associate learning. In contrast, retrieval of Functional/Associative knowledge (both Animate and Inanimate) was consistent and paired-associate learning was influenced by connection strength. This study provides strong evidence to support the validity of both ''knowledge type'' and ''category'' based accounts of the organisation of semantic memory.

INTRODUCTION

A fundamental question for any model of memory concerns the number of semantic systems required to describe the phenomena of knowledge storage and retrieval. Consideration of the number (and type) of systems is not new. Indeed, there was a debate in the nineteenth century as to whether representations for

---

Requests for reprints should be sent to Jennie Powell, University Department of Geriatric Medicine, Academic Centre, Llandough Hospital, Penarth, South Glamorgan, CF64 2XX, UK.

object knowledge are modality based (for example, visual or verbal codes) or whether they are represented in an amodal form (see Eysenck & Keane, 1990). The early evidence in support of modality-based coding of knowledge (Charcot, 1883; Freund, 1889) was not good; consequently, in the first three-quarters of this century, the more parsimonious view that object knowledge ("semantic") representations have a unitary (amodal) code became the norm. Thus, neuropsychological models for the organisation of semantic memory became more likely to contrast concrete aspects of objects with abstract ideas (Goldstein, 1948; Marshall & Newcombe, 1973; Warrington, 1975) rather than, say, visual *vs* verbal coding. The position changed after findings in both normal research (Paivio, 1971) and with patients (Warrington, 1975) reasserted modality-based differences. These assertions were quickly challenged and the dispute between modality-based semantics and unitary semantics re-emerged (Humphreys & Riddoch, 1988; Paivio, 1971; Pylyshyn, 1979; Warrington, 1975).

Modality-specific memory impairments are now debated with accounts that have become more theoretically sophisticated. Authors wishing to posit unitary semantics allow modality-specific entry recognition systems with substantial processing capacity. They place the locus of modality-specific loss of knowledge at these primary contacts (object form/structural description) with stored object knowledge rather than at more central semantic representations (Humphreys & Riddoch, 1988; Ratcliff & Newcombe, 1982). In what may be a similar theoretical position, Caramazza, Hillis, Rapp, and Romani (1990) hold that unitary semantics can account for data from studies that apparently show modality specificity if they are combined with procedures for access of semantic information that are not identical for different types of input. Nevertheless, others still prefer to explain modality specificity by more separable stores or connections within semantics itself (see Shallice, 1988). The argument continues (Rapp, Hillis, & Caramazza, 1993; Shallice, 1993).

Somewhat separate from concerns about the modality of storage are reports of patients who display highly specific deficits or preservation of certain categories of object. The first quantitative investigation of category specificity (Goodglass, Klein, Carey, & Jones, 1966) reported dissociable word-comprehension deficits for body parts, objects, actions, colours, letters, and numbers. Other subsequent reports include claims for the selective deficits or preservation of specific object categories for colour names and indoor objects (Yamadori & Albert, 1973), countries (McKenna & Warrington 1978), geographical place names (Wapner & Gardener, 1979), specific person names (McKenna & Warrington, 1980), inanimate objects compared to some aspects of animate objects and food (Hart, Berndt, & Caramazza, 1985; Sartori & Job, 1988; Temple, 1986; Warrington & McCarthy, 1983, 1987; Warrington & Shallice, 1984), proper names (Semenza & Zettin, 1988), and large objects compared to manipulable man-made objects (Warrington & McCarthy, 1987).

The specific category deficits of greatest relevance to the present paper are the animate *vs* inanimate deficits such as those documented by Warrington and co-workers. Warrington and McCarthy (1983) observed, in spoken word to picture matching tasks, a pattern of selective preservation of animals, flowers, and foods in comparison with objects. The opposite dissociation was observed in another globally dysphasic patient (Warrington & McCarthy, 1987). These authors claim that variables such as word frequency, age of acquisition, and familiarity cannot account for this relative preservation of the inanimate category. Warrington and McCarthy (1987) suggest that performance discrepancies, such as those reported earlier for animate *vs* inanimate objects, may reflect different weighting values from various sensory channels. They suggest that animate representation may be more weighted towards sensory attributes than functional attributes. Conversely, inanimate object representation may be more dependent on functional than on sensory attributes. Thus, inanimate objects may be distinguished primarily in terms of their functional significance (e.g. shoes *vs* slippers; handbag *vs* briefcase; gate *vs* stile) whereas animate objects may be differentiated in terms of their physical attributes (e.g. carrot *vs* parsnip; canary *vs* robin; snowdrop *vs* crocus). Warrington and McCarthy (1987) thus imply that disorders of animate and inanimate objects may be the incidental result of selective damage to sensory or to functional representations. Similar theoretical interpretations have been given by other authors (Basso, Capitani, & Laiacona, 1988; Davidoff, 1991; Flores d'Arcais & Schreuder, 1987; Kelter et al., 1984; Sartori & Job, 1988; Silveri & Gainotti, 1988). However, data from most of the empirical papers are potentially ambiguous in their interpretation, in that there is either an absence of control data regarding task-difficulty level, or, where control data are provided, ceiling effects for control subjects are likely to be hiding differences in task-difficulty level.

Farah, Hammond, Mehta, and Ratcliff (1989) address the question of task-difficulty level in their report of selective impairment of animate-visual knowledge in patient L.H., who was presented with written questions concerning (a) living-visual object knowledge, (b) living-nonvisual object knowledge, (c) nonliving-visual object knowledge, and (d) nonliving-nonvisual object knowledge. He was required to circle "y" or "n" to signify "yes" or "no". Although Farah et al. (1989) claim that the four question groups were of equal difficulty level in that there were no control data ceiling effects, their control subjects' accuracy level for the living-visual group of questions (80.4%) was in fact lower than for the other three question groups (88.5%, 88.0%, 91.6%). They hypothesise a selective deficit of animate-visual knowledge on the basis that L.H.'s performance differed significantly from that of the controls only on the living-visual question group. However, the fact that the controls also found this group of questions more difficult could suggest that living-visual questions are generally more difficult. As brain damage may have the effect of making what is more difficult proportionately even more difficult, failure to adequately match question groups for accuracy and failure to take into account the difficulty level involved in the process of obtaining a correct answer may result in false conclusions regarding divisions of knowledge. Similar questions concerning level of difficulty have been raised by Stewart, Parkin, and Hunkin (1992). A further difficulty with the Farah et al. study was raised by Funnell and Sheridan (1992) who found, when re-analysing the data, that the 12 control subjects had more difficulty with visual questions about low-familiarity animate items. L.H.'s performance may therefore merely reflect control subjects' poor knowledge of the visual attributes of animate items with which they are not familiar.

The empirical work that follows considers whether, when assessed through the verbal medium, visual knowledge regarding aspects of the appearance of an object is distinguishable from functional-associative knowledge. Because the current literature suggests that animacy may be a factor that interacts with these two knowledge types, the investigations will distinguish between four possible divisions of knowledge: Animate-Visual attribute knowledge; Animate-Functional/Associative knowledge; Inanimate-Visual attribute knowledge; Inanimate-Functional/Associative knowledge. Data were obtained from control subjects (correct *vs* incorrect) to ensure that the four knowledge groups were matched for accuracy. In addition, control latency data were obtained as a measure of the degree of difficulty involved in the process of obtaining a correct answer.

Our investigation was pursued in a cortically blind patient who had had normal vision until the time of her accident. Her performance was compared to those of normal control subjects and also to a control patient with acquired peripheral blindness due to diabetes.

CASE HISTORY

N.B., born in 1961, sustained a head injury as the result of a traffic accident while on holiday in France on 9.9.82. She had obtained six 'O' levels but had failed one 'A' level taken just before her accident. On 13.10.82 N.B. was transferred to hospital in England. Examination at that time showed that she opened her eyes to command and flexed limbs to painful stimuli. On 31.03.83, N.B. was discharged into the care of her parents in the family home. She was quadriplegic, cortically blind, and dependent on others for activities of daily living.

A CT scan in June 1987 (4 years, 11 months post-onset) showed that the cerebral ventricles were dilated and very gross stigmata of parenchymatous dissolution were present in both hemispheres. On the right, the entire hemisphere had a mottled, flocculent or marmoreal hypodensity, sparing only the basal ganglia and being most severe in the anterior parietal sub-cortex. On the left there were similar changes in the temporal lobe, and the fronto-parietal convexity sulci were widened, although the hemisphere as a whole was relatively better preserved. In the occipital poles of both hemispheres there were particularly gross atrophic changes, more or less symmetrical on the two sides of the brain, and clearly implicating the calcarine and post-calcarine cortex and sub-cortex, i.e. the specific cerebral substrate for vision. A well-placed shunt catheter was lying in the right lateral ventricle, its tip being probably at the foramen of Monro. The trephine defect had partly re-ossified. The shunt had been placed following the development of post-traumatic hydrocephalus probably due to "ex-vacuo" factors or to dissolution of cerebral substrate rather than to hydrodynamic obstruction.

N.B. was 27 years of age (six and a half years post onset) when the current series of investigations were initiated in March 1989 (Month 1). She remained cortically blind except for a rough appreciation of luminance level. With some difficulty, she was able to hold objects and feed herself. N.B. presented with a moderate dysarthria and dysphonia and with impaired respiratory control for speech. She was, however, usually understandable, even if it was sometimes necessary to ask her to repeat what she had said. There was no indication of any receptive or expressive dysphasia in general conversation. Nevertheless, N.B.'s parents described her language as "flowery" and commented that it was not like this before the accident when she used more normal words. N.B.'s family reported that they did not see her as a different person and that her essential character had not been changed by the accident.

Formal Assessment of Orientation

An orientation test was devised to measure N.B.'s orientation in time, place, and person, and in relation to social environment. The test was administered eight times in eight sessions over five days during Month 7. The results showed that N.B. was not orientated in time. On 7/8 occasions she stated that the day was Monday. However, when incorrect at giving the month, she was only one month out. Incorrect answers for the year (correct = 1989) were 1907, 1966, 1969, 1986, 1988, 1988, and one "don't know" response. N.B. was consistently able to give her name, date and month of birth, but not her year of birth (one "1975" response; seven "don't know" responses). She correctly gave her age on 4/8 occasions and when incorrect was only one year out. She could consistently give her address, including town and country, and could consistently state with whom she lived. She could also consistently give the names of her father, mother, and brother, and the number of siblings she had. Although she was inconsistent in her ability to provide her brother's age (correct = 42), incorrect responses were at most six years more than the correct age. She was always able to name the Prime Minister, the Prime Minister's Political Party, and the name of the leader of the opposition party.

EXPERIMENTAL INVESTIGATIONS

Stimuli

The stimuli incorporated into the assessments designed for this investigation were drawn, wherever possible, from a core set of 130 objects. This core set was selected from the 260 black and white line drawings designed by Snodgrass and Vanderwart (1980) to be used in experiments investigating differences and similarities in the processing of pictures and words. Although assessment was to be conducted using the spoken word and not pictures, the stimuli were selected from this set of pictures because frequency and familiarity ratings were available for all items. Familiarity and frequency have been considered confounding variables in some studies using the spoken word. Familiarity ratings were obtained (Snodgrass & Vanderwart, 1980) by asking subjects to judge the familiarity of each picture, according to how usual or unusual the object was in their realm of experience, and the degree to which they came into contact with or thought about the concept. On a 5-point scale, a rating of 1 indicated low agreement and a rating of 5 indicated high agreement. The frequency ratings recorded by Snodgrass and Vanderwart (1980) are those of Kučera and Francis (1967). The 130 stimuli selected for the core set was drawn from two broad object categories, namely, the Animate category (N = 72) and the Inanimate category (N = 58). Each of these broad categories was sub-divided into six specific object categories. For the Animate group these specific object categories were: Body Parts (BP: N = 12), Vegetables (VEG: N = 8), Fruits (FRU: N = 11), Insects (INS: N = 7), Animals (ANI: N = 25), and Birds (BIR: N = 9). For the Inanimate group the specific categories were: Furniture (FUR: N = 8), Kitchen Utensils (KU: N = 11), Clothes (CLO: N = 15), Vehicles and Transport (VT: N = 8), Tools (TOO: N = 7), and Musical Instruments (MI: N = 9).

Provisional Experimental Investigations: "Legs Test"

Patient N.B. was first tested by asking questions concerning the legs of objects. Historically, the interrogation of Visual knowledge by asking questions about parts of animals was first incorporated into tests of semantic disturbance by Warrington (1975). Subsequent tests concerning heads and tails of animals have also proved informative (Chertkow, Bub, & Kaplan, 1992).

107 of the 130 items comprising the "core set" (see "Stimuli") were incorporated into the legs test. In addition, seven living creatures without legs (worm, snake, dolphin, shark, snail, whale, and salmon) were added to the core set. N.B. was asked whether each of the items had legs. If the response was "yes" she was then asked how many legs: "2", "4", "6", "8", or "more". The test was administered twice in Month 1. The results are summarised in Table 1.

TABLE 1
Legs Test

	Questions for which "Yes" is correct (n = 43)	Questions for which "Yes" is correct + giving correct number of legs (n = 43)	Questions for which "No" is correct (n = 71)
Correct on 1st administration	91	24	62
Correct on 2nd administration	95	33	61
Correct on both administrations	88	16	48

N.B.'s performance (% correct).

N.B.'s performance on the questions for which "yes" is the correct answer appeared good (88% correct). However, when asked to state the exact number of legs, performance was poor (16% correct). She stated, for example, that a peacock, a camel, and a tiger have six legs, a fox has eight legs, and a zebra "eight or more". N.B.'s performance on the questions for which "no" is the correct answer was poorer than that for the "yes" questions (48% correct). Errors included giving an apple, a shirt, a pumpkin and a lettuce two legs, a chisel and a guitar four legs, and a worm and a snake eight legs. A longer account of her difficulty in visualising objects and her introspection is given in Powell and Davidoff (1992). From these introspections and the results of the legs test, it was considered worthwhile to examine in detail her ability to retrieve visual knowledge compared with her ability to retrieve non-visual knowledge.

MAIN EXPERIMENTAL INVESTIGATIONS

Forced-choice Knowledge Test

General Method

A forced-choice test was constructed to examine, using auditory-verbal input, the state of N.B.'s object knowledge. The assessment was designed to make orthogonal comparisons between two "knowledge-types" ("Visual" knowledge and "Functional/Associative") and two "knowledge categories" ("Animate" and "Inanimate"). The four types of question will be referred to as Animate-Visual (Anim-Vis), Animate Functional/Associative (Anim-F/A), Inanimate-Visual (Inan-Vis), and Inanimate-Functional/Associative (Inan-F/A) knowledge.

Test Construction

In this test, the subject is presented with a question and is then required to select the appropriate answer out of two possible alternatives (i.e. target and distractor). To overcome problems of ceiling effects, the forced-choice test was to be devised with all sets of questions (Anim-Vis; Anim-F/A; Inan-Vis; Inan-F/A) matched by latency as well as accuracy for control subjects. For each of the 130 items (72 Animate and 58 Inanimate) constituting the "core set", two questions were devised. One of the questions concerned Visual attributes of the object and the other tapped Functional/Associative knowledge. Examples of the questions are as follows. Anim-Vis: "Which is black in colour—a camel or a gorilla?". Anim-F/A: "Which is thought to be a quite intelligent animal—a gorilla or a pig?". Inan-Vis: "Which has a body that has a round hole in the centre—a harp or a guitar?". Inan-F/A: "Which do pop groups often use—a guitar or a french horn?". Target and distractor objects within each question were always from the same specific object category (see "Stimuli"). The position of the target (first or second) was balanced and target items did not occur in either position on more than three consecutive occasions. In addition, no pairing of items was repeated within the test, and no two questions concerning items from the same specific object category occurred consecutively. Two administrations of the test were prepared, allowing the position of target and distractor to be reversed for a second presentation.

Procedure

The forced-choice test was administered to N.B. twice over four sessions in two days in Month 9. Each question was presented auditorily with repeats allowed of any question.

Control latency data were obtained for 20 subjects (10 male); all were undergraduates or postgraduates. Overall mean age was 27.3 (s.d. 5.80) years. Mean age for males was 27.4 (s.d. 3.89) years and for females 27.2 (s.d. 7.48) years. The 260 questions comprising the forced-choice test were incorporated into a BBC computer programme designed to record latency data for each question and to simulate the temporal sequence of the administration to N.B. Questions were presented in written form in order to obtain reliable latency data. There is a small possibility that the relative time to read targets and distractors differed from the relative time to required for aural comprehension of these words. However, given the overall response latencies, these differences must be of minimal significance.

Subjects were told that a question would appear on the screen; they should read it carefully and, when ready, ask for the space-bar to be pressed by the examiner. It was then explained that two possible answers would appear, one above the other on the screen, and that they should choose quickly by pressing an upper or lower key corresponding to the position of the chosen answer on the screen. The following minor changes to question format were required in this computerised written version of the test: first, the answers did not include the article "a" preceding presentation of singular target and distractor items; second, the first modification necessitated changing the item "pepper" to the plural form to avoid confusion with the condiment "pepper". Subjects were asked to choose which hand they wished to place on which key, and not to change hands. They were also asked to keep their hands on the keys throughout the experiment. The instructions were given orally and then displayed in written form on the computer screen for subjects to read before commencing a set of trial questions. Subjects were told that they should take their time reading the question but should respond quickly and accurately to the answers once they appeared. Reaction time was measured in milliseconds from the time of appearance of the target and distractor items on the screen to the time of response. Ten subjects (five male) were presented with the first administration of the test and 10 (five male) the second administration, thus balancing the position of targets and distractors. Each subject completed the test over two sessions.

A sub-set of the forced-choice test (see later text) was administered once in one session to a blind control subject (P.W.). P.W. had been blind due to diabetes since the age of 25. At the time of testing, she was eight years post-onset.

Results for Controls

The control group's mean reaction times and accuracy levels for the Anim-Vis, Anim-F/A, Inan-Vis, and Inan-F/A sets of questions are shown in Table 2. Reaction times falling outside 3 standard deviations from the mean were excluded, although if the corresponding answer was correct, it was included in the accuracy counts.

The accuracy levels recorded for controls in Table 2 were obtained under time pressure but the reduction from (presumed) perfect accuracy affects all categories equally. The four sets of questions would appear to be well matched

TABLE 2
Forced Choice Test

	Animate Visual	Animate F/A	Inanimate Visual	Inanimate F/A
Control Group	1365.2	1112.9	1471.2	1169.9
Mean RT	(s.d.393.0)	(s.d.332.3)	(s.d.376.8)	(s.d.389.1)
Control Group Accuracy	91.9	94.8	92.3	91.8
Blind Control Accuracy	94	94	92	94

Control data—Overall mean reaction time (msec) and accuracy level (%) for each of the four question sets of the full test. Accuracy levels for blind control.

POWELL AND DAVIDOFF

for accuracy. This was confirmed by a 2(Animate *vs* Inanimate) × 2(Visual *vs* Functional/Associative) ANOVA which revealed no reliable main effects or interaction (all *F* values < 1). However, the latency data show that the answers to Functional/Associative questions are easier to retrieve than answers to Visual questions. A 2(Animate *vs* Inanimate) × 2(Visual *vs* Functional/Associative) ANOVA on the latency data confirmed that Visual questions were responded to more slowly than the Functional/Associative questions, $F(1,256) = 35.20$, $P < 0.001$. There were no other reliable effects.

Before proceeding further, it was necessary to extract, from the 260 questions, four new sets of questions that were matched for both accuracy and latency. Extracting all questions within the latency band 1000–1699 created four sets of questions that were matched for both latency and accuracy (Table 3). In the 1000–1699 band there were 55 Anim-Vis questions, 40 Anim-F/A questions, 42 Inan-Vis questions, and 25 Inan F/A questions (see Appendix 1). Separate one-way analyses of variance on the latencies and accuracies of these four question sets from the 1000–1699 band revealed no differences in latency, $F(3,158 < 1$, or accuracy, $(F(3,158) < 1$. It was also possible to obtain a reasonable corpus of matched Anim-F/A and Inan-F/A questions (*t* values < 1) that were responded to within 800–999msec (Table 3).

The accuracy scores for blind control P.W. for each of the four full sets of questions are given in Table 2. P.W.'s accuracy scores for the four extracted sets of questions from the 1000–1699 latency band and for the two extracted Functional/Associative sets from the 800–999 latency band are given in Table 3. P.W.'s performance clearly does not differ from that of the sighted control group.

TABLE 3
Forced Choice Test

		Animate Visual	Animate F/A	Inanimate Visual	Inanimate F/A
1000–1699		(n = 55)	(n = 40)	(n = 42)	(n = 25)
Latency:	Control Group	1274.0	1290.0	1320.5	1292.8
		(s.d.180.8)	(s.d.204.4)	(s.d.203.6)	(s.d.193.3)
Accuracy:	Control Group	94.7	94.6	95.0	94.8
	Blind Control	98.0	93.0	98.0	100.0
	N.B.	64.6	86.3	70.2	60.0
800–999			(n = 17)		(n = 22)
Latency:	Control Group	—	929.5	—	903.9
			(s.d.57.4)		(s.d.61.4)
Accuracy:	Control Group	—	97.1	—	96.6
	Blind Control	—	96.0	—	90.0
	N.B.	—	97.1	—	95.5

Mean reaction time (msec) for controls and accuracy (%) for control group, blind control and N.B. on sub-sets 800–999 and 1000–1699.

Results for Patient N.B.

Performance Levels. The mean scores obtained by N.B. for each set of questions within the 800–999 and 1000–1699 latency bands over the two administrations of the test are recorded in Table 3. Within the 800–999 latency band, both Anim-F/A knowledge and Inan-F/A knowledge were recalled better than chance ($z = 3.88$, $P < 0.001$; $z = 4.26$, $P < 0.001$). Indeed, N.B.'s performance does not differ from the control group, although they were under time pressure. Within the 1000–1699 latency band, N.B.'s Anim-Vis knowledge and Inan-Vis knowledge differed significantly from chance ($z = 2.16$, $P < 0.05$, and $z = 2.62$, $P < 0.01$ respectively). Anim-F/A knowledge also differed significantly from chance ($z = 4.59$, $P < 0.001$). However, Inan-F/A knowledge was at chance ($z = 1.00$, $P > 0.05$) but see later under "Consistency".

Visual vs Functional/Associative Knowledge—Animate. Within the 1000–1699 latency band, a significant "knowledge-type" deficit was demonstrated, with Anim-Vis knowledge significantly impaired relative to Anim-F/A knowledge, $\chi^2(1) = 4.56$, $P < 0.05$. The analysis by latency band does, of course, mean that Visual and Functional/Associative knowledge were not requested of exactly the same items (as would have been the case had it been possible to use all 260 questions in the full test). However, for the 1000–1699 question set, there were 33 objects for which both Anim-Vis and Anim-F/A knowledge were tested. Analysis of only these items verified the superior retention of Anim-F/A knowledge over Anim-Vis knowledge: for these 33 Animate items, 19 were answered more accurately for the Functional/Associative question, six for the Visual question, and eight were equal ($P < 0.05$). An analysis of the control latencies and accuracy levels for these 33 Animate *vs* Inanimate questions revealed no significant differences. In fact, Controls answered the Functional/Associative questions more slowly and less accurately than the Visual questions (Anim-Vis 1270.3, 96.1%; Anim-F/A 1313.3, 94.4%).

Visual vs Functional/Associative Knowledge—Inanimate. For the Inanimate category, retrieval of Visual knowledge did not differ significantly from retrieval of Functional/Associative knowledge, $\chi^2(1) < 1$. For Inanimate objects, there were 16 items for which both Visual and Functional/Associative knowledge was tested; four were answered more accurately for the Functional/Associative question, seven for the Visual question, and five were equal ($P > 0.05$). An analysis of the control latencies and accuracy levels for these 16 Animate *vs* Inanimate questions revealed no significant differences (Inan-Vis 1325.1, 93.4%; Inan-F/A 1307.4, 96.6%).

Animate vs Inanimate Knowledge—Visual. Within the 1000–1699 latency band, there was no significant difference in retrieval for the Animate category in comparison with the Inanimate category $\chi^2(1) < 1$.

Animate vs Inanimate Knowledge—Functional/Associative. Anim-F/A knowledge was significantly preserved relative to Inan-F/A knowledge (1) = 4.48, $P < 0.05$. Superior retention of Anim-F/A knowledge in comparison with Inan-F/A knowledge is further supported by a reliable drop in performance between the 800–999 and 1000–1699 latency band (see Table 3) for Inanimate objects (1) = 6.35, $P < 0.05$, but not for Animate objects (1) < 1.

Frequency and Familiarity. Preserved Anim-F/A knowledge was shown, in two post-hoc analyses, not to depend on item frequency or item familiarity (see Table 4). A 2 (Animate *vs* Inanimate) × 2 (Knowledge Type: Visual *vs* Functional/Associative) ANOVA on the frequency of the target names revealed that Animate frequencies were lower, $F(1,154) = 4.25$, $P < 0.05$. For distractor names, there was a trend in the same direction, $F(1,157) = 2.32$, $P < 0.2$. Similar analyses on the familiarity of the target and distractor items revealed that both were less familiar for Animate items, $F(1,158) = 15.17$, $P < 0.001$, and $F(1,158) = 15.72$, $P < 0.001$, respectively. All other F ratios were less than 1. The lower familiarity and frequency of the Animate target and distractor items is unlikely to explain their preserved Functional/Associative knowledge. One might also add that it is not really either the frequency or the familiarity of the targets and distractors that is the crucial issue in this test, but the familiarity with the particular aspect of knowledge; one could have arcane aspects of knowledge associated with very familiar objects.

Response Consistency. Consistency of N.B.'s performance from the first to the second presentation of the test could not be evaluated for the 800–999 latency band over the first and second administrations because of the ceiling effect. However, it was possible to consider performance consistency for the 1000–1699 latency band. A binomial expansion based on the probability of a correct answer on the first session, considered deviations from the expected values of 0, 1, or 2 correct. Consistency was observed in N.B.'s responses (see Table 5) for Anim-F/A knowledge, $\chi^2(2) = 6.01$, $P < 0.05$, and for Inan-F/A

TABLE 4
Forced Choice Test

	Animate Visual		Animate F/A		Inanimate Visual		Inanimate F/A	
	Targets	Distractors	Targets	Distractors	Targets	Distractors	Targets	Distractors
Familiarity	2.92	3.02	2.96	2.99	3.65	3.71	3.31	3.44
Mean	(s.d.1.04)	(s.d.1.04)	(s.d.1.01)	(s.d.1.02)	(s.d.0.77)	(s.d.0.79)	(s.d.0.80)	(s.d.0.79)
Frequency	19.70	27.70	16.70	20.90	36.50	44.40	27.50	33.40
Mean	(s.d.31.3)	(s.d.62.5)	(s.d.29.1)	(s.d.32.7)	(s.d.63.6)	(s.d.73.9)	(s.d.44.8)	(s.d.72.4)

Mean Familiarity and frequency scores for the items in the 1000–1699 sub-set when used as targets and distractors.

TABLE 5
Forced Choice Test

	Animate Visual	Animate F/A		Inanimate Visual	Inanimate F/A	
	1000–1699	*800–999*	*1000–1699*	*1000–1699*	*800–999*	*1000–1699*
Correct on:						
Both administrations	45	94	80	52	86	48
One administration	38	6	13	36	9	24
Neither administration	16	0	8	12	0	28

Percentage of questions answered correctly by N.B. on both administrations, on one administration only, and on neither administration for each question set within the 1000–1699 sub-set and within the 800–999 sub-set.

knowledge, $\chi^2(2) = 8.04$, $P < 0.02$. In contrast, for Anim-Vis knowledge and for Inan-Vis knowledge, observed responses did not differ from chance predictions, $\chi^2(2) = 1.48$, $P > 0.05$, and $\chi^2(2)$ $P < 1$ respectively.

Discussion

Analysis of the control group's latencies revealed that it took longer to respond to questions concerning Visual properties of objects than Functional/Associative properties. In fact, only eight of the Visual questions compared to 57 of the Functional/Associative questions were answered in less than one second. These results emphasise the need to match tasks for latency as well as accuracy.

N.B. would appear to have relatively preserved Animate Functional/Associative knowledge. However, the consistency data showed reliable access to her knowledge of the Functional/Associative aspects of both Animate and Inanimate objects—even though her knowledge of the Functional/Associative aspects of Inanimate objects from the 1000–1699 band is severely limited, she tends to give the same correct or wrong answer. In contrast, even though N.B.'s Visual knowledge was shown to be above chance on the forced-choice test, it was inconsistent for both Animate and Inanimate items. Thus, qualitative differences in retrieval occurred across knowledge type (Visual *vs* Functional/Associative) but not across category type (Animate *vs* Inanimate). The difference in consistency cannot be explained away by the differences in overall recall (Funnell & Sheridan, 1992) because N.B.'s retrieval levels for Visual knowledge fell between those for the two types of Functional/Associative knowledge.

Warrington and Shallice (1984) have argued that when an impaired performance is associated with consistent responses, the patient has a degraded store of knowledge. They further argue that inconsistent responses are associated with problems of access to knowledge representations. However, the argument with respect to access has been disputed (Mayes, 1988). We were also concerned that there might be other explanations for N.B.'s inconsistent responses because we were not convinced that she retrieved Visual information by the same procedures as controls. To pursue the issue of the impaired status of Visual Knowledge, a paired-word recall test was devised; it considered the question of implicit vs explicit knowledge.

Paired-word Recall Test

Studies of brain-damaged patients have shown that overt procedures may underestimate the preservation of knowledge. Therefore, N.B. was tested with a procedure that could covertly tap the status of her knowledge. A paired-associate technique was used, similar to that which has demonstrated implicit knowledge for faces in prosopagnosia (Bruyer et al., 1983; De Haan, Young, & Newcombe, 1987). The method chosen for the examination of the status of N.B.'s implicit knowledge was the comparison of her ability to learn and recall highly/strongly connected word pairs vs ability learn low/weakly connected word pairs. High-connectedness pairs are easier to learn than Low-connectedness pairs (Warrington & Weiskrantz, 1982), provided the connection is present within the subject's knowledge store. If N.B. was able to learn High-connectedness word pairs, even though she had not previously been able to demonstrate the same connection explicitly, it may be hypothesised that the deficit is one of access to knowledge rather than loss of knowledge.

Test Construction

In designing this experiment, the intention had been to construct groups of word pairs for all combinations of knowledge category (Animate vs Inanimate), connection strength (High vs Low Connectedness), knowledge type (Visual vs Functional/Associative), and N.B.'s explicit knowledge (Consistently present vs Inconsistently present). However, it was only possible to construct the following groups of word pairs: Group 1 (Visual Inconsistently Correct)—High and Low Connectedness Animate and Inanimate Visual word-pairs for which N.B. did not appear to have consistent explicit knowledge; Group 2 (Visual Consistently Correct)—High and Low Connectedness Animate and Inanimate Visual word pairs for which N.B. did appear to have explicit knowledge; and Group 3 (Functional/Associative Consistently Correct)—High and Low Connectedness Animate and Inanimate Functional/Associative word pairs for which N.B. did appear to have explicit knowledge. It proved impossible to construct a group of Functional/Associative pairs where explicit knowledge was not consistently demonstrated because N.B. did not fail on a sufficient number of questions in the explicit knowledge component of this assessment (see later). A fourth ("filler") group of Functional/Associative pairs was used to balance the number of Visual to Functional/Associative questions; this group was not, however, considered in the final analysis.

As the Functional/Associative word pairs in this test were those for which N.B. had demonstrated consistently present explicit knowledge, it was not expected that the category-specific deficit (Animate *vs* Inanimate) found in the forced-choice test could be verified in this experiment. Nevertheless, the animacy factor was included because it is important to verify that N.B. can successfully learn word pairs for Inanimate Functional/Associative items—in the forced-choice test Inanimate-Functional/Associative knowledge, though limited, was consistent and reliable.

The choice of the particular word pairs to be included in each of the Groups (1, 2, 3) was based on two factors: (1) ratings of the degree of connectedness between stimulus and target words; (b) N.B.'s performance on explicit testing of knowledge of the connection between the two words in each word pair. In order to provide a large pool of words from which the word pairs could be selected, appropriate "core-set" words (see earlier) along with an additional eight new objects were allocated Visual and Functional/Associative properties with either a High or a Low degree of connectedness with the object (e.g. onion–round; onion–hollow; onion–cry; onion–jump). A total of 388 word pairs were created, from which a final 96 word pairs could be selected for inclusion in the paired-word recall test based on these criteria.

Ratings of the degree of connectedness between stimulus and target words were obtained for 20 control subjects (10 male, 10 female; mean age 28.1 years) with a comparable level of education to N.B. The word pairs were presented in written form, and subjects were asked to rate the connectedness of each word pair on a scale from 0 (low) to 10. In order to test N.B.'s explicit knowledge of the word pairs, each pair of words was placed into sentences with four different formats: (i) Is/Is Not Statement: e.g. "Which is correct? A lion is striped. A lion is not striped"; (ii) True/False Test: e.g. "A lion is striped. True or False"; (iii) Is/Or Not Question Test: e.g. "Is a lion striped or not striped?"; (iv) Yes/No Test: e.g. "Is a lion striped?" (Yes or No). "Do you know that for sure or are you just guessing?".

Formats (i), (ii), and (iii) were each administered once, and Format (iv) twice over nine sessions in four days during Month 25, with great care taken to ensure that N.B. did not tire. Word pairs for Group 2 (Visual Consistently Correct) and Group 3 (Functional/Associative Consistently Correct) were selected from word pairs for which N.B. showed correct explicit knowledge on all presentations of each of the explicit Formats (i.e. a total of five correct explicit responses to each word pair). Word pairs for Group 1 (Visual Inconsistently Correct) were selected from explicit questions that were answered sometimes correctly and sometimes incorrectly. It was decided to use Inconsistently Correct word pairs rather than "Always Incorrect" word pairs because N.B. showed a strong tendency to answer "yes" to Visual questions. N.B. thus achieved a high "success rate" of

86% for sentences derived from High Connectedness word pairs and a low "success rate" of 48% for sentences derived from Low Connectedness word pairs. We were concerned that her consistent wrong answers to Visual questions might reflect stable wrong information and contain pairings that would be easy for her to learn. Thus, if word pairs were selected from sentences that were consistently failed (i.e. answered "yes" to "no" questions), it would be impossible to determine whether correct recall of Low Connectedness word pairs had been assisted by consistent false-positive connections.

Twenty-four word pairs were assigned to each of the groups described earlier. These were divided into four sub-sets each comprising six word pairs (see Appendix 2); sub-set A (six Animate High Connectedness word pairs); sub-set B (six Animate Low Connectedness word pairs); sub-set C (six Inanimate High Connectedness word pairs); and sub-set D (six Inanimate Low Connectedness word pairs). Sub-set B of Group 1 consisted of only five word pairs as there were insufficient explicit questions answered correctly to obtain six word pairs. An extra filler word pair was added to this sub-set but eliminated from analysis of N.B.'s results.

A preliminary test revealed that, provided lists of word pairs were restricted to four pairs, N.B. was able to demonstrate some learning. The 96 word pairs were therefore divided into 24 lists, so that each contained four word pairs. In each list, there was one each of the following types of word pairs: Anim-Vis, Inan-Vis, Anim-F/A, and Inan-F/A. There were equal numbers of High and Low Connectedness word pairs in each list. In addition, each list contained three word pairs on which N.B. had been consistently correct, and one word pair on which N.B. was inconsistently correct on the corresponding sentences in the testing of explicit knowledge. The order of presentation of word pairs was balanced with respect to Group type (1,2,3) and Sub-set type (A,B,C,D).

Procedure

Following the presentation of a list, N.B. was asked the probe question "What word went with [stimulus word]? N.B. was encouraged to reply "Pass" if she could not recall a target word, so that the next stimulus could be presented without delay. Recall of target words was requested in the same order as presentation. Each list was presented 10 times in succession before proceeding to the next list. Two administrations of the test were prepared, with the second administration reversing the order of presentation of the four word pairs within each list. The paired-word recall test was administered twice over eight sessions in three days during Month 27. Stimulus and target words of a word pair were presented at one-second intervals, with two seconds between the presentation of a target word and the presentation of the stimulus word of the next word pair.

Predictions

The following predictions were made concerning N.B.'s performance on this test. First, where a given knowledge type has been consistently demonstrated to be present explicitly (Groups 2 and 3), performance should follow a normal pattern of greater success for High than for Low Connectedness word pairs. Second, where Visual knowledge has previously been shown to be inconsistently present explicitly (Group 1), performance on High Connectedness word pairs should not differ from performance on Low Connectedness word pairs.

Results

The overall mean scores obtained by N.B. on each of the four sub-sets within each of the three word pair groups are shown in Table 6. A 3 (Group Type) × 2 (Animate *vs* Inanimate) × 2 (High *vs* Low Connectedness) ANOVA revealed a main effect of connectedness, $F(1,60) = 9.52$, $P < 0.001$, that interacted with group, $F(2,60) = 9.12$, $P < 0.001$. Analysis of the interaction revealed that recall scores differed by connectedness for Group 3 (Functional/Associative Consistently correct), $t(21) = 5.87$, $P < 0.0001$, but not for either of the other groups ($t < 1$ in both cases). All effects involving the Animacy factor produced F ratios less than 1.

Discussion

We predicted that N.B. would find it easier to learn the word pairs that were highly connected and for which she showed explicit knowledge (Groups 2 & 3). Absence of covert Visual knowledge would be confirmed by failure to

TABLE 6
Word Pair Recall Test

	Group 1 Visual Inconsistently Correct	Group 2 Visual Correct	Group 3 Functional/ Associative Correct
Sub-set Animate High Connectedness	3.58 (s.d.2.94)	6.50 (s.d.2.35)	8.67 (s.d.2.54)
Sub-set Animate Low Connectedness	6.50 (s.d.0.84)	5.70 (s.d.2.95)	4.00 (s.d.2.28)
Sub-set Inanimate High Connectedness	5.17 (s.d.2.73)	6.00 (s.d.2.19)	7.90 (s.d.1.59
Sub-set Inanimate Low Connectedness	3.58 (s.d.2.58)	5.08 (s.d.2.63)	2.83 (s.d.1.69)

N.B.'s mean score (max = 10) on the four sub-sets within each word-pair group.

demonstrate a connectedness effect in Group 1. The results actually obtained were somewhat different. For Functional/Associative knowledge (Group 3), N.B. did indeed show an effect of connectedness. This result is in agreement with N.B.'s consistency data for Functional/Associative questions on the forced-choice test, i.e. Functional/Associative knowledge operates in the paired-word recall experiment as would be expected where knowledge representations are stable. However, consistency (Group 2) or inconsistency (Group 1) of explicitly demonstrated Visual knowledge did not differentially affect recall.

The absence of a connectedness effect for Group 2 could indicate a complete absence of intact Visual knowledge, although this would appear to be in contradiction to N.B.'s performance on the forced-choice test where N.B.'s Visual performance differed significantly from chance. Thus some retrieval process other than random generation of responses must have been in operation in that test. The slower pace of the forced-choice test may allow N.B. to use a compensatory retrieval process. Evidence for N.B.'s ability to use of compensatory strategies was recorded in the "legs test": for example, N.B. stated that she didn't know how many legs an elephant had but that she thought it was a lot because an elephant is heavy. It is likely that she used similar compensatory knowledge in the forced-choice test and also for the explicit questions from which word pairs for Group 2 were taken. However, the way in which N.B. uses compensatory knowledge suggests that it is a reasoning process that requires time. Thus, the first word of a word pair may not have had sufficient time to activate, or even to initiate activation of, compensatory knowledge, thereby eliminating the possibility of assisted recall in the paired-word recall test. It is therefore suggested that the most likely explanation of N.B.'s Visual knowledge deficit is that knowledge is lost, and that N.B. is able to answer some Visual questions with the use of compensatory non-visual knowledge which relates to visual properties (cf congenitally blind people's knowledge of the colours of some objects; Wyke & Holgate, 1973).

GENERAL DISCUSSION

From our results we wish to comment on two aspects of the functional organisation of the semantic system. First, the structure of semantics in patient N.B. allows selective preservation of Animate Functional/Associative knowledge. This result is established within a context in which questions were of equal difficulty, as measured by both latency and accuracy, and uncontaminated by effects of frequency and familiarity. Second, there was a qualitative difference in patterns of knowledge retrieval for Visual compared to Functional/Associate knowledge. Retrieval of Visual knowledge, both Animate and Inanimate, was inconsistent and the strength of association of a Visual property to an object did not promote paired-associate learning in a paired-word recall test. In contrast, retrieval of Functional/Associative knowledge (both Animate and Inanimate) was consistent and paired-associate learning was influenced by connection strength.

The relative ability to retrieve Functional but not Visual knowledge has been noted previously (Davidoff & Wilson, 1985; Goldenberg, 1992; Wilson & Davidoff, 1993). N.B.'s loss of Visual knowledge may be total (see Powell & Davidoff, 1992, for N.B.'s introspective reports). Given the location and extent of the brain damage, this might be predicted if activation of visually coded representations is required to retrieve Visual object knowledge (Farah, 1985). The loss of Visual knowledge may have an interesting consequence. It appears that concrete descriptions now play a smaller part in her conversation. N.B.'s inability to use visual descriptors could explain why her parents consider that her language has become more "flowery" (see earlier). It is noteworthy that Freund (1889; Beaton, Davidoff, & Erstfeld, 1991, p.27) made a similar observation concerning patients with impairments "in relation to the visual memory pictures". The opposite dissociation (i.e. a Functional knowledge deficit) may affect the ability to think conceptually and result in a preference for concrete expression (see Meltzer, 1983).

We now turn to consider whether N.B.'s preserved Animate Functional/ Associative knowledge could be artifactual. It could be argued that the preservation results from pre-morbid differences in the relative strengths of knowledge representation in N.B. that do not correspond to the organisation of knowledge in the majority of individuals. Perhaps, before her accident, N.B. was a teenage girl who had weakly established Functional/Associative knowledge of inanimate objects. Brain damage could serve to exacerbate differing strengths of knowledge representation. Admittedly, N.B. had been interested in biology, and this interest was still evident following her accident; but it is hard to understand why this interest should have been restricted to functional/associative aspects. There is also no evidence to suggest that she was particularly uninterested in inanimate objects. However, as a precautionary measure, we carried out a post-hoc male vs female evaluation of the 100–1699 Matched Latency and Accuracy sub-set of the forced-choice test. The results of a 2(male vs female) × 4(Anim-Vis; Anim-F/A; Inan-Vis; Inan-F/A) ANOVA on the accuracy data, and a comparable analysis on the latency data revealed no significant effects and no interactions. As a further precautionary measure, the performance of the control subject (female) who made the greatest number of errors (n = 28) on the forced-choice test was examined. This control subject's performance on animate-visual questions (45/55: 82%), Animate-Functional/Associative questions (33/40: 83%), Inanimate-Visual questions (36/42: 86%), and Inanimate-Functional/ Associative questions (20/25: 80%) provides no evidence to suggest that she has any particular difficulty with any knowledge type. The mean RTs for correct responses for each of the four knowledge types were 1242 (s.d. 413), 1264 (s.d. 507), 1399 (s.d. 510), and 1231 (s.d. 362) milliseconds respectively. A 2(Animate vs Inanimate) × 2(Visual vs Functional/Associative) ANOVA on the latency data revealed no significant effects and no interaction. Overall, it is difficult to conclude that differences in pre-morbid strength of association for N.B. in comparison with the control subjects could be so great as to give rise to a selective preservation of Animate-Functional/Associative knowledge.

Another possible artifact is that inanimate objects are represented in a more visual fashion than supposed by Warrington and McCarthy (1987); thus, loss of visual knowledge alone could have produced the selective preservation of Animate Functional/Associative knowledge. For example, it could be argued that functional/associative properties of inanimate objects require visualisation of certain features of their structure. Consider the following questions that are comparable in terms of latency and accuracy for control subjects in the forced-choice test: "Which is used for undoing something, a saw or a spanner?" and "Which are often eaten with cheese after a meal, apples or bananas?". One could also argue that the visual-sensory features of animate objects may play little, if any, role in establishing animate functional/associative information, whereas visual-sensory features are important for establishing functional/associative representations of inanimate objects. Thus, the functional/associative information relating to inanimate objects may have a stronger bias towards visual representation than does the functional/associative representation of inanimate objects. The consequence of such an organisation could be that disruption to a visual store may have a greater impact on Inanimate Functional/Associative knowledge than on Animate Functional/Associative knowledge.

This explanation of the preserved Animate Functional/Associative knowledge is unlikely. If Inanimate Functional/Associative knowledge depends on visual representations, the pattern of consistency of N.B.'s Inanimate Functional/Associative knowledge performance on the forced-choice test should reflect the pattern for Animate and Inanimate Visual knowledge, i.e. it should be inconsistent. This was not the case. However, to reassure ourselves that the questions concerning Inanimate Functional/Associative knowledge did not require more visual imagery for their solution, we carried out a control experiment. Ten undergraduate subjects were asked to rate, on a 5-point scale, the visual imagery used in answering the Animate and Inanimate Functional/Associative questions. The mean ratings were: Animate, 3.13, Inanimate 3.0, t (9) = 1.52, $P > 0.1$. The lack of difference in the latencies to answer the questions was confirmed on the same subjects; this produced no reliable difference ($t < 1$). Thus, there is no evidence to support the hypothesis that N.B.'s preserved Animate Functional/Associative knowledge is due to the fact that Inanimate Functional/Associative knowledge is more dependent on visual representations than is Animate Functional/Associative knowledge.

(In conclusion, it is suggested that this paper provides strong evidence to support a multiple-store model of knowledge representation and the division of semantics by knowledge type (Visual vs Functional/Associative) and by knowledge category (Animate vs Inanimate).)

REFERENCES

Basso, A., Capitani, E., & Laiacona, M. (1988). Progressive language impairment without dementia: a case with isolated category specific semantic defect. *Journal of Neurology, Neurosurgery and Psychiatry, 51*, 1201–1207.

Beaton, A., Davidoff, J.B., & Erstfeld, U. (1991). Freund, C.S. (1889): On optic aphasia and visual agnosia: Translation and commentary. *Cognitive Neuropsychology, 8*, 21–38.

Bruyer, R., Laterre, C., Seron, X., Feyereisen, P., Strypstein, E., Pierrard, E., & Rectem, D. (1983). A case of prosopagnosia with some preserved covert remembrance of familiar faces. *Brain and Cognition, 2*, 257–284.

Caramazza, A., Hillis, A.E., Rapp, B.S., & Romani, C. (1990). The multiple semantics hypothesis: Multiple confusions? *Cognitive Neuropsychology, 7*, 161–189.

Charcot, J.M. (1883). Un cas de suppression brusque et isolee de la vision mentale des signes et des objets (formes et couleurs). *Progres Medical, 11*, 568–571.

Chertkow, H., Bub, D., & Caplan, D. (1992). Constraining theories of semantic memory processing: Evidence from dementia. *Cognitive Neuropsychology, 9*, 327–365.

Davidoff, J. (1991). *Cognition through color.* Cambridge, MA: MIT Press.

Davidoff, J., & Wilson, B.A. (1985). A case of visual associative agnosia showing a disorder of pre-semantic categorisation. *Cortex, 21*, 121–134.

De Haan, E.H.F., Young, A., & Newcombe, F. (1987). Face recognition without awareness. *Cognitive Neuropsychology, 4*, 385–415.

Eysenck, M.W., & Keane, M.T. (1990). *Cognitive psychology* London: Lawrence Erlbaum Associates Ltd.

Farah, M.J. (1985). Psychophysical evidence for a shared representational medium for visual images and percepts. *Journal of Experimental Psychology: General, 114*, 93–105.

Farah, M.J., Hammond, K.M., Mehta, Z., & Ratcliff, G. (1989). Category-specificity and modality-specificity in semantic memory. *Neuropsychologia, 27*(2), 193–200.

Flores d'Arcais, G.B., & Schreuder, R. (1987). Semantic activation during object naming. *Psychological Research, 39*, 153–159.

Freund, C.S. (1889). On optic aphasia and visual agnosia. [Translation and commentary by: Beaton, A., Davidoff, J., & Erstfeld, U. (1991). *Cognitive Neuropsychology, 8*(1), 21–38].

Funnell, E., & Sheridan, J. (1992). Categories of knowledge? Unfamiliar aspects of living and nonliving things. *Cognitive Neuropsychology, 9*(2), 135–153.

Goldenberg, G. (1992). Loss of visual imagery and loss of visual knowledge. *Neuropsychologia, 30*, 1081–1099.

Goldstein, K. (1948). *Language and language disturbances: aphasic symptom complexes and their significance for medicine and theory of language.* New York: Grune & Stratton.

Goodglass, H., Klein, B., Carey, P., & Jones, K. (1966). Specific semantic word categories in aphasia. *Cortex, 2*, 74–89.

Hart, J., Berndt, R.S., & Caramazza, A. (1985). Category specific naming deficit following cerebral infarction. *Nature, 316*, 439–440.

Humphreys, G.W., & Riddoch, M.J. (1988). On the case for multiple semantic systems: A reply to Shallice. *Cognitive Neuropsychology, 5*, 143–150.

Kelter, S., Groetzbach, H., Freiheit, R., Hoehle, B., Wutzig, G., & Diesch, E. (1984). Object identification: The mental representation of physical and conceptual attributes. *Memory and Cognition, 12*, 123–133.

Kučera, H., & Francis, W.N. (1967). *Computational analysis of present-day American English.* Providence, RI: Brown University Press.

Marshall, J.C., & Newcombe, F. (1973). Patterns of paralexia: a psycholinguistic approach. *Journal of Psycholinguistic Research, 2*, 175–199.

Mayes, A.R. (1988). *Human organic memory disorders.* Cambridge: Cambridge University Press.

McKenna, P., & Warrington, E. (1978). Category-specific naming preservation: a single case study. *Journal of Neurology, Neurosurgery, and Psychiatry, 41*, 571–574.

McKenna, P., & Warrington, E.K. (1980). Testing for nominal dysphasia. *Journal of Neurology, Neurosurgery & Psychiatry, 43*, 781–788.

Meltzer, M.L. (1983). Poor memory: A case report. *Journal of Clinical Psychology, 39*, 3–10.

Paivio, A. (1971). *Imagery and verbal processes*. New York: Holt, Rinehart & Winston.

Powell, J., & Davidoff, J. (1992). The two legged apple. In R. Campbell (Ed.), *Mental lives*. Oxford: Basil Blackwell Ltd.

Pylyshyn, Z. (1979). Imagery theory: Not mysterious–just wrong. *Behavioral and Brain Sciences, 2*, 561–563.

Rapp, B.C., Hillis, A.E., & Caramazza, A. (1993). The role of representations in cognitive theory: More on multiple semantics and the agnosias. *Cognitive Neuropsychology, 10*, 235–249.

Ratcliff, G., & Newcombe, F. (1982). Object recognition: some deductions from the clinical evidence. In A.W. Ellis (Ed.), *Normality and pathology in cognitive functions*. London: Academic Press.

Sartori, G., & Job. R. (1988). The oyster with four legs: a neuropsychological study on the interaction of visual and semantic information. *Cognitive Neuropsychology, 5*(1), 105–132.

Semenza, C., & Denes, G. (1988). Modality and category specific aphasias. *Aphasiology, 2*(3/4), 405–410.

Semenza, C., & Zettin, M. (1988). Generating proper names: A case of selective inability. *Cognitive Neuropsychology, 5*, 711–721.

Shallice, T. (1988). *From neuropsychology to mental structure*. Cambridge: Cambridge University Press.

Shallice, T. (1993). Multiple semantics: Whose confusions? *Cognitive Neuropsychology, 10*, 251–261.

Silveri, M.C., & Gainotti, G. (1988). Interaction between vision and language in category specific semantic impairment. *Cognitive Neuropsychology, 5*, 677–709.

Snodgrass, J.G., & Vanderwart, M. (1980). A standardised set of 260 pictures: Norms for name agreement, image agreement, familiarity and visual complexity. *Journal of Experimental Psychology: Human Learning and Memory, 6*(2), 174–215.

Stewart, F., Parkin, A.J., & Hunkin, N.M. (1992). Naming impairments following recovery from herpes simplex encephalitis: Category-specific? *Quarterly Journal of Experimental Psychology, 44A*(2), 261–284.

Temple, C.M. (1986). Anomia for animals in a child. *Brain, 109*, 1225–1242.

Wapner, W., & Gardner, H. (1979). A note on patterns of comprehension and recovery in global aphasia. *Journal of Speech and Hearing Research, 29*, 765–771.

Warrington, E.K. (1975). The selective impairment of semantic memory. *Quarterly Journal of Experimental Psychology, 27*, 635–657.

Warrington, E.K., & McCarthy, R. (1983). Category specific access dysphasia. *Brain, 106*, 859–878.

Warrington, E.K., & McCarthy, R.A. (1987). Categories of knowledge. Further fractionations and an attempted integration. *Brain, 110*, 1273–1296.

Warrington, E.K., & Shallice, T. (1984). Category specific semantic impairments. *Brain, 107*, 829–854.

Warrington, E.K., & Weiskrantz, L. (1982). Amnesia: a disconnection syndrome? *Neuropsychologia, 20*, 233–248.

Wilson, B.A., & Davidoff, J. (1993). Partial recovery from visual object agnosia: a ten year follow-up study. *Cortex, 29*, 529–542.

Wyke, M., & Holgate, D. (1973). Colour-naming defects in dysphasic patients. A qualitative analysis. *Neuropsychologia, 11*, 451–461.

Yamadori, A., & Albert, M.L. (1973). Word category aphasia. *Cortex, 9*, 112–125.

APPENDIX 1

Animate-Visual Questions: 1000–1699 Sub-set

Which has very short legs?   a PENGUIN or a chicken
Which has a body that is long and thin in shape?   a CATERPILLAR or a fly
Which has a pattern on its body?   a TIGER or a sheep
Which tapers to a point at one end?   a lettuce or a CARROT
Which has black and white stripes on its tail?   a horse or a ZEBRA
Which has skin that looks smooth on the outside?   a strawberry or a BANANA
Which could be black and white in colour?   a squirrel or a COW
Which has an outer skin that looks like very thin paper?   an ONION or a potato
Which part of an adult is between two and three inches in length?   a THUMB or an arm
Which usually has a whitish body: a SHEEP or an elephant
Which has legs that are covered in feathers all the way down?   a duck or an EAGLE
Which has big thick legs?   a BEAR or a zebra
Which has a skin that has a diamond-shaped pattern on it?   a PINEAPPLE or an orange
Which is very smooth and almost shiny on the outside?   a CHERRY or a peach
Which has a long tail?   a pig or a MOUSE
Which has wings that are much bigger than its body?   a BUTTERFLY or a grasshopper
Which is taller than it is long?   a cow or a GIRAFFE
Which has holes at the end of it?   a NOSE or a finger
Which are sometimes completely red on the outside?   APPLES or pineapples
Which has coloured patches shaped a bit like a circle on its feathers?   a PEACOCK or an ostrich
Which has ears that stick up from the top of its head?   a gorilla or a KANGAROO
Which is long and thin in shape?   an ARM or a foot
Which has a large and full tail?   a SQUIRREL or a goat
Which has a very fine fur over the outside of it?   a PEACH or a banana
Which sometimes have lots of curly hair around their face and down their neck?   LIONS or foxes
Which has a back that looks hard?   a spider or a BEETLE
Which could look almost silver in colour?   a hand or the HAIR
Which could be brown in colour?   a MONKEY or a leopard
Which are fairly often blackish in colour?   butterflies or FLIES
Which stands about twelve inches high?   a peacock or a CHICKEN
Which is black in colour?   a camel or a GORILLA
Which is much fatter at the bottom than at the top?   a PEAR or a lemon
Which has very long thin legs?   an owl or an OSTRICH
Which is hollow in the middle   a tomato or a PEPPER
Which is shaped like a thin solid tube?   an ear or a FINGER
Which has legs that are quite thin?   a tiger or a DEER
Which is quite slim?   a LEOPARD or a donkey
Which part of an adult could be between one and two inches in length?   a TOE or a leg
Which is usually grey in colour?   a dog or a DONKEY
Which has hair on its tail?   a DOG or a rhinoceros
Which is usually brownish in colour on the outside?   a celery or a POTATO
Which has a very long thin neck?   an eagle or a SWAN
Which has a part that is white in colour?   the nose or an EYE
Which tapers to a point at both ends?   a watermelon or a LEMON
Which has very long thin ears sticking up from the top of its head?   a mouse or a RABBIT
Which has a thick and full tail?   a FOX or a monkey
Which has a zig-zag shaped piece sticking up from the top of its head?   a penguin or a COCKEREL

Which could be between six and seven feet tall?   a CAMEL or a lion
Which are usually pinkish in colour?   the eyes or the LIPS
Which sometimes have skin that we can almost see through?   apples or GRAPES
Which has a curved white piece sticking up from its face?   a RHINOCEROS or a cat
Which has a body that looks wrinkled?   an ELEPHANT or a bear
Which part of an adult is more than nine inches in length?   a LEG or a thumb
Which is green on the outside and red on the inside?   a pear or a WATERMELON
Which is round and fat in shape?   a PUMPKIN or a pepper

Animate-Functional/Associative Questions: 1000–1699 Sub-set

Which stops particles of dirt from getting inside us?   an ear or a NOSE
Which are often eaten with cheese after a meal?   APPLES or bananas
Which can be used as a source of alcohol?   POTATOES or lettuces
Which is it quite common in this country to keep for pleasure?   monkeys or MICE
Which are kept as a hobby when they're dead?   BUTTERFLIES or beetles
Which was traditionally used to measure material years ago?   an ARM or the hair
Which are probably more popular abroad than in Britain?   apples or WATERMELONS
Which provides us with something we can eat for breakfast?   a CHICKEN or an ostrich
Which do people traditionally throw at people they don't like?   TOMATOES or potatoes
Which have some members of their species that damage the wood in our houses?   grasshoppers or BEETLES
Which eats mainly grass and twigs?   a bear or a GIRAFFE
Which is sometimes baked in the oven?   a celery or a PEPPER
Which have certain members of their species that give humans a disease called sleeping sickness?   Bees or FLIES
Which helps to keep the head warm?   a leg or the HAIR
Which sometimes provides us with something we can use to make cheese?   a SHEEP or a deer
Which would someone in Ancient Egypt have been put to death for killing?   a CAT or a mouse
Which sometimes provide us with something we can use to make jumpers?   dogs or GOATS
Which is thought to be a quite intelligent animal?   a GORILLA or a pig
Which is it quite difficult to find being sold in a shop in the Winter?   oranges or STRAWBERRIES
Which do people in this country sometimes eat?   a DEER or a fox
Which sometimes provides us with something we can use to make pillows with?   a swan or a DUCK
Which do people on a diet often eat?   an onion or a CELERY
Which help us to keep our balance?   the lips or the TOES
Which can people in this country grow quite easily?   PEARS or pineapples
Which is sometimes used to carry people's belongings long distances?   a rabbit or a CAMEL
Which came originally from India and Africa?   RHINOCEROSES or kangaroos
Which do people traditionally give to someone who is sick?   GRAPES or cherries
Which can be used to show someone the way they should go?   a FINGER or a toe
Which is sometimes used to carry people's belongings over mountains?   a DONKEY or a rhinoceros
Which are often eaten for dessert in this country?   PEACHES or watermelons
Which do people in Britain often grow in the garden?   pumpkins or CARROTS
Which is sometimes used to wake people up in the morning?   a peacock or a COCKEREL
Which can fly?   a penguin or a SWAN
Which have some members of their species that go to sleep for long periods in the Winter?   lions or BEARS

Which do we often eat in this country?   goats or PIGS
Which has remains that are thought to cause people to fall?   a BANANA or a grape
Which eats animals?   an EAGLE or a chicken
Which was used to determine a unit of measurement still in use today?   a THUMB or an eye
Which eats only grasses and plants?   a ZEBRA or a cat
Which is also called a panther?   a tiger or a LEOPARD

Inanimate-Visual Questions: 1000–1699 Sub-set

Which are usually less than four feet wide?   MOTOR-BIKES or trains
Which might have, on the underneath of it, a very fine continuous groove forming a coil shape?   a glass or a SAUCEPAN
Which could have a main surface that is square and about 18 inches by 18 inches?   a CHAIR or a sofa
Which has a piece about two feet long coming out from each side of it?   a BLOUSE or a glove
Which has a body that has a round hole in the middle of it?   a harp or a GUITAR
Which is quite long and thin in shape?   a helicopter or a TRAIN
Which has a piece about two feet long coming out from each side of it?   a sock or a COAT
Which are usually brownish in colour?   DESKS or beds
Which has one edge with very small zig-zag shaped slits running along its length?   a hammer or a SAW
Which, if you look down on it, is like a circle in shape?   a CAP or a skirt
Which has lots of thin black and white pieces running along its length?   a PIANO or a flute
Which has a piece about two feet long coming out from each side of it?   a SHIRT or a tie
Which has two handles?   a screwdriver or a PLIERS
Which, if you look down on it, has a top that is shaped like a circle?   a DRUM or a violin
Which has a kind of loop on one side of it?   a CUP or a rolling-pin
Which sometimes have a brightly coloured flowery pattern on them?   chests of drawers or SOFAS
Which is usually more than ten feet long?   a motor-bike or a BUS
Which do men tend to have in black?   jumpers or TROUSERS
Which could have a hollow tube-shaped piece sticking out from the side of it?   a KETTLE or a bowl
Which is usually gold in colour?   a FRENCH HORN or a drum
Which has a piece sticking out from each side which is shaped roughly like a triangle?   an AEROPLANE or a lorry
Which has a body that is a bit like a figure eight in shape?   a trumpet or a VIOLIN
Which is less than three feet wide?   a bus or a BICYCLE
Which has one end like a very very thin solid tube?   a SCREWDRIVER or a saw
Which sometimes have little notches running along one edge?   spoons or KNIVES
Which, if you look down on it, is a bit like a circle in shape?   a HAT or a coat
Which is more than two feet long when belonging to an adult?   a cap or a DRESS
Which gradually flattens out at the very tip of it?   a CHISEL or a spanner
Which could be 6 feet long and 4 feet wide?   a chair or a TABLE
Which divides into four thin narrow pieces at one end?   a knife or a FORK
Which, if you look down on it, could be shaped like a circle?   a desk or a STOOL
Which could be nine inches long when belonging to an adult?   a shirt or a SOCK
Which could be ten feet high?   a LORRY or a bicycle
Which are often silver in colour?   cups or SPOONS
Which is long and thin in shape?   a guitar or a FLUTE
Which is usually gold in colour?   a TRUMPET or a piano
Which has two large curved pieces at the bottom?   a ROCKING-CHAIR or a stool
Which is like a solid tube in shape?   a ROLLING-PIN or a jug

Which has a number of thin narrow parts sticking out from it?   a GLOVE or a waistcoat
Which is very long and thin in shape?   a TIE or a blouse
Which often has the front of it rounded?   a HELICOPTER or a car
Which is similar in shape to a very large box?   a CHEST OF DRAWERS or a table

Inanimate-Functional/Associative Questions: 1000–1699 Sub-set

Which do women sometimes wear when working inside an office?   gloves or JACKETS
Which is used for undoing something?   a saw or a SPANNER
Which are there normally four of in a symphony orchestra?   pianos or FRENCH HORNS
Which do women often wear to a wedding?   socks or DRESSES
Which do people often eat meals off?   a stool or a TABLE
Which can be used for twisting wire?   a PLIERS or a hammer
Which do soldiers sometimes use when they're on parade?   a guitar or a DRUM
Which officially started carrying mail from London to Paris in November 1919?   AEROPLANES or helicopters
Which are the most ancient form of seating?   STOOLS or beds
Which do men usually wear when they're at home?   a SHIRT or a waistcoat
Which became less popular with men after the First World War?   HATS or trousers
Which is quite likely to be used for people to sing along to in a social club?   an ACCORDIAN or a flute
Which is a woman quite likely to wear when working inside an office?   SKIRTS or mittens
Which is used for putting something into a piece of wood?   a SCREWDRIVER or a spanner
Which is sometimes used to remove something from a piece of wood?   a HAMMER or an axe
Which, at the beginning of this century, did men wear to dress formally?   skirts or GLOVES
Which is there usually more than one of in an orchestra?   a VIOLIN or a harp
Which do children today tend to wear to school?   a cap or a TIE
Which is often used to rescue people?   a HELICOPTER or a lorry
Which do people tend to make for new-born babies?   MITTENS or dresses
Which do men tend to wear to a wedding?   WAISTCOATS or jumpers
Which do people sometimes use to accompany themselves while singing?   a HARP or a trumpet
Which is often used on stone and brick?   a pliers or a CHISEL
Which were certainly used in Ancient Egypt?   chests of drawers or CHAIRS
Which is usually used for cold drinks?   a GLASS or a cup

APPENDIX 2

Implicit Knowledge Test Word Pairs with Mean Connectedness Ratings for each Sub-set

	Group 1 Visual Inconsistently Correct	Group 2 Visual Correct	Group 3 Functional/ Associative Correct
Sub-Set A Animate High Connectedness	strawberry–red grasshopper–green zebra–patterned elephant–wrinkled tiger–patterned beetle–dark	banana–yellow bee–striped sheep–white apple–round monkey–brown giraffe–patterned	owl–night caterpillar–leaf goat–milk onion–cry penguin–swim celery–diet
Mean Connectedness	8.17 (s.d.1.02)	8.50 (s.d.0.72)	8.79 (s.d.0.62)
Sub-Set B Animate Low Connectedness	horse–short dog–striped pig–narrow gorilla–yellow cat–wrinkled	fox–blue squirrel–tall swan–red duck–square cherry–straight donkey–pink	ostrich–cry lion–nuts leopard–shopping grapes–angry carrot–sky peacock–honey
Mean Connectedness	0.63 (s.d.0.64)	0.18 (s.d.0.18)	0.29 (s.d.0.25)
Sub-Set C Inanimate High Connectedness	button–circular saucepan–round french-horn–shiny violin–brown pencil–thin fork–silvery	drum–circular saucer–round trumpet–shiny pin–long bed–oblong screwdriver–thin	table–meals shirt–man sock–warmth sofa–relax coat–outside piano–accompany
Mean Connectedness	8.35 (s.d.0.38)	8.03 (s.d.0.77)	8.69 (s.d.0.54)
Sub-Set D Inanimate Low Connectedness	blouse–curly bowl–straight hat–long motor-bike–fluffy car–spiky bicycle–thick	spanner–wide guitar–purple axe–hollow chair–shallow kettle–narrow glove–high	stool–accompany harp–nail pliers–stir bus–eat skirt–drink jacket–earth
Mean Connectedness	0.33 (s.d.0.48)	0.49 (s.d.0.41)	0.44 (s.d.0.41)

MEMORY, 1995, *3* (3/4), 463–495

Charting the Progression in Semantic Dementia: Implications for the Organisation of Semantic Memory

John R. Hodges

University of Cambridge, UK

Naida Graham

University of Cambridge, UK

Karalyn Patterson

MRC Applied Psychology Unit, Cambridge, UK

A patient, JL, with the syndrome of semantic dementia was assessed longitudinally over a two-year period. The data presented here address the controversy concerning the hierarchical organisation of semantic memory. On a range of category fluency tests, when first tested JL was just within the normal range on the broadest categories of animals and household items, but was virtually unable to produce any instances of specific categories such as breeds of dog or musical instruments. Longitudinal fluency data for the animal category demonstrate that while JL continued to produce the most prototypical responses (cat, dog, horse), other animal labels dropped out early from his vocabulary. On the picture-sorting tests from our semantic memory test battery, JL's discrimination between living things and man-made objects was preserved for a substantial time in conjunction with a marked decline in his sorting ability for more specific categories, particularly features or attributes (e.g. size, foreign-ness, or ferocity of animals).

An analysis of naming responses to the 260 Snodgrass and Vanderwart pictures on four occasions suggests a progressive loss of the features of semantic representations that enable discrimination between specific category instances. There was a progressive decline in circumlocutory and category co-ordinate responses with a rise in broad superordinate and cross-category errors. The latter are of particular theoretical interest; on session I, all cross-category errors respected the living/man-made distinction, but by session IV almost half of such errors failed to respect this distinction. The emergence of category prototypes was another notable feature, particularly in the living domain: at one stage, land (or

Requests for reprints should be sent to John R. Hodges, Department of Neurology, University of Cambridge Clinical School, Addenbrooke's Hospital, Hills Road, Cambridge CB2 2QQ, UK.

This research was supported by a MRC project grant to JRH. We are grateful for the helpful suggestions made by Roz McCarthy, Alfonso Caramazza, and an anonymous reviewer.

four-legged) animals were all named either cat, dog, or horse. By contrast, within the man-made domain, items were frequently described in terms of their broad use or function, until eventually no defining features were produced. These findings are discussed in the context of competing theories of semantic organisation.

INTRODUCTION

An attempt to understand how knowledge about the world is represented and organised in the brain has been a major goal of cognitive neuropsychology. In studies of brain-injured subjects with disorders of world knowledge or semantic memory (Kintsch, 1982; Tulving, 1972, 1983), particular attention has been devoted in recent years to issues concerning the internal architecture of semantic memory, for instance, whether there is separate representation of knowledge relating to different sensory modalities, or to different conceptual categories, or both (e.g. Caramazza, Hillis, Rapp, & Romani, 1990; Chertkow, Bub, & Caplan, 1992; Hillis & Caramazza, 1991a; McCarthy & Warrington, 1990; Saffran & Schwartz, 1994; Sheridan & Humphreys, 1993; Warrington & Shallice, 1984). Although the question of how such knowledge is actually represented has been a topic of intense interest among experimental cognitive psychologists (for review see Chang 1986), this topic has received relatively less attention from neuropsychologists, and at present there is no consensus (see Caramazza et al., 1990).

A fuller account of the competing theories will follow in the discussion. In brief, two main hypotheses have been proposed to explain the observation that patients with semantic memory loss often show a preservation of broad superordinate information but a loss of finer grained knowledge (e.g. when asked questions about an elephant, such patients are able to answer correctly that it is an animal, but are unable to answer more specific questions about its habitat, size, ferocity, etc.). The first explanation, and perhaps the most intuitively appealing, is that this finding actually reflects the hierarchical manner in which knowledge is organised (Collins & Quillian, 1969), with more specific aspects of the hierarchy more vulnerable to brain damage (Shallice, 1988). The second explanation is that degraded semantic information is better able to support general than specific distinctions (McClelland & Rumelhart, 1985; Rapp & Caramazza, 1989, 1993). This view requires no assumptions about hierarchical forms of representation. If one's knowledge about an elephant consists of a network of semantic features, then, even when a substantial number of these have been lost, it is possible that the remaining information would permit the classification of an elephant as an animal (rather than a man-made object), because almost any "animal" feature distinguishes it from a non-living thing.

A third explanation advanced more recently to explain the apparent preservation of superordinate information locates the effect in the form of testing, rather than in the form of knowledge representation. By this account, as words used to describe higher levels of the putative tree (e.g. "animal", "bird", etc.) are more common vocabulary items than those for more specific distinctions (e.g. "foreign", "fierce"), the apparently hierarchical loss of knowledge might indicate nothing more than the fact that subjects only understand the verbal labels applied to more general, "higher" levels (Funnell, this issue).

We have had the opportunity to address this issue in a study of JL, a patient with semantic dementia, a disorder that causes a progressive and profound, yet relatively selective, loss of semantic knowledge. Longitudinal data from his performance at naming a large corpus of objects produced a pattern of errors that provides significant insights into both this specific hierarchical question and also other aspects of semantic organisation.

Selective impairment of semantic memory was first clearly described by Warrington (1975), who reported three patients with cerebral atrophy presenting with progressive anomia and impaired word comprehension. Detailed neuropsychological testing revealed a loss of receptive and expressive vocabulary, and impoverished knowledge of a wide range of living things and inanimate objects; specific subordinate (attributional) knowledge was particularly affected. Warrington, drawing on a distinction made by Tulving (1972), identified the deficit as one of semantic memory. Since this seminal paper, a number of other patients with selective semantic memory impairment have been reported (e.g. Schwartz, Marin, & Saffran, 1979). The majority have occurred in the context of extensive neocortical damage, for instance following herpes simplex virus encephalitis (e.g. De Renzi, Liotti, & Nichelli, 1987; Pietrini et al., 1988; Sartori & Job, 1988; Sheridan & Humphreys, 1993; Warrington & Shallice, 1984). Other cases with a progressive loss of semantic memory have been subsumed under the rubric of "primary progressive aphasia". As we have discussed before (Hodges, Patterson, Oxbury, & Funnell, 1992), the majority of patients reported in the literature as cases of PPA, like the original Mesulam (1982) cases, have presented with a progressive non-fluent aphasia with prominent impairment of the phonological and syntactic aspects of language, but relatively preserved comprehension. Other cases, by contrast, have had clear semantic memory loss causing deficits in both word production and comprehension, but with relative sparing of other components of language (e.g. Basso, Capitani, & Laiacona, 1988; Poeck & Luzzatti, 1988; Tyrrell, Warrington, Frackowiak, & Rossor, 1990).

To avoid confusion, and to encapsulate the key component of the disorder, we have adopted the term "semantic dementia" (Hodges, Patterson, Oxbury, & Funnell, 1992; Hodges, Patterson, & Tyler, 1994; Patterson & Hodges, 1992) which was first proposed by the Manchester group (Snowden, Goulding, & Neary, 1989) and is now being adopted by other workers in the field (e.g. Saffran & Schwartz, 1994). This term describes a form of progressive fluent aphasia with the following characteristics: (i) selective impairment of semantic memory causing severe anomia, impaired single-word comprehension (both spoken and written), reduced generation of exemplars on category fluency tests, and an impoverished fund of general knowledge; (ii) relative sparing of other components of language output, notably syntax and phonology; (iii) normal perceptual skills and non-verbal problem-solving abilities; and (iv) relatively preserved autobiographical and day-to-day (episodic) memory.

One of our patients, JL, was studied at regular intervals from the time of his presentation in the spring of 1991 until his death in January 1994. His performance on a semantic memory test battery and, in particular, the pattern of his naming errors on multiple administrations of all of the 260 Snodgrass and Vanderwart pictures, provides neuropsychological data pertinent to issues concerning the organisation of semantic memory.

CASE REPORT

JL, a 60-year-old company director, presented in April 1991 with a two-year history of difficulty remembering the names of people and places. More recently his vocabulary had diminished causing word finding difficulty in conversation. The family had noted problems understanding the meaning of words that had previously been well within his vocabulary, for instance the names of foods. He was no longer familiar with the names of the local villages in the region where he had lived all his life. The deficit also affected his ability to recognise people by face, name, or description. He had also exhibited problems identifying real objects and animals, for instance he had been frightened by finding a snail in the back yard and thought that a goat was a strange creature. Despite these difficulties, his day-to-day and autobiographical memory remained relatively very good.

His family suggested that there had also been subtle changes in personality behaviour, and judgement. Having previously been very financially shrewd and adept, he had made a number of recent disastrous deals, provoking his sons to take over the company. Also, he had become uncharacteristically generous, giving money to charities and offering use of his holiday home to relative strangers.

Examination revealed that his spontaneous speech was fluent with normal articulation and grammar. Occasional word-finding difficulties were apparent, but there were no phonemic paraphasic errors and only occasional semantic substitutions. Confrontational naming was severely impaired. Comprehension of conversation appeared good, and responses to syntactically complex three-part commands were normal. In contrast, understanding of nominal terms was impaired. Repetition of single words and sentences was normal. Reading of prose passages was unimpaired, but he made regularisation errors to low-frequency irregular words. Writing was poorer than expected with numerous spelling errors, especially for irregular words. He was fully orientated in time and place. Recall of autobiographical details was good. Drawing of abstract geometric and representational figures (e.g. a house, clock etc.) could not be faulted. He was, however, able to correctly locate only 8 of 20 previously familiar cities (e.g. London, Cambridge, Norwich etc.) or holiday areas (e.g. the Norfolk Broads, Lake District etc.) on an outline map of Great Britain.

MRI revealed striking focal atrophy of the temporal region, more marked on the right, which was particularly evident on the coronal slices (see Hodges, Patterson, Oxbury, & Funnell, 1992). A SPECT scan also showed bilateral hypoperfusion confined to the temporal lobes.

On follow-up, over the next two years, JL deteriorated rapidly with increasing anomia and a striking reduction in his receptive vocabulary. His recognition of objects also declined. For instance, he would ask his wife what common food items were, and kept enquiring about "this stuff" growing on his face every day. He became very rigid in his habits and insisted on going to the same restaurant every Saturday and eating the same food. In his impatience to get to the restaurant, on Saturdays he would sometimes set his watch, and all the clocks in the house, ahead to the usual departure time. This behaviour reveals an intriguing combination of preserved and disrupted cognition: on the preserved side, it indicates that JL was aware of the day of the week, and also retained some knowledge of the passage of time and of what clocks are for; on the degraded side, it shows his lack of understanding of the relationship between clock-time and "real-world" time. In 1993 hyperphagia and other features of the Kluver-Bucy syndrome became a major problem; he ate the entire contents of the fridge on several occasions and gained 60lb in weight. He also began to consume non-food items including a table-mat and newspaper. There was a decline in self-care and general hygiene. When last assessed by our team in October 1993, he was unable to comply with any verbal or written instructions and was extremely distractible. His verbal output had become extremely limited; although syntactically correct, his speech was empty, often irrelevant, and poorly articulated. Throughout the second half of 1993 his condition declined and he died in January 1994. Post-mortem brain examination revealed a degree of generalised cerebral atrophy with marked temporal lobe accentuation. Histologically, there was severe neuronal loss and occasional intraneuronal inclusions with the staining characteristics of Pick's cells. Alzheimer's disease changes were absent.

LONGITUDINAL NEUROPSYCHOLOGICAL ASSESSMENT

The results of general neuropsychological testing between March 1991 and September 1992 are summarised in Table 1. When first seen, JL was administered a slightly shortened version of the WAIS on which he showed the same pattern of subtest scores as seen in other patients with semantic

TABLE 1
Basic Neuropsychological Data

	March 91	Sept 91	March 92	Sept 92
Raven's Col. Prog. Matrices (36)	29	NT	25	24
Rey Figure Copy (36)	34	34	34	32
45min delayed recall	16	8	3	0
Face Matching Test (54)	NT	50	46	NT
Judgement of Line Orientation (30)	27	27	27	23
Object matching "unusual views" (40)	36	37	35	28
Object decision test (64)	NT	51	NT	35
Digit Span Forward	7	7	7	7
Backward	5	5	4	6
Logical Memory WMS				
Immediate (21)	10.5	3.0	1.5	NT
30min delayed	9.0	2.0	0.5	NT
Boston Naming Test (60)	10	9	NT	0
Semantic Battery Naming Test (48)	17	9	8	5
Naming to description (24)	6	4	3	0
Word–picture matching (48)	31	27	25	16
Fluency:				
Letter (F,A,S)	14	14	15	6
Category (animals)	10	6	3	3
Word–picture matching from PALPA (40)	30	29	25	15
Token Test (36)	NT	30	28	NT
TROG	76	73	76	65

NT = Not tested, WMS = Wechsler Memory Scale, TROG = Test for the Reception of Grammar.
Figures in brackets indicate maximum scores.

dementia (JL age-scaled scores: Vocabulary 1, Information 2, Similarities 1, Digit Span 8, Arithmetic 11, Block Design 9, Digit Symbol 8, Picture Completion 4).

When first tested, basic visuo-spatial and perceptual abilities were well preserved, as illustrated by JL's near-perfect copy of the complex Rey-Osterrieth figure and his normal performance on Benton's Face Matching and Line Orientation Judgement Tests (Benton, Hamsher, Varney, & Spreen, 1983). On follow-up over the next 18 months these scores declined minimally, which contrasts strikingly with the progressive decline in semantic memory.

On the Humphreys and Riddoch (1987) object matching test in which one photograph—showing a prototypical view of a common object (e.g. comb, knife, hammer etc.)—is presented along with an atypical view of the target object (e.g. from above or one end) and a different but visually similar item, his performance was within the normal range (JL 36; controls 37.3 ± 3.1) and remained at this level until the last test session in September 1992 (see Table 1), even though he could not name or identify many of the objects. In contrast, JL was impaired on the object decision test of Riddoch and Humphreys (1987) which depends on the integrity of the putative structural description system; half of the 64 pictures in this test are line drawings of real objects (e.g. a pair of scissors, a tiger) while the other half are chimeric objects (e.g. the body of a tiger with the head of a mouse, the blades of a pair of scissors on the handle of a screwdriver). Control subjects perform well in discriminating between real and unreal objects (58.7 ± 2.4) whereas JL's performance was clearly impaired in September 1991 and fell to chance level one year later (see Table 1).

Assessment of verbal memory was confounded by the language disorder. Initially JL demonstrated normal recall of the prose passage from the Wechsler Memory Scale (Wechsler, 1945), but his score then declined precipitously. His recall of the complex Rey figure was, at first, within the normal range for his age and even on the second assessment it was clearly superior to his verbal recall.

Picture description using the "cookie theft scene" from the BDAE (Goodglass & Kaplan, 1976) produced fluent, normally articulated and grammatically correct, but factually empty discourse, punctuated by frequent word-finding difficulty. Performance on naming tests (both a sub-set of 48 pictures from the Snodgrass and Vanderwart pictures used in the semantic battery and the Boston Naming Test) was severely impaired. Apart from omissions, the errors were almost entirely semantic in type, being either category co-ordinate, superordinate, or cross-category errors. No phonemic errors were observed. The evolving pattern of the errors over time will be described in detail later. In fluency tests, the observed dissociation between reasonable performance on initial letters (F, A, and S) and severely impaired performance on categories has been noted in our other patients with semantic dementia (Hodges, Patterson, Oxbury, & Funnell, 1992).

On language comprehension tests, there was a marked discrepancy between those stressing semantic as opposed to syntactic comprehension. For instance on the Test for the Reception of Grammar (TROG, Bishop, 1989) on which subjects point to one of four pictures in response to statements of increasing syntactic complexity while vocabulary remains very simple (e.g. "the boys pick the apples", "the dog the boy is chasing is brown" etc.), JL's performance was essentially normal until the final occasion when even the lexical contrasts (horse/boy etc.) presented in the TROG caused confusion. In contrast, vocabulary comprehension was severely impaired from the start. On the word–picture matching test from the PALPA battery (Kay, Lesser, & Coltheart, 1992) in which subjects are asked to point to one of five alternative pictures (i.e. the target, a close semantic, a distant semantic, a visual, and an unrelated foil) in response to the spoken word, JL's performance was clearly impaired with the majority of errors being semantically related. By September 1992 (session four) his performance was approaching chance level.

On tests of oral reading, JL showed a somewhat weak pattern of surface dyslexia: he was significantly better at reading regular words than exception words, and a number of his errors on exception words were phonologically plausible (regularisation) errors (e.g. PINT pronounced to rhyme with "mint"). However, unlike some of the more striking examples of surface dyslexia associated with semantic memory loss reported both by us (Patterson & Hodges, 1992) and by others (e.g. Behrmann & Bub, 1992; McCarthy & Warrington, 1986; Shallice, Warrington, & McCarthy, 1983), JL had a mild deficit in reading regular words and nonwords as well as the more pronounced problem with exception words. We have also recently documented an item-by-item correspondence between JL's word comprehension and reading ability specifically for exception words. Using imageable regular and exception words, matched for frequency, we demonstrated that failure on word–picture matching tests for exception words was significantly correlated with the tendency to misread that word, whereas comprehension performance for regular words did not predict reading performance of these words (Graham, Hodges, & Patterson, 1994). This result replicated that obtained by Hillis and Caramazza (1991b) in their stroke patient JJ.

LONGITUDINAL ASSESSMENT OF SEMANTIC MEMORY

To assess JL's performance over time we have used a semantic memory test battery that employs a consistent set of stimulus items and is designed to assess input to and output from central representational knowledge about the same group of items via different sensory modalities (see Hodges, Salmon, & Butters, 1992). It contains 48 items selected to represent three categories of animals (land animals, sea creatures, and birds) and three categories of man-made items (household items, vehicles, and musical instruments) matched for category prototypicality. They were chosen from the corpus of line drawings by Snodgrass and Vanderwart (1980). In brief, the seven sub-tests consist of:

1. Category fluency for each of the six main categories plus two lower-order categories (breeds of dog and types of boat).
2. Naming of all 48 line drawings.
3. Naming in response to verbal descriptions (e.g. "what do we call the large African animal with a curved horn on its head").
4. Picture sorting at superordinate, category, and subordinate levels.
5. Word–picture matching using within-category arrays of pictures (e.g. eight land animals).
6. Semantic feature questions: for each of the items in the battery we designed

eight questions, such that four questions explore knowledge of physical features (size, shape, colour etc.) and four tap knowledge of more non-perceptual attributes (habitat, ferocity, diet, uses etc.). One half of the questions posed should receive "yes" answers and the other half "no" answers (e.g. "does a zebra have stripes", "does a zebra eat meat" etc.).
7. Generation of verbal definitions in response to the spoken name of the item.

JL's performance is contrasted with that of 25 similarly aged (69.7 ± 7.8) controls with a range of educational levels, who were recruited from the MRC Applied Psychology Unit's subject panel as part of an investigation into semantic memory in dementia of the Alzheimer's type (Hodges & Patterson, 1995).

The progressive decline in JL's performance on the semantic battery is illustrated in Fig. 1. In category fluency (see Table 2 for a comparison of JL's and control subjects' fluency performance), the normal subjects produced a mean total of 58.3 items (± 12.3) for the four living categories combined, and 55.4 items (± 8.6) for the four man-made categories. Considering performance as a whole, JL was well outside the normal range even on initial testing, and his ability to generate instances of these categories declined dramatically over the subsequent 1.5 years. The most dramatic difference between JL and controls, however, was on the more specific categories; for the two broadest categories (animals and household items), on initial testing JL was actually just within the normal range (taken as 2 SDs from the mean). This, then, is the first indication in JL's data of a performance discrepancy between broader and more detailed information. Note that JL's greater success when asked to generate instances of the broader categories cannot be explained, or at least not

TABLE 2
Category Fluency Test

	April 1991	Sept 1991	March 1992	Sept 1992	Controls mean (±SD)	
Animals	10	6	3	3	17.5	(4.0)
Birds	6	4	0	0	15.9	(4.6)
Sea creatures	4	3	1	0	14.0	(4.5)
Dogs	1	0	0	0	10.9	(3.5)
Household items	9	7	1	0	17.5	(3.4)
Vehicles	5	3	2	0	11.8	(2.6)
Musical Instruments	0	0	0	0	15.3	(3.4)
Boats	2	2	0	0	10.9	(3.4)

JL's performance on the category fluency test from the semantic memory test battery compared to 25 age- and education-matched control subjects.

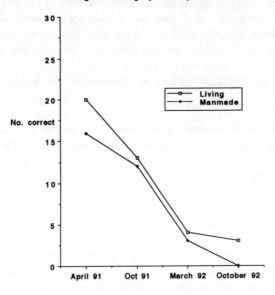

Change on Category Fluency Test

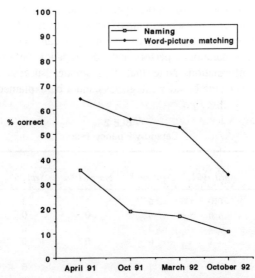

Naming & Word-Picture Matching

FIG. 1. JL's performance over time on the following subtests from the semantic memory test battery: (i) category fluency, showing the total number of correct items for the four living and four man-made categories, (ii) naming and word-picture matching, and (iii) the picture sorting test. Key for iii: levels I, II, and III = living *vs* man-made, superordinate (category), and subordinate-level sorting, respectively (see text for details).

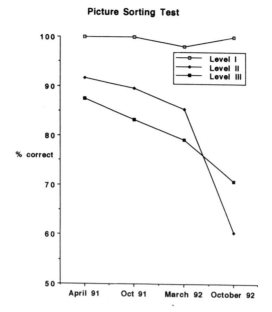

Picture Sorting Test

FIG. 1. *continued*

entirely, on the basis that this is an easier task. Normal subjects produced more animals than types of dog, too, but only about half-again as many (roughly 18 *vs* 11) whereas for JL's initial session this ratio was 10:1. In another example, normal subjects produced hardly any more household items than musical instruments, whereas for JL this contrast was a dramatic 9:0. We will discuss our interpretation of this finding later, following more data substantiating the discrepancy between levels. Finally with regard to category fluency, Table 3 shows the consistency of JL's responses to the animal category on the four testing occasions. Of the three responses produced on the final occasion, horse was given on every previous test as well, and dog and cat each on two of the three. Indeed, as we shall see, these three items gradually became his stereotyped animal naming responses.

Naming on the semantic battery was impaired to a very severe degree even on initial testing (JL 17/48 = 0.35, controls 0.91 ± 0.05) and then deteriorated until, in September 1992, he was able to name only 5 of the 48 line drawings. Naming was in fact administered a fifth time, in March 1993, when his score was 2/48. An analysis of the pattern of responses over five test sessions showed a striking item-by-item consistency (Table 4); there were only three instances (out of a total possible of 157) where a naming error on a particular item was followed by a correct response; in all other instances a naming error was followed by an error on all subsequent occasions. Stated another way, once a name dropped out of

TABLE 3
Animal Fluency Test

April 1991	Sept 1991	March 1992	Sept 1992	March 1993
cow	horse	horse	dogs	—
bullock	cows	cows	cats	
sheep	bullock	birds	horses	
lamb	duck	bird (P)		
pig	cats			
dog	dog			
horse	bullock (P)			
cat	cows (P)			
birds				
geese				

JL's performance on the animal fluency test from the semantic memory test battery.
(P) = preservation.

TABLE 4
Naming Consistency

	April 91	Sept 91	March 92	Sept 92	March 93
lorry	+	+	+	+	+
bike	+	+	+	+	+
telephone	+	+	+	+	−
aeroplane	+	+	+	+	−
motorcycle	+	−	+	+	−
bus	+	+	+	−	−
fish	+	+	+	−	−
monkey	+	+	−	−	−
duck	+	+	−	−	−
cooker	+	−	−	−	−
toaster	+	−	−	−	−
helicopter	+	−	−	−	−
deer	+	−	−	−	−
rabbit	+	−	−	−	−
mouse	+	−	−	−	−
tiger	+	−	−	−	−
chicken	+	−	−	−	−
kettle	−	+	−	−	−
Total Correct	17	9	7	5	2

JL's naming consistency on the 18 pictures (of the 48 used in semantic memory test battery) for which he ever produced a correct response; for the remaining 30 items, he was incorrect on the first and every subsequent testing. + correct, − incorrect.

JL's repertoire, it essentially never returned. A more detailed analysis of the evolving pattern of error types on a much larger corpus is given later.

On the naming to description subtest from the semantic battery JL initially named 6 of the 24 items. His performance then deteriorated on successive test sessions until, in September 1992, he failed to name any items correctly.

Word–picture matching is clearly an easier task than picture naming; controls obtain a near perfect score (0.99 ± 0.01). This is also reflected in JL's differential performance levels on the two tests (see Fig. 1). Over time, however, the rate of decline on the word–picture matching test parallelled that in naming and, by September 1992, his performance on the matching test was extremely poor.

The results of the picture sorting test showed a pattern observed in other patients with semantic dementia (Hodges, Patterson, Oxbury, & Funnell, 1992). At the beginning, on level I (living vs man-made) JL obtained a perfect score. At level II (household item vs musical instrument vs vehicle; land animal vs sea creature vs bird), his performance was just below normal (JL 0.91, controls 0.97 ± 0.02, chance 0.33). At level III (British vs foreign animal; fierce vs non-fierce animal etc.), his performance was clearly impaired (JL 0.83, controls 0.95 ± 0.03, chance 0.5). This pattern of completely preserved superordinate level and relatively preserved category level sorting was maintained for the first year, although (as shown in Fig. 1) there was a gradual decline at the lower two levels. Then, in 1992, his ability to perform anything other than the level I sorting task plummeted. In view of the fact that the chance values at levels II and III are different (0.3 and 0.5, respectively), it could be argued that this pattern still reflected better performance at the category than at the subordinate level of the task.

The semantic features questionnaire was designed after we had initially assessed JL and was given on the first occasion in September 1991 at the time of the second round of testing: he answered correctly only 118 of 192 questions which was well below the normal controls' range (controls 178 ± 5.1). On subsequent test sessions, his performance fell and on the third test session, March 1992, his score was no better than chance (106/192). His performance on the physical and non-perceptual questions was equivalent throughout.

The definitions subtest was also given to JL on three occasions. He never produced a detailed and rich definition of the type given by normal subjects, but we were able to classify his responses into four different qualities of definitions, as follows:

(i) reasonable: containing some details specific to the target
   bicycle—"Two wheels, a seat, a steering "thingummy", two pedals, chain to drive the back wheel, metal and rubber on the wheels."
   swan—"They're white. Not allowed to shoot them. I got a lot of them in my swimming pools and rivers."

(ii) minimal: usually superordinate information only

mouse—"A small animal."

accordion—"A musical instrument."

(iii) don't know

(iv) errors:

cooker—"Somebody who can cook. Cookers are people who can produce marvellous meals."

seahorse—"I didn't think there was horses that go in the sea. I didn't know there was such a thing, seahorses going in the sea."

JL's performance on the definitions and naming subtests is compared in Table 5. It can be seen that there was a striking concordance between his failure to name items and the production of don't knows or gross errors on the definition tests: of the 98 responses in these categories he named only one (1%). By contrast, of the 14 items for which he produced reasonably detailed definitions, 11 (78%) were successfully named, and of the 32 items for which he produced minimal or superordinate information he named 13 (41%).

The Pyramids and Palm Trees Test (Howard & Patterson, 1992) requires subjects to match conceptually related pictures (or, in the word version, their written or spoken names). For instance, the target picture of an Egyptian pyramid is presented above two drawings depicting a palm tree and a fir tree, and the subject is asked to judge which one goes with the pyramid. Other examples are spectacles with eye and ear, saddle with goat and horse. In September 1991 JL scored 36/52 (=0.69 *vs* controls 0.98 ± 0.03). When re-tested in March 1992, his performance was at chance (26/52) on both the three-picture and three-word versions of the test.

TABLE 5
Definitions Subtest

	Sept 91		March 92		Sept 92		Total	
	Named		Named		Named		Named	
	Yes	No	Yes	No	Yes	No	Yes	No
Reasonable	6	1	5	1	0	1	11	3
Minimal	5	6	3	6	5	7	13	19
Don't know	0	21	0	25	0	28	0	74
Errors	1	8	0	8	0	7	1	23

JL's performance on the definitions subtest of the semantic memory test battery with responses classified according to their information content and whether the same items were named correctly on the picture naming subtest.

PATTERN OF NAMING ERRORS OVER TIME

In order to examine, in more detail, the consistency of JL's naming responses, we administered the entire Snodgrass and Vanderwart corpus of 260 line drawings on four occasions between October 1991 and March 1993. The same pseudo-random order of presentation was used each time; blocks of items from the same category were avoided by presenting one example from one category followed by one from a different category, and so on. JL's errors were classified using a modification of a classification previously described (Hodges, Salmon, & Butters, 1991) as follows:

1. *Category co-ordinate:* an item from the same category as the target (e.g. "violin" for trumpet, "dog" for elephant, etc.). For the purposes of this analysis, the small number of items that might be considered to belong in a different bin (e.g. "cat" for lion could be an intermediate-level superordinate) were classified as category co-ordinates.
2. *Superordinate:* an error that refers to the superordinate category of the target (e.g. "bird" for eagle, "animal" for lion; "musical machine" for violin).
3. *Circumlocution:* a response that reflects item-specific knowledge about the target (e.g. "a seat for two people" for couch; "what you cook water in" for kettle; "what you use for the rain, you carry it over your head" for umbrella; "climbing steps" for ladder). Only responses that unambiguously refer to the target were classified as circumlocutions.
4. *Semantic associative:* an error that is semantically related to the target but neither a category co-ordinate nor superordinate (e.g. "light" for candle; "time" for watch) nor—in the case of a short phrase—specific enough to be considered a circumlocution (e.g. "in garden" for flower; "carry water" for glass).
5. *Cross-category:* these were of two types: (a) errors that respect the living/ man-made distinction but come from the wrong category (e.g. "dog" for swan; "bird" for spider; "musical machine" for traffic light), and (b) errors that do not respect this division ("vehicle" for deer; "animal" for telephone). Also included in this category were a number of anthropomorphic errors (e.g. "man" for doll; "a man" for trousers and dress, etc.).
6. *Visual:* a response that clearly reflects a perceptual rather than semantic recognition error ("row of books" for accordion; "part of a brush" for volcano; "a box" for toaster).
7. *Phonological:* a response that shares at least one phoneme with the intended target. JL made no such errors.
8. *Other:* these were largely vague or bizarre unclassifiable responses devoid of information ("one of them things"; "you take it out" etc.).
9. *Don't knows.*

JL's overall naming accuracy fell progressively over the four test sessions from 94 (0.36) to 75 (0.28), 41 (0.15), and 17/260 (0.006), which produced a corpus of 806 errors. A Chi squared goodness of fit test showed that there was a significant change in JL's performance over time ($\chi^2 = 59.13$, $P < 0.0001$). Fortunately the rate of don't know responses remained relatively low (0.13 on session I, 0.20 on session IV) and the vast majority of the remaining errors were classifiable into one of the categories given here. A categorisation of the errors for each of the test sessions is shown in Fig. 2. It can be seen that on the first two assessments, by far the most frequent error type was a category co-ordinate response; these constituted approximately a third of the total errors on session I and 40% on session II. By session IV, however, the proportion of this error type had fallen to 0.14. There was a similar fall in the proportion of circumlocutory errors, which initially made up almost a tenth of all errors, but by session IV there were virtually no responses of this type. This progressive decline in category co-ordinate and circumlocutory errors was accompanied by a rise in the proportion of superordinate (0.09 to 0.16) and cross-category errors (0.08 to 0.19). It is notable that the latter actually constituted the largest category (apart from "don't knows") on session IV. There was also a rise in the proportion of vague and bizarre unclassifiable responses (0.03 to 0.13). The proportion of semantic-associative and visual errors was relatively constant throughout. The cross-category errors are of particular interest. Of the 18 such errors on session I, all respected the living/man-made distinction, and the number of errors of this type remained fairly constant over the four sessions. By contrast, there was a steady rise in cross-category errors breaking the living/man-made boundary; of the 46 cross-category errors on session IV, 21 failed to respect this distinction. Some examples of this pattern are given later.

Examination of the individual errors in each category showed an even more striking and consistent picture. Within both the living and man-made domains, JL's knowledge about some categories (e.g. insects, musical instruments) was already severely impoverished when first tested, while others (e.g. land animals, vehicles) appeared to be much better preserved. The fact that, on session I, some categories elicited largely category co-ordinate or circumlocutory errors, but others gave superordinate errors, means that the evolving pattern is somewhat masked by grouping together the errors from all categories.

This longitudinal pattern of errors is illustrated for selected categories in the Appendix. The first thing to note is that, for those items ever named correctly, an error on the next session was virtually always a category co-ordinate or superordinate or, more rarely, a circumlocution. That is, when JL's early performance demonstrated reasonable knowledge of an object, the first error step was typically to one of these three error types, reflecting at least some preserved information. Errors indicative of either a relative absence of knowledge about the object (vague responses like "not made" plus don't knows) or some factually incorrect information (cross-category and visual errors) occurred, with very few exceptions, only as a subsequent step along the error trajectory.

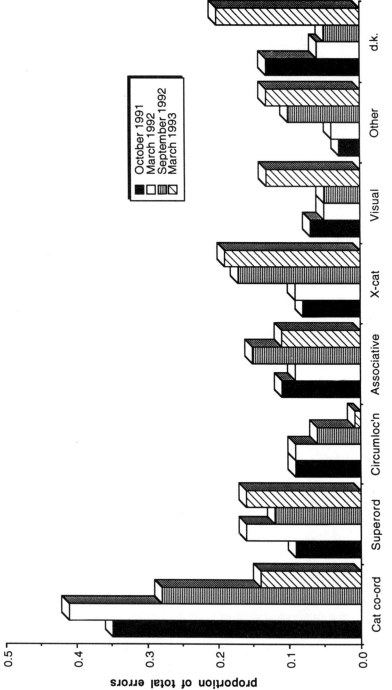

FIG. 2. Distribution of the error types produced by JL when naming the entire corpus of 260 Snodgrass and Vanderwart line drawings on four successive occasions. The following error classification was used: category co-ordinate (cat co-ord), superordinate (superord), circumlocution (circumloc'n), associative, cross-category (X-cat), visual, other, and don't know (d.k.).

The emergence of category prototypes is another notable feature. In the category land (or four-legged) animals there was a gradual reduction in the repertoire of category co-ordinate errors until all land animals were either "cat", "dog", or "horse" (note that these were also his most consistent and longest-surviving responses on the category fluency test). There also appeared, at one stage (sessions II and II), to be a size effect, in that almost all of the large animals like elephant and camel were named as "horse", whereas the smaller animals such as racoon and fox were called either "dog" or "cat". On the final session, however, the labels were applied in a more arbitrary way, many responses were superordinate labels ("animal"), and there was even one cross-domain response (deer → "vehicle").

In the category of birds, all errors in session I were category co-ordinates ("duck", "swan", "chicken"). On session II, the accuracy rate had halved and all of the errors were superordinates ("bird") except one. On the next session (III), only the undifferentiated prototype BIRD was named correctly, and three of the errors were of a cross-category type ("cat"), though still within the domain of living things. On the final session, the label bird seemed to have disappeared from his vocabulary, the most common response was now "animal", and there was one cross-category error of the cross-domain type ("vehicle").

The category of insects appeared from the start to have been subsumed under birds; on session I, six of the eight responses were "bird" and, interestingly, one was a bird exemplar ("pheasant"[1]). As in the bird category, there was a steady increase in less specific responses over successive test sessions ("animal") and eventually a total disappearance of the label bird.

The same pattern of category co-ordinate and superordinate errors followed by cross-category responses was also apparent in the categories fruits and vegetables. On sessions I and II, virtually all fruits and vegetables were named as "apple" or "egg". The superordinate label vegetable was used, but never fruit. On several occasions JL said "vegetable, not an apple is it?". The sequence of responses over sessions for BANANA and PUMPKIN are particularly instructive. The former elicited the following sequence: (i) "banana", (ii) "yellow thing you eat, you pull off the outside and eat the stuff inside", (iii) "something you eat", (iv) "part of an animal"; and for PUMPKIN: (i) "vegetable, not an apple is it?", (ii) "could be an egg", (iii) "an animal", (iv) "came from a vehicle".

The emergence of stereotyped category co-ordinate responses and of typical superordinate labels was, not surprisingly, less clear-cut in the man-made categories, but the same general pattern can be observed. As shown in the

[1] It is interesting that when given the supermarket fluency test from the Dementia Rating Scale (Mattis, 1973) in 1991, JL produced the following examples of things you buy in a supermarket: bread, cheese, potatoes, and pheasants!

Appendix, the majority of the household items and vehicles were either correctly named or elicited circumlocutory responses on session I. With the progressive decline in accuracy, the errors became semantic-associative responses and eventually cross-category errors emerged. For instance, HANGER was initially called "a piece to hang your coats and shirt over" and eventually "some form of vehicle". The term "machine" was used to label a wide range of man-made items (e.g. PLIERS, CANNON, CLOTHESPEG, ARROW, LOCK, etc.). It is also notable how often items from these categories were described in terms of their use or function; with the exception of a very few responses like "to eat" for fruit and vegetables, functional descriptions were never offered for the natural kind of items. In the category of tools (e.g. SCISSORS "to cut things"; RULER "for measurement"; SCREWDRIVER "unscrew things"), this type of response occurred even when there was clearly an error in identification (e.g. PAINTBRUSH "to dig holes"). The same tendency was apparent in the category of containers (FRYING PAN "to carry water").

The occurrence of anthropomorphic errors was an intriguing feature. These were particularly common in the category clothing (see Appendix). It can be seen that on several occasions JL produced names of body parts for articles of clothing; "hand" for GLOVE or "foot" for SOCK could be explained as visual errors, but "a man" for COAT and for BLOUSE are more difficult to explain on this basis, as the pictures portray the clothing item only and do not show any body parts. Such errors occurred in other categories; CLOWN, DOLL, and SNOWMAN were also named as man or woman, as were MONKEY and GORILLA. This may suggest an inability to distinguish between inanimate items with a person-like shape (e.g. COAT), higher primates, and human beings, although of course one must always take account of possible limitations in the words available for speech production in a case of progressive aphasia like this.

It is also striking that although JL produced a limited repertoire of category exemplars, which at one stage were applied to most members of the appropriate category, he was not always correct when attempting to name the real instance of his own category prototype. This can be seen in the categories land animals, fruit, and clothing; "cat", "dog", "apple", "coat", and "jacket" were frequent error responses on sessions where JL failed to name these drawings correctly.

NAMING AND WORD–PICTURE MATCHING CONSISTENCY

To examine the consistency between naming and single-word comprehension on an item-by-item basis, we compared JL's performance at naming the entire Snodgrass and Vanderwart corpus (see earlier section) with his word–picture matching ability for the same items, on four occasions between October 1991 and March 1993. To test comprehension, we presented JL with arrays consisting of four items from the same category (e.g. fruit, vehicles etc.) and asked him to point to the item named by the examiner. The test sequence was arranged so that each item was followed by one from a different category.

In parallel with his progressive anomia, there was a steady decline in accuracy on the word–picture matching task from 192 (0.74) to 106 (0.41) over the four test sessions. As shown in Table 6, there was a striking item-specific correspondence across the two tests. As word–picture matching is easier than picture naming, we expected that a high proportion of the items not correctly named would have correct responses on the word–picture matching test, as was indeed the case. More critical for the current analysis is the opposite dissociation, i.e. correct naming but incorrect word-picture matching. For the 225 items (over four sessions) that JL correctly named, there were only 21 (0.093) occasions when he selected the wrong item on the comprehension test. The overall consistency between naming and word–picture matching was highly significant on each test session (Chi squared analyses: session one, $\chi^2 = 26.68$, $P < 0.0001$; session two, $\chi^2 = 38.47$, $P < 0.0001$; session three, $\chi^2 = 26.59$, $P < 0.0001$; session four, $\chi^2 = 5.37$, $P = 0.02$).

DISCUSSION

In common with the other reported cases of semantic dementia, JL showed an inexorable loss of semantic memory, which resulted in progressive anomia as well as a decline in receptive vocabulary. One facet that we have not explored in detail here was the very significant item-by-item correspondence across tests

TABLE 6
Word–picture Matching Test

Oct 1991		Naming			March 1992		Naming		
		+	–	Total			+	–	Total
Word-Picture	+	87	105	192	Word-Picture	+	70	104	174
Matching	–	7	61	68	Matching	–	3	83	86
Total		94	167	260	Total		73	187	260

Sept 1992		Naming			March 1993		Naming		
		+	–	Total			+	–	Total
Word-Picture	+	35	95	130	Word-Picture	+	12	94	106
Matching	–	5	125	130	Matching	–	6	148	154
Total		40	220	260	Total		18	242	260

JL's performance on the word-picture matching test on four occasions, with responses classified according to whether the same items were named correctly on the picture naming test. The entire Snodgrass and Vanderwart corpus (n = 260) was used on each occasion.

shown by JL. That is to say, if he was able to name an item correctly, he almost never made mistakes on that item in word–picture matching or on the other tasks from the semantic battery. Examples of this item-specific concordance are illustrated in Tables 5 and 6, which show the striking correlation between JL's performance on the naming and definitions subtests of the semantic battery and between naming and word–picture matching using the entire Snodgrass and Vanderwart corpus. Furthermore, the deficit was not confined to verbal semantic knowledge: for example, within the first year of longitudinal testing, JL's performance fell to chance level on the three-picture version of the Pyramids and Palm Trees Test (Howard & Patterson, 1992). We have reported in other patients the pattern shown by JL of a dissociation between normal performance on tests of object matching (or unusual views) and severely impaired performance on object decision using photographs of real and chimeric items (see Hodges, Patterson, Oxbury, & Funnell, 1992; Hodges, Patterson, & Tyler, 1994). In contrast to his rapid decline on all measures from the semantic battery, JL's performance on tests of visuo-spatial and non-verbal problem-solving ability, syntactic comprehension and auditory verbal short-term memory remained intact, at least during the first 12 months of follow-up. Exactly the same pattern was observed in one of our other patients with semantic dementia, PP (Hodges, Patterson, & Tyler, 1994), although the degree of anomia in her case was so profound from the inception of our investigations that we could not use naming to study the dissolution of her semantic system in the way illustrated here for JL. Having established that JL does indeed show a progressive disorder of the semantic system, we will concentrate here on the implications of his longitudinal data for the organisation of semantic memory.

JL's performance on the semantic battery provides a pattern of data suggesting loss of specific semantic information with preservation of superordinate knowledge (for reviews of a similar pattern in other cases, see Patterson & Hodges, 1994; Rapp & Caramazza, 1993; Shallice, 1988). In JL's case, this pattern was demonstrable both within a particular test session, in the contrast between performance on sub-tests tapping these different "levels" of knowledge, and across test sessions, in the longitudinal data. His performance on three different tests fits this pattern: (i) On the category fluency tests, on initial testing JL was just about within normal limits on the broadest categories of animals and household objects, but was virtually unable to produce any instances of specific categories such as breeds of dog or musical instruments. Also, longitudinal fluency data for the broadest categories demonstrate that, although he could still produce the most prototypical animal names (cat, dog, horse) very late in the progression of his disease, more specific animal labels (e.g. lamb, bullock) dropped out early. (ii) On the sorting tests, JL's discrimination between living things and man-made objects was preserved for a substantial period of time in parallel with a marked decline in his sorting on the basis of more specific categories and particularly of features or attributes (e.g.

foreign-ness or ferocity of animals). (iii) Finally, the longitudinal pattern of JL's naming responses to the 260 Snodgrass pictures on four occasions over 1.5 years is very suggestive of a progressive loss of the features of semantic representations that enable discrimination between specific category instances.

To explore this notion in a little more detail, let us take JL's sequence of responses to two items over the four sessions: *elephant* → (1)"elephant" (2) "horse" (3) "horse" (4) "animal"; *rhinoceros* → (1) "elephant" (2) "horse" (3) "horse" (4) "dog". On session 1, it appears that the pictures could contact a semantic representation with sufficient distinguishing features to enable identification at least as members of a fairly constrained sub-set (large African animals); note however that at this stage, other African animals (zebra and giraffe) were already failing to reach this level of specificity. On the next two sessions, by which time no foreign-animal labels remained in JL's repertoire, both elephant and giraffe could only contact a semantic representation of an animal specified with regard to size; JL's prototypical large animal label was "horse". On the final occasion, neither picture any longer reached even a size differentiation; one was simply subsumed under the generic "animal" response, and the other was assigned JL's most prototypical animal name, "dog". Of his total set of responses to four-legged animals on the final session, four were "horse", six were "animal", and a total of 11 different animals were called "dog" (though not including the dog which was called a "cat"!). We have no ready explanation for the fact that elephant ended up as "animal" but rhinoceros as "dog", nor would we necessarily expect these to have been stable responses to these particular items if JL had been asked to name them again a day or an hour later. The longitudinal progression towards the broadest response "animal" is however notable: this response entered his repertoire rather early for a few insects and water creatures; but for land animals, even on session III every animal picture was called cat, dog, or horse (except for mon-key → "boy"), with six "animal" responses coming in only at session IV.

One alternative explanation to the loss of distinguishing features has been proposed by Funnell (this issue): she claims that the apparent levels effect on the sorting task, for e:..... ₁le, may reflect the fact that the patient can still understand general, high-frequency concept labels like "animal" and "man-made object" but can no longer comprehend terms like "fierce" or "foreign". In our view, Funnell is correct to emphasise the gradual loss of vocabulary (both in comprehension and production) but wrong to offer this a: ¬ account of the data suggesting preservation of broader distinctions with impairment to more specific information. Vocabulary loss is not an explanation but rather another deficit to be explained. It seems clear to us that *both* the loss of vocabulary *and* the poor performance on tasks requiring specific discriminations can be explained by the gradual degradation of features of semantic representations. Why is this kind of central semantic disintegration the most plausible account of JL's performance (and that of other similar patients)? There are a number of reasons for this, but perhaps the most compelling is the fact that these patients show a parallel decline in tests of comprehension and production. Apart from the sorting tests, we have mainly concentrated here on two speech production tasks, fluency and naming; but it must not be forgotten that, absolutely in tandem with JL's declining performance on these production tasks, his performance on tests requiring comprehension of both words and pictures (e.g. the word–picture matching task and the Pyramids and Palm Trees Test with either pictures or words) was gradually falling to chance. The only parsimonious explanation of this parallel decline in comprehension and production is a central semantic deficit; and the conception of semantic impairment most congruent with the longitudinal pattern of JL's performance seems to be the gradual loss of specific features of semantic representations.

Another aspect highlighted by Funnell (this issue) is the fact that the patients' gradual loss of receptive vocabulary is strongly modulated by word frequency or familiarity. We entirely agree with this point, and note that it applies to expressive as well as receptive vocabulary: JL's longest surviving naming responses to animals (''dog'', ''cat'', and ''horse'') are probably the most familiar and frequent animal words in the English language (indeed, according to written-word frequency norms, ''dog'' is more frequent than ''animal'', and we suspect that the discrepancy favouring ''dog'' is probably even greater in spoken word frequency). Once again, while agreeing with the importance of Funnell's observation, we argue that this familiarity effect (a) is not an explanation but is rather a phenomenon to be explained, and (b) is entirely consonant with, and indeed is to be predicted from, a loss of semantic features. The behaviour of both human subjects and simulation models leads to the view that the transcoding or computation between one type of representation and another (here, between semantic and phonological representations) is highly frequency-sensitive. Normal subjects are more accurate and faster to name objects with high-frequency names (Newcombe, Oldfield, & Wingfield, 1965; Rochford & Williams, 1965), and patients with progressive semantic deficits all show a massive frequency/familiarity effect on naming accuracy (see for example Parkin, 1993; Patterson & Hodges, 1992; Warrington, 1975). Our proposal is that the links from semantic memory to spoken word representations are weighted in a way that will make less familiar words more vulnerable to partial loss of semantic information. It is thus predictable that, if degraded semantic representations of animals are only distinguished by a size feature, the activation of these representations by any animal picture should result in production of the common words ''dog'' (for a small animal) and ''horse'' (for a large one), rather than, say, ''skunk'' and ''zebra'' with much lower frequencies of usage. For ''dog'' and ''horse'', the link between meaning and speech production will have been both learned early and repeatedly exercised throughout the person's life, resulting in damage-resistant weights on these connections.

Although much of this discussion has relied on examples of JL's performance in the domain of natural kinds, similar conclusions apply to his performance with man-made objects. Here, his responses often reflected knowledge of the broad function of the target objects (e.g. "to carry things", "fill it up", "to cut up", "for measuring", etc.) but without specific identifying features. Once again, this points to the preservation of general knowledge applicable to the general category in the face of degraded item-specific information. It is also noteworthy that, for the man-made objects, no "default" responses emerged to mirror either the superordinates ("animal", "vegetable") or prototype exemplars ("dog", "apple") that he applied to natural kinds. This difference is exactly what one would predict from analyses showing significantly greater structural similarities among natural kinds than man-made objects (Humphreys, Riddoch, & Quinlan, 1988).

The final issue to be addressed is whether the phenomenon of loss of specific semantic information, which we have concluded is real rather than artifactual, finds a more satisfactory account in terms of a hierarchical organisation (Warrington, 1975) or a distributed-feature network concept (Allport, 1985) of semantic memory. Unfortunately, it is not clear that anything in the present data would properly distinguish between these two accounts, partly because neither has been described in sufficient detail to yield specific predictions. The same point regarding under-specification in models of semantic representation has been made by the Baltimore group (Hillis, Rapp, Romani, & Caramazza, 1990; Rapp & Caramazza, 1989; Caramazza et al., 1990), and is addressed by Tippett et al. (this issue). It has been argued that prototypicality effects are more compatible with distributed networks than with hierarchical organisations (Chang, 1986); thus, the fact that JL eventually labelled almost all animals as "dog", "cat", or "horse" seems generally to support the network approach. It also seems, intuitively, that networks of features are a more natural way for semantic memory to be organised than strictly hierarchical trees. Two aspects of such feature networks seem particularly appealing: (i) the notion that the meaning of a concept, based on a loose collection of semantic features, is computed on-line and differs from one situation/context to another; (ii) the notion that higher (superordinate) levels are emergent properties reflecting many shared features of physically or functionally similar objects, rather than explicitly represented at the top of a tree. Intuition is, however, no basis for scientific progress, and a resolution of this issue awaits further empirical and particularly theoretical precision.

REFERENCES

Allport, D.A. (1985). Distributed memory, modular subsystems and dysphasia. In S.K. Newman & R. Epstein (Eds.), *Current perspectives in dysphasia*. Edinburgh: Churchill Livingstone.

Basso, A., Capitani, E., & Laiacona, M. (1988). Progressive language impairment without dementia: a case with isolated category specific semantic defect. *Journal of Neurology, Neurosurgery and Psychiatry, 5*, 1201–1207.

Behrmann, M., & Bub, D. (1992). Surface dyslexia and dysgraphia: Dual routes, single lexicon. *Cognitive Neuropsychology, 9*, 209–251.

Benton, A.L. de S., Hamsher, K., Varney, N.R., & Spreen, O. (1983). *Contributions to neuropsychological assessment*. New York: Oxford University Press.

Bishop, D.V.M. (1989). *Test for the reception of grammar*. UK: Medical Research Council.

Caramazza, A., Hillis, A.E., Rapp, B.C., & Romani, C. (1990). The multiple semantics hypothesis: Multiple confusions? *Cognitive Neuropsychology, 7*, 161–189.

Chang, T. (1986). Semantic memory: Facts and models. *Psychological Bulletin, 99*, 199–220.

Chertkow, H., Bub, D., & Caplan, D. (1992). Constraining theories of semantic memory processing: Evidence from dementia. *Cognitive Neuropsychology, 9*, 327–365.

Collins, A.M., & Quillian, M.R. (1969). Retrieval time from semantic memory. *Journal of Verbal Learning and Verbal Behavior, 8*, 240–247.

De Renzi, E., Liotti, M., & Nichelli, P. (1987). Semantic amnesia with preservation of autobiographical memory: A case report. *Cortex, 23*, 575–597.

Funnell, E. (this issue). Objects and properties: A study of the breakdown of semantic memory. *Memory, 3*(3/4).

Goodglass, H., & Kaplan, E. (1983). *The assessment of aphasia and related disorders*, 2nd edn. Philadelphia: Lea and Febiger.

Graham, K.S., Hodges, J.R., & Patterson K. (1994). The relationship between comprehension and oral reading in progressive fluent aphasia. *Neuropsychologia, 32*, 299–316.

Hillis, A.E., & Caramazza, A. (1991a). Category-specific naming and comprehension impairment: A double dissociation. *Brain, 114*, 2081–2094.

Hillis, A.E., & Caramazza, A. (1991b). Mechanisms for accessing lexical representations for output: Evidence from a category-specific deficit. *Brain and Language, 40*, 106–144.

Hillis, A.E., Rapp, B., Romani, C., & Caramazza, A. (1990). Selective impairment of semantics in lexical processing. *Cognitive Neuropsychology, 7*, 191–243.

Hodges, J.R., & Patterson, K. (1995). Is semantic memory consistently impaired early in the course of Alzheimer's disease? Neuroanatomical and diagnostic implications. *Neuropsychologia, 33*, 441–459.

Hodges, J.R., Patterson, K., Oxbury, S., & Funnell, E. (1992). Semantic dementia. Progressive fluent aphasia with temporal lobe atrophy. *Brain, 115*, 1783–1806.

Hodges, J.R., Patterson, K., & Tyler, L.K. (1994). Loss of semantic memory: Implications for the modularity of mind. *Cognitive Neuropsychology, 11*, 505–542.

Hodges, J.R., Salmon, D.P., & Butters, N. (1991). The nature of the naming deficit in Alzheimer's and Huntington's disease. *Brain, 114*, 1547–1558.

Hodges, J.R., Salmon, D.P., & Butters, N. (1992). Semantic memory impairment in Alzheimer's disease: Failure of access or degraded knowledge? *Neuropsychologia, 30*, 301–314.

Howard, D., & Patterson, K. (1992). *Pyramids and palm trees, A test of semantic access from pictures and words*. Bury St Edmunds, UK: Thames Valley Publishing Company.

Humphreys, G.W., & Riddoch, M.J. (1987). The fractionation of visual agnosia. In G.W. Humphreys & M.J. Riddoch (Eds.), *Visual object processing*. London: Lawrence Erlbaum Associates Ltd.

Humphreys, G.W., Riddoch, M.J., & Quinlan, P.T. (1988). Cascade processes in picture identification. *Cognitive Neuropsychology, 5*, 67–103.

488   HODGES, GRAHAM, PATTERSON

Kay, J.M., Lesser, R., & Coltheart, M. (1992). *PALPA: Psycholinguistic Assessment of Language Performance in Aphasia*. London: Lawrence Erlbaum Associates Ltd.

Kintsch, W. (1982). Semantic memory: A tutorial. In R.S. Nickerson (Ed.), *Attention & performance VIII*. Hillsdale NJ: Lawrence Erlbaum Associates Inc.

Mattis, S. (1973). *Dementia Rating Scale*. Windsor, UK: NFER-Nelson.

McCarthy, R.A., & Warrington, E.K. (1986). Phonological reading: Phenomena and paradoxes. *Cortex, 22*, 359–380.

McCarthy, R.A., Warrington, E.K. (1990). Evidence for modality-specific meaning systems in the brain. *Nature, 334*, 428–430.

McClelland, J.L., & Rumelhart, D.E. (1985). Distributed memory and the representation of general and specific information. *Journal of Experimental Psychology: General, 114*, 159–188.

Mesulam, M.M. (1982). Slowly progressive aphasia without dementia. *Annals of Neurology, 11*, 592–598.

Newcombe, F., Oldfield, R.C., & Wingfield, A. (1965). Object naming by dysphasic patients. *Nature, 207*, 1217–1218.

Parkin, A.J. (1993). Progressive aphasia without dementia—a clinical and cognitive neuropsychological analysis. *Brain and Language, 44*, 201–220.

Patterson, K., & Hodges, J.R. (1992). Deterioration of word meaning: implications for reading. *Neuropsychologia, 30*, 1025–1040.

Patterson, K., & Hodges, J.R. (1994). Disorders of semantic memory. In A. Baddeley, B. Wilson, & F. Watts (Eds.), *Handbook of memory disorders*. Chichester, UK: John Wiley.

Pietrini, V., Nertempi, P., Vaglia, A., Revello, M.G., Pinna, V., & Ferro-Milone, F. (1988). Recovery from herpes simplex encephalitis: Selective impairment of specific semantic categories with neuroradiological correlation. *Journal of Neurology, Neurosurgery and Psychiatry, 51*, 1284–1293.

Poeck, K., & Luzzatti, C. (1988). Slowly progressive aphasia in three patients: The problem of accompanying neuropsychological deficit. *Brain, 111*, 151–168.

Rapp, B., & Caramazza, A. (1993). On the distinction between deficits of access and deficits of storage: A question of theory. *Cognitive Neuropsychology, 10*, 113–142.

Rapp, B.A., & Caramazza, A. (1989). General to specific access to word meaning: A claim re-examined. *Cognitive Neuropsychology, 6*, 251–272.

Riddoch, M.J., & Humphreys, G.W. (1987). Visual object processing in optic aphasia: A case of semantic access agnosia. *Cognitive Neuropsychology, 4*, 131–185.

Rochford, E., & Williams, M. (1965). The development and breakdown of the use of names Part IV. The effects of word frequency. *Journal of Neurology, Neurosurgery and Psychiatry, 28*, 407–443.

Sartori, G., & Job, R. (1988). The oyster with four legs: A neuropsychological study on the interaction of visual and semantic information. *Cognitive Neuropsychology, 5*, 105–132.

Saffran, E.M., & Schwartz, M.F. (1994). Of cabbages and things: Semantic memory from a neuropsychological perspective—a tutorial review. In C. Umilta & M. Moscovitch (Eds.), *Attention & Performance XV*. Cambridge, MA: MIT Press.

Schwartz, M.F., Marin, O.S.M., & Saffran, E.M. (1979). Dissociation of language function in dementia: a case study. *Brain and Language, 7*, 277–306.

Shallice, T. (1988). *From Neuropsychology to mental structure*. Cambridge: Cambridge University Press.

Shallice, T., Warrington, E.K., & McCarthy, R.A. (1983). Reading without semantics. *Quarterly Journal of Experimental Psychology, 35*, 111–138.

Sheridan, J., & Humphreys, G.W. (1993). A verbal-semantic category specific recognition impairment. *Cognitive Neuropsychology, 10*, 143–184.

Snodgrass, J.G., & Vanderwart, M. (1980). A standardised set of 260 pictures: norms for name agreement, familiarity and visual complexity. *Journal of Experimental Psychology: General, 6*, 174–215.

Snowden, J.S., Goulding, P.J., & Neary, D. (1989). Semantic dementia: a form of circumscribed cerebral atrophy. *Behavioural Neurology*, 2, 167–182.

Tippett, L.J., McAuliffe, S., & Farah, M.J. (this issue). Preservation of categorical knowledge in Alzheimer's disease: A computational account. *Memory*, 3(3/4).

Tulving, E. (1972). Episodic and semantic memory. In E. Tulving & W. Donaldson (Eds.), *Organization of memory*. New York and London: Academic Press.

Tulving, E. (1983). *Elements of episodic memory*. New York: Oxford University Press.

Tyrrell, P.J., Warrington, E.K., Frackowiak, R.S.J., & Rossor, M.N. (1990). Heterogeneity in progressive aphasia due to focal cortical atrophy: A clinical and PET study. *Brain*, 113, 1321–1336.

Warrington, E.K. (1975). Selective impairment of semantic memory. *Quarterly Journal of Experimental Psychology*, 27, 635–657.

Warrington, E.K., & McCarthy, R.A. (1983). Category specific access dysphasia. *Brain*, 106, 859–878.

Warrington, E.K., & Shallice, T. (1984). Category specific semantic impairments. *Brain*, 107, 829–854.

Wechsler, D. (1945). A standardized memory scale for clinical use. *Journal of Psychology*, 19, 85–95.

APPENDIX

The evolving pattern of JL's naming responses on items from the Snodgrass and Vanderwart corpus which was administered on four occasions. (Cross-category errors are in italics.) Key: dk = don't know; pt = part; pce = piece; circumloc = circumlocution; + = correct.

Land Animals

	Sept 91	March 92	Sept 92	March 93
horse	+	+	+	+
dog	+	+	+	cat
cat	+	+	+	animal
cow	+	+	horse	horse
pig	+	on farms	dog	dog
deer	+	horse	cow	*vehicle*
rabbit	+	cat	cat	cat
sheep	+	dog	dog	dog
elephant	+	horse	horse	animal
mouse	cat	cat	cat	animal
monkey	pig	cat	*boy*	animal
gorilla	a big animal	dog	dog	*man*
tiger	dog	dog	dog	dog
squirrel	cat	chicken	cat	dog
racoon	dog	cat	dog	animal
lion	dog	dog	dog	animal
fox	dog	dog	cat	dog
bear	dog	big animal	dog	dog
goat	dog	dog	dog	dog
leopard	dog	dog	dog	cat
skunk	dog	cat	cat	cat
donkey	pony	horse	horse	horse
zebra	horse	horse	dog	dog

	Sept 91	March 92	Sept 92	March 93
camel	horse	horse	horse	dog
kangaroo	pig	horse	dog	dog
rhinoceros	elephant	horse	horse	dog
giraffe	big, tall an.	horse	horse	horse

Birds

	Sept 91	March 92	Sept 92	March 93
bird (generic)	+	+	+	animal
chicken	+	+	bird	animal
duck	+	bird	bird	*dog*
swan	+	bird	bird	animal
eagle	duck	bird	bird	*horse*
ostrich	swan	bird	*cat*	animal
peacock	duck	bird	*cat*	*vehicle*
penguin	duck	bird	*cat*	pt of animal
rooster	chicken	chicken	bird	*dog*

Insects

	Sept 91	March 92	Sept 92	March 93
ant	bird	bird	*cat*	animal
bee	bird	animal	*cat*	d.k.
beetle	bird	bird	*cat*	animal
butterfly	bird	bird	bird	animal
caterpillar	animal	animal	animal	side piece
fly	bird	bird	bird	animal
grasshopper	bird	bird	*cat*	animal
spider	*pheasant*	bird	animal	d.k.

Water Creatures

	Sept 91	March 92	Sept 92	March 93
fish	+	+	bird	*vehicle*
alligator	small dog	fish	cat	animal
frog	cat	cat	cat	animal
lobster	for eating	d.k.	d.k.	d.k.
seahorse	animal	animal	cat	animal
seal	animal	dog	cat	dog
turtle	eat it	animal	animal	d.k.

Others

	Sept 91	March 92	Sept 92	March 93
snail	small fish	fish	dog	dog
snake	d.k.	animal	animal	animal

Fruit

	Sept 91	March 92	Sept 92	March 93
apple	+	+	egg	to eat
pear	+	apple	egg	food
banana	+	circumloc	to eat	*pt animal*
cherry	egg	apple	apple	to cook
grapes	apples	eggs	apples	pieces

	Sept 91	March 92	Sept 92	March 93
lemon	egg	apple	egg	*a head*
orange	apple	apple	d.k.	for food
peach	apple	apple	d.k.	material
pineapple	food	food	growing	d.k.
strawberry	*vegetable*	apple	eat it	used
tomato	apple	apple	eat it	use it
watermelon	*clothes*	d.k.	material	d.k.

Vegetables

	Sept 91	March 92	Sept 92	March 93
carrot	+	yellow, eat it	food	d.k.
artichoke	flowers	eggs	grows	d.k.
asparagus	vegetable	*a machine*	eat it	*cut holes*
celery	flowers	flower	pt tree	d.k.
lettuce	vegetable	flowers	in garden	d.k.
onion	apple	apple	egg	round
pepper	d .k.	eat it	3 eggs	animal
potato	vegetable	egg	*building*	*for the wet*
pumpkin	vegetable	egg	*animal*	*vehicle*

Foods

	Sept 91	March 92	Sept 92	March 93
bread	+	+	+	business hall
cake	+	food	to be cooked	d.k.
peanut	+	nut	food	*room for animal*
sandwich	+	d.k.	used for it	*place for animals*

Body parts

	Sept 91	March 92	Sept 92	March 93
arm	+	+	+	+
foot	+	+	+	+
hand	+	+	+	+
leg	+	+	+	+
ear	+	+	+	a head
eye	+	+	+	to see out of there
finger	+	+	hand	hand
lips	+	+	to eat	*a hole*
thumb	circumloc	+	circumloc	*animal*
hair	vegetable	d.k.	d.k.	d.k.
nose	piece of wire	+	used	a human
toe	finger	finger	finger	*place for animal*

Other Natural Kinds

	Sept 91	March 92	Sept 92	March 93
tree	+	+	in the woods	+
cloud	+	+	material	pce of food
flower	+	+	s'thing grown	growing up
sun	+	+	from garden	d.k.
leaf	+	pce off tree	pce off tree	d.k.
star	+	a picture	not made yet	d.k.

	Sept 91	March 92	Sept 92	March 93
moon	d.k.	d.k.	not made	*pt of vehicle*
mountain	pt of bush	hill	d.k.	d.k.

Household items

	Sept 91	March 92	Sept 92	March 93
bed	+	+	+	+
door	+	+	+	window
spoon	+	+	+	tool
table	+	+	+	sit at it
window	+	+	+	door
television	+	+	+	a square
telephone	+	+	wire thing	*animal*
broom	+	+	tool, clean	d.k.
chair	+	+	table to sit on	to sit on
clock	+	+	circumloc	the time
fork	+	+	use w knife	digs holes
toaster	+	box	box	*material*
cooker	radio	radio	box	d.k.
couch	circumloc	circumloc	circumloc	sit down
desk	circumloc	circumloc	holds things	*building*
dresser	circumloc	loading box	put things	table
fridge	box	box	box	d.k.
hanger	circumloc	circumloc	metal thing	*vehicle*
iron	circumloc	circumloc	flatten things	d.k.
kettle	circumloc	circumloc	cook tea	d.k.
lamp	light	light	light	d.k.
record player	makes music	music	does things	d.k.
salt cellar	bowl	bottle	holds things	use it
stool	seat	sit on	sit on	sit on
plug	business	d.k.	for measuring	d.k.

Vehicles

	Sept 91	March 92	Sept 92	March 93
bicycle	+	+	+	+
car	+	+	+	+
lorry	+	+	+	+
aeroplane	+	+	+	d.k.
train	+	+	+	thing
motorbike	+	+	+	ride on it
bus	+	+	car	lorry
helicopter	circumloc	circumloc	aeroplane	d.k.
pram	circumloc	circumloc	push child	truck
sledge	seat	d.k.	d.k.	d.k.
wagon	push it	a machine	4-wheeled	mobile

Musical Instruments

	Sept 91	March 92	Sept 92	March 93
accordion	music	m. machine	been made up	d.k.
drum	round box	box	to keep things	d.k.
flute	metal stick	metal stick	metal rod	rod

	Sept 91	March 92	Sept 92	March 93
French horn	music player	music player	*water thing*	a bit
guitar	make music	music player	music	a thing
harp	for music	*fence*	*fence*	*house*
piano	make music	music	reduce things	*animal*
trumpet	make music	blow it	music thing	d.k.
violin	music	m. machine	music	d.k.

Buildings

	Sept 91	March 92	Sept 92	March 93
house	+	+	+	pt house
church	+	+	building	pt building
barn	garage	building	building	pt building
well	d.k.	supply water	*for music*	d.k.
windmill	d.k.	building	building	bit of work

Clothing

	Sept 91	March 92	Sept 92	March 93
boot	+	+	+	+
hat	+	+	+	+
trousers	+	+	*two legs*	+
tie	+	+	d.k.	d.k.
coat	+	+	jacket	*a man*
shoe	+	+	circumloc	boot
jacket	+	coat	coat	coat
skirt	+	dress	in house	*animal pt*
belt	leather tape	+	circumloc	circle
dress	suit	+	jacket	clothes
blouse	coat	coat	jacket	*a man*
bow	clothes	clothing	clothes	d.k.
button	coin	ball	hand-made	for something
cap	shoes	hat	hat	*of paper*
glove	*a hand*	*a hand*	*a hand*	*a hand*
jumper	jacket	coat	jacket	coat
mitten	d.k.	*nose*	*a head*	*a face*
shirt	coat	coat	jacket	suit
sock	boot	boot	shoe	*a foot*
waistcoat	shirt	jacket	jacket	coat

Jewellery

	Sept 91	March 92	Sept 92	March 93
crown	to sit in	d.k.	d.k.	material
necklace	metal rings	metal ball	tiny nuts	d.k.
ring	steel tube	metal ring	round picture	to fill up

Containers

	Sept 91	March 92	Sept 92	March 93
bottle	+	+	+	+
box	+	+	+	+
cup	+	+	+	+
bowl	+	+	empty bottle	fill it up

	Sept 91	March 92	Sept 92	March 93
glass	+	+	glass bottle	fill with drink
wine glass	+	+	bottle for wine	to drink out of
barrel	bucket	box	made for it	d.k.
basket	a bag	bag	fill it up	fill it up
frying pan	cookin' pan	mean bucket	to carry water	to fill up
dustbin	bucket	metal bowl	bottle	water bottle
jug	cup	bowl	cup	to up things in
pot	cookin' pan	bowl	carry water in	to eat out of
suitcase	case to carry	circumloc	carry about	a house
vase	d.k.	bottle	food bowl	to hold something
watering can	circumloc	water bottle	water bottle	bit added on

Tools

knife	+	+	+	+
hammer	+	+	+	thing to cut
nut	+	+	to lock up	to be used
saw	+	+	to saw things	you saw things
scissors	+	+	to cut things	a machine
pen	+	spoon	+	a rod
pencil	+	pen	pen	rod
nail	+	pin	pencil	tighten things
axe	circumloc	circumloc	knife	to cut up
chisel	d.k.	machine	pen	to do things
clothespeg	d.k.	open & undo	machine	machine
ladder	to climb up	steps to climb	circumloc	to walk up
paintbrush	knife	to dig holes	pencil	*pce of a vehicle*
pliers	d.k.	a machine	pen	machine
ruler	measurement	measures	nothing	to lock up
screw	screw it in	pin	screwed in	pushed in
screwdriver	unscrew things	knife	knife	something

Toys

gun	+	+	+	shoot with it
ball	+	+	d.k.	*to eat*
balloon	pce of rope	ball	egg	*food*
bat	d.k.	meal	d.k.	*eatable*
clown	*man's face*	*a man*	*gentleman*	d.k.
doll	*baby girl*	*little girl*	*yg. lady*	*woman*
football	d.k.	d.k.	d.k.	d.k.
helmet	put on head	d.k.	*eatable*	*pt of animal*
kite	d.k.	d.k.	in garden	*to eat*
racquet	tennis	circumloc	knock ball	*a meal*
roller skate	little ridin'	ride it	ride on	*small animal*
snowman	*little man*	*male boy*	*human being*	*animal*
swing	sheet	fence	table	d.k.
top	d.k.	d.k.	d.k.	d.k.
whistle	d.k.	water shooter	keep food in	a bit

	Sept 91	March 92	Sept 92	March 93
cannon	for shooting	d.k.	machine	use it
chain	steel rings	metal rings	pce metal	d.k.

Other Man-made

	Sept 91	March 92	Sept 92	March 93
wheel	+	+	+	a bit
book	+	+	+	old door
brush	+	+	+	to wipe
comb	+	+	for hair	do your hair
glasses	+	+	things	d.k.
envelope	+	letter	book	d.k.
flat	+	pce of paper	a sign	d.k.
arrow	+	circumloc	circumloc	machine
key	+	knife	knife	d.k.
toothbrush	+	brush	hold & rub	pce of rod
watch	+	the time	one of them	used once
cigarette	+	pipe	a rod	d.k.
heart	hat	+	d.k.	used again
anchor	used for work	machine	material	bit of material
ashtray	d.k.	d.k.	4 places here	4 corners on it
pipe	you smoke it	smoke with	one of these	d.k.
bell	d.k.	a light	holds drink	d.k.
lock	to lock door	lock up	machine	tighten up
nail file	knife	knife	metal	to make a hole
needle	knife	knife	metal	d.k.
purse	bag	bag	to carry	carry about
spool	string holder	black thing	d.k.	*cook & eat*
thimble	bottle	bottle	holds drinks	d.k.
traffic light	d.k.	music machine	9 places	for waiting
umbrella	circumloc	circumloc	circumloc	on head

MEMORY, 1995, *3* (3/4), 497–518

Objects and Properties: A Study of the Breakdown of Semantic Memory

Elaine Funnell

Royal Holloway University of London, UK

This paper reports a study of the breakdown of semantic memory in the case of a subject with semantic dementia. The first experiment shows that the subject failed to comprehend words of low familiarity and word frequency, even though the spoken word forms were recognised as familiar. Experiments 2 and 3 showed (a) that the recall of word meanings in definition tasks did not vary with the generality of the word meaning (e.g. category, basic level, or subordinate property) but varied instead with the concept familiarity and frequency of the name; (b) that the ability to verify properties of basic-level objects was not affected by the ability to comprehend the property name, but depended instead on the degree of knowledge demonstrated for the object name in definition tasks; (c) that properties were frequently verified correctly when the object had been defined only to the superordinate level. It is argued that the results do not support the widely held view that, in general, specific information is lost first when semantic memory breaks down. The selective failure to recall specific information for some word meanings is discussed with reference to two theoretical accounts.

INTRODUCTION

Semantic memory contains the knowledge a person has about words, their meaning, what they refer to, and how words relate to each other (Tulving, 1972). Early models of semantic memory (such as that proposed by Collins & Quillian, 1969) represented word meanings as a hierarchy of features arranged in levels from the most general (e.g. living thing) to the most specific (e.g. robin). Properties of objects were stored in a hierarchy from most general to most specific. Properties true of animals in general (e.g. has skin, breathes) were stored at the animal category level, while properties true of particular animals (e.g. long ears) were stored at more specific levels (e.g. rabbit). Information in

---

Requests for reprints should be sent to Elaine Funnell, Department of Psychology, Royal Holloway University of London, Egham, Surrey TW20 0EX, UK. E-mail: E.FUNNELL@RHBNC.AC.UK

I should like to thank EP and her family for their support of this research, and Roz McCarthy and two anonymous referees for perceptive comments on an earlier draft of this paper. The writing up of this research was supported by a grant from the Medical Research Council.

the hierarchy could be accessed at any level: at the most specific (e.g. robin), or at any of the more general levels (bird, animal, living thing).

The hierarchical model was subsequently modified by Collins and Loftus (1975) when it was found that responses to negative statements (e.g. a Robin is a fish), and effects of typicality, did not fit the predictions of the hierarchical model (Collins & Quillian, 1969; Shaeffer & Wallace, 1970). They abandoned the hierarchical arrangement and proposed instead that semantic memory was organised as a network in which items close in meaning were located close together, with strong links connecting them.

In a seminal study of three subjects with a disorder of semantic memory, Warrington (1975) found that although the patients had lost the meanings of some words entirely, the broad meaning of other words seemed to be retained. So, for example, when asked to define the word *geese* one patient described it only as "An animal". When the patients were asked a series of probe questions, such as "Is this an animal?"; "Is it black?"; "Is it found indoors?"; "Is it bigger than a cat?", the subjects were more successful at deciding whether a word or picture named an animal or an object, than whether the items had particular properties such as size, colour, black. To explain these findings, Warrington (1975) suggested that the subjects had lost the more specific defining-feature knowledge required for identifying the meaning precisely. Most importantly, she suggested that when an object concept breaks down, the specific-feature knowledge is lost first.

Warrington argued that this pattern of breakdown supported the hierarchical model of Collins and Quillian (1969), in which an object concept is represented in memory across levels of increasing specificity. But in order to account for the selective loss of specific knowledge in semantic memory disorders, Warrington suggested one notable departure to this model: whereas Collins and Quillian (1969) proposed that access to a concept could occur at any level, Warrington suggested that information in semantic memory had to be accessed from the most general information to the most specific. In other words, the meanings of words were processed first at the superordinate level, and only later at more specific levels. When explaining how the data from her patients fits with this theory, Warrington (1975, p. 655) wrote:

The present evidence for hierarchical organization is the relative preservation of broad category information and the relative vulnerability of specific attribute and specific associative information. Using multi-choice methods and probe techniques there is some evidence from both the visual and auditory modality that for a given concept superordinate information may be accessible when subordinate information is not ... This leads one to question the precise operation of the hierarchical organization proposed by Collins and Quillian. In their model it is possible to move in either direction from any given word concept, the node in a hierarchy, from the general to the specific or *vice versa* ... Here the converse is proposed; with the concept "mallard", either the word or the object would first be categorized as living then as an animal then as a bird then as a duck and so on *down* the hierarchy.

Warrington's general to specific access theory predicted that people should be faster to make decisions about the general category of an object than more specific decisions. However, Rosch et al. (1976) found that adults were faster to decide that a picture matches a spoken basic-level name (e.g. *dog*), than either the superordinate name (*animal*) or the subordinate-level name (e.g. *poodle*). They also showed that young children of 3 and 4 years could sort pictures into basic-level groups (e.g. four tables, four cars) before they could sort pictures into superordinate categories (e.g. four items of furniture, four vehicles). They could also pick out the odd picture from groups of basic-level items (e.g. cat1, cat2, dog) more successfully than from groups in which differences in superordinate category membership were important (e.g. cat, dog, car). Thus, the results of experimental studies have not supported the revised hierarchical theory of semantic memory suggested by Warrington (1975).

Rapp and Caramazza (1989) argued that the theory does not explain how a specific concept would be located in semantic memory once the superordinate had been activated. They point out that very different concepts share the same superordinate concept (for example *fern* and *collie dog* are both living things) and that the theory does not explain how a search for a particular concept proceeds once the superordinate category has been accessed. They suggested that the general to specific access theory would predict that subjects with a semantic access disorder should find it more difficult to distinguish between words that share a common superordinate than those that do not, but when they tested the prediction with an appropriate subject, the theory was not confirmed.

Warrington's findings have been supported by studies conducted by Chertkow, Bub, and Seidenberg (1989) who reported similar dissociations between retained knowledge of the superordinate category and loss of the specific defining features of object concepts. However, other studies have either produced contradictory results across different categories (Bub, Black, Hampson, & Kertesz, 1988), or have shown that the ability to answer category and property questions was equally impaired and declined over time at the same rate (Funnell, 1992).

One reason why superordinate knowledge may sometimes produce enhanced performance relative to subordinate information may be because questions about categories are intrinsically easier than questions about properties. Bayles, Tomoeda, and Trosset (1990) suggested that questions about object properties, for example ''Is it bigger than a cat?'' tend to be more complex than questions about category membership; ''Is it an animal?'' In Warrington's study, control subjects found questions in which properties of an object had to be compared to other objects (e.g. Is it heavier than a telephone directory? Is it bigger than a cat?) significantly harder than more direct questions about properties (e.g. Is it black? is it found indoors?). Using a measure that standardised task difficulty, Bayles et al. (1990) showed that moderately impaired subjects with dementia were better at recalling the specific names of pictured objects (a task that they assumed entails knowledge of specific properties) than either recalling, or recognising, the category name; a finding at odds with the general to specific access hypothesis. It was also noted that when subjects with dementia misnamed a picture, they were more likely to give an attribute, for example "to write with", than to give the name of another object from the same category. The authors argued that, in total, the evidence refutes the theory that more specific knowledge is lost before more general knowledge when semantic memory breaks down. However, it could be argued that comments such as "To write with" are substitutes for superordinate terms (i.e. writing utensils) and may, after all, offer some support for a hierarchical theory of semantic access.

A further problem with probe questions is that the understanding of the words used may differ across question types. Recent studies have shown that semantic memory disorders are susceptible to differences in the familiarity of the concept: lower familiarity items being more likely to be degraded (Funnell & Sheridan, 1992, Hirsh & Funnell, 1994; Stewart, Parkin, & Hunkin, 1992). If feature questions tend to use words of lower familiarity than superordinate questions, a difference in performance might follow which reflects the general difficulty that arises when degraded concepts are used to investigate the functional level of further concepts.

Although most of the available evidence suggests that semantic memory is not organised as a strict hierarchy, some classes of words do appear to form hierarchical relationships. Quillian (1968) observed that a word may be a superordinate of one hierarchy and yet lie within the hierarchy of other word concepts. Miller and Johnson-Laird (1976) make the same point when they discuss the way in which groups of words form semantic fields which vary in scope from generic to specific. They observe that these relations are often characterised as a hierarchy in which generic properties are entailed within the more specific. These hierarchical relations are asymmetric, for example taxonomic relationships imply "is a" links from the item to the immediate superordinate (and not in the reverse direction). The word *poodle* entails the notion of *dog*, and the word *dog* entails the notion of *animal*. Part/whole relationships require 'has a" links from objects to properties. For example, a *knife* entails a *blade*, and a *blade* entails an *edge*. These uni-directional "is a" and "has a" links reflect the way labels include each other and are featured in the spreading activation network theory of semantic memory (Collins & Loftus, 1975; see also Quillian, 1968).

However, network models are vague about important theoretical details. Concepts are represented in an interconnected network of associated concepts, but the referential meanings of particular items are not represented (Miller & Johnson Laird, 1976). Furthermore, it is not clear that the meaning of a word is represented by the properties typically associated with the concept. So far, all attempts to isolate the defining features of concepts have failed. At best, concepts appear to share networks of overlapping similarities, characterised as family resemblances (Rosch & Mervis, 1975; Wittgenstein, 1953). Thus it is not clear exactly what a failure to verify an object property might mean for a theory of the representation of concepts in which any particular property is redundant to the meaning.

Although there is some doubt concerning the strength of the evidence derived from tests using probe questions for the particular loss of specific knowledge, the ability to retrieve only superordinate information to items in word-definition tasks that was reported by Warrington (1975) is seen commonly in the clinic. However, it is not clear whether items on which subjects derive only superordinate information are those items for which subjects cannot verify specific object properties. In general, independent measures of knowledge of the object have not been collected to compare with performance on probe questions. One notable exception is a study conducted by Chertkow et al. (1989), which found that a group of subjects with Alzheimer's disease were no better at making judgments about semantic relatedness to particular items (e.g. Is a lemon more like a lime or like a plum?) for items that yielded correct responses to probe questions and those that did not. Thus it is not clear that measures of the degree of semantic knowledge available about particular items produce consistent evidence for comprehension across different sorts of tests.

This paper will attempt to clarify some of these issues in a study of a patient with a progressive disorder of semantic memory. In particular, the paper will address the question of whether specific semantic information is particularly vulnerable following brain damage; whether the ability to define words and answer probe questions is affected by the familiarity level of the words; and whether the degree of knowledge revealed is consistent for particular items across tests in which word meanings are defined or probed.

CASE HISTORY

The case of EP has been reported by Hodges, Patterson, Oxbury, and Funnell (1992), and only brief details will be provided here. EP was referred for investigation of a 12-month history of progressive word-finding difficulty in November 1989. On investigation she was found to have a severe naming disorder and a difficulty in understanding many words. Spontaneous speech was fluent. Oral reading and written spelling showed a pattern of surface dyslexia and dysgraphia. Her memory for events was good. She ran the house efficiently, and was an accomplished dressmaker. A CT scan demonstrated focal left temporal atrophy. Hodges et al. (1992) have classified EP as a case of semantic dementia.

EXPERIMENTAL INVESTIGATION

Experiment 1

Introduction

The first set of experiments establish the cardinal features of EP's semantic memory disorder. A set of spoken words that vary in word frequency and concept familiarity (as defined by Snodgrass & Wanderwart, 1980) were defined by EP in tests spaced two years apart. The words were also presented in an auditory lexical decision test. The results show that EP's ability to define words varied with differences in word frequency and concept familiarity, and that she recognised as familiar the spoken forms of words she could not define. Her performance deteriorated markedly over time.

Method

Definitions.   Thirty-six nouns and thirty-six adjectives were selected from three bands of name frequency (Kucera & Francis, 1967): high frequency (> 100 words per million); medium frequency (49–60 words per million); and low frequency (4–6 words per million). Twelve nouns and twelve adjectives were selected for each frequency band. The mean familiarity rating was calculated for those nouns in each frequency band for which a rating could be found using available norms. The familiarity ratings showed the same trend as word frequency: high-frequency nouns, mean familiarity 4.14; medium-frequency nouns, mean familiarity 3.24; low-frequency nouns, mean familiarity 2.01. The nouns and adjectives were mixed together in a list and presented in spoken form for EP to define. The test was presented over two sessions in May 1990 and repeated in the early months of 1992.

Auditory Lexical Decisions.   Forty-eight words, comprising all the nouns and adjectives in the low-frequency definitions set, and half the nouns and adjectives in the medium- and high-frequency sets were mixed with an equal number of word-like nonsense words, e.g. *taffle, mabe, manter*. The auditory lexical decision test was carried out over three sessions from June to September 1990.

Results

Defining Words.   Definitions were classed as *correct* if specific information relevant to the item was mentioned, e.g. *garden* "Outside the house where you can plant things"; *tall* "Quite high up I think". Definitions were classed as *superordinate* if category information was mentioned either directly, e.g. *kitten* "An animal", or inferred, e.g. *scarf* "What you can wear", or if the response suggested that only general information had been derived e.g. *pool* "Water, like the river Thames". Definitions were classed as incorrect if the word was wrongly defined, e.g. *hotel* "A place where children can go to learn quite a lot of things, might be 16 or more" (such errors were very rare), or if EP failed to respond, e.g. *bald* "Don't know"; *clumsy* "What on earth does that mean?".

EP's ability to define words declined with the frequency and familiarity of the name (see Table 1). In 1990, she defined perfectly the nouns and adjectives of high and medium familiarity/frequency, but failed to define many of the least common items. In 1992 her performance had worsened; she failed to define the great majority of the low familiarity/frequency words, and also made errors on words in both sets of more familiar/frequent words. No item defined incorrectly in 1990 was defined correctly in 1992. Some examples illustrating the changes in her definitions are provided in Table 2.

Lexical Decision.   EP accepted 47/48 words and rejected 47/48 nonwords, indicating an almost perfect ability to distinguish spoken words from nonwords ($d' = 4.1$). It is of particular interest that she distinguished from nonwords 23/24 (96%; $d' = 3.5$) of the low-frequency words, of which she defined only 10/24 (42%) correctly.

Discussion

EP's ability to define words varied with differences in the familiarity and frequency of the name. Familiarity is a measure of the frequency with which a named object is thought about, or used (Snodgrass & Wanderwart, 1980) whereas word frequency is a measure of the incidence of a particular word in the language (in this case, the written language). Differences in word frequency are known to correlate highly with variations in the familiarity of the concept

TABLE 1
EP's Ability to Define Words

Frequency	Nouns	Adjectives
High	$\overline{X}$ 326 (sd 275) e.g. people, town	$\overline{X}$ 322 (sd 263) e.g. good, short
1990	1.00	1.00
1992	0.83	0.83
Medium	$\overline{X}$ 57 (sd 5) e.g. garden, wheel	$\overline{X}$ 57 (sd 5) e.g. slow, wild
1990	1.00	1.00
1992	0.75	0.75
Low	$\overline{X}$ 5 (sd 0.8) e.g. feather, cart	$\overline{X}$ 5 (sd 0.8) e.g. clumsy, tame
1990	0.25	0.50
1992	0.08	0.08

The proportion of nouns and adjectives varying in word frequency, which were defined correctly by EP in two test sessions spaced two years apart. Twelve words were presented in each set.

TABLE 2
Defining Spoken Words

Frequency	1990	1992
High		
Hotel	Place where you can stay when you go away somewhere for a holiday or business. You'd sleep there and have meals and drinks. There are bars; you can watch TV etc.	Place where children can go to learn quite a lot of things, might be 16 or more.
Hard	This is hard [taps table top]. Something which can't bend.	Something difficult to deal with, feels hard not soft.
Medium		
Island	Small place in the sea with water all the way round. Could be bigger. People could visit it or live on it.	Could be quite small, and lives in the water; might be a bit bigger. Nobody might be living on it.
Rude	Someone who makes upleasant remarks.	Don't know.
Low		
Kitten	A baby cat.	An animal.
Tame	Animals which might not be too wild—friendly with people they live with or see.	Don't know
Cherry	Is that a tree?	Don't know.
Bald	What on earth does that mean? I've forgotten that.	Don't know.

A selection of responses across test sessions, spaced two years apart.

(Snodgrass & Vanderwart, 1980). However, a recent analysis of EP's longitudinal naming performance across a range of tests has shown that concept familiarity is the only reliable predictor of her naming performance (Hirsh & Funnell, in press).

Although EP was unable to define most of the words of low familiarity and frequency, she could nevertheless recognise these words reliably in an auditory lexical decision task. Thus the lexical forms of words that she could not understand nevertheless appeared to be intact. Differences in frequency and familiarity did not affect her ability to recognise the spoken word forms, only to define the meanings of the words. This experiment therefore establishes that EP had a semantic, rather than a lexical disorder.

Experiment 2

Introduction

This experiment examined EP's ability to define category names and basic-level names, and to verify the properties of the basic-level names. The interest of this experiment was to discover to what extent definitions of concepts and probe decisions were affected by differences in word frequency and familiarity. If the meanings of superordinate names were generally better preserved, they should also be better defined than the basic-level names, and possibly less susceptible to differences in word frequency and familiarity than were the names of basic-level items. On the other hand, the ability to define superordinate and basic-level terms, and to verify the properties of basic-level terms, might vary with differences in frequency and familiarity.

The study was also designed to investigate the relationship between the ability to define words and the ability to verify the properties of these words. It was predicted that EP should verify correctly the properties of objects she defined correctly, but fail to verify properties of objects for which she demonstrated no comprehension. Her ability to verify the properties of any object she might happen to define only to category level would be of particular interest, because the failure to recall specific information might suggest that property knowledge had been lost selectively.

Method

Ten names of superordinate categories, varying subjectively in familiarity, were selected. These names varied widely in word frequency (Kucera & Francis, 1967); building 110; animal 68; vehicle 35; fish 35; weapon 42; occupation 24; clothing 20; beverage 5; cutlery 0; and crockery 0.

For each category, two basic-level members were selected, one of which was judged subjectively to be higher in concept familiarity; for example, knife/ladle; shirt/vest; horse/bear (the full set is listed in Appendix 1). The mean word-frequency counts of the more familiar term of each pair was 125.4 (sd 181) and of the less familiar term it was 11 (sd 16.7).

For each basic-level term, two properties were selected, one more familiar than the other: for example, eyes/hooves (horse); eyes/fur (bear); engine/clutch (car and jeep). Mean word-frequency count for the more familiar properties of each pair was 115.1 (sd 142) and for the less familiar properties it was 4.2 (sd 3.8). As far as possible the same properties were used for each basic-level pair, although this was easier to carry out for the higher-frequency properties, which tended to be typical of category members as a whole, than for low-frequency properties, which tended to be typical of subsets of animals, and were not always shared by the basic-level pair. In total, 65% of the properties were used for both items in the basic-level pairs.

Four probe questions about the properties of each basic-level term were derived; two questions about related properties e.g. "Does a knife have a handle?", "Does a knife have a blade?", and two questions about unrelated properties e.g. "Is a knife round?", "Does a knife have a rim?". The full set of 48 questions (24 related pairings, 24 unrelated pairings) were mixed together in a list, with questions about the same item spaced well apart.

Procedure

The spoken names of the superordinate and basic-level items were presented in separate lists for EP to define. Three weeks later, an auditory lexical decision task was given, in which the spoken names of the superordinate category names and basic-level names were presented with an equal number of spoken word-like nonwords, e.g. *glisper, yert, spone, mebble*. A week later EP was presented with the set of spoken property questions to verify.

Results

Defining Superordinate and Subordinate Names.   EP correctly defined 6/10 superordinate names, responding "Don't know" to the remaining four items *occupation, weapon, crockery*, and *beverage*. The mean word-frequency count of those words correctly defined was 44.7 (sd 39), and for those words incorrectly defined it was 16 (sd 16.4).

Definitions of basic-level terms were classified as correct or incorrect, using the criteria described in Experiment 1. In this experiment EP produced no superordinate responses, but made one paraphasic error (see below). EP correctly defined 10/20 basic-level names: (8/10 high-familiarity/frequency [f/f] names of each pair, and 2/10 low-f/f names), a difference that was significant (Fisher Exact test: $z = 2.179$ $P < 0.05$). For example, she defined the word *horse* correctly as "An animal, quite big, that people can get on top of and ride", but to the words *haddock* and *jeep* she replied "I don't know". To one item, *bomb*, she produced a semantic paraphasia "Something that somebody shoots and kills birds or animals". She produced no responses in which only superordinate information was recalled.

Auditory Lexical Decision.   EP correctly accepted all (30/30) spoken superordinate category and basic-level object names and correctly rejected 93% (28/30) of the spoken nonwords. Her ability to distinguish spoken words from nonwords was highly significant ($d' = 3.87$; binomial $P < 0.001$).

Verifying Features of Subordinate Items.   Overall, EP correctly accepted 28/40 (binomial $P < 0.01$) related properties and correctly rejected 28/40 (binomial $P < 0.01$) unrelated properties. Her ability to discriminate related from unrelated properties was significant ($d' = 1.05$; $z = 3.33$, $P > 0.001$). Differences in the relative f/f of the properties did not affect performance significantly: related properties, high f/f 15/21, low f/f 13/19 ($z = 0.67$, $P > 0.05$); unrelated properties: high f/f 16/22, low f/f 12/18 ($z = 0.069$, $P > 0.05$).

A meaningful pattern emerged when EP's knowledge of the meaning of the basic-level object name was taken into account. As Table 3 shows, for those items EP defined to a specific level, probe properties were verified to a significant level. However, for those items that she failed to define, she verified probe questions at chance level (related properties 9/18; unrelated properties 10/ 18). The properties of the single item to which EP gave a semantic paraphasia were correctly verified.

Discussion

When EP defined spoken words, the meanings of superordinate names were not spared relative to the names of basic-level terms drawn from a similar range of word frequency: she defined 60% of superordinate names and 50% of basic-level names. Knowing the meaning of superordinate and basic-level names varied with the familiarity and frequency of the words, supporting the view that the less familiar concepts were most susceptible to damage at both the superordinate and the basic level. Thus, these results do not support the view that, in definition tasks, more specific levels of information were most vulnerable to brain damage; instead the results suggest that information at every

TABLE 3
Experiment 2

Objects	Property Name	Related Properties		Unrelated Properties		χ^2 df = 1
		Accept	Reject	Accept	Reject	
1) Defined	High FF	7	2	2	9	
correctly	Low FF	10	1	2	7	
(n = 10)	Total	(17)	(3)	(4)	(16)	z = 3.97
2) Paraphasia	High FF	–	–	0	1	
(n = 1)	Low FF	2	2	0	1	
	Total	(2)	(2)	(0)	(2)	
3) Not	High FF	8	4	4	6	
defined	Low FF	1	5	4	4	
(n = 9)	Total	(9)	(9)	(8)	(10)	z = 0.15
Overall (n = 22)		(28)	(12)	(12)	(28)	z = 3.33

Number of correct decisions about related and unrelated properties according to the level of knowledge of the object in a definition task. Two related and two unrelated properties were paired with each object. Property decisions are reported separately for property names differing in frequency and familiarity (high or low).

level was vulnerable to disruption. EP recognised all the superordinate and basic-level terms as familiar words in the auditory lexical decision task, and reliably distinguished these words from nonwords, so her failure to define words of lower frequency and familiarity was not because she no longer recognised the auditory forms of the words.

It is of interest that EP's ability to define the basic-level object names was unrelated to her ability to define the associated superordinate-category label; she defined exactly half the basic-level names belonging to category labels that she either could or could not define. Instead, the ability to define superordinate and basic-level terms depended on the f/f of the word.

In contrast, EP's ability to *verify* the properties of basic-level object names was unaffected by the f/f of the property names, but depended instead on whether or not she had been able to define the basic-level name in the previous test. EP verified correctly most properties of objects that she had defined correctly, or for which she had provided a paraphasic response, but defined at chance the properties of objects she had failed to define. Rather surprisingly, this finding suggests that EP correctly verified properties with low f/f names that she was unlikely to have understood, when these names were paired with object names that she could define.

Unfortunately, EP produced no responses in which only superordinate information was recalled, so it was not possible to determine whether such responses reflected a loss of property knowledge.

Experiment 3

Introduction

Experiment 2 suggested that EP could verify object properties when the names of the properties were unlikely to have been understood. This experiment investigated this possibility by comparing EP's ability to define property names and to then verify these names as associated properties of objects. The experiment was also designed to see whether the differing effects of word frequency and familiarity on tasks of definition and verification would be replicated, and whether the systematic relationship between the ability to define a word and verify its properties would be sustained. It was also hoped that, by using fresh stimuli, the likelihood would be increased of obtaining some definitions given to basic-level names in which only superordinate information was recalled. This would allow the relationship between recalling superordinate information and verifying specific properties to be investigated. If EP were able to verify the properties of objects that she could define only to superordinate level, this would indicate that specific property knowledge had not been lost, but that, for some reason, it was more difficult to recall information about properties than information about superordinate category. In this experiment, identical properties were selected for each high f/f and low f/f pair of basic-level objects.

Method

Materials. Eleven pairs of basic-level objects were selected, each pair belonging to a particular semantic category. One item of each pair was considered to be relatively more familiar than the other, e.g. *horse–zebra*; *rose–dahlia*; *house–cottage*. In many cases this difference was also reflected in marked differences in word frequency. Overall, the more familiar items had a mean frequency of 125.1 (sd 176.3) and the less familiar items had a mean word frequency of 6.3 (sd 7.1), although in some pairs the differences in word frequency were small, and there was some overlap in frequency ranges across high- and low-familiarity sets (see Appendix 2).

Two related properties were selected for each pair of items; one judged to be more familiar and one less familiar. Each property was shared by *both* members of the pair, for example, the properties *head* and *hooves* were selected for the item pair *horse–zebra*; *leaves* and *petals* for the item pair *rose–dahlia*. In most cases, the more familiar property also had a higher name frequency. Overall, the more familiar property had a mean name frequency of 136 (sd 155.3) and the less familiar property had a mean frequency of 7.4 (sd 4.4).

The properties were also paired with basic-level objects to which they did not belong, for example the property names *eyes* and *whiskers* were paired with the items *car* and *jeep*, and the property names *handle* and *blade* were paired with *horse* and *zebra*. Care was taken to ensure that the properties in these unrelated pairs were not shared by any members of the category from which the basic-level objects were drawn.

Procedure

Object and property names were mixed together in a list and spoken to EP for her to define. EP was then asked to verify short spoken sentences linking each object name with either a related or unrelated property. Two related properties and two unrelated properties were presented with each item, for example "Does a horse have a head?", "Does a horse have a blade?". The four questions for each object were spread throughout the list and spaced well apart. The experiment was conducted within one testing session, and was presented twice, once in May 1991 and again in May 1992. At the end of the second presentation of the list, in May 1992, and immediately after the sentences had been verified, the items that had not been defined correctly at the start of the test were presented again for defining.

Results

Defining Basic-level Objects and Properties. EP's definitions were classified into three groups along the lines described in Experiment 1. In this

510   FUNNELL

experiment, a substantial proportion of responses provide superordinate-category information only for example, *mouse* "An animal", *rose* "A plant". It is clear from Table 4 that on both occasions tested, the differences in f/f strongly affected EP's ability to define both the basic-level object names and the names of properties. Moreover, there was no difference in EP's ability to correctly define basic-level object names (1991: 8/22; 1992: 6/22) and property names (1991: 8/22; 1992: 5/22).

It should be noted that the basic-level names and property names were presented again for definition following the second presentation of the verification questions in 1992. No significant improvement was observed in EP's ability to define the items and properties at this subsequent test. Of the 21 basic-level objects and properties EP had not been able to define before the verification questions had been posed, she was subsequently able to define only two items: one to a specific level and one to the superordinate level. Thus there was no evidence that experience with correct pairings of object and property names in the verification task in some way activated an explicit memory for objects and properties not available before the verification test was presented.

Verifying Properties of Objects. For the purposes of this analysis, definitions of property names were classified as either known (correct) or not

TABLE 4
Experiment 3

Year	Objects defined	Frequency/Familiarity High (n = 11)	Low (n = 11)	Kendall's Tau B
1991	correct	6	2	
	category	4	4	
	not defined	1	5	$T_B = 0.43 \ P < 0.05$
1992	correct	6	0	
	category	4	6	
	not defined	1	5	$T_B = 0.58 \ P < 0.01$
Year	Properties defined	(n = 11)	(n = 11)	Kendall's Tau B
1991	correct	7	1	
	category	2	1	
	not defined	2	9	$T_B = 0.62 \ P < 0.01$
1992	correct	4	1	
	category	2	0	
	not defined	5	10	$T_B = 0.45 \ P < 0.05$

Number of object and property names defined correctly to category level, or not defined, in two presentations of the list. Responses for names of high and low frequency and familiarity are reported separately.

known (incorrect); the few superordinate-level responses given to properties (see Table 4) were classified as "known" because the superordinate-level response indicated that some information was available.

There was no difference in EP's ability to verify known and unknown properties, she verified these equally well: 1991—known 36/44 (82%) correct, unknown 31/44 (71%) correct ($z = 1.0$, $P > 0.05$); 1992—known 21/28 (75%) correct, unknown 48/60 (80%) correct ($z = 0.25$, $P > 0.05$). EP also verified properties of high and low f/f equally well: 1991—high f/f 35/44, low f/f 32/44 ($z = 0.3$, $P > 0.05$); 1992—high f/f 33/44, low f/f 36/44 ($z = 0.03$, $P > 0.05$).

Table 5 presents the proportion of properties verified correctly given either

TABLE 5
Experiment 3

		Properties				
		Related		Unrelated		χ^2
	Properties	Accept	Reject	Accept	Reject	(df = 1)
1991						
objects defined	known	8	0	0	8	
(n = 8)	unknown	8	0	1	7	***
	(overall)	(16)	(0)	(1)	(15)	z = 4.88
objects category	known	8	0	5	2	
(n = 8)	unknown	5	3	3	6	
	(overall)	(13)	(3)	(8)	(8)	z = 1.46 ns
objects not	known	4	2	1	6	
defined	unknown	1	5	1	4	
(n = 6)	(overall)	(5)	(7)	(2)	(10)	z = 0.63 ns
	Overall total	(34)	(10)	(11)	(33)	
1992						
objects defined	known	4	0	0	4	
(n = 6)	unknown	7	1	1	7	***
	(overall)	(11)	(1)	(1)	(11)	z = 3.60
objects category	known	5	2	2	3	
(n = 10)	unknown	11	2	2	13	***
	(overall)	(16)	(4)	(4)	(16)	z = 3.44
objects not	known	3	0	3	2	
defined	unknown	3	6	0	7	
(n = 6)	(overall)	(6)	(6)	(3)	(9)	z = 0.83 ns
	Overall total	(33)	(11)	(8)	(36)	

*** $P < 0.001$

Number of correct decisions about related and unrelated properties according to the level of knowledge of the object in a definition task. Two related and two unrelated properties were paired with each object. Property decisions are reported separately for property names that (a) were defined correctly (known) or (b) were not defined (unknown).

related properties, e.g. "Does a horse have a head?", and unrelated properties, e.g. "Does a horse have a handle?", according to (a) whether or not the object name was defined to a specific level, superordinate level, or not defined; and (b) whether the properties were defined correctly (known) or incorrectly (not known). The results from the tests given in 1991 and 1992 are presented separately.

Overall, EP successfully distinguished between related and unrelated properties: in 1991 she accepted correctly 34/44 related properties and correctly rejected 33/44 unrelated properties (d' 1.413; $z = 4.58$, $P < 0.001$), and in 1992 she accepted correctly 33/44 related properties and correctly rejected 36/44 unrelated properties ($d' = 1.41$; $z = 5.1$, $P < 0.001$).

EP's ability to verify properties varied systematically with her understanding of the basic-level object name (see Table 5). The properties of *objects she defined correctly* were verified virtually perfectly: in 1991 she accepted 16/16 related properties and rejected 15/16 unrelated properties (Fisher exact: $z = 4.88$, $P < 0.001$) and in 1992 she accepted 11/12 related properties and rejected 11/12 unrelated properties (Fisher exact: [df = 1] $z = 3.60$, $P < 0.001$).

The properties of *objects she defined to superordinate level* were verified less reliably: in 1991 she accepted 13/16 related properties (a score that is significantly above chance, binomial $P < 0.01$) but rejected only 8/16 unrelated properties (a score that is at chance), so that overall her performance did not reach significance ($z = 1.46$ $P > 0.05$). However, in 1992 she accepted 16/20 related properties and rejected 16/20 unrelated properties, a level of performance that in each case was significant when related and unrelated properties were analysed separately (Binomial $z = 2.46$, $P > 0.01$) and when analysed overall ($z = 3.44$ $P < 0.001$).

The properties of *objects she failed to define* were verified overall at chance: in 1991 she accepted 5/12 related properties and rejected 9/11 unrelated properties ($z = 0.63$ $P > 0.05$). Similarly, in 1992 she accepted 6/12 related properties and rejected 9/12 unrelated properties ($z = 0.83$, $P > 0.05$). Although she rejected significant numbers of unrelated properties of objects she could not define, she also rejected related properties, the effect being more marked for unknown properties of related objects (1991: known related properties rejected 2/6 [33%], unknown related properties rejected 5/6 [83%]; 1992: known properties rejected 0/3, unknown properties rejected 6/9 [33%]). It is interesting to note that the results of Experiment 2 showed a similar tendency to reject the names of unknown related properties for object names for which no meaning was recalled: known related properties rejected 4/12 (33%), unknown properties rejected 5/6 (83%). However, the numbers involved in all these comparisons were too small for reliable statistical analysis.

Discussion

The results of this experiment confirmed and extended the findings of Experiment 2. It was again the case that EP's ability to *define* words was affected by differences in word frequency/familiarity and that this was true not only for basic-level names (demonstrated initially in Experiment 2), but also for the names of properties. Moreover, EP's ability to correctly define basic-level object and property names was equally impaired, indicating that knowledge of properties *per se* was not especially vulnerable to the effects of brain disease.

Nevertheless, when properties were verified, neither the frequency/familiarity of the property names, nor EP's ability to define the property names had any significant effect on performance. Again, as Experiment 2 indicated, the ability to verify a property of an object depended on EP's ability to define the basic-level object name (at least to some level).

EP's ability to verify the properties of objects that she defined to superordinate level was particularly relevant to this investigation, as performance here should reveal if knowledge of properties was lost when only superordinate information was recalled in a definition task. Although the findings were not unequivocal, the results overall favoured the view that knowledge of properties was generally retained when the object was defined by EP to superordinate level only.

GENERAL DISCUSSION

The studies reported here of the breakdown of semantic memory in a single subject, EP, have shown that the integrity of word meanings has been impaired to equivalent levels across different levels of word meaning: at the superordinate level; the basic level; and the level of object properties. Thus, when words are defined, there is no evidence from EP's performance that knowledge of properties is selectively impaired. Instead, at every level of word meaning, the ability to define words varies with word frequency and the familiarity of the object concept.

Concept familiarity has been isolated as the variable that most reliably predicts EP's comprehension of words (Hirsh & Funnell, in press). Ratings of object familiarity have also been shown to be related to semantic memory impairments (Funnell & Sheridan, 1992; Stewart et al., 1992) and have been argued to reflect the level and frequency of experience with an object, which may in turn influence the breadth and strength of the representation of the concept in memory (Funnell & Sheridan, 1992). Studies of the decline of semantic memory in dementia have suggested that the efficiency of the semantic memory system declines as a whole (Funnell, 1992), and it is likely that knowledge for the least familiar objects, with the least well represented concepts, will be affected first. Furthermore, it seems likely that the level of knowledge of word meaning (i.e. of superordinate category, basic-level object, or object property) will be immaterial to this decline.

Although EP defined words of different specificity to an equivalent level, suggesting that the more specific, property-level information was not selectively impaired, nevertheless, she was sometimes able to recall only superordinate information in word definition tasks (see also Warrington, 1975). However, although specific knowledge was not recalled, it was not entirely lost, as EP was able to verify the properties of these objects to a level above chance in most tests.

Two theories might account for EP's ability to verify the properties of objects for which only superordinate information was recalled in word definitions. First, it could be argued that superordinate and subordinate property information is represented separately by "is a" links to semantic category, which are stronger than "has a" links to properties, perhaps because, as Collins and Loftus (1975) proposed, links more central to the concept are shorter, or possibly stronger because they are used more often. When a semantic representation is degraded, the "has a" links will be intrinsically more vulnerable than the "is a" links, with the result that only category information will be recalled. Property links will be activated when the name is provided, as long as the links are still relatively intact. This account is similar to the account provided originally by Warrington (1975) except that, in the account given here, the relative sparing of superordinate knowledge is reflected by the superior strength of category links (cf Collins & Loftus, 1975) rather than priority of access to category information in a semantic hierarchy (Warrington, 1975).

Alternatively, it could be argued that object concepts are not composed of separable types of properties but are represented instead as complete entities in a competitive network in which related concepts are linked closely together. As semantic memory breaks down, the ability to keep the representations of less familiar concepts distinct from related concepts becomes increasingly difficult, either because these representations cannot inhibit closely related representations, or because the less familiar representation cannot emerge completely from within a distributed network. The result is that a degraded concept cannot be distinguished from its related neighbours (Funnell, 1992). However, superordinate-category knowledge emerges from the activated set of related concepts, which is then labelled by the superordinate term. When related properties are paired directly with these object names, the associations of these weakly activated object concepts are energised, but not to a level that allows the object name to be defined fully on a subsequent test.

These two theories make different predictions about the relative sparing of knowledge of unfamiliar objects with few semantically related neighbours and those with many neighbours. Although the first theory predicts that there should be no difference in the recall of concepts of objects with few or many neighbours, because the integrity of the "has a" links of these should not be affected differently, the second theory predicts that recall of concepts of objects with few or no neighbours should be more likely to be achieved because these degraded object concepts will suffer less competition from related neighbours.

In summary, this paper has shown: (1) that more specific information is not more vulnerable than more general information to the effects of brain disease when performance across different word types is compared in definition tasks; (2) that the ability to define words depends on the frequency/familiarity level of the word meaning (this experiment did not attempt to separate out these two factors, but further work has shown that familiarity is the best predictor of EP's memory for words); (3) that the ability to verify properties of objects depends only on the level of understanding of the object name, and not on understanding the names of the properties; and (4) that the ability to verify properties of objects is related to the ability to define the object. On the whole, property information seems to be retained when objects can be defined only to the superordinate level.

REFERENCES

Bayles, K.A., Tomoeda, C.K., & Trosset, M.W. (1990). Naming and categorical knowledge in Alzheimer's disease: The process of semantic memory deterioration. *Brain and Language, 39,* 498–510.

Bub, D.N., Black, S., Hampson, E., & Kertesz, A. (1988). Semantic encoding of pictures and words: Some neuropsychological observations. *Cognitive Neuropsychology, 5*(1), 27–66.

Chertkow, H., Bub, D., & Seidenberg, M. (1989). Priming and semantic memory loss in Alzheimer's disease. *Brain and Language, 36,* 420–446.

Collins, A.M. & Loftus, E.F. (1975). A spreading activation theory of semantic processing. *Psychological Review, 82,* 407–428.

Collins, A.M., & Quillian, M.R. (1969). Retrieval time from semantic memory. *Journal of Verbal Learning and Verbal Behavior, 8,* 240–247.

Funnell, E. (1992). Progressive loss of semantic memory in a case of Alzheimer's disease. *Proceedings of the Royal Society, 249,* 287–291.

Funnell, E., & Sheridan, J. (1992). Categories of knowledge? Unfamiliar aspects of living and nonliving things. *Cognitive Neuropsychology, 9,* 135–153.

Hirsh, K.W., & Funnell, E. (in press). Age of name acquisition and concept familiarity: Evidence for differing effects upon naming in progressive anomia. *Journal of Psycholinguistics.*

Hodges, J.R., Patterson, K., Oxbury, S., & Funnell, E. (1992). Semantic dementia. Progressive fluent aphasia with temporal lobe atrophy. *Brain, 118,* 1781–1806.

Kucera, H., & Francis, W.N. (1967). *Computational analysis of present-day American English.* Providence, RI: Brown University Press.

Miller, G., & Johnson-Laird, P.N. (1976). *Language and perception.* Cambridge: Cambridge University Press.

Quillian, M.R. (1968). Semantic memory. In M. Minsky (Ed.), *Semantic information processing.* Cambridge, MA: MIT Press.

Rapp, B., & Caramazza, A. (1989). General to specific access to word meaning: A claim re-examined. *Cognitive Neuropsychology, 6,* 251–272.

Rosch, E., & Mervis, C.B. (1975). Family resemblances: Studies in the internal structure of categories. *Cognitive Psychology, 7,* 573–605.

Rosch, E., Mervis, C.B., Gray, W.D., Johnson, D.M., & Boyes-Braem, P. (1976). Basic objects in natural categories. *Cognitive Psychology, 8,* 382–439.

Shaeffer, B., & Wallace, R. (1970). The comparison of word meanings. *Journal of Experimental Psychology, 86,* 144–152.

Snodgrass, J.G., & Vanderwart, M. (1980). A standardised set of 260 pictures. Norms for name agreement, image agreement, familiarity, and visual complexity. *Journal of Experimental Psychology: Human Learning and Memory, 6,* 174–215.

Stewart, F., Parkin, A.J., & Hunkin, N.M. (1992). Naming impairments following recovery from herpes simplex encephalitis: Category-specific? *Quarterly Journal of Experimental Psychology,* *44A*, 261–284.

Tulving, E. (1972). Episodic and semantic memory. In E. Tulving & W. Donaldson (Eds.), *Organization of memory.* New York: Academic Press.

Warrington, E. (1975). The selective impairment of semantic memory. *Quarterly Journal of Experimental Psychology, 27*, 635–657.

Wittgenstein, L. (1953). *Philosophical investigations* [Translated by G.E.M. Anscombe]. New York: Macmillan.

APPENDIX 1

Experiment 2: Names of basic-level objects and related and unrelated properties, classified according to the *relative* concept familiarity of the items (word-frequency counts are given in parentheses).

Basic-level object	Related properties		Basic-level object	Related properties	
Higher familiarity	Higher familiarity (HFam) Lower familiarity (LFam)		Lower familiarity	Higher familiarity (HFam) Lower familiarity (LFam)	
knife (76)	HFam	handle (53)	ladle (1)	HFam	handle (53)
	LFam	blade (13)		LFam	soup (16)
plate (22)	HFam	round (81)	tumbler (2)	HFam	glass (99)
	LFam	rim (5)		LFam	rim (5)
house (591)	HFam	roof (59)	shack (59)	HFam	roof (59)
	LFam	eaves (1)		LFam	eaves (1)
coffee (78)	HFam	brown (176)	cocoa (2)	HFam	brown (176)
	LFam	bitter (53)		LFam	powder (28)
trout (4)	HFam	head (424)	haddock (1)	HFam	head (424)
	LFam	scales (5)		LFam	scales (5)
car (274)	HFam	engine (50)	jeep (16)	HFam	engine (50)
	LFam	clutch (5)		LFam	clutch (5)
bomb (36)	HFam	kill (63)	missile (48)	HFam	kill (63)
	LFam	explode (6)		LFam	projected (4)
horse (117)	HFam	eyes (401)	beaver (3)	HFam	eyes (401)
	LFam	hooves (2)		LFam	fur (13)
builder (29)	HFam	brick (18)	clerk (34)	HFam	pen (18)
	LFam	shovel (0)		LFam	ledger (7)
shirt (27)	HFam	sleeves (8)	vest (4)	HFam	sleeves (8)
	LFam	cuffs (2)		LFam	cuffs (2)

APPENDIX 2

Experiment 3: Names of basic-level objects and related properties selected according to the relative concept familiarity of the item (word-frequency counts are given in parentheses).

Basic level objects Concept familiarity		Related properties Concept familiarity	
Higher	Lower	Higher	Lower
horse (117)	zebra (1)	head (424)	hooves (2)
person (175)	skeleton (2)	feet (283)	spine (6)
cat (23)	mouse (10)	fur (13)	whiskers (3)
bull (14)	deer (13)	teeth (103)	horns (8)
rose (86)	dahlia (0)	leaves (49)	petals (4)
oak (15)	poplar (0)	leaves (49)	bark (14)
car (274)	jeep (16)	engine (50)	clutch (5)
salmon (3)	herring (2)	eyes (401)	scales (5)
robin (2)	chaffinch (0)	wings (27)	feathers (14)
house (591)	cottage (19)	roof (59)	chimney (7)
knife (76)	axe (5)	handle (53)	blade (13)

MEMORY, 1995, 3 (3/4), 519–533

Preservation of Categorical Knowledge in Alzheimer's Disease: A Computational Account

Lynette J. Tippett, Sean McAuliffe, and Martha J. Farah

University of Pennsylvania, USA

The distinction between knowledge of specific exemplars and knowledge of their general categories is central to much theorising on the nature of semantic memory. The dissociation between exemplar and category knowledge observed in Alzheimer's Disease (AD) would appear to support this distinction, and to suggest that different neural systems are involved in the representation of exemplar and category knowledge. We review the evidence for preserved category knowledge in the semantic memory impairment of AD, and propose an alternative interpretation, according to which category and exemplar knowledge are both represented in the same distributed neural substrate. The relative preservation of category knowledge is a consequence of the greater frequency, and hence greater robustness, of the representation of attributes shared by all or most members of a category, compared to exemplar-unique attributes. We test and confirm the computational adequacy of this hypothesis in two computer simulations.

INTRODUCTION

Among the kinds of knowledge that we label as semantic memory is knowledge of category membership. The information that dogs are animals and chairs are furniture are prototypical examples of the kind of fact that psychologists would attribute to semantic memory. Indeed, knowledge of category membership is central to semantic memory because it enables knowledge to be represented and accessed efficiently. For example, once we have learned that animals breathe, we can infer that all exemplars of that category breathe, without having to represent explicit associations between breathing and all of the animals we know

Requests for reprints should be sent to Lynette J. Tippett, Department of Psychology, University of Auckland, Private Bag 92019, Auckland, New Zealand.

This research was supported by Alzheimer's Association/Hearst Corporation Research Grant PRG-93-153, ONR grant N00014-93-I0621, NIMH grant R01 MH48274, NINDS grant R01 NS34030, an NSF STC grant to the Institute for Research in Cognitive Science at the University of Pennsylvania, and the University of Pennsylvania Research Foundation. The authors thank Glyn Humphreys and an anonymous reviewer for helpful comments, and Rosaleen McCarthy for additional guidance in the revision of this paper.

520 TIPPETT, McAULIFFE, FARAH

(Collins & Quillian, 1969). Perhaps for this reason, most research on semantic memory has been research on categorisation and category representation.

In early models of semantic memory, distinctions between categories and exemplars were represented explicitly. For example in Collins and Quillian's model, representations are organised hierarchically, with knowledge of exemplars functionally separate from knowledge of categories. The psychological reality of the category–exemplar distinction was also implicit in Rosch's theorising on the "basic object level" (e.g. Rosch et al., 1976), corresponding to categories such as "chair", "apple", or "car". Rosch proposed that this level of categorical aggregation of exemplars is psychologically basic, in that objects are identified first in terms of their basic category membership, and only after additional processing can they be identified at the exemplar level (e.g. "folding chair") or the superordinate level (e.g. "furniture"). Among the implications of this theory is that knowledge of the basic-level category is special and distinct from knowledge of the exemplar level.

Recent theorising in cognitive neuroscience also emphasises the distinction between the representations of categories and exemplars, and further suggests that the brain honours this distinction. For example, Damasio (1989) suggests that the identification of objects at the basic category level can proceed within a given brain area (e.g. a visual stimulus can be categorised within the visual areas), whereas identification of particular exemplars requires that multiple brain areas can be activated and coordinated. To recognise a particular car, Damasio and colleagues hypothesise that in addition to the visual appearance of the car, associated representations in other modalities such as the sound and feel of the car must also be activated, by way of anterior temporal "convergence zones". Thus, according to this view category and exemplar representations are physically as well as functionally different.

One of the most striking dissociations between knowledge of categories and exemplars comes from the study of patients with Alzheimer's Disease (AD). Over the past decade, it has become clear that semantic memory is a major locus of cognitive impairment in AD (see Nebes, 1989, 1992 for reviews). Numerous studies have found that AD subjects are impaired on tasks presumed to measure semantic knowledge such as attribute listing tasks (e.g. Martin & Fedio, 1983; Warrington, 1975), category fluency tasks (e.g. Butters et al., 1987; Martin & Fedio, 1983; Ober et al., 1986; Ober, Koss, Freidland, & Delis, 1985; Tröster, Salmon, McCullough, & Butters, 1989), confrontation naming tasks (e.g. Bayles & Tomoeda, 1983; Hodges, Salmon, & Butters, 1991; Martin & Fedio, 1983), picture–name matching tasks (e.g. Chertkow, Bub & Seidenberg, 1989; Huff, Corkin, & Growdon, 1986), and semantic priming tasks (e.g. Margolin, 1987; Ober & Shenaut, 1988).

More specifically relevant to the present issue, semantic knowledge of exemplars often appears disproportionately impaired in patients with AD, relative to their knowledge of categories. The dissociation between exemplar and category knowledge can be seen in various measures of semantic memory, including confrontation naming, category and attribute verification, picture–name matching, and category fluency.

On confrontation naming tasks, the nature of the errors made by AD patients suggests that they are able to recognise the category of the to-be-named object more often than they recognise its specific exemplar identity. In some cases the object is simply called by the name of its category (e.g. "animal" instead of "cow"); in others the name of a different object from the same category is given (e.g. "horse" instead of "cow"; Bayles & Tomoeda, 1983; Martin, 1987; Martin & Fedio, 1983). Hodges, Salmon, and Butters (1991) found that AD subjects' pattern of naming errors involved significantly more category names, as well as nonresponses and related concepts (such as "painting" for easel), than age-matched controls. In all cases these findings suggest that semantic category knowledge is available, but that identification of specific exemplars is impaired.

Martin (1987) devised a verification task in which category and exemplar knowledge could be contrasted in AD patients and normal controls. He reports that AD patients were nearly perfect at verifying category membership of depicted objects, but had great difficulty verifying the physical and functional attributes of these same objects.

Performance on picture–name matching tasks also supports the view that AD results in difficulty discriminating among exemplars within a semantic category, but does not impair discrimination between categories. For example, Huff et al. (1986) found that on a true–false test of picture-to-name pairings, AD subjects were impaired at rejecting incorrect names of pictures when the names were other items from the same category. In contrast, they successfully rejected incorrect category names for the same set of items. Similarly, Chertkow et al. (1989) found that AD subjects made considerably more errors than control subjects when selecting the picture of a named object when the distractors were from the same semantic category. In addition, Chertkow et al. showed that this result was not attributable to the generally high level of similarity of within-category exemplars, by administering the same type of task with perceptually similar distractors from different categories. AD patients performed normally in this condition, showing that their problem is specific to discrimination of exemplars within a semantic category.

Findings from verbal fluency tasks also provide converging evidence for a loss of exemplar-level semantic information in AD. Most commonly in fluency tasks, subjects are either given a letter and asked to generate words beginning with that letter, or they are given a semantic category and asked to generate exemplars of the category. AD subjects are usually impaired on these tasks, producing markedly fewer items even early in the disease process (e.g. Nebes, 1989, 1992). Of course, these two tasks require semantic, lexical, and executive functions, and it is not clear what type of impairment underlies the poor verbal fluency performances of AD subjects. A third type of fluency task is more informative, however, because the pattern of responses shown by AD subjects shows a dissociation between category and exemplar knowledge. In this type of fluency task, subjects are asked to name items they might find in a supermarket. Normal controls typically name four or more items from each of a number of categories such as fruit and vegetables. In contrast, AD subjects give relatively few responses and frequently give only the category names themselves (Martin & Fedio, 1983; Ober et al., 1985; Tröster et al., 1989). Like the results from confrontation naming and picture–name matching tasks, this result suggests that knowledge of individual exemplars within a category is impaired relative to knowledge of the category itself.

In sum, AD patients' performance in a number of different tasks reveals a semantic memory impairment in which knowledge of categories is relatively preserved while knowledge of exemplars is impaired. What implications does this have for the neural organisation of semantic memory? There are two possible answers to this question, with very different implications for brain organisation in general, and the underlying nature of AD patients' impairment in particular. One answer is that the brain honours the distinction between different levels of a hierarchical, categorical knowledge system. According to this interpretation of preserved category knowledge, AD primarily affects the neural systems subserving exemplar knowledge. This interpretation is consistent with the theorising in cognitive psychology and cognitive neuroscience reviewed earlier, in which knowledge of categories and knowledge of exemplars are hypothesised to be functionally and physically distinct.

A second interpretation of the dissociation between category and exemplar knowledge in AD does not involve separate systems for representing these two kinds of knowledge. According to this interpretation, semantic memory is a distributed system of knowledge representation, in which the same physical substrate represents both categorical and exemplar information. From this perspective, the dissociation can be explained by hypothesising that category information is more robustly represented than exemplar information. This type of explanation has been applied to the preservation of category knowledge in AD by Martin (1987). He proposed that a generalised degradation of semantic knowledge might be expected to affect the relatively fine discriminations required to arrive at the correct within-category identification more than the coarser discriminations required for arriving at the correct general category.

In this article we provide an explicit computational formulation of this second type of interpretation of preserved category knowledge. Specifically, we offer an explicit explanation of why category knowledge would be more robust to damage in a system in which both exemplar and category knowledge are implemented in the same distributed representational substrate, and we test this explanation using computer simulation. Before detailing the explanation, we will briefly review the concept of distributed representation, and the nature of learning and computation in distributed neural networks.

Perhaps the easiest way to explain the concept of distributed representation is to begin by explaining its opposite, local representation. Local representations are like "grandmother cells", in that there is a one-to-one mapping of things represented onto things doing the representing. For example, your grandmother and only your grandmother would be represented by activation of one particular neuron. In contrast, with distributed representations there is a many-to-many mapping of things represented onto things doing the representing. For example, a distributed representation of your grandmother would be a pattern of activation over a number of neurons. Those same neurons, when entertaining different patterns of activation, would also represent other things. Note that representations can be said to be distributed or local only with respect to a given domain of represented things. If neurons were to represent locally things like grey hair and propensity to knit, then an ensemble of these neurons could function as a distributed representation of your grandmother. In this case, the representations are distributed with respect to people, and local with respect to attributes of people such as hair colour and hobbies. Of course, it is unlikely that individual neurons represent nameable attributes; we probably do not have conscious access to the basic elements of representation.

There is reason to believe that the brain uses distributed representation. Computationally, it is an efficient way to represent and retrieve information in a network of highly interconnected representational units like the brain. In addition to allowing a larger number of entities to be represented with a given number of units, distributed representation has two other major advantages over local representation: first, systems of distributed representations degrade "gracefully" when damaged. Instead of losing knowledge of entire entities when damaged, the system maintains knowledge of all entities albeit in degraded form, because no unit of representation is crucial to the representation of any entity. Second, systems of distributed representation tend automatically to generalise knowledge about one entity to other similar entities. This is because similar entities have attributes in common, and are therefore represented by activation of partly overlapping sets of units. Any learning that associates activation of those units with others representing other information will do so for any entity whose representation includes activation of those units (see Hinton, McClelland, & Rumelhart, 1986, for a full discussion of distributed representation). In addition to these a priori considerations favouring distributed representation, there is also empirical evidence from single unit recordings of distributed representation in monkeys' motor cortex (Georgopoulos, Schwartz, & Kettner, 1986), temporal cortex (Young & Yamane, 1992) and superior colliculus (Sparks, Lee, & Rohrer, 1990).

Finally, we must preface the presentation of our computational hypothesis with a brief description of pattern association and learning in distributed neural nets. As already noted, representations in such a system consist of a pattern of activation over a set of highly interconnected neuron-like units. The extent to which the activation of one unit causes an increase or decrease in the activation of a neighbouring unit depends on the "weight" of the connection between them; positive weights cause units to excite each other and negative weights cause units to inhibit each other. Upon representation of the input pattern to the input units, all of the units connected with those input units will begin to change their activation under the influence of two kinds of constraints: the activation value of the units to which they are connected, and the weights on the connections. These units might in turn connect to others, and influence their activation levels in the same way. In recurrent, or attractor, networks, such as the model to be presented here, the units downstream will also begin to influence the activation levels of the earlier units. Eventually, these shifting activation levels across the units of the network settle into a stable pattern of activation. That pattern is determined jointly by the input activation and the weights of the network.

Learning consists of adjusting the pattern of weights in the network so that the desired output pattern is obtained for each given input pattern. For the network to learn that a certain name representation goes with a certain visual stimulus representation, the weights are adjusted so that presentation of either the visual pattern in the visual units or the name pattern in the name units causes the corresponding other pattern to become activated.

We are now in a position to explain why category knowledge might be expected to be more robust to damage in a system of distributed representation. Consider a category such as "animal". Certain properties are shared by all or most animals, such as breathing, eating, moving, etc. Other properties are possessed by just one exemplar of the category, such as the elephant's trunk. Units that participate in the representation of the shared properties will be active for all members of the category, whereas units that participate in the representation of exemplar-unique properties will be active only for those exemplars. Every time the network learns about an animal, it learns about the exemplar-unique properties and the categorical properties. This means that, over the course of learning about a number of animals, each of the categorical properties will have been presented many more times than each of the exemplar properties. This greater amount of learning is the basis for the greater robustness of category knowledge.

We demonstrated the greater robustness of category knowledge in a distributed neural network using computer simulation. Specifically, we trained a network to produce "name" patterns when presented with "visual" patterns by way of an intermediate set of "semantic" patterns. The semantic patterns were designed so that a portion of the pattern represents category knowledge, and a portion of the pattern represents knowledge that is unique to a specific exemplar. It is important to note that the exemplar and category portions of the patterns did not map systematically onto particular units in the semantic layer. The units that represented category properties for one category represented exemplar properties for other categories. Therefore, there was no architectural or hardware distinction between category and exemplar knowledge in the model. We tested two predictions with the model: first, that damage to the semantic layer will cause more within-category errors than expected by chance, as found with AD patients. Second, that the semantic knowledge activated by presentation of pictures or names of exemplars will be more accurate at the category level than at the exemplar level.

THE MODEL

Figure 1 shows the architecture of the model, which was used in an earlier study of confrontation naming in AD (Tippett & Farah, 1994). As before, there are five layers of units. The 16 "visual units" subserve visual representations of objects. The 32 "semantic units" subserve representations of the semantic knowledge that can be activated either by "visual inputs", or by "name inputs". The 16 "name units" subserve the representation of names associated with objects. Of course, there is nothing intrinsically visual, semantic, or verbal about these pools of units, aside from the fact that their patterns of mutual connectivity conform to the general notion that semantic representations must be accessed in order to mediate between visual and name representations. In particular, we have not attempted to assign interpretations to the individual units as, for example, Hinton and Shallice (1991) did in their model of semantic and visual errors in deep dyslexic reading.

The network was trained to associate the patterns of activity between these three layers. The learning of these associations was assisted by the presence of the remaining two layers of "hidden units" (Rumelhart, Hinton, & Williams, 1986). These are located between the visual and semantic layers (the "visual hidden units") and the name and semantic layers (the "name hidden units"). All units within each layer are connected to each other, and all connections, both between and within layers, are bidirectional. In addition to weights between units, there were bias weights for each unit, which encode the relative likelihood of each unit's being activated over all trained patterns.

Twenty patterns consisting of patterns in the visual layer, semantic layer, and name layer were generated. As before, visual representations and names of objects are represented by randomly generated patterns of activity (−1s and +1s) over the 16 units in each pool, with the constraint that each pattern shared the same value on no more than 10 of the 16 units. The 20 semantic-layer patterns were constructed so that four categories were represented, each with five exemplars. Half of each semantic pattern, that is 16 of the 32 units of the semantic representation, represented the properties shared across exemplars within a category. This portion of the pattern was therefore identical across the

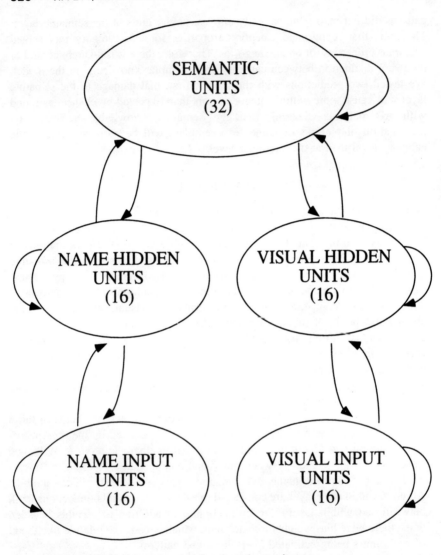

FIG. 1.   Functional architecture of model of confrontation naming.

five exemplars. The other 16 units represented the individual exemplar knowledge for each item and overlapped with other exemplars within the category by only 8 of the 16 units. An example is provided in Fig. 2, which shows the semantic patterns of the five members of Categories 1 and 2. The other categories were constructed in a similar manner except that they shared different sets of 16 units. Specifically, the category portion of the semantic patterns for Category 1 involved semantic units 1–16, Category 2 involved

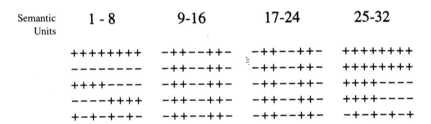

CATEGORY 1

Semantic Units	1 - 8	9-16	17-24	25-32
	+-+-+-+-	+-+-+-+-	++++++++	++++++++
	+-+-+-+-	+-+-+-+-	--------	++++++++
	+-+-+-+-	+-+-+-+-	++++----	++++----
	+-+-+-+-	+-+-+-+-	----++++	++++----
	+-+-+-+-	+-+-+-+-	+-+-+-+-	-+-+-+-+

CATEGORY 2

Semantic Units	1 - 8	9-16	17-24	25-32
	++++++++	-++--++-	-++--++-	++++++++
	--------	-++--++-	-++--++-	++++++++
	++++----	-++--++-	-++--++-	++++----
	----++++	-++--++-	-++--++-	++++----
	+-+-+-+-	-++--++-	-++--++-	-+-+-+-+

FIG. 2.   Semantic patterns of the five members of Category 1 and the five members of Category 2. Note that units 1–16 carry the category information for Category 1, and units 9–24 carry the category information for Category 2.

semantic units 9–24, Category 3 involved semantic units 17–32, and Category 4 involved semantic units 1–8 and 24–31. Thus, all units functioned equally often to represent category and exemplar knowledge. There is no division of labour, within the semantic layer, for category versus exemplar knowledge.

The same network parameters and learning algorithms were used in this study as in the previous model of confrontation naming in AD (Tippett & Farah, 1994). Thus units in this model can take on continuous activation values between −1 and +1. The weights on the connections between units can take on any real values. Activation levels are updated according to a nonlinear activation function (a hyperbolic tangent). The network was trained to correctly associate the patterns of activity between the three layers, such that when an input pattern was presented to one of the layers (e.g. the visual layer), it was able to produce the correct patterns of activity at the other two layers (the semantic layer and the name layer). During training as well as test, inputs were soft-clamped, that is their activation values were not fixed, but were the result of input activation along with activation from other units to which they were connected. Noise was injected into each layer to facilitate robustness of learning. To assess the generality of the results, multiple networks were trained with the same semantic patterns but different random starting weights. The learning procedure used during training was the Contrastive Hebbian Learning (CHL) algorithm (Movellan, 1990). Note that we are using CHL as a means of setting the weights in the network to enable it to perform naming; we are not concerned with the psychological reality of the training procedure as a model of learning.

SIMULATION 1

The goal of this simulation was to test the prediction that erroneous names will more frequently be from the same category than a different category as the correct name, after damage to distributed semantic representations in which there is not explicit architectural distinction between categorical and exemplar-unique knowledge.

Methods

Ten networks were trained to associate 20 patterns of activity on the visual, naming, and semantic layers. Each network was trained with semantic patterns described earlier, but the visual and naming patterns were different for each of the 10 networks.

Damage to semantic memory was simulated by removing randomly chosen subsets of the semantic units. Four levels of damage were used, to explore the effects of increasingly severe damage: two units, four units, six units and eight units, or 6.25%, 12.5%, 18.75%, and 25% of the semantic layer. At each of these levels of damage, each network was lesioned in 20 different ways, that is, with 20 different random patterns of semantic units eliminated. Although the neuropathological changes in AD are more complex than a simple loss of cells, we chose this means of lesioning the network because it was the simplest and most straightforward. Furthermore, Patterson, Seidenberg, and McClelland (1989) compared the effects on network performance of deleting units, deleting weights, and adding noise, and found them to be similar.

Confrontation naming was simulated by presenting just the visual pattern to the visual input layer, allowing the network to settle, then looking at the pattern of activation on the name units to see which of the 20 name patterns it matched most closely. In effect, this procedure simulated a 20-alternative forced-choice naming task. The degree of pattern match was simply the number of units whose values (+1 and –1) matched. Partial activations, such as –0.7, were converted to maximum activations, such as –1, for this computation. If the network made a naming error, we classified the erroneous name as coming from the same category or a different category.

Results and Discussion

Table 1 shows the average number of naming errors overall, the average number of within-category naming errors expected by chance alone, and the average number of within-category errors observed, at each level of damage to the semantic layer. Not surprisingly, as damage increases, errors also increase. The expected number of errors was calculated by multiplying the total number of errors by 4/19, because there are 19 possible erroneous names and four of these are within the same category as the correct name. At each level of damage, within-category errors exceed the expected number, $P < 0.001$ by binomal test. Of the 40 individual cases of the 10 networks at the four levels of damage, 24 showed more within-category errors than expected by chance at the $P = 0.05$ level.

SIMULATION 2

The results of the first simulation can be summarised thus: After damage, the system showed a stronger tendency to within-category errors than between-category errors, as do patients with AD, even though the damaged representations do not separately implement category and exemplar knowledge. However, the reason for these results is ambiguous. The hypothesis proposed earlier is that the preponderance of within-category errors results from the greater robustness of category-level knowledge to damage, because this knowledge is common to all members of the category and is therefore experienced or trained more often than exemplar-unique knowledge. It is also possible that the results of the previous simulation simply reflect the greater similarity among exemplars of a category than among exemplars of different categories. It is well known that similar patterns may be confused with one another after network damage (e.g. Hinton & Shallice, 1991; Plaut & Shallice, 1993). Similar semantic patterns will have a tendency to activate each other's name patterns because to the extent that they activate the same units in

TABLE 1
Simulation 1

Level of Damage to Semantic Layer (%)	Average Overall Errors	Expected Within-category Errors	Observed Within-category Errors	Significance Level (Binomial Test)
6.25	2.50	0.53	0.79	0.001
12.50	5.58	1.17	1.76	0.001
18.75	7.97	1.68	2.39	0.001
25.00	10.64	2.24	2.91	0.001

Average number of multiple choice naming errors out of 20, at four levels of damage, showing expected and observed within-category errors semantics, they also propagate activation along the same semantics–name connections. Can the errors made by our network be characterised simply as "semantic errors", that is, confusions between patterns that share similar semantic subpatterns, or do they also reflect the greater robustness of the categorical portion of the semantic subpattern?

In order to distinguish between these two possible mechanisms causing the error patterns in our simulation, we carried out a new simulation to assess the state of category and exemplar knowledge after semantic layer damage directly, that is, without using confusions among patterns as the measure of knowledge preservation. With the same patterns, networks, and lesionings as Simulation 1, we measured the error, or discrepancy between the correct pattern and obtained pattern, for the categorical and exemplar portions of the patterns after damage.

Methods

The same architecture, learning rule, and patterns used in the previous simulation were used again here. The random lesionings were also determined using the same seed for the random number generator, so that the same lesions were also used again.

Visual input patterns were also presented as before. After the network had settled, the activation values of the units in the semantic layer were rounded to +1 or −1, and the number of units that mismatched the correct semantic pattern (the Hamming distance) were counted for the category and exemplar portions separately.

Results and Discussion

Table 2 shows the average error in category and exemplar portions of the patterns in 10 different networks after 20 different random lesionings at each level of damage. There is a consistent tendency for the categorical information to be more robust to damage than the exemplar-unique information. Even

TABLE 2
Simulation 2

Level of Damage to Semantic Layer (%)	Category Unit Errors	Exemplar Unit Errors	Significance Level (Binomial Test)
6.25	0.20	0.29	0.001
12.50	0.48	0.59	0.001
18.75	0.80	0.88	0.001
25.00	1.04	1.12	0.001

Average number of erroneous unit activation values per pattern in category and exemplar portions of semantic patterns at four levels of damage though errors in category and exemplar units should be equally likely by chance, they are in fact less likely to occur in category units, $P < 0.001$ at each level of damage by binomial test. Of the 40 individual cases of the 10 networks at the four levels of damage, 20 showed greater preservation of categorical semantic information than expected by chance at the $P = 0.05$ level.

In this simulation we assessed the preservation of categorical and exemplar-unique semantic knowledge directly, without the confounding influence of the greater number of similar and hence confusable patterns within a category than between categories on our error measure. The results support the claim that categorical information is robust to damage because of the greater degree of experience or training enjoyed by categorical information.

GENERAL DISCUSSION

Neuropsychological dissociations often reflect the organisation of our cognitive systems fairly directly. For example, the dissociation between declarative and nondeclarative forms of memory appears to result from the existence of separate components of the functional architecture dedicated to these different forms of memory, and vulnerability of the declarative memory system to medial temporal and thalamic damage. However, dissociations do not invariably and transparently reflect the structure of the underlying cognitive architecture (Farah, 1994; Shallice, 1988), and this is particularly true for single dissociations, in which two abilities may rely on the same architectural component but one may be more resistant to damage than the other (Teuber, 1955).

In the case of the dissociation between category and exemplar knowledge observed in AD, we suggest that it is not necessary to hypothesise that semantic memory is compartmentalised into category-level knowledge and exemplar knowledge. In very general terms, our alternative explanation is an instance of the type of explanation noted by both Teuber (1955) and Shallice (1988), in which the relatively impaired ability is simply "easier" or more "robust" than the relatively spared ability. However, our more specific computational interpretation is by no means superfluous. "Easy" and "robust" are not mechanistic terms, and should therefore be regarded as placeholders, at best, in an incomplete explanation. The advantage of the model presented here is that it replaces these nonspecific concepts with an explicit, mechanistic account of the preservation of category-level knowledge when semantic memory is degraded.

Our mechanistic account of preserved category knowledge in AD draws on two features of neural network computation, namely distributed representation and graded learning. With distributed representations of knowledge, the category is implicitly represented by the attributes shared by all or most members of the category (see Fig. 2). The categorical portion of each exemplar's representation is therefore encountered more frequently, during learning, than the exemplar-unique portions. Because learning is not all-or-none in connectionist networks, but is a matter of degree that depends on, among other factors, frequency of training, category knowledge is more overlearned in a trained network than exemplar knowledge.

Further research is needed to determine whether this account is correct. Because the model is explicit, it can make specific predictions. One such prediction is that the preservation of categorical knowledge should be greater for larger and more frequent categories, and relatively homogeneous categories. In this connection, it is encouraging to note that Bayles, Tomoeda, and Trosset (1990) failed to find preservation of categorical knowledge when the categories in question were relatively heterogeneous, such as games and cooking utensils.

REFERENCES

Bayles, K.A., & Tomoeda, C.K. (1983). Confrontation naming impairment in dementia. *Brain and Language*, *19*, 98–114.

Bayles, K.A., Tomoeda, C.K., & Trosset, M.W. (1990). Naming and categorical knowledge in Alzheimer's disease: The process of semantic memory deterioration. *Brain and Language*, *39*, 498–510.

Butters, N., Granholm, E., Salmon, D.P., Grant, I., & Wolfe, J. (1987). Episodic and semantic memory: A comparison of amnesic and demented patients. *Journal of Clinical and Experimental Neuropsychology*, *9*, 479–497.

Chertkow, H., Bub, D., & Seidenberg, M. (1989). Priming and semantic memory loss in Alzheimer's disease. *Brain and Language*, *36*, 420–446.

Collins, A.M., & Quillian, M.R. (1969). Retrieval time from semantic memory. *Journal of Verbal Learning and Verbal Behavior*, *8*, 240–247.

Damasio, A.R. (1989). Time-locked multiregional retroactivation: A systems-level proposal for the neural substrates of recall and recognition. *Cognition*, *33*, 25–62.

Farah, M.J. (1994). Neuropsychological inference with an interactive brain. *Behavioral and Brain Sciences*, *17*, 43–104.

Georgopoulos, A.P., Schwartz, A.B., & Kettner, R.E. (1986). Neuronal population coding of movement direction. *Science*, *233*, 1416.

Hinton, G.E., McClelland, J.L., & Rumelhart, D.E. (1986). Distributed representations. In D. Rumelhart, J.L., McClelland, & the PDP research group (Eds.), *Parallel distributed processing: Explorations in the microstructure of cognition, Vol. 1* (pp.77–109). Cambridge, MA: MIT Press.

Hinton, G.E., & Shallice, T. (1991). Lesioning an attractor network: Investigations of acquired dyslexia. *Psychological Review*, *98*, 74–75.

Hodges, J.R., Salmon, D.P., & Butters, N. (1991). The nature of the naming deficit in Alzheimer's and Huntington's disease. *Brain*, *114*, 1547–1558.

Huff, J.F., Corkin, S., & Growdon, J.H. (1986). Semantic impairment and anomia in Alzheimer's disease. *Brain and Language*, *28*, 235–249.

Margolin, D.I. (1987). Lexical priming by pictures and words in aging, stroke and dementia (Doctoral dissertation, University of Oregon). *Dissertation Abstracts International*, *49*, 1416B.

Martin, A. (1987). Representation of semantic and spatial knowledge in Alzheimer's patients: Implications for models of preserved learning in amnesia. *Journal of Clinical and Experimental Neuropsychology*, *9*, 191–224.

Martin, A., & Fedio, P. (1983). Word production and comprehension in Alzheimer's Disease: The breakdown of semantic knowledge. *Brain and Language*, *19*, 124–141.

Movellan, J. (1990). Contrastive Hebbian learning in the continuous Hopfield model. In D.S. Touretzky, G.E. Hinton, & T.J. Sejnowski (Eds.), *Proceedings of the 1989 Connectionist Models Summer School* (pp.10–17). San Mateo, CA: Morgan Kaufman.

Nebes, R.D. (1989). Semantic memory in Alzheimer's disease. *Psychological Bulletin, 106*, 377–394.

Nebes, R.D. (1992). Cognitive dysfunction in Alzheimer's disease. In F.I.M. Craik & T.A. Salthouse (Eds.), *The handbook of aging and cognition* (pp.373–446). Hillsdale, NJ: Lawrence Erlbaum Associates Inc.

Ober, B.A., Dronkers, N.F., Koss, E., Delis, D.C. & Friedland, R.P. (1986). Retrieval from semantic memory in Alzheimer-type dementia. *Journal of Clinical and Experimental Neuropsychology, 8*, 75–92.

Ober, B.A., Koss, E., Friedland, R.P., & Delis, D.C. (1985). Processes of verbal memory failure in Alzheimer-type dementia. *Brain and Cognition, 4*, 90–103.

Ober, B.A., & Shenaut, G.K. (1988). Lexical decision and priming in Alzheimer's disease. *Neuropsychologia, 26*, 273–286.

Patterson, K.E., Seidenberg, M.S., & McClelland, J.L. (1989). Connections and disconnections: Acquired dyslexia in a computational model of reading processes. In R.G.M. Morris (Ed.), *Parallel distributed processing: Implications for psychology and neurobiology.* Oxford: Oxford University Press.

Plaut, D.C., & Shallice, T. (1993). Perseverative and semantic influences on visual object naming errors in optic aphasia: A connectionist account. *Journal of Cognitive Neuroscience, 5*, 89–117.

Rosch, E., Mervis, C.B., Gray, W.D., Johnson, D.M., & Boyes-Braem, P. (1976). Basic objects in natural categories. *Cognitive Psychology, 8*, 382–439.

Rumelhart, D.E., Hinton, G.E. & Williams, R.J. (1986). Learning internal representations by error propagation. In D. Rumelhart, J.L. McClelland, & the PDP research group (Eds.), *Parallel distributed processing: Explorations in the microstructure of cognition, Vol. 1* (pp. 318–362). Cambridge, MA: MIT Press.

Shallice, T. (1988). *From neuropsychology to mental structure.* Cambridge: Cambridge University Press.

Sparks, D.L., Lee, C., & Rohrer, W.H. (1990). Population coding of the direction, amplitude and velocity of saccadic eye movements by neurons in the superior colliculus. *Cold Spring Harbor Symposium on Quantitative Biology, LV*, 805–811.

Teuber, H.L. (1955). Physiological psychology. *Annual Review of Psychology, 6*, 267–296.

Tippett, L.J., & Farah, M.J. (1994). A computational model of naming in Alzheimer's disease: Unitary or multiple impairments? *Neuropsychology, 8*, 3–13.

Tröster, A.I., Salmon, D.P., McCullough, D., & Butters, N. (1989). A comparison of category fluency deficits associated with Alzheimer's and Huntington's disease. *Brain and Language, 37*, 500–513.

Warrington, E.K. (1975). The selective impairment of semantic memory. *Quarterly Journal of Experimental Psychology, 27*, 635–657.

Young, M.P., & Yamane, S. (1992). Sparse population coding of faces in the inferotemporal cortex. *Science, 256*, 1327–1331.

MEMORY, 1995, 3 (3/4), 535–586

An Interactive Activation Approach to Object Processing: Effects of Structural Similarity, Name Frequency, and Task in Normality and Pathology

Glyn W. Humphreys

University of Birmingham, UK

Christian Lamote

University of Leuven, Belgium

Toby J. Lloyd-Jones

University of Birmingham, UK

We present a computational model of the processes involved in retrieving stored semantic and name information from objects, using a simple interactive activation and competition architecture. We simulate evidence showing a cross-over in normal reaction times to make semantic classification and identification responses to objects from categories with either structurally similar or structurally dissimilar exemplars, and that identification times to objects from these two different classes correlate differentially with measures of the structural similarity of objects within the category and the frequency of the object's name. Structural similarity exerts a negative effect on object decision as well as naming, though this effect is larger on naming. Also, on naming, structural similarity interacts with the effects of name frequency, captured in the model by varying the weight on connections from semantic to name units; frequency effects are larger with structurally dissimilar items. In addition, (1) the range of potential errors for objects from these two classes, when responses are elicited before activation reached a stable state, differ—a wider range of errors occur to objects from categories with structurally similar exemplars; and (2) simulated lesions to different locations within the model produce selective impairments to identification but not to semantic classification responses to objects from categories with structurally similar exemplars. We discuss the results in relation to data on visual object processing in both normality and pathology.

Requests for reprints should be sent to Glyn W. Humphreys, Cognitive Science Research Centre, School of Psychology, University of Birmingham, Edgbaston, Birmingham B15 2TT, UK.

The work reported in the paper was supported by a grant from the Economic and Social Research Council of Great Britain, and from a European Union Erasmus studentship exchange.

INTRODUCTION

Historically, most attempts to provide theoretical treatments of visual object processing have focused on the nature of the visual information used to "index" stored visual knowledge about objects (e.g. Biederman, 1987; Marr, 1982; Marr & Nishihara, 1978; Ullman, 1989), and relatively little attention has been paid to the procedures mediating the retrieval of other forms of stored knowledge which are required for object recognition (as measured in semantic classification tasks) and identification (as measured in object-naming tasks). For example, while most theories of visual object naming assume that this requires access to stored visual or structural representations ("structural descriptions"; cf. Humphreys, Riddoch, & Quinlan, 1988; Seymour, 1979; Warren & Morton, 1982), stored semantic representations (specifying functional and associative knowledge about objects), and stored name representations (specifying the stored phonological description for the object's name; see Bruce & Humphreys, 1994, for a review), the consequences for object identification of having information mapped between these representations in different ways has not been extensively explored. Nevertheless, as we review here, there is clear evidence indicating that object identification and classification responses vary directly as a function of the nature of the stored knowledge that must be retrieved, and object identification and classification can be disrupted by lesions affecting either particular stored representations or processes mapping between the various stored representations. To provide a full understanding of object processing, we need to develop models in which the procedures involved in accessing different forms of stored knowledge are articulated fully. In the present article, we aim to take one stop towards this by presenting an explicit computational model of object classification and identification, using a simple interactive activation-competition architecture (cf. McClelland, 1981). The model is then applied to data on normal object processing, and to account for disorders of object identification associated with lesions either to different forms of stored knowledge or to the procedures involved in mapping between different knowledge representations.

To generate a framework for the model, we first outline the relevant literature on object processing in both normal and brain-injured subjects, before we go on to report the model.

Basic-level Classification

Rosch and her colleagues (e.g. Rosch et al., 1976) noted that, for normal subjects, reaction times (RTs) varied as a function of the nature of the classification decision made to objects; RTs were faster if "basic-level" classifications were performed than if sub-ordinate classifications were made. "Basic-level" classifications involve assigning objects to a class in which the stimuli have substantial perceptual overlap with other members of their category, have a common set of functional properties, can be given a common name, and involve a grouping together of objects without specific referents. Within a category such as "animal", basic-level representations correspond to different types of animal (e.g. dogs, cats). Sub-ordinate classifications involved assignments of objects to categories with specific referents, such as particular types of dog or cat. People classify a particular dog more quickly as a "basic-level" dog than as a "sub-ordinate level" alsation (for example). From this, Rosch argued that stored knowledge about objects was accessed first at a basic level, and that sub-ordinate information was contacted only after access was achieved to basic-level knowledge. The form that basic-level representations took, and how such stored representations related to the visual information used to index them, was not clearly specified.

Subsequent research however has shown that access to stored knowledge about objects is not determined by fixed procedures in which basic-level representations are always contacted before sub-ordinate representations. For example, Jolicoeur, Gluck, and Kosslyn (1984) noted that times to make basic-level and sub-ordinate classifications varied as a function of the typicality of the object. Basic-level classifications were made more quickly than sub-ordinate classifications for objects that were typical members of their category (e.g. for an alsation), but sub-ordinate classifications were made more quickly than basic-level classifications for atypical objects (e.g. a racing car is classified more quickly as a racing car than as a car). Typicality here may be multiply determined, involving (for instance) the visual similarity of the object to other members of the same category or the frequency with which an object is assigned to a particular category. Rather than suggesting a fixed order for accessing basic-level and sub-ordinate knowledge, such results indicate that decision times vary as a function of the relationships between a target object and other members of its category, and how these relationships map onto different decisions. For instance, high visual similarity between a target object and other members of its category (e.g. with typical category members) may be helpful for responses that can be based on information common to the category (e.g. a basic-level response) and it may be unhelpful for responses contingent on the differentiation of an individual exemplar from other category members (e.g. a sub-ordinate response). In contrast, low visual similarity between an object and other members of its category (e.g. with atypical category members) may impair responses contingent on information common to a category and facilitate those contingent on knowledge of the individual exemplar, so that sub-ordinate naming is faster than basic-level naming. Note that the variance in RTs for basic-level and sub-ordinate decisions may even be accounted for by a model in which there are no fixed representations for basic-level and sub-ordinate knowledge, but rather differential patterns of overlap in activation levels in representations of individual exemplars produced respectively by typical and atypical category members. We elaborate such a model in this article.

Structural Similarity, Identification, and Semantic Classification

The time taken by subjects to make super-ordinate classification responses to objects (e.g. animal) is typically shorter than the time taken to give such objects names corresponding even to their basic-level representations (e.g. cow; see Potter & Faulconer, 1975). This pattern of fast super-ordinate classification relative to slow naming is the opposite pattern to that found when words are presented rather than objects. The data with words can be accommodated by models of reading which hold that words can be named via either a non-lexical or a direct (non-semantic) lexical route, in addition to naming being mediated by access to super-ordinate, semantic knowledge (e.g. Patterson & Coltheart, 1987; Patterson & Morton, 1985; Seidenberg & McClelland, 1989). For words, naming will be faster than super-ordinate classification because either the non-lexical or the direct lexical route to phonology can be quicker than the route to phonology via the semantic system. For objects, however, the data demonstrate that access to super-ordinate semantic knowledge is faster than access to stored phonological representations (for naming). Indeed, access to the names of objects seems only to proceed via access to stored semantic information about the object's category and function. For example, unlike neuropsychological studies of reading (e.g. Schwarz, Marin, & Saffran, 1979), there is (at least to date) little good neuropsychological evidence of patients being able to name objects without being able to retrieve associated semantic information; rather patients typically show knowledge of super-ordinate category without being able to identify the object (e.g. Warrington, 1975; see Riddoch & Humphreys, 1987a, for a review). Also, when normal subjects are required to name objects to an RT deadline that is faster than their usual naming time, a preponderance of semantic errors is generated, consistent with the names being selected following the activation of semantic representations (e.g. Vitkovitch & Humphreys, 1991; Vitkovitch, Humphreys, & Lloyd-Jones, 1993). These results suggest a model of object naming in which semantic representations are contacted on route to access to name representations

Interestingly, when classification times with words and objects are compared, objects can be advantaged (Potter & Faulconer, 1975). This last finding suggests either that there is some form of privileged access to semantics from objects (Caramazza, Hillis, Rapp, & Romani, 1990), or that semantic classification for objects can benefit from the correlation between the physical form of the stimulus and its semantic category. Objects from the same semantic class tend also to have similar physical structures (e.g. see Carr, McCauley, Sperber, & Parmalee, 1982). Semantic classification times to objects can be advantaged if there is co-activation of the representations of objects with similar structures, leading to enhanced activation of representation across category members. As words have no necessary correlation between their physical structure and the category of object they represent, semantic classification for words cannot benefit from correlated effects of physical similarity between category members. Evidence that supports this last interpretation of the "object benefit" for semantic classification is that the magnitude of the benefit varies as a function of whether physical similarity between category exemplars correlates with the classification decision. With a super-ordinate classification task such as living *vs.* non-living, there is a substantial benefit for classifying objects relative to words (Potter & Faulconer, 1975); with a classification task requiring discrimination between objects that have similar perceptual structures across the to-be-discriminated categories (e.g. discriminating fruits from vegetables), the object benefit can be eliminated (Lloyd-Jones & Humphreys, submitted) or even reversed (Snodgrass & McCullough, 1986). In this case, visual similarity between object exemplars that have to be assigned to different categories can impair performance.

Additional evidence for physical similarity between object exemplars having either beneficial or detrimental effects on performance, depending on the task, comes from studies of processing differences between objects from different categories. Riddoch and Humphreys (1987a) and Humphreys et al. (1988) made a distinction between objects belonging to categories in which the exemplars have similar perceptual structures ("structurally similar" categories, such as animals, birds, insects, fruits, and vegetables) and those belonging to categories with perceptually more dissimilar exemplars (e.g. clothing, tools, furniture). Objects belonging to categories with structurally similar exemplars are assigned to their super-ordinate category faster than objects from categories with structurally dissimilar exemplars (Riddoch & Humphreys, 1987a). In contrast, in a task requiring differentiation between category members, object naming, responses are slower to structurally similar objects (Humphreys et al., 1988).

Fast semantic responses, when physical similarity correlates with the classification decision, can arise either if responses are based on the activation of pre-semantic physical representations (e.g. on the activation of "stored structural descriptions"; cf. Riddoch & Humphreys, 1987a; Seymour, 1979) or if activation is transmitted to the semantic system continuously (in cascade; cf. McClelland, 1979; Humphreys et al., 1988). In this last case, an object from a category where the exemplars share visual features will generate activation within the semantic representations of many category members; this is because, in addition to any general spread of activation within the semantic system (cf. Meyer & Schvaneveldt, 1971), the structural descriptions of perceptual "neighbours" will initially be activated by the target, with this activation being passed on to the semantic system before processing at the structural level is completed. Were evidence to be transmitted to the semantic system only following the completion of processing at the structural level, semantic activation should not vary according to the structural similarity within a category.

Evidence consistent with a cascade approach comes from various sources. For example, consider studies on object naming to deadline. In addition to there being a general increase in semantic errors under these conditions, subjects are also likely to make "perseverative" errors in which they misname target objects by giving the name of an earlier object (a prime) that had previously been named and that came from the same category as the target object. Thus having named the picture of a cup earlier, people are likely to produce the perseverative response "cup" when required to name the related item "jug" under deadline conditions. These prime-related, perseverative errors do not occur if the previous stimuli have been named words or if they have been objects categorised semantically (Vitkovitch & Humphreys, 1991). These last findings indicate that the perseverative errors reflect the operation of a particular processing stage, one that is required for naming objects but not for naming words or for classifying objects.

The task of naming words can tap access to stored phonological representations (in fact converging evidence for this was provided by Vitkovitch & Humphreys, 1991, in the form of faster naming responses for printed words than for nonwords: cf. McCann & Besner, 1987). Semantic classification requires access to semantic representations. In contrast to both of the latter tasks, only object naming requires that activation at the semantic level is mapped onto name representations. Prime-related, perseverative errors may arise because primes change the weights in the mappings from the semantic to the name level of representation. When targets are subsequently presented that are related to primes, then the representations of primes are re-activated (e.g. due to spreading semantic activation). Because weights on the connections mapping semantic to name representations have been changed to favour primes over any other stimuli, related primes become strong competitors for name selection with targets, generating perseverative errors to these stimuli. Vitkovitch et al. (1993) further showed that these prime-related perseverative errors were uniformly both visually and semantically related to targets. Given that these errors reflect a stage of processing mapping from semantic to name representations, it follows that this stage is influenced by joint visual and semantic relations between primes and targets. The activation of semantic information thus appears to be constrained by the visual characteristics of objects. This would happen if activation at a pre-semantic, structural level modulates that at a semantic level.

Vitkovitch et al. (1993) also found that, when naming to deadline was compared for objects from categories with structurally similar and dissimilar exemplars, a broader range of error responses occurred for structurally similar than for structurally dissimilar objects. To the extent that naming to deadline limits a relatively late stage in object identification (mapping from a semantic to a name representation), this result suggests that a broader range of semantic and name representations are activated by structurally similar relative to structurally dissimilar objects.

A second piece of evidence favouring a cascade approach was reported by Humphreys et al. (1988). In their examination of object naming, structurally similar and dissimilar exemplars could have names that occurred either relatively frequently or relatively infrequently in the language. Previous studies of object naming suggest that name frequency affects name retrieval processes (e.g. Oldfield 1966; Wingfield, 1968)[1]. Humphreys et al. found that the effects of name frequency, on name retrieval, varied according to the structural similarity of the objects: objects from categories with structurally similar exemplars showed weaker effects of name frequency than objects from categories with structurally dissimilar exemplars. Such modulation of a variable affecting a "late" stage of processing (name retrieval) by another variable affecting an "early" stage (the similarity between a target object and its perceptual neighbours) counters a discrete stage account, in which processing at one level (e.g. access to a stored structural description) is completed prior to processing at a subsequent stage (name retrieval) being set underway. If that were the case, then structural similarity and name frequency should have combined additively, as effects of structural similarity on accessing stored structural knowledge should have been completed before name retrieval was set underway. Instead of this, the data suggest that the effects of frequency on name retrieval are lessened when access to stored structural knowledge is delayed; for example, when access to structural knowledge is slow there may be sufficient time for a number of candidate names to be selected, reducing any benefits for high-frequency names which may be selected first.

These data from studies of object classification and naming in normal subjects suggest an account of object naming in which there is activation of stored structural, semantic, and name representations, with activation at each level influencing the degree (and spread) of activation at each subsequent level, consistent with activation being transmitted in cascade.

Neuropsychological Disorders of Object Processing

(i) Separating Structural, Semantic and Name Information.   Over the past 15 or so years, a number of case reports have been documented of patients with impaired object recognition and naming, with the impairments being shown to have arisen from lesions to discrete functional sites within the object processing

---

[1] Although whether these effects are due solely to the frequency of occurrence of an object's name, or to a correlated variable such as the familiarity of the name or the age at which the name was acquired, remains unclear (cf. Morrison, Ellis, & Quinlan, 1992). Whichever of these factors is critical is not relevant here; all that is important is that a variable can be identified that exerts an effect specifically on name retrieval rather than on object recognition. Consistent with this, neither name frequency nor age of acquisition effects are apparent when subjects make semantic classification responses to objects (Morrison et al., 1992).

system (e.g. see Farah, 1990; Humphreys & Riddoch, 1993, 1994; Warrington, 1982, for reviews). Such cases can throw light on the nature of the object processing system, by highlighting functionally isolatable components of the system. Of particular relevance here are cases where the problems seem to be "central" in origin, affecting either the representation of particular types of stored knowledge about objects or the retrieval of information after access to some forms of stored knowledge (e.g. to stored structural descriptions) have been achieved relatively successfully.

For example, at least three patients have been reported who have been able to discriminate between real objects and novel "non-objects" made by inter-changing the parts of real objects (i.e. in object decision tasks; Riddoch & Humphreys, 1987b; Sheridan & Humphreys, 1993; Stewart, Parkin, & Hunkin, 1992), but who were impaired at accessing knowledge about the functional characteristics of objects, or about inter-object associations, when the objects were visually presented. For example, JB (Riddoch & Humphreys, 1987b) was poor at judging which two of three real objects would be used together (e.g. a cup, a saucer, and a knife) when shown them visually, although he was able to perform the same task at normal levels when given the names of the objects. This last result indicates that JB understood the task and had the appropriate semantic knowledge to match the objects (when accessed verbally); however he was impaired at accessing this knowledge from vision. Nevertheless, JB was able to discriminate between real objects and non-objects that did not differ in terms of perceptual properties such as closure or goodness of shape (note that differences in such properties could have supported discrimination without access to stored knowledge). This dissociation, between good performance in difficult object decision tasks, and poor performance in associative matching tasks, is consistent with a functional lesion that separates stored structural descriptions from semantic knowledge. A patient may perform object decisions well due to the activation of structural knowledge, but be impaired at associative matching because a lesion disrupts the mapping of structural knowledge onto semantic knowledge.

In JB's case, it can be argued that the lesion did not affect semantic knowledge, because he remained able to perform associative match tests when the information was accessed from other modalities. For other patients, however, the deficit seems to affect semantic knowledge itself. For example, the patient reported by Sheridan and Humphreys (1993), SB, was impaired at retrieving functional and associative knowledge about objects. For example, she was poor at judging which food might be eaten with which meals or which objects might be used for particular tasks. In her case, the deficit seemed to reside within the semantic system. Such a semantic deficit also seems separable from deficits affecting either the retrieval of structural knowledge or name information appropriate to objects. Sartori and Job (1988; see also Sartori, Job, & Coltheart, 1993; Sartori, Miozzo, & Job, 1993) reported a patient with selectively impaired object decision performance but whose ability to retrieve verbal knowledge about objects was good. Basso, Capitani, and Laiacona (1988), and Silveri and Gainotti (1988), have presented similar cases, where the problem lies in the activation of appropriate visual-perceptual knowledge about objects. Silveri and Gainotti's patient, for instance, was able to provide the names to definitions that stressed verbal knowledge about objects (e.g. "the king of the jungle", for lion) but not to definitions that stressed visual-perceptual knowledge (e.g. "a white and black striped wild horse", for zebra). Contrasting with this are anomic patients who seem to have intact access to both structural and semantic knowledge, and whose difficulties seem confined to the retrieval of object names (e.g. Kay & Ellis, 1987). Such cases demonstrate the dissociation of structural and semantic knowledge from the process of name retrieval.

(ii) Category-specific Deficits in Object Processing. Orthogonal to the issue of whether neuropsychological deficits can be isolated at different functional stages within the object processing system, is the issue of category-specific deficits in object processing. Perhaps most commonly, patients have been documented with deficits in recognising animate objects along with relatively good recognition of inanimate objects (e.g. Basso et al., 1988; Farah, McMullen, & Meyer, 1991; Riddoch & Humphreys, 1987b; Sartori & Job, 1988; Sheridan & Humphreys, 1993; Silveri & Gainotti, 1988; Warrington & Shallice, 1984), although patients with the opposite pattern of impairment have also been documented (e.g. Hillis & Caramazza, 1990; Sacchett & Humphreys, 1992; Warrington & McCarthy, 1983, 1987). Category-specific deficits in object recognition have been attributed to several causes. For example, it has been argued that problems isolated to animate objects are due to: animate objects being less familiar or more complex than inanimate objects (Funnell & Sheridan, 1992; Stewart et al., 1992); impaired visual processing, leading to confusion between visually similar objects (e.g. Riddoch & Humphreys, 1987c); impaired stored visual perceptual knowledge, again leading to confusion between stimuli with similar perceptual structures (e.g. Riddoch & Humphreys, 1987a; Silveri & Gainotti, 1988); impaired semantic knowledge concerning the specific object categories over and above effects due to visual-perceptual similarity (Farah et al., 1991); impaired semantic knowledge that is sub-divided according to both the category of object and the nature of the information being represented (i.e. perceptual *vs.* functional; Warrington & McCarthy, 1987; Warrington & Shallice, 1984). As the opposite pattern of dissociation has also been reported (Hillis & Caramazza, 1990; Sacchett & Humphreys, 1992; Warrington & McCarthy, 1983, 1987), it is unlikely that some of the arguments can account for the complete pattern of category-specific disturbances (e.g. if animate objects are less familiar or more complex than inanimate objects, a deficit with inanimate objects is unlikely to be due to the same cause), although

such arguments may still account for the impairments with some kinds of objects in some patients (e.g. Riddoch & Humphreys, 1987c).

It is possible to link some of these category-specific deficits to particular loci within the object processing system. Effects linked to impaired stored visual/ perceptual knowledge have been isolated by showing that patients are selectively poor at object decisions to objects within the affected categories (e.g. Sartori & Job, 1988). In addition, in some patients the category-specific impairments seem to be isolated to stages in object identification occurring after access to stored visual knowledge has been achieved. As noted earlier, the patients described by Stewart et al. (1992) and Sheridan and Humphreys (1993) were able to carry out difficult object decision tasks at a normal level, but both patients had a selective problem in identifying animate objects. Sheridan and Humphreys' patient SB, for example, was particularly impaired at naming fruits and vegetables, but was able to distinguish pictures and real fruits and vegetables from those of "conglomerate" fruit/vegetables formed by interchanging the features of similar objects. As SB was impaired at retrieving functional knowledge about objects (see earlier), the data indicate that functional/semantic knowledge can be differentially impaired for different categories of object. Effects have also been isolated on procedures subsequent to access to semantic knowledge. Hart, Berndt, and Caramazza (1985) first documented a patient, MD, whose problem was confined to identifying fruits and vegetables. However, when given the names of the objects he performed well at judgements concerning the objects' category, size, colour, and texture. These last results suggest that MD had intact semantic knowledge about the stimuli. However, it should be noted that MD did not perform perfectly when asked to sort visually presented fruits and vegetables into their categories, suggesting perhaps some residual impairment in gaining visual access to semantic knowledge. More recently, Farah and Wallace (1992) have reported a similar case. Their patient was impaired at giving the name to verbal definitions of fruits and vegetables, in addition to showing poor naming to visual instances, but he was able to give adequate definitions of fruits and vegetables when given their names (e.g. "it's juicy, starts out green, then turns red, used for foods like spaghetti sauce", for tomato) and his naming was improved if he was given a phonemic cue. Sartori et al. (1993) also reported one patient with a selective problem in identifying animate objects whose naming was helped by the examiner providing phonemic cues to the object's name. This patient was also good at object decision tasks for stimuli within his impaired categories. In contrast, Sartori et al. found that a patient with a similar category-specific deficit but with selectively impaired object decision was not helped in naming by phonemic cues. The beneficial effects of phonemic cues found by Farah and Wallace and by Sartori et al. might be expected if the problem was primarily one of retrieval of the phonemic form of the word.

These results suggest that category-specific impairments in object identification can arise from lesions affecting a number of apparently separate loci within the object processing system, including lesions producing impairments in (1) visual perceptual processing (Riddoch & Humphreys, 1987c), (2) stored visual perceptual knowledge (Sartori & Job, 1988), (3) stored semantic/functional knowledge (Sheridan & Humphreys, 1993), and (4) name retrieval (Farah & Wallace, 1992).

How might these category-specific deficits, at different apparent levels in the object processing system, be accounted for? Several proposals have been made. One suggestion is that the representations at each level in the object processing system are categorically organised; for example, representations of animate and inanimate objects are coded independently at the structural, semantic, and name representations (e.g. Sartori & Job, 1988). For such an account to provide something more than a re-description of the data, however, there needs to be a satisfactory explanation of how representations putatively representing solely visual/structural or phonological (name) features take on a categorical structure; for instance, how do the phonological representations of "cap" and "cat" come to be represented independently of each other but (respectively) represented conjointly with the phonological representations of "glove" and "dog"? One account of how such categorical organisation might come about was posited by Farah and Wallace (1992). In line with recent accounts of learning in connectionist models (e.g. Hinton, McClelland, & Rumelhart, 1986), they suggested that the formation of arbitrary associations between semantic and phonological (name) representations may depend on the existence of "hidden units" which themselves are "semantically bound". A lesion to these hidden units could produce a deficit isolated to naming but which remains categorical in nature. Presumably the same argument could be extended to the associations formed between structural and semantic representations, although this would have difficulty explaining why patients may have selective difficulty in performing object decisions on stimuli from the affected categories (Sartori & Job, 1988; Sartori et al., 1993). Note that patients may perform object decisions well without being able to retrieve functional and associative (semantic) knowledge (Riddoch & Humphreys, 1987a; Sheridan & Humphreys, 1993; Stewart et al., 1992; see earlier text); if structural knowledge were intact (and only the hidden units used in mapping associations between structural and semantic representations affected) patients might be expected to succeed at object decisions even with stimuli from the affected categories (see Sheridan & Humphreys, 1993, for evidence on this).

A rather different approach, illustrated in the model presented here, is to suggest that category-specific deficits can be found at different levels within the object processing system because of how processing operates rather than because of the way in which representations at each level are organised. As we have already stated, if processing operates in cascade, then activation at one processing level will constrain the magnitude and spread of activation at other levels in the system. For normal subjects, objects from some categories are more difficult to identify than objects from others; for example, identification is relatively slow for objects from categories with many structurally similar exemplars, presumably because perceptual similarity between category members leads to the activation of a broad range of neighbours when stored structural knowledge is contacted (Humphreys et al., 1988; Price & Humphreys, 1989). This in turn may lead to the activation of more semantic neighbours (as evidenced by the relatively fast semantic classification responses for these stimuli; Riddoch & Humphreys, 1987b) and more competitors for name selection (as evidenced by the greater spread of errors under conditions of naming to deadline; Vitkovitch et al., 1993). Neuropsychological patients may have lesions affecting object processing at different levels of representation. Also, representations at these different levels might have contrasting forms of internal organisation. In a disturbed system, similar structural representations will be those sharing common structural features, similar semantic representations will be those sharing functional features and similar phonological representations will be those sharing phonological features; representations at a structural or at a name level need not be semantically "bound" (cf. Farah & Wallace, 1992). Nevertheless, despite the functional independence of the lesion sites, and the different forms of representation at each level, similar category-specific deficits might emerge after lesions at each level; in particular, identification may prove more difficult for objects from categories with structurally similar exemplars than for objects from categories with structurally dissimilar exemplars. For example, even if a lesion only affects the mapping of semantic information onto name representations, structurally similar objects might suffer most because these items are subject to more competition for name selection. Similarly if a lesion affects only the structural description system, the processing of structurally similar items might again be expected to be affected most severely because these items require more perceptual differentiation for the identification of individual exemplars. In essence, at least some forms of category-specific impairment may be manifest following lesions at different loci in the object processing system because there are knock-on consequences of processing efficiency at one level to other levels in the system.

Of course, such an argument will not provide a complete account of all forms of category-specific impairment. For instance, deficits are predicted for objects that are difficult to identify for normal subjects, but not for objects that are normally identified relatively efficiently (e.g. objects belonging to categories with structurally dissimilar exemplars). As we have already noted, patients have been reported with problems confined to such objects (e.g. Hillis & Caramazza, 1990; Sacchett & Humphreys, 1992; Warrington & McCarthy, 1983, 1987). Such findings suggest that it is false to assume that all forms of category-specific impairment arise in the same way. For example, we believe that some forms of category-specific deficit could arise if lesions affect representations important to the identification of particular types of stimulus (e.g. if representations for certain functional features were damaged within the semantic system; see Warrington & McCarthy, 1987). In this case, patients may find it difficult to identify affected objects, even if such objects are normally identified efficiently. We return to this point following our simulations of category-specific deficits for objects from structurally similar categories. Category-specific deficits due to processing differences between stimuli, and category-specific deficits due to selective impairment of particular representations, are not mutually exclusive. Here we examine how category-specific deficits due to processing differences between stimuli might arise.

Prior Simulations

As we have already noted, there have been relatively few attempts to model high-level processes in object recognition and identification, concerned with the retrieval of stored structural, semantic, and name representations[2]. Within the closely related field of face recognition and identification, some attempts have been made. In particular, Burton, Bruce, and Johnston (1990; Burton, 1990; Burton, 1994; Burton & Bruce, 1992, 1993) developed a connectionist model of face processing using a simple interactive activation and competition (IAC) architecture that incorporates the main information processing assumptions made by the earlier "box and arrow" model of Bruce and Young (1986). For example, in early versions of this IAC model, face recognition units, person identification nodes, and semantic information units were represented locally within a pool of units at each processing level, with there being inhibitory connections between the units within a level and excitatory ones between compatible representations at different levels. Different decisions were assumed to require access to different levels of representation; for example, familiarity decisions were assumed to be taken at the level of person identity units whereas other decisions such as naming required access to further representations (e.g. those for face names). This simple architecture was shown capable of simulating several effects influencing normal face processing, such as priming from one related face onto another and the faster recognition of known distinctive faces than known faces with a "typical" set of facial features (we discuss this last result in more detail later, when we introduce our IAC model of object naming). Also, by assuming that brain lesions could affect different loci within the model, Burton et al. (1991) were able to simulate some of the evidence from studies of neurological impairments of face processing. For example, when weights on the connections from the face recognition units to the person identity nodes were lowered, the model was impaired at making familiarity decisions, nevertheless

---

[2] For example, the connectionist model of Hummel and Biederman (1992) dealt with the processes leading to the activation of stored structural representations for objects, but not with how activation at the structural level constrains the retrieval of semantic and name information.

"covert" recognition was shown in face–word interference tasks because the face recognition units were intact. This mirrors the performance of at least some patients with face processing deficits (e.g. de Haan, Young, & Newcombe, 1987). More recently, Burton (1994) has demonstrated how the model can be extended to use distributed representations of faces and to incorporate learning procedures. The present model is closely related to this IAC model of face processing and uses a similar architecture. One difference between the models is that although the present model uses a localist scheme, the input given to the model creates distributed patterns of activation which vary across object classes. It is this distributed pattern of activation that leads to differences in identification and categorisation efficiency for structurally similar and dissimilar objects.

One prior attempt to simulate one of the effects on object processing that we are interested in, namely the emergence of category-specific deficits after brain damage, was reported by Farah and McClelland (1991). They used a distributed associative memory system (after McClelland & Rumelhart, 1985) in which a single pool of inter-linked "semantic" units was trained to become associated with vectors corresponding to "visual" and to "verbal" inputs. The semantic units were themselves arbitrarily divided into units representing "functional" properties and those representing "perceptual" properties of objects. Definitions of "living things" contain more perceptual descriptors than do definitions of non-living artefacts, whereas definitions of the latter contain more functional descriptors than do definitions of living things. Category-specific deficits affecting living things may arise because of damage to units representing perceptual properties, and category-specific deficits affecting artefacts may arise because of damage to units representing functional properties of objects (see Warrington & Shallice, 1984; see also our earlier remark about category-specific deficits due to damage to certain semantic features). In their simulation, Farah and McClelland differentially activated different numbers of functional and perceptual units to represent living things and artefacts. They found that, after damage to the perceptual units, the model was less able to recall the names of living things than it was those of artefacts, when given "visual" input (the visual input vector used to represent a given object during training); in contrast, damaging the functional units produced the opposite effects, with performance being worse on artefacts than on living things. This model, then, was able to capture the double dissociation between the recognition of living things and artefacts in different patients, even though a single memory system was used to represent both classes of objects. In addition, the effects of lesions to different processing levels in the model may be captured in terms of lesioning "input and output" connections between the visual and verbal units, on the one hand, and the semantic units, on the other.

However, one caveat is that, due to the use of a distributed associative memory to represent both artefacts and living things, category-specific deficits are partial rather than absolute. Even though living things tend to be most strongly represented by patterns of activation across the perceptual units, they have some representation across the functional units, and damage to the perceptual units will produce some noise in the retrieval of the full representation of living things across the functional as well as the perceptual units (albeit less severe). Farah and McClelland suggested that this was a strength of the model, as many patients with deficits in (e.g.) the visual recognition of living things are also poor at retrieving functional knowledge about the stimuli from their names, consistent with there being knock-on deficits in the retrieval of functional as well as perceptual semantic knowledge (e.g. Farah et al., 1991). Against this, Riddoch and Humphreys (1993) presented a brief report on a patient with very good functional knowledge about living things (when accessed verbally) despite being markedly poor at visual identification of the same stimuli (and rather better at identifying artefacts). Thus this patient performed at control levels when required to produce names to definitions stressing the functional attributes of living things, but he was impaired at object decision, retrieving item-specific semantic information, and naming the same objects presented visually. Retrieval of relevant functional knowledge should have been affected by a lesion of perceptual knowledge sufficient to produce a severe category-specific recognition deficit for living things. A second caveat concerns the emergence of category-specific deficits following lesions to different levels of the object processing system (see earlier a review of the evidence). Farah and McClelland used bidirectional connections between units in the semantic system and the visual and the verbal units. Lesioning the connections between the semantic system and either the visual or the verbal units enables some of the effects apparent at different processing levels to be captured, but it is limited if the same connections are used for inputs as well as outputs. For example, by lesioning connections between the verbal units and the perceptual-semantic units, Farah and McClelland were able to simulate data from a patient reported by McCarthy and Warrington (1988), who showed a problem retrieving semantic information about living things, but only when given a name verbally. If the same connections are used to map semantic activation onto verbal units for an output task (e.g. for naming), then the same lesion would also produce a selective problem in naming living things presented visually. On the other hand, patients with putative category-specific deficits confined to naming can perform well when given the names of the objects (e.g. Farah & Wallace, 1992; Hart et al., 1985). That is, category-specific deficits for verbal output responses do not necessarily co-occur with category-specific deficits for verbal inputs. It is not clear that the distributed memory approach can capture deficits at an apparent output locus as well as deficits within the semantic system. A third caveat is that the model was not designed to simulate the time course of normal object naming, and so could not be applied to category differences in object processing in normal subjects. The present simulation, in contrast, attempts to capture both normal and pathological object processing. As far as normal object naming is concerned, we provide the first formal simulation that, within a model operating in cascade, a variable affecting access to an early level of processing (the structural similarity of the object) can interact with a variable affecting a late processing stage (the frequency of the object's name).

THE IAC MODEL OF OBJECT PROCESSING

Basic Architecture

The model aimed to capture data on object classification and naming in normal subjects, and on object processing impairments in patients with neurological damage, using a simple architecture. Following accounts of object processing such as those proposed by Humphreys et al. (1988), Riddoch and Humphreys (1987a) and Seymour (1979), we used three central pools of units, corresponding to different forms of stored knowledge within the object processing system: one pool for structural units (corresponding to the structural description system)[3], one for semantic units (corresponding to the semantic system), and one for name units (corresponding to the phonological output lexicon). These units were sequentially arranged, with activation at the structural level propagated through to semantic units, and activation at the semantic level propagated through to name units. In order to keep the modelling as simple as possible, and in order to avoid making assumptions about the nature of the representations at each level in the model, representations at each level were local: one unit stood for either the structural, semantic, or name description of an object. After presenting the model we discuss how it could be extended to incorporate distributed representations. Within each pool, the units were inhibitory, and between pools there were bi-directional excitatory connections between units corresponding to the same objects (see Burton et al., 1990; McClelland & Rumelhart, 1981, 1988). The model aimed to assess a range of tasks including: object naming, object decision, and semantic classification. One problem in comparing the relative speed of such responses within a continuous processing model is that activation values take longer to accumulate within "output" units the more processing levels intervene between the input and the output. For this reason, comparisons of the time course of activation at the semantic and name units would differ simply because more processing levels intervene between input and output for name responses than for responses based on activation at the semantic level. To make a more valid comparison, that is not confounded with the number

---

[3] Although we will term these units structural units, and we term the system they are represented in, the structural description system, this is simply to have the least level of commitment towards the nature of the stored representations at this level in the object processing system. For example, such units may represent more than structural knowledge about objects, including (e.g.) other forms of visual knowledge (object colour, size, texture).

of intervening processing levels, a further set of units were added to the model, corresponding to the super-ordinate category names for objects, and these served as the "output" units to signal which semantic classification responses should be made. The super-ordinate units were placed at the same level within the model as the name units (for both sets of units, activation was propagated to them after the activation of semantic units, passing through a single set of weights), facilitating direct comparisons between semantic classification and naming responses. The full architecture of the model is shown in Fig. 1.

Input to the model is at the level of structural descriptions, and activation then propagates from there through to the semantic units, and from there to the name and super-ordinate response units. From the structural description to the semantic system, and from the semantic system to the name system, units corresponding to single objects are directly and individually connected. In contrast, many units in the semantic system are connected to the same super-ordinate classification units, so that super-ordinate knowledge is based on pooled activation across a category. As with other IAC models of information processing (e.g. Burton et al., 1990; Grossberg, 1978; McClelland & Rumelhart, 1981), activation values at each level are updated after each cycle of activation values through the model, and after many cycles activation values of units tend to stabilise.

Activation values within such networks can be calculated in several ways, and different formulations have been presented by Grossberg (1978) and by McClelland and Rumelhart (1981, 1988). For comparability to other similar simulations (e.g. the IAC model of face processing), we used the activation functions given by McClelland and Rumelhart (1981, 1988; see Appendix 1 for details). Units receive inputs from two sources: external input from the experimenter (in this case, simulating the presentation of an object to the model) and internal input from other units connecting to them. The value propagated from one unit to another is proportional to the product of activation of the "input" unit and the weight on the connection between the two units. Activation values in each unit are changed on every cycle of the model, as units are driven to take on maximum or minimum values, depending on whether the net input to a unit is positive or negative. The changes in activation values are modulated by a further decay component, which tends to force activation values back down to a resting point.

Responses can be measured in various ways. One procedure is to measure the probability that a given response is made. We calculated response probabilities in two ways, using formulations of Luce's (1959) choice theorem. In one case, the activation of a target unit was compared with the activation values in all possible output units; in the other, output units with a negative activation value were assigned a zero response strength, the rationale being that negatively activated units may be considered to be inhibited preventing any type of response (see Appendix 1 for details). For direct comparisons of response

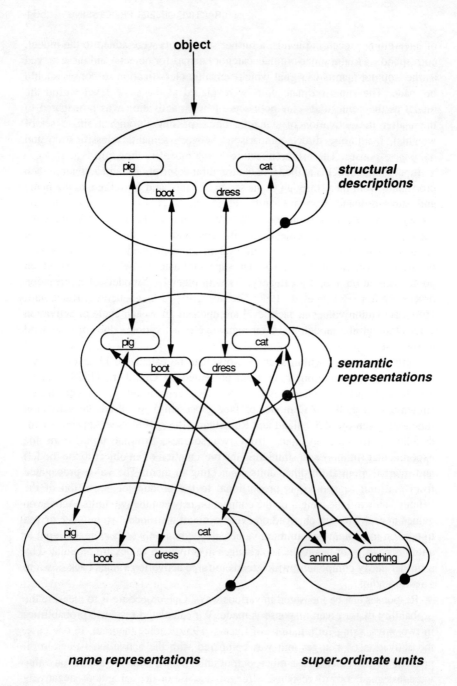

FIG. 1. Framework illustrating the IAC model of object processing. → for excitatory connections; —● for inhibitory connections.

552

probabilities we mainly used the uncorrected response measure (using negatively activated units), as this provided a reasonable spread of performance across all the tasks examined (e.g. semantic classification and naming) as a function of the number of cycles of the model. The accuracy trends using the two response probability measures were in all cases very similar, however. For RT measures we assessed the number of cycles taken to reach an arbitrary threshold level of activation (a value of 0.2 was taken; see Burton et al., 1990, for a precedent). Using the corrected response probability measure (eliminating negatively activated units), response probabilities had typically reached their maximum level of 1.0 when this level of activation occurred, ensuring that RT measures were based on correct responses. However, to ensure that non-cross over interactions (in Simulations 2 and 3) were not due to the specific threshold chosen, we replicated the findings using a threshold of 0.35 (see later further discussion).

There were 20 units within each of the structural, semantic, and name pools, and 2 units within the super-ordinate classification response pool (for animals and clothing). Stimuli were drawn from the categories animals and clothing in order to simulate data on processing differences between objects drawn from categories with structurally similar exemplars (animals) and those from categories with structurally dissimilar exemplars (clothing). As already noted, we did not wish to pre-judge the nature of the internal representations at each level of the model (and hence used local representations). However, in order to capture the effects of structural similarity, we used as input to the structural units vectors that reflected the visual similarity between a given stimulus and other stimuli from the chosen categories, with visual similarity values based on ratings given by a set of 10 independent judges (half male, half female). There were 10 animals and 10 items of clothing used, to represent structurally similar and structurally dissimilar categories respectively (camel, cat, cow, deer, donkey, fox, horse, pig, squirrel, tiger; belt, blouse, boot, coat, dress, pants, ring, sweater, tie, watch). For these judgements, the subjects were given pairs of object names in random order (190 pairs in total, for all combinations of 10 animals and 10 items of clothing), and asked to rate the visual similarity between imagined typical exemplars corresponding to the object name using a seven point scale (1 = not similar, 7 = very similar). Ratings were elicited from object names rather than from pictures of the objects because we wanted subjects to provide a measure of similarity generalised across individual examplars; with pictures it is possible that subjects simply rate the particular depictions. Subjects were told that their judgements should be independent of differences in size, colour, texture, and touch between the objects. The mean judged similarity between each pair of objects was used as part of the input vector for each object, with the means (from 1 to 7) scaled down to a −1 to +1 interval. Input vectors for each stimulus are given in Appendix 2. Essentially, animals were judged to have higher levels of within-category visual similarity than items of clothing, and levels of between-category visual similarity were judged to be relatively low. This meant that input vectors for animals led to the activation of a number of structural units in addition to the activation of the structural unit corresponding to the input stimulus; this was less the case with items of clothing. Analyses of the simulations were based on the performance of the model across the items within a category, rather than on specific example stimuli, as we wished to ensure that any differences between categories were not specific to a few items that (for example) had particularly high similarity values (and therefore very similar input vectors) (cf. Burton et al., 1990).

Parameters in the model were set in order to provide stable naming performance when the model was unlesioned, with correct responses being given to each item after a maximum of 50 cycles using the corrected response probability measure (see earlier; see also Appendix 1 for a full list of parameter values). Connections from the semantic to the name units were set differentially in order to reflect the frequency of occurrence of the object's name. Connections were set at this level so that it was the frequency of the object's name, rather than its visual frequency, that was captured in the model. Note the psychological evidence indicates that the name frequency/familiarity variable affects name retrieval rather than object recognition (Wingfield, 1968). Semantic-name weights were based on the rated familiarity of each item as given in the Snodgrass and Vanderwart (1980) norms. Although familiarity does not correspond exactly with name frequency, the two measures correlate and, for the present stimuli, familiarity gives a measure of occurrence that is better matched across the structurally similar and dissimilar object sets than is raw name frequency. Nevertheless, in subsequent tests of the model we have found qualitatively similar results (and in particular the interaction between structural similarity of object and name frequency) when weights are set to a raw frequency count, and here we show that the same patterns of data occur even when just two frequency values are used (high and low) and frequencies are identical for structurally similar and dissimilar objects. Throughout the rest of the paper we refer to variations in the weights between the semantic and name systems as reflecting name frequency. Frequency and within-category similarity values for the stimuli used in the simulations are given in Table 1.

Aims of the Simulations

The simulations aimed to capture four main results from the literature on object naming in both normality and pathology:

1. The dissociation between semantic classification and naming for objects from categories with structurally similar and structurally dissimilar exemplars, found in normal subjects; semantic classification is faster for structurally similar

TABLE 1
Name Frequency and Visual Similarity Values for the Stimuli Used in the Simulations

Structurally similar items			Structurally dissimilar items		
Item	Frequency	Similarity	Item	Frequency	Similarity
cat	4.22	4.60	belt	4.12	2.92
tiger	2.10	4.76	blouse	4.18	3.17
cow	2.42	4.83	boot	3.38	2.16
fox	1.95	4.75	coat	3.88	3.22
horse	3.55	4.99	dress	3.62	3.17
squirrel	3.82	3.53	pants	4.55	2.57
donkey	1.88	4.79	ring	3.48	2.46
camel	2.08	4.35	tie	3.80	2.68
deer	2.22	4.68	watch	4.58	2.47
pig	2.18	4.34	sweater	4.48	2.96
Mean:	2.64	4.56	Mean:	4.01	2.78

The frequency values ranged from 1–5, with 5 being high. The similarity values ranged from 1–7, with 7 being high.

Name frequency values were based on the familiarity ratings for these objects given in Snodgrass and Vanderwart (1980)

objects, whereas naming is faster for structurally dissimilar objects (Riddoch & Humphreys, 1987a) (Simulation 1).

2. The interaction between structural similarity and name frequency in object naming, with the effects of name frequency being larger on structurally dissimilar objects (Humphreys et al., 1988) (Simulation 3).

3. The greater spread in naming errors across category members when normal subjects name structurally similar objects to a deadline faster than their normal naming responses (Vitkovitch et al., 1993) (Simulation 4).

4. The emergence of category-specific deficits for structurally similar objects when the model is "lesioned", with such effects being apparent when the model is lesioned at a number of different levels (cf. Farah & Wallace, 1992; Sartori et al., 1993) (Simulation 5).

In addition, we sought to simulate an effect reported by Lloyd-Jones and Humphreys (submitted). They assessed latency differences for normal subjects between objects from categories with structurally similar and dissimilar members in naming and object decision tasks (the stimuli belonged to the categories fruits, vegetables, clothing, and furniture). In the object decision tasks, non-objects were created by interchanging the parts of real objects, with all substitutions being within-class (see Fig. 2 for examples of non-objects). They found that category differences in object decision were massively reduced relative to those found in naming, even though it might be thought that both

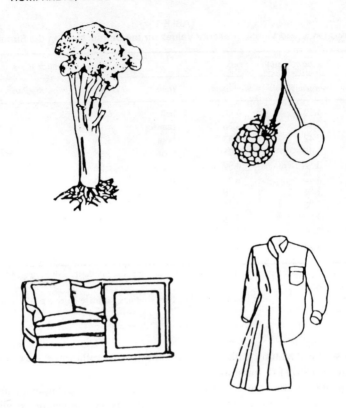

FIG. 2.   Example non-objects used by Lloyd-Jones and Humphreys (1994).

tasks require access to specific knowledge about the individual target objects. For example, to distinguish a leek from a leek/broccoli (non-object) in an object decision task, information specific to the target object has to be accessed; information concerning the general category of the stimulus [vegetable] is not sufficient; the same holds true for object naming. Nevertheless, in two experiments, differences in naming between structurally similar objects (fruits and vegetables) and structurally dissimilar objects (clothing and furniture) were 301 and 418msec respectively, whereas differences in object decision were 44 and 34msec. The effects of structural similarity on naming were very large in this study because fruits and vegetables were used, which have high levels of perceptual overlap. Even so, the same items were employed in object decision and yet clear differences emerged between the effects of structural similarity on the two tasks (though the effects on both tasks were reliable).

Lloyd-Jones and Humphreys interpreted their results in terms of a model of object processing operating in cascade (Humphreys et al., 1988). They argued that naming responses required access to representations at a later stage in the model than object decisions; for instance, object decisions require access to stored structural knowledge about objects, whereas naming requires access to both semantic and name representations (Riddoch & Humphreys, 1987a). In a model operating in cascade, effects due to the slow access to stored structural knowledge for objects from structurally similar categories might be propagated to subsequent processing stages, leading to increased delays in tasks requiring access to these subsequent stages (such as naming). For example, if a number of perceptual neighbours in the structural description system are initially activated by structurally similar objects, then this can lead to both a number of alternative semantic representations and a number of competitor name representations being activated, producing greater slowing on naming tasks than on object decision (requiring only access to structural knowledge). Responses based on activation at the structural description level cannot be reasonably assessed in the model as simulated, because activation at this level had a rapid rise making any differences difficult to measure. However, it is possible to monitor activation values at the semantic level in the model, as well as those at the level of the name and super-ordinate classification units. Note that, as semantic information in the model is represented locally, activation at this level needs to be specific to the individual object in order to provide response evidence for one object over others (using Luce's, 1959, choice theorem); conjoint activation of a number of alternative semantic representations for members of the same category will not do. Hence activation at both the semantic and name levels is equivalent in this sense. In order to compare "yes" responses for object decision with naming performance, we assessed response latencies and probabilities for units at the semantic level with those at the name level (Simulation 2)[4].

Some researchers (e.g. Chertkow, Bub, & Caplan, 1992) have argued that object decisions are indeed made on the basis of semantic activation, and so our simulations here assess this proposal. An alternative is that people can make object decisions on the basis of activation at the structural level (Humphreys et al., 1988; Riddoch & Humphreys, 1987a). This proposal is not assessed here if we interpret the sequentially labelled sets of units within our IAC model literally as structural descriptions, semantic representations, and name representations. However it should be stressed that we took measures of object decision from the semantic units on pragmatic not theoretical grounds. Within the localist architecture of the model, the semantic units could equally well correspond to structural descriptions of individual objects, and the structural descriptions as data-driven perceptual representations of the stimuli, so arguments about how

---

[4] Our measures of object decision were based purely on 'yes' responses and non-objects were not presented for 'no' responses. The input to the model does not comprise of either visual features or any other decomposable attributes of objects, hence performance with non-objects derived from the parts of real objects could not be simulated.

the locus of our measure of object decision relates to particular stages within theoretical models of object recognition are not straightforward. What is important is that the measure derives from representations coded at a level of processing prior to that involving name representations. Hence comparisons of object decision and naming assess whether the magnitude of the category effect increases as activation is traced through the object processing system, even when the representations involved are coded at the individual object level. Also our main interest is not to compare the absolute response latencies for object decision and either naming or semantic classification; we have already indicated that these will differ for object decision and for the naming and semantic classification responses as measured here, as the number of connections between the input and output differ for the response types (making naming and semantic classification slower in absolute terms). Our interest is whether there is any variation across tasks in the magnitude of differences between RTs to objects from structurally similar and dissimilar categories.

Simulation 1: Semantic Classification and Object Naming

Time Course of Activation.   For these simulations, each "object" was presented once to the network, and activation values in the semantic classification and name units was monitored. The mean probability of a correct response, as a function of the time course for the activation across the structurally similar (animal) and structurally dissimilar objects (items of clothing), is shown for both classification responses in Fig. 3a and for naming responses in Fig. 3b. For illustration purposes, we present the equivalent response probabilities for naming calculated using the corrected response probability measure in Fig. 3c.

These graphs indicate that semantic classification responses were considerably easier than naming responses, reaching asymptote after about 20 as opposed to nearly 50 cycles using the uncorrected response probability measure. For semantic classification, the rise in the probability of a correct response was faster for structurally similar than for structurally dissimilar items, whereas the opposite was true for naming responses. The advantage for naming structurally dissimilar over structurally similar objects is qualitatively similar when the corrected response probability measure is used (Fig. 3c). This advantage for structurally dissimilar items reflects the differential overlap in the input values for the structurally similar and dissimilar stimulus sets, not any differences in name frequency. In Simulation 3 we show the same advantage with name frequencies exactly matched across the two categories.

Response Latencies.   Studies of object classification and naming in normal subjects have typically used RT measures. To provide such a measure, we

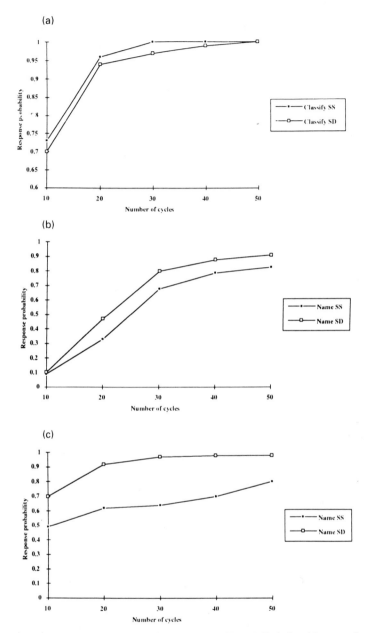

FIG. 3. Probability of a correct response to structurally similar and dissimilar objects as a function of network cycle: (a) super-ordinate classification response using the uncorrected measure of response probability; (b) naming response using the uncorrected measure of response probability; (c) naming response using the corrected measure of response probability. SS = structurally similar objects; SD = structurally dissimilar objects.

559

evaluated the time taken for classification and name units to attain threshold activation levels. Mean RTs (measured in terms of network cycles) are shown in Fig. 4a. To show the relations between the simulated data and comparable data from human subjects, in Fig. 4b we show naming and super-ordinate classification times for human subjects presented with standardised line drawings of objects. The naming data are taken from Humphreys et al. (1988) and the classification data from Riddoch and Humphreys (1987a).

One methodological issue concerns the appropriate way to assess RT functions generated by such simulations. IAC simulations use a non-linear but monotonically increasing update function (Appendix 1), so that over a number of cycles activation values in a unit rise quickly and then asymptote. This means that differences in the time to reach a given threshold level of activation will depend on where that threshold is set. Because of this, experimenters have typically used such models to make only ordinal predictions (e.g. Burton et al., 1990). Even so it is the case that units that initially gain rapidly in activation values are generally those that end with the highest asymptotic levels of activation, and that differences between structurally similar and dissimilar items occur consistently across the whole range of processing cycles (see Figs. 3b and 3c). In Simulation 1 we report a cross-over interaction, with super-ordinate classification being faster for structurally similar than for structurally dissimilar items, and with the opposite pattern for naming. Such a cross-over result is not affected by the absolute threshold value chosen. However, Simulations 2 and 3 are concerned with non-cross-over interactions, which might vary according to where the activation threshold is set. In practice we found this not to be the case, but nevertheless we report results for those simulations in which a second threshold measure was used (0.35 as well as 0.2).

Our simulations also differed from several previous IAC simulations in that we used distributed input, that varied across the population of category members according to the visual similarity ratings provided by independent judges. Analyses of variance were conducted to ensure that any differences between category members held across the populations of stimuli. Analyses of covariance were conducted to ensure that differences were not due to some co-varying factor (e.g. name frequency, when differences across the categories are evaluated).

For Simulation 1, performance as a function of the task (semantic classification vs. naming) and the type of object (structurally similar vs. structurally dissimilar) was assessed using a between-items analysis of co-variance, taking the mean time to reach threshold for each object as the measure of performance[5] and the name frequency of the object as the co-variate. There was a reliable overall effect of stimulus category $F(1,16) = 4.87$, $P < 0.05$, which

---

[5] For this analysis, the response to the item donkey was omitted, as the naming RT to this item fell more than 2 SDs away from the mean of the other items in the structurally similar set.

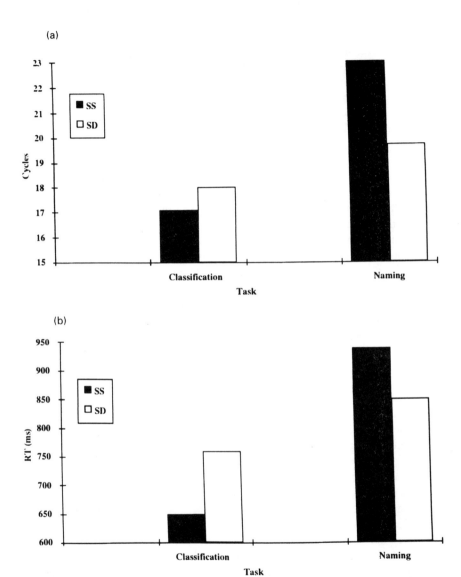

FIG. 4. Mean times to make super-ordinate classification and naming responses to structurally similar and dissimilar objects: (a) the IAC model; (b) human subjects (human data taken from Humphreys et al., 1988; and Riddoch & Humphreys, 1987a). SS = structurally similar objects; SD = structurally dissimilar objects.

was qualified by a reliable interac:ion between the stimulus and the task, $F(1,16) = 6.73$, $P < 0.025$. Categorisation responses were faster to structurally similar items than to structurally dissimilar items, $t(18) = -2.39$, $P < 0.02$, whereas naming responses were faster to structurally dissimilar items than to structurally similar items, $t(17) = 3.45$, $P < 0.01$. This pattern of results generalised across the members of the stimulus sets.

This pattern of results conforms to that found in the literature of object processing by normal observers (Riddoch & Humphreys, 1987a): there is a cross-over interaction between the category of the stimulus and the nature of the response. Within the IAC model this is because visual similarity between stimuli is helpful for super-ordinate classification but harmful for naming. Structurally similar objects activate a broader range of representations than structurally dissimilar objects within the structural description system and subsequently within the semantic and name representation systems. Because all semantic representations within a category feed into the same super-ordinate unit, the co-activation of units at the semantic level for structurally similar objects facilitates semantic classification. In contrast, for naming to occur, there must be differentiation between activated name and semantic representations in order for the name appropriate to the target object to emerge as the winner. This takes longer the more competitor items there are, and hence is longer for structurally similar than for structurally dissimilar items.

Simulation 2: Object Decision and Object Naming

In the second simulation we explored a further comparison of the effects of structural similarity across different tasks, using object decision and naming responses. Lloyd-Jones and Humphreys (submitted) found that the effects of structural similarity were greater on naming than on object decision tasks for normal observers, even though in both cases responses were contingent on the activation of item-specific information (as object decisions could not be based on the perceptual goodness of the figures; see Fig. 2). In the simulations presented here, only "yes" responses for object decision were measured, based on activation levels within the semantic system for each object, and the same activation threshold was adopted as for the naming responses (either 0.2 or 0.35). Mean RTs (in network cycles) for the object decision and naming responses for each class of stimulus, and for each threshold setting, are shown in Fig. 5.

RTs were analysed as in Simulation 1 (with name frequency as a co-variate). Irrespective of the threshold adopted, there was an interaction between the stimulus and the type of task, $F(1,16) = 4.55$ and 5.21, both $P < 0.05$ for the 0.2 and 0.35 thresholds respectively. We have already shown that RTs are slower for naming responses to structurally similar than to structurally dissimilar items (Simulation 1). In object decision, the same held true, $t(18) = 3.43$ and 4.18, both

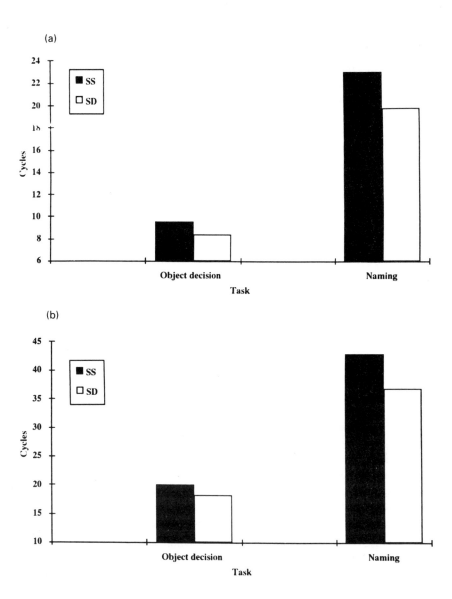

FIG. 5.   Mean latencies (in network cycles) for the IAC model to make object decision and naming responses to structurally similar and dissimilar objects. (a) with a 0.2 activation threshold setting; (b) with a 0.35 activation threshold setting. SS = structurally similar objects; SD = structurally dissimilar objects.

$P < 0.01$ for the 0.2 and 0.35 thresholds. The interaction between the stimulus and the task demonstrates that the magnitude of the difference between structurally similar and dissimilar items is increased for naming relative to object decision, and this holds across items and different threshold settings. This pattern matches that reported by Lloyd-Jones and Humphreys (submitted) for human subjects. The fact that the detrimental effect of structural similarity on performance is increased in naming, is what might be expected from a system operating in cascade, in which processing differences between stimuli are exacerbated as activation is mapped through a hierarchy of processes. It holds even though representations for individual items need to be differentiated for both object decision and naming responses to be made (Lloyd-Jones & Humphreys, submitted), and even though the response thresholds were the same at each level in the hierarchy.

Simulation 3: Effects of Structural Similarity and Name Frequency on Naming

Humphreys et al. (1988) reported that, in an object naming task, the structural similarity of the object interacted with the object's name frequency, with structurally similar objects showing a smaller name frequency effect than structurally dissimilar objects[6]. This finding was used as evidence that object naming operated in cascade. Whether such a pattern of results really emerges in a cascade system can be evaluated by examining the joint effects of structural similarity and name frequency in the IAC model.

(a) Unmatched Name Frequencies.   We first examined the effects of name frequency and structural similarity using as frequency values the familiarity ratings reported by Snodgrass and Vanderwart (1980). These values were not matched across the stimuli, however. In a second set of simulations, frequency values were arbitrarily fixed by the experimenter as either "high" or "low" for half the items within each of the two object classes. For the first set of simulations, performance was analysed by (1) using an analysis of variance, taking median splits of the items with "high" and "low" name frequency items within each category (as in Humphreys et al., 1988), and (2) correlating naming times with the rated visual similarity of the item and with the item's name frequency (operationalised here as the weight on the connections between the semantic and the name units). Riddoch and Humphreys (1987a) reported different patterns of

---

[6] In fact in several studies of picture naming with normal human subjects, using stimuli that are not highly infrequent, we have found that structurally similar objects with low name frequencies may even be named faster than those with higher name frequencies. Such an effect might occur because name frequency co-varies to some degree with structural similarity; within many structurally similar object classes (e.g. animals), stimuli with low name frequencies are also those with more distinctive perceptual structures (e.g. elephant, giraffe, ostrich).

correlation between object naming latencies for normal human observers and frequency and visual similarity measures[7], for structurally similar and dissimilar objects. Naming times to structurally similar objects correlated reliably with the measure of visual similarity between the target and other category members and not with the object's name frequency; naming times to structurally dissimilar objects correlated with their name frequency rather than their visual similarity to other category members. Here we assess whether similar patterns of correlation emerge across the items used in the structurally similar and dissimilar categories. Similar analyses were performed when the stimuli were frequency-matched across the categories, except that the items within each category then divided directly into those with high-and those with low-frequency names.

Figure 6a gives the mean correct RTs (in network cycles) for naming responses to structurally similar and dissimilar items not matched for frequency (using median splits to form the name frequency groups within each category). The outlier item within the structurally similar set (donkey) was again omitted for all analyses. Figure 6b gives the same results when the name frequencies of the structurally similar and dissimilar objects were matched and half were arbitrarily set to high and low levels.

There was a reliable effect of name frequency on response latencies for structurally dissimilar items: $t(8) = -4$ and $t = -4.3$, $P < 0.01$ for the 0.2 and 0.35 threshold settings; for structurally similar items the effect of frequency was not reliable, $t(7) = 1$ and $t < 1.0$, both $P > 0.05$.

The correlations between naming times (0.2 threshold) and name frequency and within-category visual similarity for structurally similar stimuli were: $r(16) = 0.05$ and 0.72, $P > 0.05$ and $P < 0.001$ respectively (for the 0.35 threshold the equivalent values were 0.07 and 0.69). For structurally dissimilar stimuli, the correlations with name frequency and within-category visual similarity for the 0.2 threshold setting were $r(18) = -0.90$ and 0.23, $P < 0.001$ and $P > 0.05$ respectively (for the 0.35 threshold setting the equivalent values were −0.87 and 0.22). Hence RTs for individual structurally similar items correlated reliably with the visual similarity of the items relative to other category members, but they did not correlate with name frequency; the opposite held true for structurally dissimilar items.

(b) Matched Name Frequencies.   When the structurally similar and dissimilar items were matched for name frequency, the assumed rating value for high frequency items was 4, and for low frequency items it was 2. These assumed frequency scores were transformed into weight values (see Appendix 1). The mean RTs are given in Fig. 6b.

---

[7] The visual similarity measure used in these analyses by Riddoch and Humphreys (1987a) was the degree of overlap in the boundary contour for a target object and for all other objects from the target's class given in Snodgrass and Vanderwart (1980).

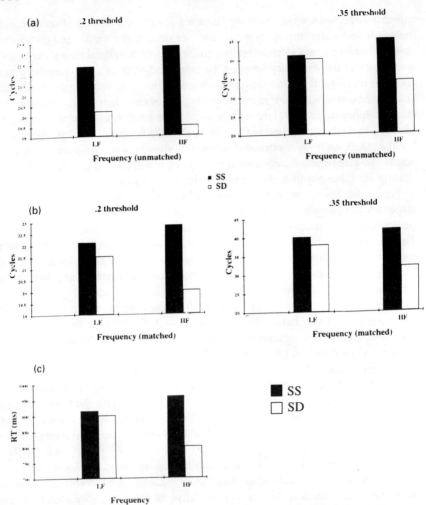

FIG. 6.   Mean times to name structurally similar and dissimilar items varying in name frequency: (a) IAC model with items unmatched for name frequencies across categories; (b) IAC model with matched name frequencies across categories; (c) human data (from Humphreys et al., 1988). SS = structurally similar objects; SD = structurally dissimilar objects; HF = high name frequencies; LF = low name frequencies.

Structurally dissimilar items showed a reliable positive effect of name frequency on RT, $t(8) = -18.54$ and -17.74; both $P < 0.001$ for the 0.2 and 0.35 threshold settings; there was no effect of name frequency on naming times for structurally similar items, $t < 1.0$ for both threshold settings.

For structurally similar objects, the coefficients for the correlations between RTs (with a 0.02 threshold setting) and name frequency and within-category visual similarity were 0.17 and 0.40 respectively, for $r(16)$; $P > 1.0$ and $P = 1.0$. For the 0.35 setting the equivalent figures were 0.14 and 0.43. For structurally dissimilar objects the correlations were -0.99 and -0.31, for $r(18)$; $P < 0.001$ and $P > 0.05$. For the 0.35 setting the equivalent values were -0.87 and -0.28[8]. Again, name frequency was a better predictor of naming latency than structural similarity for structurally dissimilar objects, and the opposite pattern of correlation occurred with structurally similar objects. Although the magnitude of any correlations found across small numbers of items, as used here, will vary according to (e.g.) the precise frequency values used, the pairings of the structural similarity and name frequency values, and the particular parameters of the model, what is important to note is that (a) the patterns of correlation hold across variations in these values, and (b) the effects of name frequency on naming are modulated by the structural similarity of the stimulus.

As might be expected from the fact that frequency only influenced the weights on the connections between the semantic and name units, name frequency had little effect on object decision and semantic classification responses in the model, and frequency effects on either stimulus category did not approach significance for these tasks (see Table 2 for the mean response latencies for each structural similarity × frequency group, for each task, using the 0.2 threshold setting).

TABLE 2

The Effects of Name Frequency on Object Decision and Super-ordinate Classification Responses (Simulation 3)

Task:	Object decision		Semantic classification	
Object:	Structurally similar	Structurally dissimilar	Structurally similar	Structurally dissimilar
Unmatched name frequencies				
High	9.52	8.43	17.07	18.00
Low	9.23	8.41	17.31	18.01
Matched name frequencies				
High	9.72	8.50	17.07	18.05
Low	9.01	8.36	17.29	18.00

Responses are measured in network cycles.

---

[8] There was a trend for a negative correlation between naming latencies and structural similarity for structurally dissimilar items here, suggesting that items with higher levels of visual similarity within their category were named faster. However, this trend was not reliable, and likely reflects an arbitrary but correlated pairing of name frequency values with structural similarity values.

Overall, these results accord well with the human data (Fig. 6c). Objects from structurally similar categories tend to be identified faster than those from structurally dissimilar categories, and naming times to these two classes of object are affected differentially by name frequency (Humphreys et al., 1988; Riddoch & Humphreys, 1987a).

Simulation 4: Naming to Deadline

Human performance under conditions where naming responses are made to a deadline that is faster than usual (Vitkovitch & Humphreys, 1991; Vitkovitch et al., 1993) can be simulated in the model by examining performance across network cycles at which activation has not reached the response threshold. Vitkovitch et al. (1993) reported that, under deadline conditions, people make a broader range of within-category errors to objects from categories with structurally similar exemplars relative to objects from categories with structurally dissimilar exemplars.

We examined the range of possible naming errors made by the model when performance was assessed at cycles prior to the response threshold being reached. Naming errors were judged by counting the number of active competitors (i.e. competitors with positive activation values) at the name output level for particular cycles of the network, (5, 7, 9, 12, and 15 cycles respectively). The mean number of competitors for structurally similar and structurally dissimilar objects is given in Table 3. A broader range of errors tended to occur for structurally similar relative to structurally dissimilar objects at the shortest deadline examined (5 cycles) $t(18) = 4.2$, $P = 0.06$.

The broader range of errors made to structurally similar relative to structurally dissimilar objects is caused by the increased number of within-category competitor representations that are activated for structurally similar items. This occurs because these items share high levels of within-class visual similarity.

TABLE 3
Mean Number of Active Competitor Name Units Available as
a Function of Network Cycles

Cycle	Structurally similar	Structurally dissimilar
5	1.4	0.7
7	0.8	0.1
9	0.7	0
12	0.6	0
15	0.3	0

Simulation 5: Lesioning the Model

In order to compare the performance of the model to that of neuropsychological patients, the model was "lesioned". Lesioning took the form of adding "noise" to either input values or weights at different locations within the model, a procedure used in other attempts to model neuropsychological disorders in connectionist systems (e.g. Humphreys, Freeman, & Müller, 1992; Patterson, Seidenberg, & McClelland, 1989)[9]. Lesioning was examined at the level of structural descriptions (adding noise to the input values), at the level of mapping from structural descriptions to semantics (adding noise to the weights on the connections between the structural and semantic units), and at the level of mapping from semantic representations to name representations (adding noise to the weights on the connections between the semantic representations and the name units). In each case, we assessed the effects of adding random noise at two levels, varying respectively from 0.1 to 0.3 and from 0.2 to 0.4, about a mean of zero. In order to ensure that any effects of lesioniong were not confounded by differences in name frequency between structurally similar and dissimilar items, lesioning was conducted on the version of the model with name frequency values matched across items within each category (with half having a high and half a low frequency of occurrence). In addition, lesions of each magnitude were conducted three times at each location within the model, in order to ensure that any effects were not due to one particular and perhaps arbitrary lesion. We report the mean performance of the model averaged across the three lesions at each site. When lesioned, the model sometimes failed to reach threshold levels of activation after 50 cycles (the arbitrary time used in fixing the parameters for the unlesioned model). In order to prevent RTs being fixed at an arbitrary ceiling, the model was allowed to iterate for 100 cycles before halting performance. Performance was evaluated on object decision, super-ordinate semantic classification, and naming by monitoring outputs at the semantic, super-ordinate, and name levels in the model.

Table 4 gives the mean percentage increase in RTs (in network cycles) for each lesion for each of the three different tasks examined (object decision, semantic classification, and naming), measured relative to the performance of the model in an unlesioned state. Note that this measure takes into account differences in baseline levels of performances across object type and task. Table 5 gives the number of trials on which activation values failed to reach threshold after 100 cycles, which were treated as errors.

The results in Table 4 are clear. First, the effects of lesioning varied across tasks. In general, semantic classification and object decision were relatively less

---

[9] Because the model used local representations at the structural, semantic, and name levels, it was not possible to remove units at random at these levels without producing obvious and complete loss of recognition for the affected items. Effects of lesioning the processing units themselves might be examined more profitably in a system with distributed representations.

TABLE 4
Percentage Increases in RTs

	Object decision		Semantic classification		Naming	
Lesion site and size	SS	SD	SS	SD	SS	SD
Structural descriptions						
Lesion: 0.1–0.3	15	5	0	0	52	7
	(0.1)	(0)	(0)	(0)	(0.5)	(0.1)
Lesion: 0.2–0.4	21	10	–3	–3	75	11
	(0.1)	(0.1)	(0.1)	(0.1)	(4.3)	(0.1)
Structural descriptions to semantics						
Lesion: 0.1–0.3	21	17	15	12	31	18
	(0.2)	(0.1)	(0.3)	(0.2)	(2.2)	(0.2)
Lesion: 0.2–0.4	30	33	22	23	34	30
	(0.2)	(0.2)	(0.1)	(0.3)	(3.2)	(0.4)
Semantics to names						
Lesion: 0.1–0.3	1	0	0	0	65	45
	(0)	(0)	(0)	(0)	(2.0)	(1.4)
Lesion: 0.2–0.4	1	1	0	0	122	130
	(0)	(0)	(0)	(0)	(10.2)	(7.5)

Percentage increases in RTs (relative to the baseline levels of performance for the unlesioned model) for each task (object decision, semantic classification and naming) after each lesion. Standard deviations (sd) for the percentage increases across the three lesions performed for each size and location are given in brackets. SS = structurally similar objects; SD = structurally dissimilar objects. Scores are given to one decimal place.

affected than naming. Second, in many cases, but not all, performance was disrupted relatively more for structurally similar than for structurally dissimilar objects. We discuss the effects in each task separately.

For semantic classification, both the effects of lesioning the structural descriptions and of lesioning the mappings between semantic and name representations, produced minimal disruption (in fact increasing the noise on the input vectors [from "lesioning" the structural descriptions] led to slight benefits in semantic classification, as any spreading of activation across category members produced by the lesions tended to lead to more rapid accumulation of activation in the super-ordinate decision units). There was an impairment to response times following lesions of the mappings between the structural description system and the semantic system, presumably because these lesions decreased the general efficiency of mapping activation through to units at later levels in the model. This impairment was of equal magnitude for structurally similar and structurally dissimilar objects.

TABLE 5
Percentage of Naming Responses Where Activation Values in the Name Units Failed to Reach Threshold After 100 Cycles

Lesion	Structurally similar	Structurally dissimilar
Structural descriptions		
Lesion: 0.1–0.3	10.0	0
Lesion: 0.2–0.4	13.3	0
Structural descriptions to semantics		
Lesion: 0.1–0.3	3.3	0
Lesion: 0.2–0.4	3.3	0
Semantics to names		
Lesion: 0.1–0.3	10.0	0
Lesion: 0.2–0.4	20.0	16.7

For object decision, performance was unaffected when the lesion affected the mapping between the semantic and output representations, as might be expected if object decision ''taps'' activation at earlier levels within the model (Riddoch & Humphreys, 1987b; Sheridan & Humphreys, 1993). There were detrimental effects on object decision from lesioning at earlier levels in the model (adding noise to the structural descriptions or to the connections mapping structural onto semantic descriptions). For the lesions to the structural description system, these effects tended to be larger on objects from structurally similar classes than on objects from structurally dissimilar classes. Presumably adding noise to input vectors led to less discrimination between the more similar items, when activation values were monitored in representations specific to individual items (as was done for object decision but not for semantic classification responses here). For lesions between the structural description and semantic systems, however, the effects on structurally similar and dissimilar items were roughly equal.

For naming, the effects of lesioning the structural descriptions, and the effects of the ''light'' lesions on the mappings between units at the structural and semantic, and at the semantic and name level, were greater on objects from categories with structurally similar exemplars. When larger lesions were introduced to the mappings from the structural to the semantic, and from the semantic to the name, levels, effects on structurally similar and dissimilar items were equal in magnitude.

Note that overall there were an increased number of trials for structurally similar objects in which activation levels failed to reach the designated response threshold within the 100-cycle time period (Table 5); on such trials it might be considered that correct naming failed to take place. Thus not only were naming times often slowed differentially for structurally similar items, but also the error rate increased[10].

(i) Effects of Lesioning on Different Tasks.   The general pattern of results was that semantic classification was affected less than object decision, and that object decision was affected less than naming. The IAC model shows this effect because super-ordinate semantic knowledge requires less differentiation within an object class than either object decision or naming, and so is less affected when noise is added to impair discrimination between individual object exemplars. This trend, for preserved ability to access super-ordinate over specific object knowledge has been noted in many neuropsychological patients, and has been taken as a marker of an impairment to stored semantic knowledge about objects (e.g. Warrington, 1975). Interestingly the IAC model shows this trend even after lesions affecting processing at pre-semantic levels in the model (e.g. affecting the structural descriptions of objects), suggesting that the effect should not necessarily be taken as a marker of problems within the semantic system.

Interestingly, object decision was affected after lesions to both the structural descriptions and to the connections between the structural description system and the semantic system. Riddoch and Humphreys (1987b) argued that it is possible for patients with the latter lesion to still perform object decisions at a normal level. As noted in the Introduction, their patient, JB, performed object decisions at a control level, while showing poor judgements of the semantic relations between visually presented stimuli. Riddoch and Humphreys proposed that this reflected a problem in accessing semantic knowledge from the structural description system, because JB was able to make accurate judgements of the semantic relations between stimuli when he was given the names of the objects auditorily. The discrepancy between JB's performance and that of the IAC model suggests that the assumption made in the IAC model (see also Chertkow et al., 1992), that object decisions are conducted on the basis of semantic activation, is wrong. In principle, the IAC model does not require that semantic activation is monitored in order for object decisions to be carried out, and, as already noted, this was done here on implementational not theoretical grounds. If activation to the structural description system were provided by an earlier set of input units (e.g. representing the features of objects), then it would

---

[10] It might be argued here that the simulations with a lesioned version of the model fail to relate to studies of neuropsychological patients because performance of the model is measured mainly in terms of RT, whereas neuropsychological data are primarily based on accuracy measures. However, this argument fails to appreciate that, as RTs lengthen, so the chances increase that a given object fails to establish a threshold level of activation within its corresponding representations. For the model, RT and accuracy are intimately related, and both can be taken as measures of processing efficiency.

be possible to use activation in the structural description system to perform object decisions; similarly, we might consider the present "semantic" units as structural units fed by a set of input perceptual descriptions (the present structural units). In either case, lesioning a site after the structural description system (e.g. the mappings from the structural description system to the superordinate semantic system) should have little effect on object decisions.

However, it should also be pointed out that, although lesions of the structural description system, and of the mappings between the structural and semantic systems, did affect object decision as well as naming responses, the effects were substantially larger on naming (Table 4). As naming responses are based on activation values in units located later within the model, there is increased time and opportunity for the effects of any noise (from lesioning) to occur and to magnify competitive interactions between processing units. As far as the testing of neuropsychological patients is concerned, this result does suggest that, if object decision tasks are not relatively stringent, patients could perform within normal limits while being impaired at naming; this might occur even if object decisions are conducted on the basis of semantic activation.

(ii) Category-specific Disorders. In many cases, when lesioned, the IAC model had more difficulty retrieving specific information for structurally similar than for structurally dissimilar items (i.e. on object decision and naming tasks rather than on semantic classification). The finding that a category-specific disorder for structurally similar items can emerge after lesions affecting a number of different processing loci within the model accords with existing neuropsychological data (see the Introduction). However, we have also shown that structurally similar objects are more difficult for the model to make object decisions to and to name than structurally dissimilar items, even when the model is unlesioned (Simulations 1–3); hence the selective effect of lesioning on structurally similar items may be little more than an effect of task difficulty. Essentially, if lesioning generally worsens performance of the object processing system, then items that are difficult in normality may well suffer more than those that are normally relatively easy. Is task difficulty all there is?

As we noted in the Introduction, several cases have now been reported in which neuropsychological patients have been reported with selective deficits in identifying structurally dissimilar items (e.g. artefacts) relative to items from categories with structurally similar members (e.g. living things) (Hillis & Caramazza, 1990; Sacchett & Humphreys, 1992; Warrington & McCarthy, 1983, 1987). Hence we do not think that a task difficulty account can be applied to all known neuropsychological cases. Also, the present simulations suggest that factors other than task difficulty are important. First, the effects on naming (the most difficult task) of "large" lesions at later levels in the model were no greater on structurally similar objects than on structurally dissimilar objects. This was not because ceiling effects were involved. The slowest average naming

RTs were 50.9 and 46.1 cycles for structurally similar and dissimilar items after a "large" lesion to the mappings between the semantic and name units, which were a long way from the ceiling of 100 cycles. Second, the effects of lesioning on structurally similar and dissimilar items varied as a function of the level of the lesion and the nature of the task. Lesioning the structural descriptions disrupted object decisions and naming more for structurally similar objects. These lesions decreased the discriminability between input vectors, with the effects being most pronounced for the more similar vectors. This affected performance for structurally similar items most when discrimination of individual representations was required for the response (with object decision and naming but not semantic classification). Lesioning the mappings between the structural description and semantic levels only affected structurally similar items more than structurally dissimilar items when naming responses were required; effects on object decision and semantic classification were equal across the categories.

The effects of lesioning the mappings between processing levels can be understood in terms of an exaggeration of the effects on normal performance. Simulations with the unlesioned version of the model have already shown that category effects are larger on naming than on object decision and semantic classification: the costs of visual similarity between category members are increased as activation is passed through more levels in the model. This is because competition at earlier stages in the model (e.g. within the semantic system) adds to the competition at later stages (e.g. in name selection), producing particularly slow naming of structurally similar objects (Simulations 1 and 2). Lesioning the mappings from structural to semantic units decreases the efficiency with which activation values are transmitted from the structural units, increasing the time taken to resolve competition at later stages in the model. As competition is greatest at the name level, and for structurally similar objects, the effects of decreased efficiency in mapping between processing levels are most apparent for naming structurally similar objects. A similar argument can be made concerning the effects of lesioning the mapping between the semantic and name units. The simulations also show, however, that any advantage for structurally dissimilar items is lost when there are relatively "large" lesions to the mappings between levels. In this case, it appears that any differentiation in the activation levels at the structural and semantic levels between structurally similar and dissimilar items is simply lost by the increased noise in mapping from these levels to the output units. These points demonstrate that what is important is not difficulty *per se*, but the nature of the different tasks (the degree of competition for selection of a specific response) and whether lesioning increases the competition at particular levels or simply loses the "normal" benefits from lessened competition for one class of object over another.

In addition, it is possible to lesion the model in ways other than the ones we have examined. For example, because the model at present has local representations, lesions to any of the levels of representation in the model, or to the connections between representations, could affect some items more than others. Hence it would be possible to disrupt the processing of structurally dissimilar items more than that of structurally similar items, to mimic the reported dissociations in the neuropsychological literature (e.g. Hillis & Caramazza, 1990; Sacchett & Humphreys, 1992; Warrington & McCarthy, 1983, 1987). To provide a more principled account for why such lesions would produce deficits across categories with structurally dissimilar members, however, we need to explain why representations of these items might be bound together functionally or anatomically. One possibility, as noted previously by Farah and McClelland (1991) and by Warrington and McCarthy (1987), is that such items may be defined in terms of their functional properties, and their semantic representations may be linked on the basis of common functions (indeed, their semantic representations may be anatomically located close to areas for particular motor actions; cf. Warrington & McCarthy, 1987). Thus a lesion affecting units corresponding to semantic representations of structurally dissimilar items could produce a category-specific deficit opposite to the impairments we have examined here. This would be similar to the lesions affecting structurally dissimilar items in Farah and McClelland's (1991) simulation.

Some patients have been reported as having difficulty in retrieving information about structurally similar items even when given their names and asked to define the objects verbally (e.g. Warrington & Shallice, 1984) or when given verbal definitions stressing the visual properties of objects and asked to provide a name (e.g. Silveri & Gainotti, 1988). That is, the deficits are not confined to the use of visual input. For the model, the last result is informative, because it suggests that, for some patients, the retrieval of information about structurally similar objects from verbal labels is most affected when stored visual/structural knowledge must be contacted. Tasks such as providing a definition of structurally similar items, or naming such items from a definition of their perceptual characteristics, may be accomplished by activation of stored visual/structural knowledge, following the verbal/name input (see Farah & McClelland, 1991, for evidence of the role of visual/perceptual characteristics in the definition of objects from structurally similar categories). The propagation of activation back from the visual/structural knowledge system through to the name system will then be affected by lesioning as we have shown, even though the original input was not visual (see Riddoch et al., 1988, for a similar proposal). Definitions stressing verbal or functional characteristics of objects, in contrast, may require only the retrieval of semantic information from the verbal label. This may not be problematic if the model is lesioned at a pre-semantic level (e.g. within the structural description system or in the mappings from the structural description system to the semantic system); hence such patients may perform well at naming functional definitions (Silveri & Gainotti, 1988).

One final point concerns the disappearance of category-specific deficits after large lesions to the mappings between structural and semantic, and semantic and name, units. Object processing deficits following lesions affecting the mappings between the structural and semantic systems remain controversial (cf. Farah, 1990, and Riddoch & Humphreys, 1987a) and have not been studied in sufficient detail to assess whether the model's performance here is appropriate. However, anomic deficits due to problems in mapping semantic to name information are well known. Mostly such deficits are not noted as being category-specific in nature. This might be due to a failure to probe for category-specific loss in some cases, but it may be that deficits for particular categories might only be apparent after quite subtle lesions (cf. Hart et al., 1985). The model suggests the latter.

GENERAL DISCUSSION

We have presented an extremely simple model of object processing using an IAC formulation that has been able to account for many of the basic results concerning the effects of within-category structural similarity on object processing by both normal and brain-injured observers. The model as presented here is in its most simple form, and, as we now outline, there may be good reasons to introduce changes of either its basic representations (from local to distributed) or even of its basic architecture (e.g. to incorporate direct connections between the structural description and name representations). However, such changes should not alter the overall operation of the model, which is determined by two main assumptions: that (1) processing operates in cascade, being transmitted from one level of the system to others before processing at the prior level has been completed; and (2) structural similarity affects the number of perceptual neighbours within the structural description system that are activated on the presentation of a given object. It is these two assumptions that have allowed us to simulate the following results:

1. The cross-over interaction between response latencies for super-ordinate semantic classification and naming tasks for structurally similar and structurally dissimilar objects (Simulation 1).

2 The emergence of stronger effects of structural similarity on naming than on object decision, even when the data are analysed with name frequency as a co-variate, when the same response thresholds are adopted for the two responses, and even though both tasks require access to item-specific representations (Simulation 2).

3. The interaction between structural similarity and name frequency, such that items from categories with structurally dissimilar members tend to show a stronger positive effect of frequency on naming times (Simulation 3).

4. The greater spread of within-category naming errors to structurally similar than to structurally dissimilar objects, when naming is required to operate to a speeded deadline (Simulation 4).

5. The emergence of category-specific deficits for objects from categories with structurally similar members when the model is lesioned at various levels (Simulation 5).

These results are not tied to the specific parameters adopted in the present simulations. Interactions between structural similarity and name frequency occur both when the weights between the semantic and name representations are differentially set for individual name frequencies and when they are set to just two frequency bands, equal across the two object classes (Simulation 3). Also, the results do not change qualitatively when different response thresholds are used.

The model extends previous simulations in several ways. First, it shows how variables affecting different levels of representation (here structural similarity and name frequency) can interact within a system operating in cascade. It also shows how a variable affecting early perceptual representations (structural similarity) can generate larger effects on performance as activation is transmitted through a hierarchical processing system (e.g. from object decision to naming). The previous simulation of category-specific deficits, provided by Farah and McClelland (1991), is extended by our demonstration that such deficits can arise after lesioning different levels of the model, including the lesioning of relatively late processing stages (e.g. mapping from semantic to name representations), and we also demonstrate that the same model can be used to account for category-specific effects on the efficiency of normal object processing. Note that such effects on normal processing make it difficult to attribute all between-category differences in object processing to emergent properties of damaged information processing systems. In addition, because this model has functionally separate visual/structural and semantic representations, it is possible to account for "pure" deficits for particular categories of item; such deficits are difficult to account for in models that employ only a single, inter-linked network to represent both visual/structural and functional/semantic information about objects (as in Farah & McClelland, 1991). For example, for the IAC model lesions to the structural description system selectively disrupt both identification and object decision responses to objects from categories with structurally similar exemplars (Simulation 5). However, such lesions will not disrupt the ability to name the stimulus from a verbal definition stressing its functional properties; this is the pattern of results reported by Riddoch and Humphreys (1993). By having a functional separation between visual/structural and semantic knowledge, the IAC model can also capture selective deficits in accessing semantic knowledge about objects along with intact object decisions (at least providing that object decisions are based on activation within the structural description system).

Distributed Representations

The model has a simple representation scheme in which one unit stands for a given object at each level of representation. Such local representations facilitate interpretation of the operation of connectionist models, but they also have certain drawbacks; for example, knowledge loss may be severe if there is neuronal degeneration, certain types of learning may be restricted, and it may be more difficult to compute similarities (and hence to generalise) across given levels of representation (e.g. Hanson & Burr, 1990; Hinton et al., 1986). In principle, we see no reason why the present model could not be extended to incorporate distributed rather than local representations. At the level of structural descriptions, distributed representations of individual objects may be built out of patterns of co-activation across units representing individual parts of objects; at the semantic level, they may be built from patterns of co-activation across units representing functional characteristics of objects; at the name level they may be built from patterns of co-activation across units representing individual phonemes. There will be particular reasons for adopting each of several candidate representations at each proposed level in the model. However, even if such a representation scheme were to be adopted, we do not believe it would fundamentally affect the operation of the model. The present localist version of the IAC model captures the effects of structural similarity on object processing by introducing patterns of co-activation across objects with similar perceptual structures; this would be much the same in a model with distributed representation, except that what is represented here as levels of activation within individual units might be expressed in terms of the spread of activation values across units in a distributed system. The net effect ought to be the same. Tasks such as super-ordinate semantic classification, which can be based on convergent activation across category members, should be most efficient when there is a spread of activation across category members (and hence increased evidence for a given categorisation). Tasks such as object decision and naming, which require differentiation between category members, should be most efficient when there is relatively little spread of activation across category members.

Although we have been able to capture several of the important characteristics of visual object processing, some further issues remain.

Direct or Indirect Object Naming?

The IAC model has a hierarchical organisation, in which structural knowledge is contacted before semantic knowledge, which is in turn contacted before name information. According to this model, semantic knowledge needs to be activated in order for object naming to take place. As we noted in the Introduction, this finding fits the current neuropsychological evidence, as there have been few convincing cases to date of patients being able to name objects without being able to retrieve some semantic knowledge. However, as the IAC model does not have discrete processing stages, it is not the case that all semantic knowledge would necessarily have to be retrieved in order for naming to take place. Indeed, for objects that do not activate many members of the same category, it may be the case that there is relatively little semantic activation prior to naming. Hence some objects may be named in a way that is more "direct" than others. For the model as it stands, naming would be more direct for objects from categories with structurally dissimilar exemplars (see also Riddoch & Humphreys, 1987a). An alternative view, however, stresses the importance of different defining characteristics for different objects. Objects from categories with structurally similar exemplars tend to be defined in terms of their perceptual characteristics, objects from categories with structurally dissimilar exemplars tend to be defined in terms of their functional characteristics (Farah & McClelland, 1991; Warrington & McCarthy, 1987; Warrington & Shallice, 1984). It might be, then, that differentiation of a target representation from other representations at the level of structural descriptions is sufficient to enable name retrieval to take place for structurally similar objects, whereas differentiation at a semantic level is necessary for name retrieval for structurally dissimilar objects. This would fit with category-specific deficits showing impaired naming of objects from categories with structurally dissimilar objects, possibly linked to poor differentiation of semantic information. Were such an account to prove valid, the model as simulated here would need to be modified to enable direct connections to be made between the structural description level and the name level. From the evidence to date, the model with direct structural-name connections is not strongly supported, and, for patients showing category-specific loss for structurally dissimilar items, it remains possible for there to be a fine-grained breakdown within the semantic system which particularly affects structurally dissimilar objects. For the present, we maintain the simpler account that maintains a strict hierarchy rather than a heterarchy of processing stages.

Modality-specific Semantics?

The IAC model makes a distinction between one knowledge system for visual/structural knowledge about objects (the structural description system) and one for functional knowledge about objects (the semantic system). This distinction is grounded in empirical dissociations between patients who show good access to structural knowledge from vision along with impaired access to functional-semantic knowledge (e.g. Riddoch & Humphreys, 1987b). Indeed in labelling one system as a structural description system rather than (say) a visual semantic system, we have attempted to maintain operational definitions of the knowledge systems mediating visual object processing, and not to step beyond the bounds of the empirical data. In particular, it is not clear that patients who can access stored structural knowledge from vision, while having impaired access to functional-semantic knowledge, can also access non-visual forms of perceptual knowledge or visual contextual knowledge, both of which might indicate access to a knowledge base specifying more than the structural descriptions of individual objects. As we have already stated, however, we assume that the structural description system is involved when we retrieve stored visual knowledge about objects even when we are only given the object's name.

McCarthy and Warrington (1988) argued for the existence of modality-specific semantic systems from a single case, TOB, who apparently showed access to contextual knowledge about objects from vision, but not when given the object's name (see the Introduction). This difficulty was most pronounced for animate objects. They proposed that TOB gained access to a visual semantic system, but failed to gain access to a verbal semantic system in which animate and inanimate objects were represented independently (perhaps in terms of perceptual and functional features respectively). TOB may be accommodated by the IAC model in much the same way as we outlined earlier for Farah and McClelland's (1991) distributed memory model. For example, deficits in retrieving information about animate objects from their names can be attributed to poor access to the structural description system from either the names (directly) or from the semantic system (e.g. due to lesions to the pathways involved in mapping activation back to the structural description level). Nevertheless, the structural description may itself be relatively intact and, along with the semantic system, accessible from visual input. The pattern of performance expected from such a deficit was simulated by Farah and McClelland (1991).

Base-level Classification Revisited

Within the IAC model, access to stored representations operates with varying degrees of efficiency according to the perceptual characteristics of the object input to the system and according to the constraints of the task. In this sense the "access code" used to retrieve different kinds of stored knowledge can be seen as flexible. For object decision and naming responses, the access code is based on the activation of the representations of individual exemplars; for super-ordinate semantic classifications, it is based on co-activation across a number of category exemplars. For objets that activate few perceptual neighbours, there will be relatively faster access to specific names than to more general names corresponding to several members from the same category; the opposite will hold for objects that activate a number of perceptual neighbours. This pattern of results fits with findings showing that atypical category members access their specific names faster than their base-level names (e.g. penguin *vs.* bird), whereas the opposite holds for typical category members (sparrows *vs.* bird) (Jolicoeur et al., 1984). Rather than thinking that such results indicate that there are different "entry level" representations for the different objects, we suggest that the stored representations contacted by typical and atypical objects are the same, and that variations across objects arise as a function of processing rather than representational constraints. The IAC model provides a natural framework for capturing such flexible access operations.

REFERENCES

Basso, A., Capitani, E., & Laiacona, M. (1988). Progressive language impairment without dementia: A case with isolated category specific semantic deficit. *Journal of Neurology, Neurosurgery and Psychiatry, 51*, 1201–1207.

Biederman, I. (1987). Recognition-by-components: A theory of human image understanding. *Psychological Review, 94*, 115–147.

Bruce, V., & Humphreys, G.W. (1994). Recognizing objects and faces. *Visual Cognition, 1*, 141–180.

Bruce, V., & Young, A.W. (1986). Understanding face recognition. *British Journal of Psychology, 77*, 305–328.

Burton, A.M. (1994). Learning new faces in an interactive activation and competition model. *Visual Cognition, 1*, 313–348.

Burton, A.M., & Bruce, V. (1992). I recognize your face but I can't remember your name: A simple explanation? *British Journal of Psychology, 83*, 45–60.

Burton, A.M., & Bruce, V. (1993). Naming faces and naming names: Exploring an interactive activation model of person recognition. *Memory, 1*, 457–480.

Burton, A.M., Bruce, V., & Johnston, R. (1990). Understanding face recognition with an interactive activation model. *British Journal of Psychology, 81*, 361–380.

Burton, A.M., Young, A.W., Bruce, V., Johnston, R., & Ellis, A.W. (1991). Understanding covert recognition. *Cognition, 39*, 129–166.

Caramazza, A., Hillis, A.E., Rapp, B.C., & Romani, C. (1990). The multiple semantics hypothesis: Multiple confusions? *Cognitive Neuropsychology, 7*, 161–189.

Carr, T.H., McCauley, C., Sperber, R.D., & Parmalee, C.M. (1982). Words, pictures and priming: On semantic activation, conscious identification and the automaticity of information processing. *Journal of Experimental Psychology: Human Perception and Performance, 8*, 757–777.

Chertkow, H., Bub, D., & Caplan, D. (1992). Constraining theories of semantic memory processing: Evidence from dementia. *Cognitive Neuropsychology, 9*, 327–365.

deHaan, E.H.F., Young, A.W., & Newcombe, F. (1987). Face recognition without awareness. *Cognitive Neuropsychology, 4*, 385–415.

Farah, M.J. (1990). *Visual agnosia: disorders of object recognition and what they tell us about normal vision.* Cambridge, MA: MIT Press.

Farah, M.J., & McClelland, J.L. (1991). A computational model of semantic memory impairment: Modality-specificity and emergent category-specificity. *Journal of Experimental Psychology: General, 120*, 339–357.

Farah, M.J., McMullen, P.A., & Meyer, M.M. (1991). Can recognition of living things be selectively impaired? *Neuropsychologia, 29*, 185–194.

Farah, M.J., & Wallace, M.A. (1992). Semantically-bounded anomia: Implications for the neural implementation of naming. *Neuropsychologia, 30*, 609–621.

Funnell, E., & Sheridan, J. (1992). Categories of knowledge: Unfamiliar aspects of living and non-living things. *Cognitive Neuropsychology, 9*, 135–154.

Grossberg, S.J. (1978). A theory of visual coding, memory and development. In E.L.J. Leeuwenberg & H.F.J.M. Buffart (Eds.), *Formal theories of visual perception.* New York: Wiley.

Hanson, S.J., & Burr, D.J. (1990). What connectionist models learn: Learning and representation in connectionist networks. *The Behavioral and Brain Sciences, 13*, 471–518.

Hart, J., Berndt, R.S., & Caramazza, A. (1985). Category-specific naming deficit following cerebral infarction. *Nature, 316,* 439–440.

Hillis, A., & Caramazza, A. (1990). Category-specific naming and comprehension impairment: A double dissociation. *Brain, 114,* 2081–2094.

Hinton, G.E., McClelland, J.L., & Rumelhart, D.E. (1986). Distributed representations. In D.E. Rumelhart & J.L. McClelland (Eds.), *Parallel distributed processing. 1. Foundations.* Cambridge, MA: MIT Press.

Hummel, J.E., & Biederman, I. (1992). Dynamic binding in a neural network for shape recognition. *Psychological Review, 99,* 480–517.

Humphreys, G.W., Freeman, T.A.C., & Müller, H.M. (1992). Lesioning a connectionist model of visual search: Selective effects on distractor grouping. *Canadian Journal of Psychology, 46,* 417–460.

Humphreys, G.W., & Riddoch, M.J. (1993). Object agnosias. In C. Kennard (Ed.), *Balliere's clinical neurology: Visual perceptual deficits.* London: Balliere Tindall.

Humphreys, G.W., & Riddoch, M.J. (1994). Neurological disturbances of vision: Approaches to assessment and treatment. In M.J. Riddoch & G.W. Humphreys (Eds.), *Cognitive neuropsychology and cognitive rehabilitation.* London: Lawrence Erlbaum Associates Ltd.

Humphreys, G.W., Riddoch, M.J., & Quinlan, P.T. (1988). Cascade processes in picture identification. *Cognitive Neuropsychology, 5,* 67–103.

Jolicoeur, P., Gluck, M., & Kosslyn, S.M. (1984). Pictures and names: Making the connection. *Cognitive Psychology, 16,* 243–275.

Kay, J., & Ellis, A.W. (1987). A cognitive neuropsychological case study of anomia: Implications for psychological models of word retrieval. *Brain, 110,* 613–629.

Lloyd-Jones, T.J., & Humphreys, G.W. (submitted). Perceptual differentiation as a source of category effects in object processing: Evidence from naming and object decision. *Memory and Cognition.*

Luce, R.D. (1959). *Individual choice behavior.* New York: Wiley.

Marr, D. (1982). *Vision.* San Francisco: W.H. Freeman.

Marr, D., & Nishihara, H.K. (1978). Representation and recognition of the spatial organization of three-dimensional shapes. *Proceedings of the Royal Society of London, B200,* 269–294.

McCann, R.S., & Besner, D. (1987). Reading pseudohomophones: Implications for models of pronunciation assembly and the locus of word frequency effects in naming. *Journal of Experimental Psychology: Human Perception and Performance, 13,* 14–24.

McCarthy, R.A., & Warrington, E.K. (1988). Evidence for modality-specific meaning systems in the brain. *Nature, 334,* 428–430.

McClelland, J.L. (1979). On the time relations of mental processes: An examination of systems of processes in cascade. *Psychological Review, 86,* 287–330.

McClelland, J.L. (1981). Retrieving general and specific information from stored knowledge of specifics. *Proceedings of the Third Annual Meeting of the Cognitive Science Society,* 170–172.

McClelland, J.L., & Rumelhart, D.E. (1981). An interactive activation model of context effects in letter perception. 1. An account of basic findings. *Psychological Review, 88,* 375–407.

McClelland, J.L., & Rumelhart, D.E. (1985). Distributed memory and the representation of general and specific information. *Journal of Experimental Psychology: General, 114,* 159–188.

McClelland, J.L., & Rumelhart, D.E. (1988). *Explorations in parallel distributed processing.* Cambridge, MA: Bradford Books.

Meyer, D.E., & Schvaneveldt, R.W. (1971). Facilitation in recognizing pairs of words: Evidence of a dependence between retrieval operations. *Journal of Experimental Psychology, 90,* 227–234.

Morrison, C.M., Ellis, A.W., & Quinlan, P.T. (1992). Age of acquisition, not word frequency, affects object naming, not object recognition. *Memory and Cognition, 20,* 705–714.

Oldfield, R.C. (1966). Things, words and the brain. *Quarterly Journal of Experimental Psychology, 18,* 340–353.

Patterson, K.E., & Coltheart, V. (1987). Phonological processes in reading: A tutorial review. In M. Coltheart (Ed.), *Attention and performance, XII*. London: Lawrence Erlbaum Associates Ltd.

Patterson, K.E., & Morton, J. (1985). From orthography to phonology: An attempt at an old interpretation. In K.E. Patterson, J.C. Marshall, & M. Coltheart (Eds.), *Surface dyslexia: Neuropsychological and cognitive studies of phonological reading*. London: Lawrence Erlbaum Associates Ltd.

Patterson, K.E., Seidenberg, M.S., & McClelland, J.L. (1989). Connections and disconnections: Acquired dyslexia in a computational model of reading processes. in R.G.M. Morris (Ed.), *Parallel distributed processing: Implications for psychology and neurobiology*. Oxford: Oxford University press.

Potter, M.C., & Faulconer, B.A. (1975). Time to understand pictures and words. *Nature, 253*, 437–438.

Price, C.J., & Humphreys, G.W. (1989). The effects of surface detail on object categorization and naming. *Quarterly Journal of Experimental Psychology, 41A*, 797–828.

Riddoch, M.J., & Humphreys, G.W. (1987a). Picture naming. In G.W. Humphreys & M.J.R. Riddoch (Eds.), *Visual object processing: A cognitive neuropsychology approach*. London: Lawrence Erlbaum Associates Ltd.

Riddoch, M.J., & Humphreys, G.W. (1987b). Visual object processing in optic aphasia: A case of semantic access agnosia. *Cognitive Neuropsychology, 4*, 131–185.

Riddoch, M.J., & Humphreys, G.W. (1987c). A case of integrative visual agnosia. *Brain, 110*, 1431–1462.

Riddoch, M.J., & Humphreys, G.W. (1993). The smiling giraffe. In R. Campbell (Ed.), *Broken lives*. Oxford: Blackwells.

Riddoch, M.J., Humphreys, G.W., Coltheart, M., & Funnell, E. (1988). Semantic systems or semantic system? Neuropsychological evidence re-examined. *Cognitive Neuropsychology, 5*, 3–25.

Rosch, E., Mervis, C.B., Gray, W.D., Johnson, D.M., & Boyes-Braem, P. (1976). Basic objects in natural categories. *Cognitive Psychology, 8*, 382–439.

Sacchett, C., & Humphreys, G.W. (1992). Calling a squirrel a squirrel but a canoe a wigwam: A category-specific deficit for artefactual objects and body parts. *Cognitive Neuropsychology, 9*, 73–86.

Sartori, G., & Job, R. (1988). The oyster with four legs: A neuropsychological study on the interaction of visual and semantic information. *Cognitive Neuropsychology, 5*, 105–132.

Sartori, G., Job, R., & Coltheart, M. (1993). The organization of object knowledge: Evidence from neuropsychology. In D.E. Meyer & S. Kornblum (Eds.), *Attention & performance XIV*. Cambridge, MA: MIT Press.

Sartori, G., Miozzo, M., & Job, R. (1993). Category-specific naming impairments? Yes. *Quarterly Journal of Experimental Psychology, 46A*, 489–504.

Schwarz, M.F., Marin, O.S.M., & Saffran, E.M. (1979). Dissociations of language function in dementia: A case study. *Brain and Language, 7*, 277–306.

Seidenberg, M.S., & McClelland, J.L. (1989). A distributed, developmental model of word recognition and naming. *Psychological Review, 96*, 523–568.

Seymour, P.H.K. (1979). *Human visual cognition*. London: Collier MacMillan.

Sheridan, J., & Humphreys, G.W. (1993). A category-specific verbal-semantic impairment. *Cognitive Neuropsychology, 10*, 143–184.

Silveri, M.C., & Gainotti, G. (1988). Interactions between vision and language in category-specific semantic impairment. *Cognitive Neuropsychology, 5*, 677–710.

Snodgrass, J.G., & McCullough, B. (1986). The role of visual similarity in picture categorization. *Journal of Experimental Psychology: Learning, Memory and Cognition, 12*, 147–154.

Snodgrass, J.G., & Vanderwart, M. (1980). A standardized set of 260 pictures: Norms for name agreement, image agreement, familiarity and visual complexity. *Journal of Experimental Psychology: Human Perception and Performance, 6*, 174–215.

Stewart, F., Parkin, A.J., & Hunkin, N.M. (1992). Naming impairments following recovery from herpes simplex encephalitis: Category-specific? *Quarterly Journal of Experimental Psychology*, *44A*, 261–284.

Ullman, S. (1989). Aligning pictorial descriptions: An approach to object recognition. *Cognition*, *32*, 193–254.

Vitkovitch, M., & Humphreys, G.W. (1991). Perseverative responding in speeded naming to pictures: Its in the links. *Journal of Experimental Psychology: Learning, Memory and Cognition*, *17*, 664–680.

Vitkovitch, M., Humphreys, G.W., & Lloyd-Jones, T.J. (1993). On naming a giraffe a zebra: Picture naming errors across different categories. *Journal of Experimental Psychology: Learning, Memory and Cognition*, *19*, 243–259.

Warren, C., & Morton, J. (1982). The effects of priming on picture recognition. *British Journal of Psychology*, *73*, 117–129.

Warrington, E.K. (1975). The selective impairment of semantic memory. *Quarterly Journal of Experimental Psychology*, *27*, 635–657.

Warrington, E.K. (1982). Neuropsychological studies of object recognition. *Philosophical Transactions of the Royal Society, London, B298*, 15–33.

Warrington, E.K., & McCarthy, R.A. (1983). Category-specific access dysphasia. *Brain*, *106*, 859–878.

Warrington, E.K., & McCarthy, R.A. (1987). Categories of knowledge: Further fractionation and an attempted integration. *Brain*, *110*, 1273–1296.

Warrington, E.K., & Shallice, T. (1984). Category-specific semantic impairment. *Brain*, *107*, 829–853.

Wingfield, A. (1968). Effects of frequency on identification and naming of objects. *American Journal of Psychology*, *81*, 226–234.

APPENDIX 1

The simulations were run using the software provided by McClelland and Rumelhart (1988).

Parameter Values

All connections had weights of either 1 or −1, with the exception of connections from the semantic level to the name level. These connections had weights that reflected the familiarity of the objects, as assessed by Snodgrass and Vanderwart (1980). The familiarity ratings, on a scale from 1 to 5, for the items we used were taken from Snodgrass and Vanderwart and scaled down to a 0.74 to 0.9 interval, which was found to give stable and accurate naming performance for the unlesioned version of the model after 50 cycles. The other parameters listed by McClelland and Rumelhart (1988) were given the following values:

$$max +1$$
$$min -1$$
$$rest\ 0$$
$$alpha = gamma = decay = 0.1$$
$$estr = 0.14$$

The estr. (external strength) parameter scales the effects of the external input on the activation functions for input units. This parameter was chosen in order to allow all objects to be named correctly when the model was unlesioned. If the estr. parameter is too high, then many objects fail to be named correctly, particularly those from categories with many visually similar competitors. Using smaller values of estr. produced qualitatively similar results to those reported here, although with less striking differences produced between structurally similar and structurally dissimilar objects.

Activation Functions

The activation functions were taken from McClelland and Rumelhart (1988).

If $(net_i > 0)$

$$\Delta a_i = (max - a_i)\, net_i - decay\, (a_i - rest)$$

If $(net_i < 0)$

$$\Delta a_i = (a_i - min)\, net_i - decay\, (a_i - rest)$$

where

$$net_i = \Sigma\, w_{ij}\, output_{\,j} + extinput_i$$

w_{ij} = weight on the connection between units i and j
$output_j$ = output activation from unit j (internal unit providing input into unit i)
$extinput_i$ = external input into unit i
net_i = net input into unit i

Response Probabilities

Uncorrected measure:

$$s_i(t) = e^{ka_i(t)}$$

Corrected measure:

$$s_i(t) = e^{ka_i(t)} \qquad \text{for } a_i(t) > 0$$
$$s_i(t) = 0 \qquad \text{else}$$

where $s_i(t)$ is an indicator of the response strength for unit i on time t

Probability of a given response, $P(s_i,t)$, at time t:

$$P(s_i,t) = \frac{s_i(t)}{\Sigma\, s_i(t)}_{jec}$$

where c is the set of competing alternative responses.

APPENDIX 2

Input Vectors

Structural unit:

	cat	tiger	cow	fox	horse	squirrel	donkey	camel	deer	pig
Stimulus:										
cat	1.00	0.57	0.23	0.47	-0.03	-0.01	-0.03	-0.13	0.10	0.20
tiger	0.57	1.00	0.33	0.33	0.27	-0.27	0.33	-0.07	0.23	-0.20
cow	0.23	0.33	1.00	0.10	0.53	-0.40	0.33	0.17	0.20	0.27
fox	0.47	0.33	0.10	1.00	0.27	-0.03	0.13	0.10	0.03	0.10
horse	-0.03	0.27	0.53	0.27	1.00	-0.43	0.83	0.20	0.53	0.13
squirrel	-0.10	-0.27	-0.40	-0.03	-0.43	1.00	-0.27	-0.43	-0.23	-0.40
donkey	-0.30	0.33	0.33	0.13	0.83	-0.27	1.00	0.27	0.33	-0.03
camel	-0.13	-0.07	0.17	0.10	0.20	-0.43	0.27	1.00	0.03	0.03
deer	0.10	0.23	0.20	0.03	0.53	-0.23	0.33	0.03	1.00	0.03
pig	0.20	-0.20	0.27	0.10	0.13	-0.40	-0.03	0.03	0.03	1.00
belt	-0.07	-0.83	-0.90	-0.83	-0.83	-0.90	-0.90	-0.87	-0.80	-0.87
blouse	-0.70	-0.70	-0.90	-0.83	-0.80	-0.90	-0.70	-0.80	-0.83	-0.80
boot	-0.90	-0.83	-0.77	-0.83	-0.77	-0.87	-0.83	-0.93	-0.80	-0.80
coat	-0.70	-0.83	-0.67	-0.77	-0.70	-0.77	-0.80	-0.60	-0.77	-0.80
dress	-0.83	-0.87	-0.83	-0.87	-0.80	-0.73	-0.77	-0.77	-0.80	-0.83
pants	-0.80	-0.80	-0.77	-0.93	-0.73	-0.97	-0.83	-0.70	-0.90	-0.90
ring	-0.83	-0.87	-0.87	-0.90	-0.83	-1.00	-0.90	-0.83	-0.80	-0.80
tie	-0.83	-0.83	-0.80	-0.77	-0.93	-0.93	-0.97	-0.90	-0.83	-0.77
watch	-0.90	-0.80	-0.97	-0.93	-0.83	-0.97	-0.83	-0.83	-0.97	-0.93
sweater	-0.73	-0.83	-0.87	-0.80	-0.80	-0.73	-0.67	-0.83	-0.90	-0.90

Structural unit:

	belt	blouse	boot	coat	dress	pants	ring	tie	watch	sweater
Input:										
cat	-0.70	-0.70	-0.90	-0.70	-0.83	-0.80	-0.83	-0.83	-0.90	-0.73
tiger	-0.83	-0.70	-0.83	-0.83	-0.87	-0.80	-0.87	-0.83	-0.80	-0.83
cow	-0.90	-0.90	-0.77	-0.67	-0.83	-0.77	-0.87	-0.77	-0.93	-0.80
fox	-0.83	-0.83	-0.83	-0.77	-0.87	-0.93	-0.90	-0.77	-0.93	-0.80
horse	-0.83	-0.80	-0.77	-0.70	-0.80	-0.73	-0.83	-0.93	-0.83	-0.80
squirrel	-0.90	-0.90	-0.87	-0.77	-0.73	-0.97	-1.00	-0.93	-0.97	-0.73
donkey	-0.90	-0.70	-0.83	-0.80	-0.77	-0.83	-0.90	-0.97	-0.83	-0.67
camel	-0.87	-0.80	-0.93	-0.60	-0.77	-0.70	-0.83	-0.90	-0.83	-0.83
deer	-0.80	-0.83	-0.80	-0.77	-0.80	-0.90	-0.80	-0.83	-0.97	-0.90
pig	-0.87	-0.80	-0.80	-0.80	-0.83	-0.90	-0.80	-0.77	-0.93	-0.90
belt	1.00	-0.83	-0.70	-0.80	-0.73	-0.80	-0.20	-0.27	0.00	-0.08
blouse	-0.83	1.00	-0.70	0.27	0.33	-0.53	-0.87	-0.80	-0.90	0.27
boot	-0.70	-0.70	1.00	-0.63	-0.87	-0.73	-0.77	-0.90	-0.87	-0.97
coat	-0.80	0.27	-0.63	1.00	0.17	-0.47	-0.70	-0.70	-0.97	0.23
dress	-0.73	0.33	-0.87	0.17	1.00	-0.40	-0.87	-0.63	-0.83	0.07
pants	-0.80	-0.53	-0.73	-0.47	-0.40	1.00	-0.80	-0.63	-0.90	-0.50
ring	-0.20	-0.87	-0.77	-0.70	-0.87	-0.80	1.00	-0.70	-0.27	-0.97
tie	0.27	-0.80	-0.90	-0.70	-0.63	-0.63	-0.70	1.00	-0.43	-0.87
watch	0.00	-0.90	-0.87	-0.97	-0.83	-0.90	-0.27	-0.43	1.00	-0.93
sweater	-0.80	0.27	-0.97	0.23	0.07	-0.50	-0.97	-0.87	-0.93	1.00

Subject Index

sorting animals by semantic attributes, 421–2
Spearman rank correlation, 426
SPECT scan, 232, 467
spoken word-picture matching tasks, 312–20, 328–31
spoken word-written word matching tasks, 315–16, 320–1, 332
stimulus modality, 278–81, 306–7
stimulus preparation (sensory and associative semantics), 401–3
storage-access
    distinction (in neuropsychology), 265–302
    impairments, 267, 361–3
storage deficits, 309–10, 323
    refractory semantics, 297, 301–2
strategic priming effects, 364, 375
structural descriptions, 344, 349, 351, 354, 399–400, 410, 536, 539, 546, 551–2, 569–74, 576–80
structural information, 541–3, 545, 550
structural similarity, 538–41, 553–63
    effects on naming, 564–8
subordinate information, 499, 506–7, 514, 537
superordinate errors, 477–81
superordinate knowledge, 268, 498–502, 505–7, 510–11, 514, 520, 538–9
superordinate units, 551–2, 557, 560–1
surface dyslexia, 470
surnames, 280, 281–2
synonym matching experiment, 274–5

tactile naming, 341
target, semantic priming, 363–5, 370–1, 375, 379, 384–5, 386
task-difficulty level, 437
temporal lobectomy, 226
temporal lobes, 252–4, 259
    injury, 409–31, 433
Test of Reception of Grammar, 231, 468–9
Thorndike-Lorge ratings, 425

3–D model, 342, 349
time course of activation (IAC model), 558, 559
token-type differentiation, 267
topographical amnesia, 412
trail making, 230, 413
TROG test, 231, 468, 469
'two parameter stochastic model', 418
type-token differentiation, 267
typicality, 537
    refractory semantics, 289–96

unmatched name frequencies, 564–7 passim

verbal comprehension impairment (in access dysphasia), 309–32
verbal definition (generation of), 471, 475–6
verbal fluency, 230, 231, 232
    test, 413, 521
verbal knowledge, 227
verbs
    category-specific disorders, 251–2
    disorders in production/comprehension (aphasic patients), 248–55
visual distractor, 276
visual errors, 477–81
visual inputs/units, 525–6, 528
visual knowledge, 227, 397–9, 406, 441–4, 457–61
    associative, 435, 438, 445–54
visual object processing, 535–81
visual object recognition, 297, 350
visual processing tasks, 342–4
visual similarity, 553
vocabulary (conversational), 227–8, 229, 233, 240
voluntary access (to semantic information), 360–3, 374, 377–8, 381, 387–8, 391

WAIS-R, 230, 311, 412–13, 467
Warrington Recognition Memory Test, 413